Hölderlin after the Catastrophe

Studies in German Literature, Linguistics, and Culture

Hölderlin after the Catastrophe

Heidegger — Adorno — Brecht

Robert Savage

CAMDEN HOUSE
Rochester, New York

First published 2008
by Camden House

Camden House is an imprint of Boydell & Brewer Inc.
668 Mt. Hope Avenue, Rochester, NY 14620, USA
www.camden-house.com
and of Boydell & Brewer Limited
PO Box 9, Woodbridge, Suffolk IP12 3DF, UK
www.boydellandbrewer.com

ISBN-13: 978–1–57113–320–5
ISBN-10: 1–57113–320–8

Library of Congress Cataloging-in-Publication Data

Savage, Robert (Robert Ian)
    Hölderlin after the catastrophe : Heidegger, Adorno, Brecht / Robert Savage.
        p. cm. — (Studies in German literature, linguistics, and culture)
    Includes bibliographical references and index.
    ISBN–13: 978–1–57113–320–5 (hardcover : alk. paper)
    ISBN–10: 1–57113–320–8 (hardcover : alk. paper)
    1. Hölderlin, Friedrich, 1770–1843—Appreciation. 2. Heidegger, Martin,
1889–1976. Abendländische Gespräch. 3. Adorno, Theodor W., 1903–1969.
Parataxis. 4. Brecht, Bertolt, 1898–1956. Antigone des Sophokles. 5. National
socialism and literature. 6. Literature and history—Germany. 7. Collective
memory—Germany. I. Title. II. Series.

PT2359.H2S345 2008
831′.6—dc22

2008011279

A catalogue record for this title is available from the British Library.

This publication is printed on acid-free paper.
Printed in the United States of America.

For Christoph Bongert and Patrick de Werra

Contents

Foreword

WHAT CAN A GERMAN UNDERSTAND about Hölderlin?"[1] The Hölderlin experts to whom this question was addressed had no doubt been expecting a more diplomatic overture from the man who posed it, Pierre Bertaux, when they invited him to appear as guest speaker at their 1968 conference. That he should begin his speech by casting doubt on their own interpretative credentials amounted to a slap in the face. In itself, the fact that they were being lectured by a foreigner on this, the most German of poets, was unusual enough. It was a moot point and, since the early twentieth century, a well-worn topos of reception, whether the work of Friedrich Hölderlin (1770–1843) even tolerated translation, whether it did not rather flout the criterion of universal communicability and intelligibility upon which any act of translation depends. Conventional wisdom suggested that no matter how diligently a non-German were to delve into the poetry's language, intertextual borrowings, historical background, or symbolism, its essential meaning would always elude him. By inverting the standard reproach, Bertaux sought to transform what had hitherto been regarded as an insurmountable barrier to understanding — the brute fact of exclusion from a tribe that still defined membership according to the *ius sanguinis* — into its prerequisite. Yet even he insisted upon the privilege of nationality, maintaining that his own insights accrued to him solely by virtue of his impeccable revolutionary pedigree.[2] Where such arguments were put into play, the counter-accusation of Gallic arrogance was not far off.

In a sense, this study drives Bertaux's question *ad absurdum* — for what can an Australian possibly understand about Hölderlin that a German or Frenchman cannot? Here, the claim to a hermeneutic home advantage pressed by Bertaux is clearly out of place; for while the poet visited many countries in the course of his imaginary sea voyages around the world, there is no record of him ever venturing further south than Tahiti. (It is both ironic and heartening, though, that one of the most distinguished Hölderlin scholars at the time Bertaux delivered his speech, Lawrence Ryan, was an Australian.) In another, less flippant, sense, this study endeavors for the first time to give Bertaux's question the full consideration it deserves. With the blanks filled in, the question now reads: After the catastrophe, what can a German no longer, or only now, understand about Hölderlin? Just as important, what can he understand about the complex I have called "Hölderlin after the catastrophe"? What do the writings of the immediate postwar generation (1945–68) reveal about the changes in the conditions of Hölderlin reception precipitated by the assisted suicide of Hitler's state? Do they represent a significant departure from the models of interpretation that prevailed before and during the Third Reich, or do they simply offer more of the same? To what extent do they affirm, reformulate, or reject the broader postwar cultural-political project of salvaging a "good" German tradition from out of the ashes and rubble of the "bad" Germany? And to what extent, if at all, do they reflect upon how their own historical contingency conditions, or even co-constitutes, the object of their investigation?

Given such parameters, the goal of this study cannot be to provide a comprehensive history of Hölderlin reception in the given period. Such a history, which remains to be written, would have to treat such seminal figures as Friedrich Beißner and Peter Szondi far more thoroughly than is possible here; on the other hand, it would have little or nothing to say about Brecht's *Die Antigone des Sophokles* (The Antigone of Sophocles), to which I devote an entire chapter. This brings me to another possible misunderstanding that needs to be addressed at the outset, that of arbitrariness in the matter of text selection. My pickings from the vast array of potential candidates — a dialogue by Heidegger, a speech by Adorno, an adaptation by Brecht — are slim indeed, and at first glance they may scarcely seem to justify the amount of critical attention I expend upon them, especially when one considers that all three authors stood apart from the Hölderlin "in-group" of the time. Whether they have anything else in common appears less than certain, given that one was a borderline fascist with latent megalomaniacal tendencies, one a maverick Marxist whose idea of revolution was gleaned from the new music (and largely confined to it), and one a stalwart supporter of the East German communist regime who demanded of art that it stimulate its audience to political action. To say that their interpersonal relationships were fraught with tension is to understate the case.[3] Any attempt to imagine them meeting on neutral territory to sort out their differences quickly degenerates into the slapstick of a Three Stooges skit: one pictures Heidegger reacting with icy disdain to Adorno's attacks while Brecht gives them both an occasional bang on the head with a saucepan. The fact that Heidegger and Adorno once attended a party together in Freiburg, as Herrmann Mörchen reports,[4] or that Adorno and Brecht were on speaking terms during their shared Californian exile does nothing to detract from this sense of absolute incompatibility. Strung together, their names form a necessarily disjointed series, as the dashes in my subtitle are meant to illustrate.

In the following pages I make no attempt to resolve that antagonism by adjudicating the three-way dispute, a task I take to be as uninteresting as it is unfeasible. Nor do I downplay the antagonism by reducing it to a lowest common denominator. On the contrary, I try to make it fruitful for analysis by grounding it in three irreconcilable paradigms of reception, to which I have given the names "conversation," "polemic," and "citation." There is a sense in which this study is nothing other than a meditation on what those labels signify. My central contention is that Heidegger, Adorno, and Brecht provide the most elaborate, theoretically self-aware, consequential, controversial, and stimulating reflections of their generation on what it means to read Hölderlin after the catastrophe. At a time when the mainstream reception was predominantly taken up with formalist and philological inquiry, these three thinkers brought to the poet their consciousness of a caesura — a cut or rip in the fabric of historical time — that radically problematized the comprehensibility of Hölderlin that their colleagues, by and large, still took for granted. Bertaux's troubling question is one that Heidegger, Adorno, and Brecht asked of themselves, albeit in different terms, before different audiences, and with vastly different critical and political ramifications.

As far as possible I refrain from offering any commentary on Hölderlin's own writings, preferring to focus on the critical and creative responses they occasioned in others. The approach ventured here is historical and problem-oriented rather than systematic. The introduction sketches the common background to the contributions of my three authors by examining the role played by Hölderlin in Nazi propaganda during the Second World War. It also examines how the aftershocks of the wartime reception came to be registered in the poetry of Günther Eich and Paul Celan, both of whom endeavored to rescue the poet from his false friends while simultaneously confronting the iniquities that had been said and done in his name. The three main chapters then extrapolate the paradigms of conversation, polemic, and citation from the work of Heidegger, Adorno, and Brecht, respectively. Each of these concepts is shown to entertain a relationship of complicity with its would-be opposite, such that conversation shades into monologue, polemic coincides with salvation, and citation proves indistinguishable from radical adaptation. In the epilogue, I argue that Bertaux inaugurates a new wave of reception that consigns all three models to the past, permitting them to be grasped in their epochal co-belonging.

Notes

[1] Pierre Bertaux, "Hölderlin und die französische Revolution," *HJb* 15 (1967/68): 1.

[2] Bertaux, "Hölderlin und die französische Revolution," 1.

[3] The chief documents of the triangular interrelationship are Adorno's numerous polemics against Heidegger; his 1962 essay on "committed" literature, which features a long analysis of epic theater; Brecht's notes and drafts for his unfinished *Tui* novel, a satire on Frankfurt School intellectuals; and a plethora of anecdotes, reminiscences, and letters.

[4] Herrmann Mörchen, *Adorno und Heidegger: Untersuchung einer philosophischen Kommunikationsverweigerung* (Stuttgart: Klett-Cotta, 1981), 7.

Acknowledgments

THE PUBLICATION OF THIS BOOK was made possible by a Research Support Grant from the Centre for Comparative Literature and Cultural Studies, Monash University, Melbourne. I am grateful to my colleagues in the Centre, especially David Roberts, for the advice and encouragement they have given me over many years.

Sections of chapter 2 of this book have previously appeared as "Adorno's Philopolemology: The 'Parataxis' Speech as Example," in the *European Journal of Social Theory* 8, no. 3 (2005): 281–95. Sections of chapter 3 have appeared as "The Precedence of Citation: On Brecht's *The Antigone of Sophocles*," in *Colloquy* 11 (2006): 99–126.

Note on References

CITATIONS OF PRIMARY WORKS in prose are given in English translation in the main text, with the original German in the endnotes. The same applies to citations from Brecht's play *Die Antigone des Sophokles*. Poems are cited in both German and English in the main text. All translations are my own except where otherwise stated. The following abbreviations have been used in the endnotes:

Theodor W. Adorno, *Gesammelte Schriften,* ed. Rolf Tiedemann, with the collaboration of Gretel Adorno, Susan Buck-Morss, and Klaus Schultz (Frankfurt: Suhrkamp, 1970–86):

GS 1	*Philosophische Frühschriften* (1973)
GS 2	*Kierkegaard: Konstruktion des Ästhetischen* (1979)
GS 3	*Dialektik der Aufklärung: Philosophische Fragmente* (1981)
GS 4	*Minima Moralia: Reflexionen aus dem beschädigten Leben* (1980)
GS 5	*Zur Metakritik der Erkenntnistheorie: Drei Studien zu Hegel* (1970)
GS 6	*Negative Dialektik* (1973)
GS 7	*Ästhetische Theorie* (1970)
GS 10.2	*Kulturkritik und Gesellschaft II: Eingriffe; Stichworte* (1977)
GS 11	*Noten zur Literatur* (1974)
GS 12	*Philosophie der neuen Musik* (1975)
GS 13	*Die musikalischen Monographien* (1971)
GS 16	*Musikalische Schriften I-III* (1978)
GS 17	*Musikalische Schriften IV: Moments musicaux; Impromptus* (1982)
GS 19	*Musikalische Schriften VI* (1984)
GS 20	*Vermischte Schriften* (1986)

Bertolt Brecht, *Große kommentierte Berliner und Frankfurter Ausgabe,* ed. Werner Hecht, Jan Knopf, Werner Mittenzwei, and Klaus-Detlef Müller (Frankfurt: Suhrkamp, 1988–98):

BFA 2	*Stücke 2* (1988)
BFA 3	*Stücke 3* (1988)
BFA 8	*Stücke 8* (1992)
BFA 12	*Gedichte 2: Sammlungen, 1938–1956* (1988)

BFA 15   *Gedichte* 5: *Gedichte und Gedichtfragmente, 1940–1956* (1993)
BFA 21   *Schriften 1: 1914–1933* (1992)
BFA 22   *Schriften 2: 1933–1942* (1993)
BFA 24   *Schriften 4: Texte zu Stücken* (1991)
BFA 25   *Schriften 5: Theatermodelle* (1994)
BFA 26   *Journale 1: 1913–1941* (1995)
BFA 27   *Journale 2: 1941–1955* (1995)
BFA 29   *Briefe 2: 1937–1949* (1998)

Martin Heidegger, *Gesamtausgabe,* ed. Friedrich-Wilhelm v. Herrmann et al. (Frankfurt: Klostermann, 1976–):

GA 2   *Sein und Zeit* (1977)
GA 4   *Erläuterungen zu Hölderlins Dichtung* (1981)
GA 5   *Holzwege* (1977)
GA 6   *Nietzsche* (1996)
GA 7   *Vorträge und Aufsätze* (2000)
GA 9   *Wegmarken* (1976)
GA 12   *Unterwegs zur Sprache* (1985)
GA 13   *Aus der Erfahrung des Denkens* (1983)
GA 16   *Reden und andere Zeugnisse eines Lebensweges* (2000)
GA 29/30   *Die Grundbegriffe der Metaphysik* (1983)
GA 32   *Hegels Phänomenologie des Geistes*
GA 39   *Hölderlins Hymnen "Germanien" und "Der Rhein"* (1980)
GA 40   *Einführung in die Metaphysik* (1983)
GA 52   *Hölderlins Hymne "Andenken"* (1982)
GA 53   *Hölderlins Hymne "Der Ister"* (1984)
GA 54   *Parmenides* (1982)
GA 65   *Beiträge zur Philosophie (vom Ereignis)* (1989)
GA 75   *Zu Hölderlin: Griechenlandreisen* (2000)
GA 77   *Feldweg-Gespräche* (1995)

Friedrich Hölderlin, *Sämtliche Werke* (= Große Stuttgarter Ausgabe), ed. Friedrich Beißner and Adolf Beck (Stuttgart: Kohlhammer, 1943–85):

StA 2   *Gedichte nach 1800* (1951)
StA 3   *Hyperion* (1957)
StA 4   *Empedokles: Aufsätze* (1961)
StA 5   *Übersetzungen* (1952)
StA 6   *Briefe* (1954)
StA 7   *Dokumente* (1968)

HJb   *Jahrbuch der Friedrich-Hölderlin-Gesellschaft*

Introduction: Hölderlin after the Catastrophe

Was bleibet aber, stiften die Dichter.

(But what remains, the poets found.)
— Hölderlin, "Andenken"

Was bleibt geht stiften.

(Whatever's left, go and found.)
— Erich Fried, "Lyrischer Winter"

Andenken 1: Souvenir de France

IN NOVEMBER 1946, GÜNTER EICH published his poem "Latrine" in *Der Ruf* (The Call), a forum established earlier that year for young, disillusioned, and often embittered German writers, many of them returning veterans. The third stanza reads:

> Irr mir im Ohre schallen
> Verse von Hölderlin.
> In schneeiger Reinheit spiegeln
> Wolken sich im Urin.[1]

> [Mad in my hearing echo
> Verses by Hölderlin.
> In snowy pureness, mirrored,
> Clouds in the urine are seen.]

The poem's narrator thinks of verses by Hölderlin while squatting over a makeshift open-air latrine. Specifically, he thinks of verses from Hölderlin's "Andenken," for the fourth and final stanza opens with a quotation from that poem:

> "Geh aber nun und grüße
> die schöne Garonne" —
> Unter den schwankenden Füßen
> schwimmen die Wolken davon.

> ["But go now with a greeting
> to the beautiful Garonne" —
> Under my tottering feet those
> Cloudlets have drifted, are gone.]

Andenken means memento, keepsake, or remembrance, and in the poem of the same name Hölderlin reflects upon his sojourn in Bordeaux, where he had spent a few months in 1801 working as house tutor for a wealthy German family. "Latrine," too, is set in southern France, where Eich underwent military training in 1940. By citing Hölderlin's line, Eich establishes a brutal contrast between their respective experiences.[2] Whereas Hölderlin's line is tinged with a wistful lyricism, Eich recalls it while crouching

> über stinkendem Graben,
> Papier voll Blut und Urin,
> Umschwirrt von funkelnden Fliegen

> [over the stinking drain ditch,
> paper all bloody, bepissed,
> with glittering flies around it].

Urged by Hölderlin to greet the River Garonne, Eich finds only the "Schlamm der Verwesung" (mire of corruption).[3] Hölderlin's vision is simply irreconcilable with what Eich sees around him, and his nod to his hallowed predecessor makes the reader aware of the vast distance that separates them, as great as that between the snowy clouds and the puddle of urine in which they are mirrored. Insofar as this distance proves to be unbridgeable, "Latrine" casts an oblique judgment on Hölderlin's own poetry. "Andenken" concludes with the endlessly cited apothegm: "Was bleibet aber, stiften die Dichter" (But what remains, the poets found).[4] Eich's *Andenken* of "Andenken" hints that Hölderlin's faith may well be misplaced: the coprolitic remains he discovers in France are surely not what the founding poet had in mind.[5]

The third stanza nonetheless suggests that we read "Latrine" as more than a graphic parable for the traumatic loss of poetic ideality experienced by an entire generation in the face of a repugnant, scatological reality; more, too, than a nostalgic backward glance at a time when a German in France could still write lyric poetry with a clear conscience. For despite the apparently absolute divide between Hölderlin's shimmeringly beautiful verses and the situation of the defecating speaking subject, Eich is interested, above all, in the nature of their *connection*. He employs two images in the stanza to figure that relationship. For now, I will pass over the second such image, that of the urine reflecting the clouds in their purity. The first has Hölderlin's verses echoing madly — *irr* — in the narrator's ear. The German verb *irren* shares with the English "to err" the double sense of the erratic and the erroneous: *irren* can mean to veer from the high road of truth into a mistake, an *Irrtum*. Furthermore, *irr* has a third meaning, which also reverberates in Eich's line: that of deviance from the path of reason. We might remember that Hölderlin himself seemed *irre*, spiritually muddled or crazy, upon his return from France, and a few years later he would in fact be delivered to an *Irrenanstalt*, a lunatic asylum. Why, then, should Eich write of Hölderlin's verses that they resound waywardly, falsely, even dementedly, in his ear? What makes them stray from their ordained path, that of undistorted communication, correct interpretation, and rational discourse? And what if that path should itself turn out to be crooked?

An earlier, shorter version of "Latrine" is also extant, probably drafted in 1940, while Eich was still in France. Its second and final stanza reads:

> Im Fieber schallen im Ohre
> Verse von Hölderlin.
> Im Spiegelbild der Latrine
> Die weißesten Wolken ziehn.[6]

> [In fever resound in my ear
> Verses by Hölderlin.
> In the mirror of the latrine
> The whitest clouds can be seen.]

Although the imagery and diction correspond almost exactly to that of the published version from 1946, the latter shows three important changes, all of which tend in the same direction: the replacement of *im Fieber* with *irr*; the rhyming of *Hölderlin* and *Urin*; and the addition of the word *Reinheit*, purity. These modifications not only accentuate the opposition between the clouds, purity, and Hölderlin, on the one hand, and the latrine, filth, and Eich, on the other. More importantly, they also implicate one in the other. For whereas the version from 1940 attributes the distortion suffered by Hölderlin's verses to the narrator's own feverish condition, the 1946 text introduces the possibility that the squalid dis-ease that pervades the poem may have infected the verses themselves. Hölderlin's poetry may have been *irrgeführt*, abducted, by an unnamed power, or become *irrsinnig*, its meaning deranged, such that it now rhymes with *Urin*. And we should not forget that the narrator squatting in the muck perceives the purity of the clouds *only in reflection*, through the urine in which they are mirrored:

> Unter den schwankenden Füßen
> schwimmen die Wolken davon

> [Under my tottering feet those
> Cloudlets have drifted, are gone].

The clouds' superlative whiteness is a mirage effect of the squalor far below, an optical illusion.[7] For Eich there can be no direct route to Hölderlin, no unperturbed gaze fixed upon the poetic word, no purity without its opposite. In short, every path or *Weg* in "Latrine" is also and above all an aberrant path, an *Irrweg*.

When comparing the draft of a poem with its definitive formulation, it is customary for the critic to explain their differences by invoking either the growing artistic command of the author or the increasing integration of the material to a central organizing idea. Submitted to a teleological reading, the draft is interpreted as the first, tentative, attempt to become what it already and unwittingly is. While it cannot be doubted that the 1946 version of "Latrine" is the stronger poem, an immanent comparative study, pursued on its own terms, will fail to account for the evolutionary process outlined above. The fact that the poem appeared just a year after the end of the Second World War is by no means irrelevant to the changes in content. In other words, the emendations that distinguish the published version from its precursor make sense only when looked at against the background of what was happening in Germany during the intervening years.

Eich wrote the final version at a time when he and many of his friends were struggling to adjust to life after the fall of the regime toward which they had come to feel neither affection nor loyalty.[8] The full title of the journal in which Eich published "Latrine" was *Der Ruf: Unabhängige Blätter der jungen Generation* (The Call: Independent Pages of the Young Generation). As the title indicates, its contributors sought to distance themselves from those they held responsible for the military, economic, and above all moral collapse of Germany. The title suggests that the blame for that collapse rested with the older generation that had voted Hitler into power in 1933. By implication, the readers of *Der Ruf* wanted nothing to do with the Germany in whose name the war had been waged. In his first editorial, Eich's friend Alfred Andersch described his journal's target audience, with some precision, as "this young German generation, the men and women between eighteen and thirty-five, separated from their seniors through their lack of responsibility for Hitler, and from their juniors through the experience of the front and captivity."[9]

While Eich did not necessarily share all his friend's views, his involvement with the journal indicates that he shared its general consciousness of epochal and generational schism. When the paper was banned by the American occupying forces the following year, Eich joined Andersch and many of his colleagues in forming *Gruppe 47*, the group of leading postwar writers. I want to suggest, therefore, that "Latrine" be understood as a response to the fact of German defeat by someone who had come to reject the Nazis by the end of their rule and was now struggling to come to terms with their legacy. More specifically, the poem is to be understood as posing the question: *how is one to read Hölderlin after the catastrophe?* If the poem is read with this question in mind, it becomes clear that what separates the draft and final versions, jutting between them and silently organizing their differences, is nothing less than the wartime experience *of* Hölderlin, whereby "Hölderlin" designates both a poet and a national myth, a clearly demarcated body of work and its systematic deformation and diffusion through the ideological apparatus of the state.

The question Eich confronted in 1946 is the same question posed by this study. In it I will look at the responses of three German writers — Martin Heidegger, Theodor W. Adorno, and Bertolt Brecht — to this question, relating their responses to their respective accounts of fascist dictatorship and their diagnoses of the postwar situation. Further, I will show

how in each case the problem of reading Hölderlin after the war is bound up with that of how Germany is to be saved from the enemy within, whether that enemy be imagined under a fascist, totalitarian, mythic, tragic, or technocratic guise. I will comment on my choice of authors a little later. For now, it is important to sketch the common background of their postwar writings on Hölderlin, the experience of what Gerhard Kurz calls the "annexation of Hölderlin by National Socialism."[10] By considering how the poet who denounced the Germans as "barbarians from the remotest past"[11] was taken into service by one of the most barbaric regimes of modern times, I hope also to shed some light on Eich's poem — and perhaps, too, on the *Irrweg* of modern German history.

Conscript Hölderlin

On 7 June 1943, on the occasion of the 100th anniversary of Hölderlin's death, the Hölderlin Society was founded in Stuttgart with the aim of conveying an "undistorted picture" of the poet to the German people and of helping him to exert a "pure influence upon our time."[12] It soon became apparent what was envisaged in these terms. The Minister for Propaganda, Joseph Goebbels, was declared honorary patron of the Society, while Hitler himself ordered that a commemorative wreath be placed in his name on Hölderlin's grave in Tübingen. The well-known poet Gerhard Schumann delivered his inaugural presidential speech before a hall packed with Party officials, local dignitaries and literary scholars. At the height of his peroration, Schumann turned to address the poet in the intimate *Du* form, appealing to his poetic vision to ennoble the relentless material warfare and mass slaughter in which the Reich was engaged at the time: "And in the storms of steel of all battles your heart is amidst us, and in your heart, the heart of the Fatherland!"[13]

On the same day a commemorative book was published in Tübingen, featuring contributions from writers of the caliber of Martin Heidegger, Walter Rehm, and Hans-Georg Gadamer. The collection was prefaced by a specially commissioned ode to Hölderlin by the Austrian poet Josef Weinheber, which swelled to a tumultuous climax in its final stanza:

> Aufbruch wieder ist nun, da du uns führst, es ist
> deutsche Zeit. Und so war keine wie diese deutsch.
> Führ uns, Genie, spür schon
> Wie Gefallene dur jauchzen, Held![14]

> [We are awakened now that you lead us, it is
> German time. And no time was as German as ours.
> Lead us, genius, feel
> How the fallen cheer you, hero!]

In his introduction to the volume, the respected Germanist Paul Kluckhohn ventured an explanation for the poet's renewed popularity: "The great political transformation that began after the [First World] War allowed, in particular, the goal of a new communal life in Hölderlin's work to step into the foreground and brought the 'singer of the people' and of sacrificial death for the Fatherland to greater influence. In the Second World War, too, . . . he is for many fighters a source of spiritual strength and a sanctifying genius."[15]

Six months later, shortly before Christmas 1943, Friedrich Beißner prepared a special field edition of Hölderlin's poems under the auspices of the Society. Despite the general paper shortage, some 100,000 copies were printed and sent to the front, although this number still fell far short of the astonishing 194,000 copies that were ordered.[16] An SS officer stationed in the East wrote back gratefully: "Mere words are probably incapable of expressing what Hölderlin means to me right now."[17] A lance corporal felt that "the war has brought Hölderlin very close to us soldiers."[18] According to Kluckhohn, letters such as these showed "how Hölderlin helps to maintain the enthusiasm and high spirits that threaten to evaporate in the long battles on the Eastern Front."[19] A direct causal link could thus be established between the poet's popularity in a time of national emergency and the ability of his readers to combat the Soviet enemy with renewed vigor. Norbert Rath is hardly exaggerating when he calls the wartime Hölderlin Society a "franchise of the Goebbels ministry."[20]

All this was very different from the picture of Hölderlin that had prevailed in the nineteenth century. Then he was remembered, with few exceptions,[21] as an incurable dreamer and romantic whose utter inability to cope with life's demands might serve as a warning to impressionable young minds.[22] When the fifteen year-old Nietzsche wrote an essay in which he declared Hölderlin to be his favorite poet, his teacher gave the essay an uncharacteristically poor grade with the advice that he stick in future to a "healthier, more German poet."[23] How then did the Nazis transform this scarcely militaristic poet, who never took up arms for his country and spent the last four decades of his life in a state of spiritual benightedness, into a paragon of Prussian masculinity and patriotic self-sacrifice? How did they successfully portray someone who never wavered in his support for the ideals of the French Revolution, heaped scorn on the backwardness of his homeland, and seriously contemplated emigrating overseas, as an enemy of the Enlightenment and nationalist icon?[24] What led them to shower on Hölderlin all the honors and accolades reserved for a hero of the movement, and how did they convince so many people that he was one of them?

The community of Hölderlin scholars would later seek to exonerate its wartime conduct with the argument that the Nazi reading of Hölderlin represented a base falsification of his poetry, and that this reading had been imposed, as if by fiat, upon a public that was not to be fooled so easily. The reality is more disconcerting. It can certainly be shown that the poet's appropriation by the Ministry of Propaganda, prosecuted with increased vigor after 1943, served pernicious ends and systematically distorted his intentions; Schumann made this blatantly obvious at the end of his presidential address, when he misquoted "Germanien" by omitting the crucial qualifier *wehrlos*, defenseless.[25] But it is important to note that the Nazi interpretation did not rest primarily upon the assumption that Hölderlin was a proto-fascist (herein lies the salient difference from the contemporary Nietzsche reception).[26] On the contrary, Hölderlin proved effective to the war effort in its final stages because he offered an inner sanctuary to which his readers could retreat to lick their wounds when confronted with the material privation, physical danger, and increasingly evident lack of freedom of everyday life under the Third Reich. Claudia Albert nicely summarizes this therapeutics of reading when she observes that the experience of reading Hölderlin was seen to compensate for the tribulations of "external reality, which was deemed insignificant in the face of the work's greatness."[27] In other words, Hölderlin proved useful to the Nazis, not because he was coarsely politicized and transformed into a mouthpiece for Hitler (although this fate was also not spared him, as Enzensberger's trite verse about those who "say Hölderlin and mean Himmler" makes clear[28]), but because, in his very purity, he provided solace to the war-weary German people at a time when their hopes of victory had been all but dashed. Whereas Kleist and Schiller, whose writings were more easily susceptible to jingoistic exploitation, had been the poets of German military success, Hölderlin became the poet of German defeat.[29] He helped obscure the real causes of the Third Reich's protracted collapse by lending it an aura of tragic grandeur and necessity. It is hardly accidental that the boom of the wartime Hölderlin cult coincided with the German capitulation at Stalingrad, nor that the poet's most frequently cited line at the time, as Gottfried Benn recalled, was

> Dir ist,
> Liebes! nicht Einer zu viel gefallen[30]
>
> [For you
> dearest! not one too many has fallen].

As such, the most disturbing aspect of Hölderlin's wartime reception is that, to extend Kurz's metaphor, the Nazis managed to conceal the fact that they had annexed Hölderlin in the first place.

If there is a key word to the Nazi reception of the poet, if there is one concept under which all its other elements were marshaled and deployed, then it is that of purity. Over and again the writings from this period refer to Hölderlin as the "purest poet and purest vessel" of his people's "authentic being."[31] There is never the slightest admission that Hölderlin was the apologist for German might into which he was surreptitiously being transformed. Indeed, we have seen how the Hölderlin Society's stated aim of helping the poet "exert a pure influence upon our time" translated, in practice, to enlisting him to increase the number of Soviet casualties. This insistence upon Hölderlin's inviolable purity, which contrasted so starkly with his function in the war effort, was by no means confined to the fascists. While the exiled Communist Party leaders in Moscow protested vociferously against the Nazi reception, they did so, much to the disgust of Brecht, by availing themselves of the same argument: that Hölderlin was the spiritual leader of the true German people.[32] Both sides used a deliberately vague notion of the Fatherland to enlist Hölderlin for their cause, as if the attribution of any particular content to the poet's sublime vision would be tantamount to its desecration.

In itself, the idea that Hölderlin was the purest of all German poets, and the most purely German of all poets, was not original to the wartime reception. The Hölderlin Society's quasi-religious transfiguration of the poet into the standard-bearer of national redemption can be traced back to the exegetical writings of Hölderlin's first modern editor, Norbert von Hellingrath, and to the mythology of the circle of poets and critics around Stefan George, to which Hellingrath made a decisive contribution. The Germanists of 1943 merely inherited patterns of interpretation first established by the Expressionist generation and proceeded to reconcile them with the political exigencies of the day. Any account of Hölderlin's fate under National Socialism must therefore begin with Hellingrath — not least because, thanks largely to Heidegger, his influence survived the demise of the Third Reich and continues to be felt in the popular image of Hölderlin still in circulation in our own day.[33]

Hellingrath's achievement was to unearth, decipher, edit, and publish many of Hölderlin's most important poems, establishing the textual foundation for a new evaluation of his significance. Heidegger would later compare the landmark fourth volume of Hellingrath's edition (1916), in which the "heart, core and summit of Hölderlin's work"[34] was unveiled for the first time, to an earthquake in terms of its impact upon the students of his generation.[35] In particular, Hellingrath succeeded in freeing the late work from the stigma of the pathological, which had stood in the way of its reception ever since Schelling had offered Hölderlin's translations of *Oedipus Rex* and *Antigone* as incontrovertible proof of his friend's ruined mental state.[36] Hellingrath's familiarity with the Expressionist avant-garde made him well-equipped to appreciate the brittle constructions and jarring syntax that had so alienated nineteenth-century sensibilities, while the Hölderlin he discovered and publicized came, in turn, to exert a profound influence upon that avant-garde, especially upon the poetry of George himself.[37]

Above and beyond his services to literary history, however, Hellingrath's most far-reaching legacy was to discover in Hölderlin a reservoir of divine experience in a godless age. In debating whether his poetry should best be chalked up to Classicism or Romanticism, and in reading it through the prism of his biography, scholars up to Wilhelm Dilthey and Ernst Cassirer had ignored the numinous quality that pulsated beneath the surface of the text and irradiated its every line.[38] For Hellingrath, Hölderlin was more than a long-neglected poet who could now take up his rightful place in the pantheon of German culture. Unique and inimitable, he was the "herald, bearer, vessel of the gods,"[39] and as such eluded all attempts to pigeonhole him in the archives. Through the force of his experience and the purity of its expression, Hölderlin shattered the categories of historical understanding and literary judgment applied by critics, exposing them to the deeper truth of myth. Hellingrath's ambition was to recover this mythic dimension in Hölderlin's poetry, to rectify the shortcomings of positivism by restoring the aura to the artwork, and to subordinate the methods of philology to the art religion of his mentor George, for whom the application of scientific principles to poetic language was equivalent to sacrilege. As a result, the historical substrate of Hölderlin's work disappeared from view, not to resurface until the 1960s.[40] The origins of his conception of the divine in a variety of factors specific to his time — his pietistic upbringing, the graecomania of his generation, the repressive political culture of late-eighteenth-century Württemberg, and the common project of the post-Kantian philosophers to skirt the twin perils of atheism and superstition — were suppressed in order that his poetry appear as the outpouring of the godhead, to be received with gratitude and wonderment by his smitten acolytes. As Henning Bothe observes in his history of Hölderlin reception in the George Circle, Hellingrath established an alternative that would have fateful repercussions in years to come: "historical-genetic investigation *or* dumbfoundedness."[41]

George had addressed Hölderlin from the beginning as the savior of the *German* people, rather than that of the Occident or a fallen modernity in general. "We call it a miracle when for generations unheeded or only as tender dreamer from ages past suddenly the great Prophet of his people steps into the light," he announced dramatically in 1908.[42] "With his unambiguous, irrefutable sooth-saying," Hölderlin was "the cornerstone of the immediate German future and the caller of the New God."[43] Under the radicalizing influence of the First World War, Hellingrath, too, came to reclaim Hölderlin for the people that had once rejected him. While he cautioned his audience that the Germany against which Hölderlin collided was "not much different back then from the people among whom we earn money, eat, and sleep today [1915],"[44] he also called the Germans "the people of Hölderlin," adding that the writings of this "most German poet . . . are probably never accessible to non-Germans."[45] On the one hand, then, the Germans are still not in a position to understand their greatest poet, condemning Hellingrath and his fellow initiates to marginality and political irrelevance. On the other, Hölderlin is the most German poet precisely by virtue of the misunderstanding and ignorance that continue to dog his reception, for "it lies deep in the German essence that its innermost glowing core, infinitely far beneath the slag crust that is its surface, only comes to light in a secret Germany."[46]

Hellingrath is here not bemoaning the fact that everyday life in the Reich failed to correspond to the Germans' spiritual essence. Rather, the infinite diremption of fiery core and immobile crust *is the German essence itself*. Were core and crust to come together in a burst of volcanic activity, were the Germans to attempt, through revolution or reform, to create a type of government that channels and satisfies their innermost drives, they would have missed the point: constitutions and parliaments will never fully express what it means to be German. Consequently, the secret Germany cannot exist without its despised official counterpart. None saw this more clearly than Walter Benjamin. In his review of Max Kommerell's *Der Dichter als Führer in der deutschen Klassik* (The Poet as Leader in German Classicism, 1928), a book that culminated in "a new *vita sanctorum*" of Hölderlin, Benjamin warned: "Hölderlin was not of the breed that is resurrected. . . . This land can become Germany once again only when it is purified, and it cannot be purified in the name of Germany — let alone the 'secret Germany' that ultimately is nothing but the arsenal of official Germany, in which the magic hood of invisibility hangs next to the steel helmet."[47]

For Hellingrath, then, the essential Germany can only come to light *as secret*, dependent on the prosaic public sphere it repudiates, just as Hölderlin can only be recognized as the poet whose fate it is to remain perennially unrecognized. According to this paradoxical figure, which we will reencounter virtually unchanged in Heidegger's doctrine of untimeliness, the vicissitudes of Hölderlin's reception testify, more tellingly than would his universal acclamation, to his archetypal Germanness. That is why the admired and celebrated Goethe, despite his "rich, rounded humanity," must cede his place as spiritual leader of his people to the neglected Hölderlin.[48] Hellingrath would have interpreted the centennial festivities of 1943, which sought to absorb the secret Germany into the Third Reich, as a sure sign that Hölderlin was now more misunderstood than ever — indeed, the "secret Germany" would become a catchword of conservative resistance to Hitler. If, for all that, Hellingrath's interpretation of Hölderlin made possible the crassly nationalist readings that flourished during the Second World War, then it was for four main reasons.

First, in a time of war, the notion that Hölderlin was the exclusive property of the Germans acquired a powerful ideological resonance at the privileged site of contestation of the German and its other: the front. Because the experience of the front was assumed to crystallize a previously indistinct awareness of German identity into existential truth, and because, for Hellingrath, Hölderlin was the "greatest exemplar of that secret kingdom, that concealed fire"[49] which flickers in every German breast, the trench became to Hölderlin what the bourgeois salon was to Goethe: the primal scene of his reception.[50] Hölderlin's ideal reader would henceforth wear a soldier's uniform and wield a bayonet. In some quarters, the *Fronterlebnis* would even be elevated to the *sine qua non* for understanding his poetry. From there, it was but a short step to the Nazis' glorification of combat in Hölderlin's name. By 1943, the war correspondent Martin Raschke was reporting from the Eastern Front: "It is an important distinction whether someone in a comfortable parlor, perhaps even plagued by boredom, sallies forth in search of the gods, or whether a heart stormed by a thousand perils and fires approaches [Hölderlin] in the face of death, which can snatch him away at any moment."[51]

Second, once there were enough initiates who shared — or thought they shared — Hölderlin's vision, the invisible church cofounded by Hellingrath could be politically activated. This is precisely what happened in the aftermath of the war, when many returning veterans found that they, too, no longer identified with "the people among whom we earn money, eat, and sleep today," not least because unprecedented economic and psychological difficulties had made it impossible for them to earn money, eat, and sleep as they had in the halcyon days before 1914.[52] Threatened from within and without, the fledgling Weimar democracy failed to correspond to the ideal of close-knit community to which their experiences at the front had given rise; tellingly, even those who lent it their support were referred to as *Vernunftrepublikaner*, republicans by power of reason. In Hölderlin — a certain Hölderlin, mediated by the likes of Kommerell — young Germans disaffected with the new regime found a patron saint and martyr for their cause.[53] By 1923, Hugo von Hofmannsthal was warning his readers about the "state of pre-messianic religiosity" with which the faithful paid homage to "this poet Friedrich Hölderlin, summoned and born again from the grave by the pressure of an entire generation."[54]

Third, if Hölderlin was the most German poet, and the Germans, despite their intolerance, philistinism, and collective myopia, his chosen people, then even Hölderlin's most vituperative attacks could be neutralized and recuperated for a deeper patriotism. This line of interpretation, opened up but never pursued by Hellingrath, would culminate in the breathtakingly mercenary homage to the poet delivered by Hermann Burte in October 1943. After quoting extensively from the *Scheltrede*, the notorious cascade of abuse with which the hero of Hölderlin's novel *Hyperion* inundates the German people, Burte resumes: "He loves his people from his streaming heart, like life, and because he loves, he does not need to be just. . . . We honor ourselves when we honor you! And no one is greater than his people!"[55] Hölderlin's stinging criticisms only fuel the narcissism of those who good-humoredly lend them an ear, although

Burte makes clear that he is not listening too closely: "Say against us what you will, you stand for us all!" (171). Burte goes further than Hellingrath in arguing that, thanks to the warmongering of the Nazis, Hölderlin has finally gained the popular recognition he deserves. "His people has caught up with him: its need in the course of two wars has accomplished what the previous century failed to achieve," namely, the insight that this poet is a shining exemplar of "the power and strength of the race" (161–62). One of Burte's most impassioned outbursts suggests that we conceive the moment in which the Germans caught up with Hölderlin less as a joyous union than as the violent climax to a hunt: "We have you, the poet Hölderlin, you are ours, flesh of our flesh, blood of our blood, spirit of our spirit!" (170). In short, Hölderlin had by 1943 been efficiently incorporated into a bombastic nationalism.

Fourth, the concept of the secret Germany eluded predication, for the simple reason that if it came out of hiding it would no longer be secret; Hellingrath immediately lapsed into metaphor whenever he broached the topic. In effect, the secret Germany derived its meaning, as well as its considerable allure, from whatever it was pitted against — typically, anything that reeked of money (especially finance capital) and institutionalized power. And therein lay the problem: there was nothing to stop the gesture of denegation with which Hellingrath conjured up the secret Germany from extending to the Jews, parliamentary democracy, or anything else the speaker happened to dislike, since Hölderlin's celebrated purity always implied purity *from* a stigmatized other. The very impulse that led Hellingrath to reject politics thereby came to serve a sinister political end.

Hellingrath had little control over a final factor that fueled the nationalist reception: his own death. When Hellingrath fell on the battlefield of Verdun in 1916, his passing was quickly assimilated into the burgeoning Hölderlin mythology. Through it, he demonstrated that his veneration for the poet had informed every aspect of his life, including and especially its ending. Hellingrath's sacrifice, demanded of him yet freely given, seemed to offer an exemplary solution to the great German (and Hölderlinian) dilemma of how spirit and deed, *Geist* and *Tat*, were to be reconciled. George set the tone in his valedictory poem "Norbert":

> Doch da dich hauch durchfuhr geheimer welt
> Tratst du wie jeder stärkste vor die schanze
> Und fielst in feuer erd und luft zerspellt.[56]

> [But grazed by winds from worlds without a name,
> Like any lusty youth you stormed ahead
> And fell, dispersed in air, and earth, and flame.]

The breath from a secret world that spurred Hellingrath to leap over the barricades stands as cipher for the inspiration provided by Hölderlin's poetry. "We all believed that a brother had fallen," recalled Ludwig von

Pigenot in 1936, introducing a collection of Hellingrath's writings released to mark the twentieth anniversary of his death. "In the trenches of the Western Front awoke the wish and vow to work further on Hellingrath's project [his Hölderlin edition], as far as strength and circumstance would allow."[57] Carl Schmitt thought Hellingrath more important than Stefan George and Rilke,[58] a view with which Heidegger would probably have concurred.[59] By 1941, the Hellingrath cult was in full swing. "He ripened unto death with humanity," attested Helmut Wocke in a hagiography published in the journal *Dichtung und Volkstum* (Poetry and Folklore), "fully aware of the necessity of sacrifice . . . . Fate of Empedocles! Spiritual sacrifice for a coming world, for the future of the Fatherland, in the struggle for its existence."[60]

And what of Hölderlin himself? Had he too been sacrificed by the likes of Wocke, Kluckhohn, Burte, Weinheber, and Schumann "for the future of the Fatherland, in the struggle for its existence"? By 1946, the lines that had once penetrated Eich's fever had been led astray by the forces of unreason and of wrong. Could the poet's sullied purity ever be restored to snowy whiteness? Or did the travesty done to his work during the war reveal that purity to have been always already compromised, tainted, soiled? How could one begin to read his poems afresh, after the catastrophe? How could one forget what had been said and done in his name?

Paper all bloody, bepissed . . .

Whitewash

The general reaction to Hölderlin's wartime reception can be gauged with considerable accuracy by perusing the publications of the Hölderlin Society in the immediate postwar period. On 14 March 1946, the advisory committee of the society voted itself out of existence. "Due to considerations of principle, the formal dissolution of the Society proved necessary," Wolfgang Binder reported later, skillfully sidestepping the fact that it had been ordered to disband by the French authorities.[61] Against the advice of Alfred Döblin, at the time a cultural attaché to the French military administration, a denazified Society was reestablished in 1947.[62] In its first yearbook, the nationalist Hölderlin has disappeared without a trace. In his place steps the Hölderlin who would dominate the journal's pages for the next two decades: a scholars' poet, a tamed object of philological discussion, jealously protected by a guild of specialists and sterilized against political or cultural-critical (mis)readings through a predominantly positivist methodology. Equipped with the imprimatur of no less an authority than the great Swiss Germanist Emil Staiger, Beißner continued his work on the Great Stuttgart Edition he had begun in the darkest days of the war. It became a monument to modern philology, standing unchallenged for over thirty years, and it enjoyed the active support of the Hölderlin Society, which had its seat in nearby Tübingen.

If the war is mentioned at all in the society's annals, then only as a regrettable aberration that need not affect the way we read Hölderlin. It is true that, in his report for the 1948–49 yearbook, Beißner's assistant Adolf Beck acknowledges a break in Hölderlin's reception mirroring that in German society as a whole: "What has appeared in Germany since [1945], stands, even if connected through its type of questioning with earlier research, yet in the most part as if on the other bank, upon another, as yet uncertain, stage of spiritual self-consciousness. We have become modest and are ready to examine, and if necessary abandon, many a myth of our spiritual life." This mood of somber reflection, however, does not lead Beck to jettison *every* myth of German spiritual life, for there is a law higher than reason, and its name is experience: "Yet we also believe to have experienced that our poet has passed the test of the breakdown. He has not been estranged from us." The "garden of his poetry" still provides "a refuge from torrential time" (*die reißende Zeit*, a term associated by Hölderlin with revolutionary turmoil); but this soothing respite, cautions Beck, should not be confused with a "flight from reality."[63] Beck thus posits a bridge connecting both sides of the river upon whose "other bank" we stand today, a river that is nothing other than *die reißende Zeit* itself: for was not the wartime experience of Hölderlin also that of a refuge that was not a flight, a temporary asylum where one could gather strength to face the trials to come? Does not his experience teach Beck that while wars may rage outside, while empires may rise and fall, Hölderlin's pure poetry continues to provide its readers with shelter and strength?

I do not wish to dispute the important contributions made by leading postwar scholars such as Beißner, Binder, and Beck to the understanding of Hölderlin's work, nor do I wish to claim that they had anything to hide: politically, all stood beyond reproach. Yet the more sober image of Hölderlin they were instrumental in disseminating was based on a silence and a fiction — a silence concerning the poet's wartime reception, and a fiction concerning its implications. One searches the yearbooks in vain for any indication that Hölderlin had once been a National Socialist icon, or any acknowledgement of the society's own involvement in the ideological manipulation of his work. Precisely in its eagerness to forget the past, however, the society failed to heed the lessons of 1943. Binder, who was to become perhaps the most distinguished Hölderlin scholar of his generation, makes this plain when he asserts in 1947 that, "through the collapse of the National Socialist state, the Hölderlin Society was liberated from those powers which, even before its foundation, had . . . made the realization of its intentions extraordinarily difficult."[64] On the patently flawed assumption that the nationalist interpretation had been imposed from outside, and hence that the integrity of both Hölderlin and the society founded in his name remained intact, the society could continue with its work as if nothing had happened. Consequently, the goals inscribed by the new society into its constitution were practically identical to those of 1943: "to awaken love for Hölderlin's work, to deepen understanding of it, and to help it exert a pure influence in Germany and in other countries."[65] The Hölderlin Society's fresh start proved as illusory as that of the defeated Germany.

The reluctance even to perceive Hölderlin's massive role in wartime propaganda was shared by many of those who had honorably refused to fete the poet of *pro patria mori*. In 1950, emerging from over a decade of inner emigration, Walter Rehm published his magisterial *Orpheus: Der Dichter und die Toten* (Orpheus: The Poet and the Dead), which featured a book-length chapter on Hölderlin. The title leaves unclear whether the dead referred to are those commemorated by the Orphic poet and redeemed through his song, or the countless victims of Hitler's aggression, who remain trapped unsung, as it were, in the underworld. Rehm's foreword suggests that he is quite conscious of this ambiguity: "The book is dedicated to a dead man. Only with sorrow do I remember the deceased, whom a dark fate allowed to become a belated victim of the war: on 11 June 1945, Walter Nestle lost his life in the Swabian homeland."[66] Rehm also discloses that the bulk of his manuscript was composed before 1945, at a time, that is, when the war's escalating fatalities must have weighed heavily on his mind. Death thus constitutes the book's subject matter and its inescapable background, its theme and its inspiration, and in investigating the "cult of death" in Novalis, Hölderlin, and Rilke, Rehm's implicit task is to find meaning in the apparently meaningless "fate" of men like Nestle.

Yet a noteworthy statement in the foreword already makes clear that Rehm is not interested in critically analyzing how the Romantic cult of death fed into Goebbels's total war, and hence in reading "the poet and the dead" as a fascist topos. Rehm explains the book's delayed publication by writing: "The final stretch of work on the book was suddenly disrupted in the summer of 1945 by" — here one expects Rehm to mention the Allied occupation, the collapse of the German economy, the revelation of the full horror, the influx of refugees from the east, the death of his friend; but no — "Kierkegaard."[67] The statement is symptomatic of the book as a whole, which is far more interested in the existential problematic of death and artistic creativity than in its intersection with, and filtration through, the social agencies of meaning-making. Unlike the Nazi Germanist Hermann Pongs,[68] or even Heidegger, Rehm can hardly be accused of a postwar "decline into profundity"[69] motivated by personal opportunism. His lack of interest in the politics of reception reflects instead his unwavering commitment to the mythology originally expounded by the George

Circle, according to which the experience of reading Hölderlin is or ought to be one of rapturous and undisturbed inwardness.

So it comes as no surprise that his chapter on Hölderlin should recapitulate the profoundly ahistorical arguments first put into circulation by Hellingrath. Rehm's panegyric could have been written in the 1920s: "He was all poet and wanted to be nothing but a poet, he fully lived out the form of the 'pure poet,'" having no other ambition than to be "wholly the tool, wholly the 'servant' of a higher power, to be solely the voice of the god."[70] "Hölderlin seems withdrawn from all external claims, from everything bourgeois," Rehm concludes, insensitive as much to the poet's political radicalism as to his reception in the Third Reich; "he is no longer to be reached for all remaining 'business.'"[71] If there is an argument against the nationalist reception here, then it rests upon the same premises greedily seized upon by fascist ideology, premises whose shakiness had been vividly highlighted in Eich's poem. Rehm's response to the German catastrophe shows scant regard for the manner in which the poetic transfiguration of death within a hallowed inner space subserves the barbaric exteriority that necessitated it in the first place.

The apparent conflict between the two predominant tendencies in West German research on Hölderlin from 1945 to 1968 — the philological or positivist approach on the one hand, the mythical or existential-ontological on the other — masks a deeper consensus that can be summarized in three points. First, both approaches either passed over the poet's wartime reception in silence or treated it as irrelevant to an understanding of his work. As late as 1965, in a speech delivered to the Hölderlin Society, Robert Minder could still castigate his audience that the "paradox" of Hölderlin's wartime reception — to wit, the fact that the murderers, "zealously served by a perverted *Germanistik*," had "set up the purest of the pure as the blood witness and herald of the Aryan soul" — had "until now remained practically unnoticed, covered up, or trivialized."[72] The silence was equally palpable in the DDR, where the nationalist reception had continued unchallenged thanks to the wartime propaganda work of the exiles stationed in Moscow. In 1952, for example, the poet and Culture Minister Johannes R. Becher counseled the youth of East Germany to do their best to "honor and creatively administer [Hölderlin's] work as a German national shrine."[73] Second, the studies that aspired to scientific rigor invariably presupposed a decision for Hölderlin not justifiable on their own terms. The choice of the object of philological investigation, as Heidegger was fond of pointing out, cannot be grounded by philological means. Scratch the surface of the scholarly articles and dissertations on Hölderlin from this period, and one soon encounters the kind of mythic claims already familiar from the writings of Hellingrath, and openly defended around the same time by the Catholic existentialist Romano Guardini and the graecophile polytheist Walter

Otto, among others.[74] Third, both philologists and mythmakers avoided discussing the political convictions informing Hölderlin's life and work, in part because the "purest of the pure" was considered to be above such mundane considerations, in part because the Nazi reception had made the political actualization of his work taboo. The controversy unleashed in 1968, when Pierre Bertaux presented his Jacobin thesis to the Hölderlin Society, only makes sense when examined in the context of the almost universal depoliticization that had prevailed hitherto. I will reserve my discussion of the post-68 reception for my epilogue, where I will use it to bring the reception of the previous generation into sharper focus.

The three authors examined in this study all belong to the immediate postwar generation, and their texts on Hölderlin all share, to a greater or lesser degree, the epoch's defining preoccupations and blind spots. Yet Heidegger's "Das abendländische Gespräch" (The Occidental Conversation, 1946–48), Adorno's address "Parataxis: Zur späten Lyrik Hölderlins" (Parataxis: On Hölderlin's Late Poetry, 1963), and Brecht's adaptation of Hölderlin's translation of *Antigone* (1948), however wildly divergent the theoretical and political concerns they bring to bear on the poet, emphatically distance themselves from the mainstream of contemporary research by taking seriously the question of how one is to read Hölderlin after the catastrophe. Heidegger, Adorno, and Brecht are all convinced of the need to reread, or even (in the case of Brecht) to rewrite Hölderlin in the light of the Second World War — not just because they are clear-sighted enough to perceive the damage so assiduously ignored by the scholarly community, but because they also recognize the catastrophe as a caesura, a cut in history compelling the urgent reevaluation of what had gone before.[75] And because all three believe Hölderlin to be in some measure still necessary, their task splits into two: that of saving Hölderlin *from* Germany, and that of saving Germany *through* (or with the help of) Hölderlin. Each uses Hölderlin, in other words, to confront the problem of the "good" and "bad" Germanys: their past collusion, their present struggle, and the possibility of their future reconciliation in a land where, in the words of the poet, "Herrschaft nirgend ist zu sehn bei Geistern und Menschen" ("Dominion is nowhere to be seen among spirits or mortals").[76]

Andenken 2: In Memoriam

While most of those who concerned themselves professionally with Hölderlin in the immediate postwar years continued to draw on prewar interpretative models, I conclude my introduction by outlining an alternative approach to Hölderlin that foreshadows the readings of Heidegger, Adorno, and Brecht to be undertaken in later chapters. Two literary texts will guide my argument. The first is a poem by Paul Celan, drafted in 1954 and published the following year in *Von Schwelle zu Schwelle* (From Threshold to Threshold). Like "Latrine," Celan's "Andenken" commemorates Hölderlin's poem of the same name by placing it in connection with what, acknowledging the inadequacy of nomination, he called "that which happened" (*das, was geschah*).[77] Celan composed "Andenken" while holidaying with his wife at the Mediterranean coastal town of La Ciotat, which perhaps explains why he felt moved to reflect at the time upon Hölderlin's homage to the south of France. At any rate, "Andenken," unlike its better known counterpiece, "Tübingen, Jänner" (Tübingen, January), makes no obvious reference to the circumstances that occasioned it:

> Feigengenährt sei das Herz,
> darin sich die Stunde besinnt
> auf das Mandelauge des Toten.
> Feigengenährt.
>
> Schroff, im Anhauch des Meers,
> die gescheiterte
> Stirne,
> die Klippenschwester.
>
> Und um dein Weißhaar vermehrt
> das Vlies
> der sömmernden Wolke.[78]
>
> [Nourished by figs be the heart
> wherein an hour thinks back
> on the deadman's almond eye.
> Nourished by figs.
>
> Steep, in the seawind's breath,
> the shipwrecked
> forehead,
> the cliff-sister.
>
> And full-blown by your white hair
> the fleece
> of the grazing cloud.]

Despite a lack of conclusive textual evidence to support an autobiographical reading, the poem is widely held to be a memorial to the poet's father, who died of typhus in a German labor camp in Ukraine in 1942. One critic traces the figs that feed the work of mourning to the Palestinian homeland to which Leo Antschel, a committed Zionist, had wanted to emigrate.[79] Another critic, Celan's biographer John Felstiner, links the almond eye of the deceased to other passages in his work in which the almond stands as a cipher for Jewishness, shoring up this philologically questionable tactic[80] with the argument: "That it is Celan's father ('the shipwrecked forehead'?) who emerges in this elegy becomes clear when a fleecy cloud surrounds 'your white hair.' (Leo Antschel's hair went gray under the duress of occupation and deportation.)"[81] Both critics alleviate the discomfort they seem to feel before the vacant, Cyclopic gaze of the dead man by supplying the eye with a body, and the body with a name (the *nom du père*, no less), reconstructing "Andenken" on this basis as a kind of kaddish, a prayer for the dead traditionally recited by the surviving child.[82] This in fact takes us quite far in clearing up some of the immediate difficulties posed by the poem, even if it is overly optimistic of Felstiner to speak of achieving final clarity when faced with a text that concludes swathed in cloud. If one pursues the line of interpretation suggested by Felstiner a little further, one notices that the poem appears as the last in the collection "Mit wechselndem Schlüssel" (With Changing Key), which opens with an epitaph to Celan's son François. The cycle is thus framed at both ends by breaks in the poet's line, breaks that paradoxically ensure the continuity of the cycle by marking it off thematically from the poems that surround it. Read in this way, "Andenken" completes a fatal breach in the cycle of generation that leaves the poet with nothing but figs — a symbol of remembrance since Augustine[83] — to nourish his doubly-bereft heart.

The role played by Hölderlin in this family tragedy is at once invisible and highly visible. It is invisible because, like the father, his name is never mentioned, an omission that has been repeated by all those who have written in the past on Celan's Hölderlin reception.[84] It is visible not only by virtue of the title, instantly recognizable to any educated German reader as an intertextual reference, but also through the various other lexical mementos of Hölderlin's "Andenken" in Celan's. The figs that sustain the poem, for example, have doubtless been plucked from the fig tree growing in the courtyard in Bordeaux, while the sea crashing against the cliff is also that upon which Hölderlin's sailors venture forth to the Indies in search of riches. Felstiner, for one, shows himself well aware of such borrowings, and yet his one-sided interest in authenticating the poem's Jewish paternity leads him to neglect evidence of mixed parentage. He overlooks the possibility that the elegy might be addressed *to Hölderlin* alongside, or in place of, the father figure. This possibility is suggested by the resemblance of the physiognomy sketched in the last two stanzas to that of the poet. Perhaps the most conspicuous feature shared by all the surviving depictions of Hölderlin, from the pencil sketch of the sixteen-year-old through to the wax relief taken shortly before his death, is the forehead rising high and straight toward the crown of his head. It would hardly represent an abuse of poetic license on Celan's part if he were to liken this forehead, which has since become something of a staple motif in fictional retellings of Hölderlin's life story,[85] to a precipitous cliff face. Nor is it surprising, in view of what we know about the last decades of Hölderlin's life, that this vaulting brow should be metonymized as "gescheitert" (shipwrecked). The image presented here is that of the senile, white-haired poet babbling away in his tower, an image Celan would later multiply and refract into a myriad of

> schwimmende Hölderlintürme, möwen-
> umschwirrt[86]
>
> [floating Hölderlintowers, gull-
> enswirled]

And indeed, something of the aphasic solitude from which Hölderlin wrested his late work seems also to trouble the speaker of these verses, as when the keyword "feigengenährt" (fig-nourished) breaks away from its functional context in the propagation of remembrance (and hence in the production of the poem) to stand alone, now nourishing only itself, at the end of the first stanza.

The phrase "gescheiterte Stirne" (shipwrecked brow) evokes death as well as madness. Both converge in the sheer barrier encountered by the breeze wafting toward it from the sea (*Anhauch*, possibly a byword for *pneuma*, the ensouling breath). This barrier marks the limit beyond which the labor of remembrance proves powerless, the point at which the intention announced in the first stanza to hold the gaze of the dead man comes face to face with its nullity. This is also the point at which the attempts to decode the poem in terms of its author's biography mentioned earlier intersect with the interpretation I am proposing here. The negative identity of Leo Antschel and Friedrich Hölderlin in the second person singular permits a speculative reading of "Andenken" as a memorial to Celan's own version of the so-called "German-Jewish synthesis" after its irrevocable failure in the camps. The disembodied eye that confronts the reader from beyond the grave may not be blue, like the eyes of the commandant in "Todesfuge" (Death fugue), but then again, neither were Hölderlin's: they were brown (or perhaps almond?). The two distinct sources of the poem, one painfully personal, the other highbrow and literary, are retroactively crossed in the act of remembrance, causing the attributes of the one to pass over to the other. In their ferment, Hölderlin is divested of his wartime role providing ideological support for those who unleashed the catastrophe, and discreetly associated with the victim of that catastrophe who stood closest to Celan himself, his own father. Peter Demetz's metaphorical description of Celan as the "heir to Hölderlin"[87] holds literally true of this poem, which has inherited family traits from *both* its progenitors.

At the same time, "Andenken" resists being reclaimed as a belated example of German-Jewish symbiosis, not only because it remains silent about whom, or what, it is commemorating — the overdetermination of the intended reference dissolves it into indeterminacy —, but also because it casts into doubt the possibility of commemoration itself, without which such synthesis cannot be effected. Hölderlin's claim to found what endures derived its apodictic certainty from the process of remembrance realized over the course of his poem, as Dieter Henrich has demonstrated in detail.[88] Celan merely expresses the *wish* to reclaim in mourning what had once been given to experience (note the optative "sei" [be] in verse one); his poem nowhere guarantees the fulfillment of that wish, nor does it hold out any prospect of consolation.[89] Instead, the concluding image of the cloud condensing from the sea spray and piling up around the ravaged brow suggests amnesia, the gradual muffling of memory or its dispersal into thin air. Celan marked a single line in the copy of Hölderlin's "Andenken" he took with him to La Ciotat:

> Es nehmet aber
> Und gibt Gedächtnis die See
>
> [But it is the sea
> That takes and gives memory].[90]

His reply to that poem underscores this reminder that the taking of memory precedes its giving, that anamnesis is predicated upon an initial forgetting, and that remembrance is a speculation on loss which by no means always results in the coming (back) to itself of consciousness, the safe return to harbor of the friends who have set sail for the Indies.

Together with Celan's other Hölderlin poems, "Andenken" implicitly rejects the pomp and ceremony of the official commemorations held in his honor during the Second World War. In effect, the poet of the secret Germany has again gone underground, this time without a hint of the messianic expectation of years past. The speaker of "Andenken" is left to perform a precarious balancing act, remaining ever mindful of Hölderlin while declining to resurrect him in memory; in a later poem, he is referred to simply as "Jener" ("that one"), as if Celan expected his readership to intuit whom he had in mind.[91] In 1970, Celan overcame some initial reservations to travel to Stuttgart to take part in the festivities marking the 200th anniversary of Hölderlin's birth. There he recited a number of unpublished poems without once mentioning by name the poet in whose memory they were being read. According to eyewitnesses, his words were greeted with blank incomprehension by the assembled Hölderlin specialists, several of whom had been members of the society since its inception.[92] Barely two months later, Celan drowned himself in the Seine. In place of a suicide note, a copy of Wilhelm Michel's Hölderlin biography was found on his writing desk, opened up to the following underlined passage: "Sometimes this genius goes dark and sinks down into the bitter well of his heart"[93] — a heart which, in its darkest hour, the figs of remembrance were no longer able to sustain.

We encounter Hölderlin exiled to a subterranean space in my second text as well, a prose poem by Eich published some twenty-two years after "Latrine" in his collection *Maulwürfe* (Moles). The year was 1968: student demonstrations rocked the streets of Paris, the United States was embroiled in the Vietnam conflict, and Bertaux had just created a furor by telling the Hölderlin Society that their hallowed poet had been a lifelong Jacobin. Amidst all this hubbub, Eich's "Hölderlin" begins on a curiously calm and detached note:

> In Fußgängertunnels denke ich: Hier ist neulich Hölderlin gegangen und hat die Auslagen betrachtet, Wäsche, Keramik, Bücher, ein Espresso. Er war außer sich, deshalb machte ihm die Zeit nichts. Diotima ist lange gestorben, aber er nicht, es schmerzt ihn.[94]

> [In pedestrian tunnels I think: Hölderlin passed though here recently and looked at the displays, linen, ceramics, books, an espresso. He was beside himself, that's why time didn't matter to him. Diotima died long ago, but he didn't; it pains him.]

The figure who wanders absentmindedly through pedestrian tunnels has little in common with the resurrected poet of the George Circle. Hellingrath's Hölderlin had been permitted decades of rest before returning from the grave to lead his people. Eich's Hölderlin never died in the first place, nor is he truly alive today: the narrator finds him haunting the catacombs of modern civilization. This is the old, mad Hölderlin invoked by Celan, the walking corpse, the spectral figure described by contemporaries as one whose spirit had been cloaked in darkness (*geistig umnachtet*). "Leben ist Tod, und Tod ist auch ein Leben" (Life is death, and death is a kind of life), he writes from out of this state of perpetual numbness, and: "Ich bin nichts mehr, ich lebe nicht mehr gerne!" (I'm nothing now, and listless I live on).[95] The historical Hölderlin would find peace in 1843, forty years after the death of his beloved Diotima. Eich's Hölderlin remains indefinitely trapped upon — or rather under — the earth.

What holds him back? "He was beside himself [with rage, that is; literally: he was outside himself], that's why time didn't matter to him" is Eich's somewhat cryptic explanation. Eich suggests that Hölderlin broke the continuum of time by becoming a stranger to himself, a meaningless sign.[96] When did this happen? In 1806, when he was committed to Dr Autenrieth's Clinic for the mentally ill? Around 1910, when his work was mythicized, voided of history and transformed into a "temple-less shrine" (Heidegger)?[97] Or after 1945, when the flood of scholarly work on Hölderlin continued unabated, proving that he could not be left to rest in peace? Eich does not say. But in the iconography of the undead, the hourglass has a double function as both enemy and redeemer. Cursed to roam the earth long after their loved ones have perished, the living dead await the time when it is time, the *kairos* that will set them free from their interminable bondage. Contrary to the claims of the Nazis, Hölderlin's time has not yet come.

In the meantime, his eyes pass over the "linen, ceramic, books and an espresso" that are up for sale in the underground passageway. Martin Walser had already used the espresso to symbolize the upwardly mobile aspirations of the West German middle class in his novel *Ehen in Philippsburg* (Marriages in Philippsburg, 1957), one of the first critical examinations of the economic miracle.[98] The products listed by Eich likewise signify the growing prosperity of the BRD. In the pedestrian tunnel, the trappings of bourgeois domesticity — the clutter of bedroom, bathroom, and kitchen — are turned outward for show, exposed to the admiring, cynical, blank, or covetous gaze of passers-by. Hölderlin's reaction is one of anger: *er war außer sich*, perhaps because the dreams given voice in his poetry have failed to materialize in consumer society. But the phrase has another meaning as well. Insofar as the commodity likewise presents itself in the tunnel as timeless and "outside itself," abstracted from the conditions of its production and the context of its use, Eich insinuates that Hölderlin has come to resemble the very wares he surveys. Indeed, his own books may well number among those set out for display. "In an essentially non-traditionalist society, aesthetic tradition is dubious a priori," Adorno wrote in the same year.[99] A generation after the war, Hölderlin's work represents just another cultural good available for exchange and ready consumption. As if in mocking inversion of the depths with which it was once credited, its purity has migrated into glazed surface and empty form. Postwar affluence has more effectively debased Hölderlin's poetry than wartime need.

From the vantage point of Eich's "Hölderlin," the two central tendencies of the postwar reception only contributed to that process. On the one hand, the philologists treated the poet's work as so much lifeless matter, which it was their duty to describe, classify, dissect, and annotate. On the other, the mythmakers transformed him, in accordance with the displacement proper to mythic speech, into the representative and sacrificial victim of a supernatural order. The blows dealt by Apollo, inexorable emissaries of a truth mere mortals could neither comprehend nor endure, had harried him from seminary to clinic to graveyard. His illness ennobled, his poverty glorified, Hölderlin could take up his place in the anthologies and feuilletons of the epoch. "Within half a century," remarked Minder in 1965, "Hölderlin has been sacralized and commodified at the same time. . . . Literary histories for schools and bourgeois households have silently put aside the military decorations and now act as cleaning ladies — Hölderlin, Rilke, Trakl their favorite objects."[100]

It should be noted, however, that Eich's position with regard to Hölderlin has undergone a significant shift since "Latrine." In 1946, there was nothing to suggest an affinity between the two poets, still less an empathetic identification. Eich considered Hölderlin to be both infinitely remote from the general morass and — to the extent that the radiance of his verses could be viewed as the function of a polluted reality — uncomfortably close to it. The opening words of "Hölderlin," by contrast, announce a new solidarity between the poets that derives from their common *resistance* to assimilation. As Michael Kohlenbach comments, pedestrian tunnels "signify places of survival as well, in which whatever is forced to disappear from the surface, and is tolerated nowhere else, can find refuge."[101] Perhaps Eich thinks of Hölderlin while passing through pedestrian tunnels because they are both moles snuffling in the underground of poetry, banished from the sunlight for speaking "a language that withdraws from all manipulation," as Eich put it in his Büchner Prize speech.[102] And just as he, in the same speech, made "critique, opposition and resistance" the sole justification for continuing to write poems,[103] so his predecessor's silent scrutiny divests the consumer goods of their reassuring solidity, making them appear in a different light. Eich continues: "That's what is characteristic of pedestrian tunnels; you go under and everything comes up. . . . The colors are gone, only yellow remains."[104] The critique may be muted, yet it is still perceptible to those accustomed to the tunnel's artificial twilight.

"Hölderlin" thus invites us to think of *two* Hölderlins: one safely canonized and exhibited for the edification of the middle class, another still susceptible to pain and gifted with vision of an almost hallucinatory clarity; one as he is judged by Germany, the other as he judges Germany. Both have achieved an immortality of sorts. But whereas the first tarries in the endless present of an empty fame, the second embodies the genuine pathos of the *Dichter in dürftiger Zeit*, the poet in a time of need.[105] It is this second figure who could rouse the Germans from out of the sleepy self-satisfaction that the mainstream reception did nothing to counteract; it is with this second figure, I would suggest, that the loyalties of Celan and Eich lie; and it is to this second figure, as we encounter him in the writings of Heidegger, Adorno and Brecht, that this study is addressed.

Notes

[1] Günter Eich. *Gesammelte Werke*, 4 vols., vol. 1: *Die Gedichte: Die Maulwürfe*, ed. Axel Vieregg (Frankfurt am Main: Suhrkamp, 1991), 37; the English translation is taken from *Pigeons and Moles: Selected Writings of Günter Eich*, trans. Michael Hamburger (Columbia, SC: Camden House, 1990), 5.

[2] Eich makes this contrast explicit in a draft to his 1947 address "Die heutige Situation der Lyrik"; see Eich, *Gesammelte Werke* vol. 4: *Vermischte Schriften*, 477. See also Eich, "Wo bleibt die deutsche Literatur?" (1948), in *Gesammelte Werke* 4:478–80.

[3] Eich, *Gesammelte Werke* 1:37; *Pigeons and Moles*, 5.

[4] Hölderlin, *StA* 2:188.

[5] Eich thereby also marks his distance from the Heideggerian reading of "Andenken," published in 1943. Martin Anderle notes the "complete incompatibility of Eich's and Heidegger's positions," even suggesting that we read "Latrine"

as a reponse to Heidegger. See Anderle, "Hölderlin in der Lyrik Günter Eichs," *Seminar: Journal of Germanic Studies* 7.2 (1971): 106–7. In the absence of evidence that Eich was familiar with Heidegger's essay at the time of writing, I have preferred to interpret "Latrine," more generally, as a reaction to the mystically tinged readings of Hölderlin that flourished during and after the Second World War.

[6] Eich, *Gesammelte Werke* 1:442.

[7] For a different interpretation, see Dieter Breuer, "Wörter so voll Licht so finster: Hölderlingedichte von Günter Eich bis Rolf Haufs." In Dieter Breuer, ed., *Deutsche Lyrik nach 1945* (Frankfurt am Main: Suhrkamp, 1988), 357.

[8] I overlook here the controversy surrounding Eich's earlier engagement for the Nazi Party.

[9] Alfred Andersch, "Das junge Europa formt sein Gesicht," in *Der Ruf: Unabhängige Blätter der jungen Generation* 1/1 (1946): 2.

[10] Gerhard Kurz, "Hölderlin 1943," in *Hölderlin und Nürtingen*, ed. Peter Härtling and Gerhard Kurz (Stuttgart: J. B. Metzler, 1994), 112.

[11] Hölderlin, *StA* 3:153; the English translation is taken from *Hyperion and Selected Poems*, ed. Eric L. Santner and Willard Trask (New York: Continuum, 1990), 128.

[12] Paul Kluckhohn, "Bericht über die Veranstaltungen," in *Iduna: Jahrbuch der Hölderlin-Gesellschaft*, ed. Friedrich Beißner and Paul Kluckhohn (Tübingen: J. C. B. Mohr, 1944), 14.

[13] Gerhard Schumann, "Ansprache des Präsidenten," in Beißner and Kluckhohn, *Iduna*, 19.

[14] Josef Weinheber, "An Hölderlin: Ode," in *Hölderlin: Gedenkschrift zu seinem 100. Todestag*, ed. Paul Kluckhohn (Tübingen: J. C. B. Mohr, 1943), 2.

[15] Paul Kluckhohn, "Zur Einführung," in *Hölderlin*, 4.

[16] Claudia Albert, ed., *Deutsche Klassiker im Nationalsozialismus: Schiller; Kleist; Hölderlin* (Stuttgart: J. B. Metzler, 1994), 228.

[17] Quoted by Kluckhohn in his essay "Hölderlin bei den Soldaten des zweiten Weltkriegs," in Beißner and Kluckhohn, *Iduna*, 193.

[18] Quoted by Kluckhohn, "Bericht über die Veranstaltungen," in Beißner and Kluckhohn, *Iduna*, 14.

[19] Kluckhohn, "Hölderlin im Bilde der Nachwelt," in Beißner and Kluckhohn, *Iduna*, 8.

[20] Norbert Rath, "Kriegskamerad Hölderlin: Zitate zur Sinngebungsgeschichte," in *Neue Wege zu Hölderlin*, ed. Uwe Beyer (Würzburg: Königshausen & Neumann, 1994), 240.

[21] Among them, however, such luminaries as Waiblinger, Mörike, Schwab, Uhland, the Arnims, Brentano, and Nietzsche.

[22] The character sketch in Otto Roquette's *Geschichte der deutschen Literatur* (2nd ed; Stuttgart: Ebnert & Seubert, 1872) is fairly representative. After a short biographical synopsis, focusing on Hölderlin's tragic love affair with Diotima and his descent into madness, Roquette turns to the poetic work, in which he does not fail

to find evidence of a pathological flight from reality: "This was entirely consumed in the enraptured admiration of ancient Greece, and in the dreamy longing to win back this beauty for the present. . . . The real foundation is obscured by his longing for the ideal. . . . The sense of longing and flame of freedom in his work never go beyond enthusiasm, and they inevitably fail when it is a question of sober seriousness and hard work" (476–77).

[23] Curt Paul Janz, *Friedrich Nietzsche: Biographie* (Munich: Carl Hanser, 1978), 1:80. The schoolboy essay is to be found in Nietzsche, *Kritische Gesamtausgabe I.2: Nachgelassene Aufzeichnungen, Herbst 1958–Herbst 1862*, ed. Johann Figl, (Berlin: Walter de Gruyter, 2000), 338–41.

[24] Kluckhohn dismissed Hölderlin's revolutionary zeal as a sign of youthful immaturity ("Hölderlin im Bilde der Nachwelt," 9). Ten years earlier, Lukács had more accurately represented Hölderlin as the only one of his contemporaries to hold fast to the principles of the Revolution even after the Thermidorian reaction had set in. See Lukács, "Hölderlins Hyperion" in *Der andere Hölderlin: Materialien zum "Hölderlin"-Stück von Peter Weiss*, ed. Thomas Beckmann and Volker Canaris (Frankfurt am Main: Suhrkamp, 1972), 22.

[25] Gerhard Schumann, "Ansprache des Präsidenten," 20.

[26] See Stanley Corngold and Geoffrey Waite, "A Question of Responsibility: Nietzsche with Hölderlin at War, 1914–1946," in *Nietzsche, Godfather of Fascism?* ed. Jacob Golomb and Robert S. Wistrich (Princeton: Princeton UP, 2002), 196–210.

[27] Claudia Albert, "'Dient Kulturarbeit dem Sieg?' Hölderlin-Rezeption von 1933–1945" in *Hölderlin und die Moderne: Eine Bestandsaufnahme*, ed. Gerhard Kurz, Valérie Lawitschka, and Jürgen Wertheimer (Tübingen: Attempto, 1995), 156.

[28] "was da Hölderlin sagt und meint Himmler." Hans Magnus Enzensberger, *Landessprache* (Frankfurt am Main: Suhrkamp, 1960), 41.

[29] See Claudia Albert, *Deutsche Klassiker im Nationalsozialismus*, 191.

[30] Benn, *Doppelleben* (Munich: dtv, 1967), 78.

[31] Hermann Burte, "Rede auf Hölderlin," in Beißner and Kluckhohn, *Iduna*, 175. Of course, not all writings on Hölderlin from the Second World War were propagandistic. Friedrich Beißner and his team, for instance, were able to continue with their Hölderlin edition after the war because of the perceived neutrality and objectivity of their wartime scholarship. Peter Szondi, who hardly stood close to Beißner philosophically, went so far as to praise his editorial work for the notorious field edition as an act of "cunning and civil courage." By this he meant that Beißner, although under considerable political pressure at the time, selected texts for the field edition that contradicted the strident image of Hölderlin being put forward by the Nazis. Peter Szondi, "Hölderlin 1943," *Die Zeit*, 20 Mar. 1970, 28.

[32] See Alfred Klein, "Im Zwielicht des Jahrhunderts: Johannes R. Bechers Hölderlinbilder," in *Im Zwielicht des Jahrhunderts: Beiträge zur Hölderlin-Rezeption*, ed. Alfred Klein, Günter Mieth, and Klaus Pezold (Leipzig: Rosa-Luxemburg-Verein, 1994), 23–26. See also Helen Fehervary, *Hölderlin and the Left: The Search for a Dialectic of Art and Life* (Heidelberg: Carl Winter, 1977), 45.

[33] On Hellingrath's influence on Heidegger's interpretation, see Henning Bothe, *"Ein Zeichen sind wir, deutungslos": Zur Rezeption Hölderlins von ihren Anfängen bis zu Stefan George* (Stuttgart: J. B. Metzler, 1992), 208–12.

[34] Norbert von Hellingrath, *Hölderlin-Vermächtnis*, ed. Ludwig von Pigenot (Munich: Bruckmann, 1936), 104.

[35] Heidegger, *GA* 12:172.

[36] Letter to Hegel, 14 July 1804; Hölderlin, *StA* 7.2:296.

[37] For a detailed account of George's Hölderlin reception, see Bothe, *"Ein Zeichen sind wir, deutungslos,"* 115–201. See also Joseph Suglia, "On the Nationalist Reconstruction of Hölderlin in the George Circle," *German Life and Letters* 55.4 (2002): 387–97.

[38] Hellingrath, *Hölderlin-Vermächtnis*, 124. See also Wilhelm Dilthey, *Das Erlebnis und die Dichtung* (Göttingen: Vandenhoeck & Ruprecht, 1965), 242–317; and Ernst Cassirer, "Hölderlin und der deutsche Idealismus," in *Hölderlin: Beiträge zu seinem Verständnis in unserm Jahrhundert*, ed. Alfred Kelletat (Tübingen: J. C. B. Mohr, 1961), 79–118.

[39] Hellingrath, *Hölderlin-Vermächtnis*, 151.

[40] This systematic inattention to Hölderlin's historical context would then be overturned on two flanks: most spectacularly, through the political revisionism of Bertaux and Minder; more effectively in the longer term, through the research of Dieter Henrich (and, later, the likes of Manfred Frank, Gerhard Kurz, and Christoph Jamme) into Hölderlin's hitherto underappreciated contribution to the philosophical debates of the age. See in particular Henrich's groundbreaking essay "Hegel und Hölderlin," in *Stuttgarter Hegel-Tage 1970*, ed. Hans-Georg Gadamer (Bonn: Bouvier, 1974), 29–52.

[41] Bothe, *"Ein Zeichen sind wir, deutungslos,"* 101.

[42] Stefan George, *Werke*, (Munich: Helmut Küpper, 1958), 1:519. The narrative implicit in such statements would recur in various guises over the course of the century. With slight variations, it may be summarized as follows: Through the happy conformity of chance to the *Zeitgeist*, something in Hölderlin's work to which his contemporaries were blind reveals itself, in all its glory, to a later readership. Like Benjamin's seed of grain unleashing its undiminished germinative power after thousands of years in storage, the poet emerges from his long oblivion into the light of his actuality, suddenly to be acclaimed as one of our own. For the silence that greeted his efforts during his lifetime can now be understood, regretted, but also excused, as the necessary corollary to his visionary mission. The poet *must* remain unheard by all who have come before, for what he says is unheard-of; it never even gets picked up on the radar screen of a "horizon of expectations," and so proves unable to bring into being the audience it requires. To Hölderlin's initiates, of course, that is precisely the sign of his authenticity. We latecomers flatter ourselves that we are uniquely placed to understand him, the clairvoyant analyst of our own condition. Hölderlin wrote *for us* and our times; honoring him, we honor our own acuity. — Thus Hellingrath barely acknowledges the entire nineteenth-century reception; thus Paul Kluckhohn, among the most brazen of the Nazi school, regrets that "Hölderlin could not escape the fate of being claimed as an advance

fighter [*Vorkämpfer*] by various modern tendencies, for example, in so-called Expressionism"; thus Heidegger ascertains the complete lack of understanding from which Hölderlin's work continues to suffer, while at the same time refusing to enter into conversation with modern philology; thus Bertaux reads Hölderlin as the poet of the 68ers. Even when the successful act of interpretation is indefinitely deferred, even when, as with Heidegger, over-hasty identifications are deplored and caution urged, the interpreter still assumes his superiority over a complacent and unappreciative tradition: he tries to wipe out his predecessors.

[43] George, *Werke* 1:521.

[44] Hellingrath, *Hölderlin-Vermächtnis*, 143.

[45] Hellingrath, *Hölderlin-Vermächtnis*, 124–25. Alfred Döblin, himself an ardent admirer of the poet (his first novel had been dedicated "in love and reverence to the *manes* of Hölderlin"), was one of the few to protest against this fateful turn. In 1923, he wrote: "Over the last few years, clever literati have tried to make him out to be the 'most German of the Germans.' . . . But Hölderlin clearly expressed what he thought about his Germans. . . . He wanted to be a Greek." Quoted in Jochen Meyer, ed., *Alfred Döblin: 1878–1978; Eine Ausstellung des Deutschen Literaturarchivs im Schiller-Nationalmuseum Marbach am Neckar* (Munich: Kösel Verlag, 1978), 75, 77.

[46] Hellingrath, *Hölderlin-Vermächtnis*, 124–25. The catchword "secret Germany," coined by Karl Wolfskehl, was widely used in the George Circle to denote an esoteric vision of national spiritual renewal diametrically opposed to the bureaucratic, rationalist Germany analyzed by Max Weber around the same time. See especially George's poem "Geheimes Deutschland" (1928). *Werke* 1:425–28; in English, *The Works of Stefan George*, trans. Olga Marx and Ernst Morwitz (Chapel Hill: U of North Carolina P, 1974), 374. The full story is told by Robert E. Norton, *Secret Germany: Stefan George and His Circle* (Ithaca, NY: Cornell UP, 2002).

[47] Walter Benjamin, "Wider ein Meisterwerk," in *Gesammelte Schriften*, vol. 3, ed. Hella Tiedemann-Bartels (Frankfurt am Main: Suhrkamp, 1972), 259; translated by Rodney Livingstone in Benjamin, *Selected Writings*, vol. 2: *1927–1934* (Cambridge, MA: Harvard UP, 1999), 384. See also the similar comments of Karl Löwith in *Mein Leben in Deutschland vor und nach 1933* (Stuttgart: Metzler, 1986), 21.

[48] Hellingrath, *Hölderlin-Vermächtnis*, 124. The antithesis between Goethe and Hölderlin that emerges around this time as a topos of Hölderlin reception persists right through to Martin Walser's 1970 address to the Hölderlin Society and beyond: "One cannot praise Hölderlin and *not* disparage Goethe." Walser, *Umgang mit Hölderlin: Zwei Reden* (Frankfurt am Main: Insel, 1997), 39.

[49] Hellingrath, *Hölderlin-Vermächtnis*, 125.

[50] See Hermann Haering, "Hölderlin im Weltkrieg, 1914–1918," in Beißner and Kluckhohn, *Iduna*, 177–92; and Hermann Burte, "Rede auf Hölderlin," 175.

[51] Quoted in Bernhard Zeller, ed. *Klassiker in finsterer Zeit, 1933–1945*, 2 vols. (Marbach: Schiller-Nationalmuseum, 1983), 2:300.

[52] Hellingrath, *Hölderlin-Vermächtnis*, 143.

[53] See Peter Gay, *Weimar Culture* (Harmondsworth, UK: Penguin, 1974), 60–63.

[54] Hugo von Hofmannsthal, *Gesammelte Werke in zehn Einzelbänden*, ed. Bernd Schoeller (Frankfurt am Main: Fischer, 1979), 9:488.

[55] Hermann Burte, "Rede auf Hölderlin," 168 and 171.

[56] George, *Werke* 1:457; *The Works of Stefan George*, 400.

[57] Ludwig von Pigenot, "Geleitwort," his introduction to Hellingrath, *Hölderlin-Vermächtnis*, 8.

[58] Carl Schmitt, *Glossarium: Aufzeichnungen der Jahre 1947–1951*, ed. Eberhard Freiherr von Medem (Berlin: Duncker & Humblot, 1991), 152.

[59] See Heidegger's prefatory note to his lecture "Hölderlins Erde und Himmel," Heidegger, *GA* 4:152.

[60] Helmut Wocke, "Norbert von Hellingrath zum Gedächtnis," *Dichtung und Volkstum* 41 (1941): 358 and 360.

[61] Wolfgang Binder, "Bericht über die Gründung der Friedrich-Hölderlin-Gesellschaft," *HJb* 2 (1947): 240.

[62] Kurz, "Hölderlin 1943," 126.

[63] Adolf Beck, "Die Hölderlin-Forschung in der Krise 1945–1947," *HJb* 3(1948/49): 212.

[64] Binder, "Bericht," 240.

[65] Binder, "Bericht," 240.

[66] Walter Rehm, *Orpheus: Der Dichter und die Toten: Selbstdeutung und Totenkult bei Novalis — Hölderlin — Rilke* (Düsseldorf: L. Schwann, 1950), 11.

[67] Rehm, *Orpheus*, 11.

[68] In 1943, Pongs was praising the anti-Semitic novelist Emil Strauß for "reaching deeper [than Hölderlin] into the biological ground of his people, which sustains the new sense of value of the 20th century." By 1966, he was preaching, against Adorno's "Parataxis" speech, that "the polar world laws of creation reach deeper than all dialectic, deeper too than the Marxist dialectic of history. He who misheeds them destroys himself in the end." A timeless creativity had thus replaced race biology as the deepest dimension that the poet can plumb. Pongs, "Einwirkungen Hölderlins auf die deutsche Dichtung seit der Jahrhundertwende," in Beißner and Kluckhohn, *Iduna*, 129; and *Dichtung im gespaltenen Deutschland* (Stuttgart: Union, 1966), 116.

[69] Lutz Niethammer, *Posthistoire: Has History Come to an End?* trans. Patrick Camiller (London: Verso, 1992), 3 and 79.

[70] Rehm, *Orpheus*, 151–52.

[71] Rehm, *Orpheus*, 162.

[72] Robert Minder, "Hölderlin unter den Deutschen," *HJb* 14 (1965/66): 5.

[73] Johannes R. Becher, *Publizistik IV: 1952–1958* (Berlin: Aufbau-Verlag, 1981), 25.

[74] See Walter Otto, "Hölderlin und die Griechen" and "Hölderlin," in *Mythos und Welt*, by Otto, ed. Kurt von Fritz (Darmstadt: Wissenschaftliche Buchgesellschaft, 1963), 120.

[75] It might be objected at this point that Heidegger refused to recognize the Second World War as an event, that his Hölderlin interpretation remained essentially unchanged after 1934, and even, as Adorno would have it, that his writings on Hölderlin are fascist through and through. I will broach these concerns in the next chapter.

[76] Hölderlin, *Poems and Fragments,* trans. Michael Hamburger (London: Routledge and Kegan Paul, 1966), 435.

[77] Paul Celan, *Gesammelte Werke,* ed. Beda Allemann and Stefan Reichert, 5 vols. (Frankfurt am Main: Suhrkamp, 1983), 3:186.

[78] Celan, *Werke,* 1:121; in English, Celan, *Selected Poems and Prose,* trans. John Felstiner (New York: Norton, 2001), 67.

[79] Otto Pöggeler, *Spur des Worts: Zur Lyrik Paul Celans* (Freiburg: Karl Alber, 1986), 387.

[80] See Peter Szondi, *Hölderlin-Studien: Mit einem Traktat über philologische Erkenntnis* (Frankfurt am Main: Insel, 1967), 16.

[81] John Felstiner, *Paul Celan: Poet, Survivor, Jew* (New Haven, CT: Yale UP, 1995), 75.

[82] See Felstiner, *Paul Celan,* 162.

[83] See Anselm Haverkamp, *Leaves of Mourning: Hölderlin's Late Work — With an Essay on Keats and Melancholy,* trans. Vernon Chadwick (Albany, NY: SUNY P, 1996), 71.

[84] Neither of Bernhard Böschenstein's two essays on Celan and Hölderlin mentions the poem. See Böschenstein, "Celan als Leser Hölderlins und Jean Pauls," in *Argumentio e Silencio: International Paul Celan Symposium,* ed. Amy D. Colin (Berlin: Walter de Gruyter, 1987), 183–98; "Hölderlin und Celan," in *Paul Celan,* ed. Werner Hamacher and Winfried Menninghaus (Frankfurt am Main: Suhrkamp, 1988), 191–200. The poem is also not discussed in Sieghild Bogumil's otherwise exhaustive analysis, "Celans Hölderlinlektüre im Gegenlicht des schlichten Wortes," *Celan-Jahrbuch* 1987 (1): 81–126.

[85] Peter Härtling emphasizes the height of the poet's brow in his *Hölderlin: Ein Roman* (Darmstadt: Luchterhand, 1976), 17 and 531, as does Stephan Hermlin in his radio play *Scardanelli,* in *Hörspiele aus der DDR,* ed. Stefan Bodo Würffel (Frankfurt am Main: Fischer, 1982), 146–67; here, 147.

[86] Celan, *Werke* 1:226; *Selected Poems and Prose,* 159. On "Tübingen, Jänner," see Philippe Lacoue-Labarthe, *Poetry as Experience,* trans. Andrea Tarnowski (Stanford, CA: Stanford UP, 1999), 1–38.

[87] Peter Demetz, *After the Fires: Recent Writing in the Germanies, Austria, and Switzerland* (San Diego: Harcourt Brace Jovanovich, 1986), 46.

[88] Dieter Henrich, *The Course of Remembrance and Other Essays on Hölderlin,* ed. Eckart Förster (Stanford, CA: Stanford UP, 1997).

[89] Around the same time, Celan transcribed a verse of Emily Dickinson: "You cannot make Remembrance grow." Quoted in Felstiner, *Paul Celan,* 96.

[90] Felstiner, *Paul Celan,* 75; Hölderlin, *StA* 2:188.

⁹¹ Celan, *Werke* 3:108: "Ich trink Wein aus zwei Gläsern / und zackere an / der Königszäsur / wie Jener / am Pindar" (I drink wine from two glasses / and plow away at / the king's caesura / like that one / at Pindar). *Selected Poems and Prose*, 367.

⁹² See the recollection of Hans Mayer, in *Das unglückliche Bewußtsein: Zur deutschen Literaturgeschichte von Lessing bis Heine* (Frankfurt am Main: Suhrkamp, 1990), 352, as well as Clara Menck's report in the *FAZ*, "Doch kein Jakobiner," *Frankfurter Allgemeiner Zeitung*, 24 Mar. 1970, 24.

⁹³ Quoted in Felstiner, *Paul Celan*, 287.

⁹⁴ Eich, *Gesammelte Werke* 1:350.

⁹⁵ Hölderlin, *StA* 2.1:267 and 374; Hölderlin, *Poems and Fragments*, 605 and 587.

⁹⁶ Cf. Hölderlin, *StA* 2.1:195.

⁹⁷ "ein tempelloser Schrein"; Heidegger, *GA* 4:7.

⁹⁸ Martin Walser, *Ehen in Philippsburg* (Frankfurt am Main: Suhrkamp, 1997), 128.

⁹⁹ "In einer wesentlich nicht-traditionalistischen Gesellschaft ist ästhetische Tradition a priori dubios" (Adorno, *GS* 7:38).

¹⁰⁰ Minder, "Hölderlin unter den Deutschen," *HJb* 14 (1965/66): 16–17.

¹⁰¹ Michael Kohlenbach, *Günter Eichs späte Prosa: Einige Merkmale der Maulwürfe* (Bonn: Bouvier Verlag, 1982), 108.

¹⁰² Eich, *Gesammelte Werke* IV, 619.

¹⁰³ Eich, *Gesammelte Werke* IV, 627.

¹⁰⁴ Eich, *Gesammelte Werke* I, 350 "Das sind die Eigenschaften von Fußgängertunnels, man taucht unter, alles taucht auf. . . . Die Farben sind dahin, nur das Gelbe bleibt."

¹⁰⁵ Hölderlin, *StA* 2.1:94.

1: Conversation: Heidegger, "Das abendländische Gespräch"

> *Irr gieng er nun; denn allzu gut sind*
> *Genien; himmlisch Gespräch ist sein nun.*
>
> [He has gone astray; for all too good are
> Genii; heavenly talk is his now.]
> — Hölderlin, "Ganymed"

MARTIN HEIDEGGER'S RECEPTION of Hölderlin's poetry is character-ized as much by its remarkable constancy and longevity as by its metamorphoses, discontinuities, and occasional U-turns. The leitmotif in the conversation is easy enough to identify: the conviction he announced in 1934, at the beginning of his first lecture course on Hölderlin, that the poet's "still space-time-less work has already overcome our petty historical affairs and founded the inception of another history, that history that commences with the struggle for the decision about the arrival or flight of the god," will never waver.[1] It animates the two other lecture courses devoted to Hölderlin that he gave during the Third Reich; it stands behind the speeches and essays collected in *Erläuterungen zu Hölderlins Dichtung* (Elucidations to Hölderlin's Poetry, 1944); it resurfaces, its eschatological tone intact, if somewhat less grandiloquently inflected, in the postwar pieces on technology, poetry, and dwelling; and it is reaffirmed in the *Spiegel* interview of 1966. In that conversation, posthumously published under the title "Nur noch ein Gott kann uns retten" (Only a God Can Save Us), Heidegger insists that his thinking "stands in an absolutely nec-essary relation to the poetry of Hölderlin."[2] The two statements find their common ground in the solemn words Heidegger had uttered over thirty years before. So it comes as no surprise that early in 1976, shortly before his death, Heidegger selected a number of verses by Hölderlin to be read aloud at his burial (*GA* 16:749). The words of the poet who had restored the possibility of divine experience resounded, prayer-like, over the grave of the thinker who had joined Nietzsche in proclaiming the death of God.

If Hölderlin's importance for Heidegger remains constant and immense, the exact nature, shifting constellations, and political implica-tions of that importance as it unfolds over time are rather more difficult to pinpoint. As ever more volumes of the monumental complete edition of Heidegger's "ways, not works"[3] emerge from the archives, we are in a bet-ter position to trace the development of his conversation with Hölderlin from 1934 to 1948, the period of his most intensive engagement with the poet. In particular, the appearance in 2000 of volume 75, which contains his previously unpublished essays, dialogues, and notes on Hölderlin, allows us to understand better the poet's role in Heidegger's thinking immediately after the collapse of Hitler's state. At this time, the crisis of the German nation went hand in hand with a personal crisis precipitated by, but not confined to, his disqualification from teaching at the recommendation of Karl Jaspers, whom he had once considered his staunchest ally in the philosophical guild. Basing my reasoning on a reading of the dialogue "Das abendländische Gespräch" (The Occidental Conversation), which he worked on intermittently between 1946 and 1948, only to set it aside unfinished, I will argue that Heidegger's conversation with Hölderlin underwent a profound and permanent transformation after the war. This transformation paved the way for the more sporadic writings on Hölderlin of the ensuing decades.

The meaning of this change, however, can only be fathomed once "Das abendländische Gespräch" is read in the political, social, and historical context of its genesis. Moreover, an appreciation of the significance of Heidegger's postwar positions requires that his earlier writings on and around Hölderlin be taken into account. Before discussing the dialogue, then, I will attempt to sketch what is at issue in their conversation through an analysis of those texts leading up to "Das abendländische Gespräch" which most obviously stand in Hölderlin's thrall (as we will see, the feudal metaphor is apposite). My interpretation of the dialogue will be guided by the questions that dominate this study as a whole: Which readings of Hölderlin became possible, which impossible, after the caesura of 1945? How could a poet misused for propagandistic purposes during the war be reclaimed for an alternative tradition? Why does Heidegger think we should still read Hölderlin, and whom does he mean by this "we"? The concluding sections of the chapter will address Heidegger's responses to these questions, briefly taking into consideration the texts following "Das abendländische Gespräch" that move in Hölderlin's orbit.

The Infinite Conversation

At first blush, conversation seems an unlikely candidate for a paradigm of reception. In a manner suspiciously in keeping with the phonocentric tradition of metaphysics analyzed by Derrida, the term generates the illusion of a face-to-face encounter between poet and thinker, held in an atmosphere of understanding, goodwill, and mutual respect. For the one-way flow of information designated by the word "reception" it substitutes a model of two-channel communication in which the indirection of writing is canceled in the immediacy and intimacy of speech. Perhaps Heidegger means simply to give voice to the hermeneutic commonplace that each generation enters into a process of dialogue with its predecessors. But just how seriously are we to take his choice of terminology? An essential requirement of any true conversation, as Heidegger himself points out, is the capacity to listen to what one's interlocutor is saying. "Being able to hear," he remarks in "Hölderlin und das Wesen der Dichtung" (Hölderlin and the Essence of Poetry, 1936), the first lecture he published on the poet, "is not merely a consequence of speaking with one another, but is, on the contrary, its presupposition."[4] In an obvious sense, this prerequisite goes unfulfilled in the case of Heidegger's conversation with Hölderlin, since the latter is neither present in person to hear what his commentator is saying nor capable of being contacted through telecommunicative means (barring the medium of the text, which is clearly unable to answer back). The conversation thus lacks a controlling instance to prevent the proliferation of interpretation and counter-interpretation, with the result that the danger of mishearing, as Heidegger concedes, is both essential and great.[5] (Or is the danger perhaps that of interrogation — *verhören* permits this alternative rendering — such that the inquisitor fails to listen to what the poet is saying precisely because he is too busy pressing him for answers? This, at any rate, will be the gist of Adorno's critique.) Consequently, there is nothing to stop one accusing Heidegger of ventriloquizing through the poet, much as the master of ceremonies at a séance hears only those responses he bids the summoned spirit say. "Dialogue is out of the question," concludes Paul de Man, a judgment shared by several later critics.[6]

Are we to see in "conversation," then, a metaphor — and an ill-chosen metaphor at that — for an interpretative maneuver more aptly described as one of selective hearing, subreption, or even violence? Before jumping to this conclusion, let us pause to examine more closely what Heidegger has in mind. Two points need to be noted here. The first is that every conversation presupposes a minimal consensus with regard to the topic being discussed, one that allows differences of opinion to emerge and make themselves heard in the first place. Heidegger rules out polemics from the outset, insisting that even the public airing of a disagreement (such as the Davos dispute with Ernst Cassirer) bears testimony to a deeper, unstated concurrence: "If there is to be *one* conversation, the essential word must remain tied to what is one and the same. Without this relation, even a quarrel is impossible."[7] So long as this common link remains in place, unanimity will prevail amidst the most vehement of altercations; once it has been severed, the conversation is over, leaving chatter to fill the void. Even when they suffer a falling out, then, the participants in a conversation must always already have *come to terms* with each other through their intuitive acquiescence to the conversation as such. The voice of the other raised in dissent is still the "voice of the friend" which, according to *Sein und Zeit* (Being and Time, 1927), each of us bears in our ear.[8]

Second, and correlatively, the interrelationship articulated by the conversationalists reflects and explicates an infrarelationship of the matter itself. Each speaker does not approach the topic with a fixed identity assured by other sources and a ready-made opinion at his disposal — this would make conversation little more than a comparison of viewpoints destined to remain forever external to what they look out on — but becomes who he is by submitting to the call that emanates from the "One and the Same." The identity of the interlocutors, that is to say, is secondary to the differentiated unity that they articulate and elucidate in the course of their discussion. So regarded, "conversation" is another, more congenial word for what Heidegger elsewhere calls *Auseinandersetzung*, the process of contestation by which the raging discord of the matter in question is taken apart in language (*GA* 6.1:xi); in the first lecture series on Hölderlin, held in 1934–35, the two terms are used almost interchangeably (*GA* 39:6 and 58). While this process necessitates a clear and measured use of words on the part of the conversationalists — despite the extravagant length of "Das abendländische Gespräch," the conversational paradigm is far removed from advocating volubility for its own sake — it also confronts them with a resistance to expression that derives from the excess of the abyssal ground of conversation over its propositional content. It is not simply the case that there is always more to be said, as if the need for conversation would vanish had we but world and time to say it all. Rather, the sayable at its limits comes up against an unsayable reserve, which is nonetheless the only thing worth saying. The appropriate rhetorical comportment when faced with such resistance is discretion. Heidegger's conversationalists endlessly, gingerly talk around what binds them together and gives their talking its characteristic shape.[9] The silences, lacunae, and pauses for breath that perforate their discourse are never simply "empty"; they intimate the presence of that which withdraws from speech in giving birth to the conversation as a whole: Being as such.

Over and above its communicative and expressive dimensions, conversation thus assumes an ontological significance that accounts for its central role in Heidegger's thinking from the early 1930s on, the period of the so-called *Kehre* or turning.[10] Notwithstanding its connotations of easy familiarity, conversation is for Heidegger an exercise in formal dictation that establishes the discursive parameters within which people(s) are free to move at any given time. It arises from, and refers back to, the epochal truth of Being in its interplay with the factual options available to Dasein in the historical world in which it finds itself; or as Heidegger remarks in "Hölderlin und das Wesen der Dichtung," "Conversation and its unity support our existence."[11] Certain topics are decreed in advance to be out of bounds, which is why it is through no fault of their own that earlier philosophers failed to pose the question of Being in an adequate fashion. Others are readmitted only after centuries of interdiction. Yet even as it sets strict limits on what is open for discussion, the conversational matrix also generates the forum in which ideas are to be introduced and debated in the first place. The anti-subjectivist implications of this model are evident. The most important is the divorce of creativity from individuality: the latter is subsumed into the dialogic relation; the former retreats into the ahistorical, utterly impersonal origin of history. The distinction between response (speaking in one's own name) and correspondence (being spoken through by what gives itself to be thought) collapses in the moment when the conversationalists co-respond to the fate prepared for them by Being.

The fate of the Germans — the *Zuspruch* assigned them by Being — is disclosed, preserved, and transcribed in the occidental tradition to which they are the sole legitimate heirs. The bond between the conversationalists, Heidegger tells his students during the war, is "the bond with the matter itself, which is one and the same from Parmenides to Hegel."[12] This fellowship guarantees the continuity of the conversation of the Occident at a time when it is threatened by the danger of nihilism, which is that of a growing estrangement from the tradition resulting in dialogic breakdown and the loss of identity. Heidegger maintains that this danger does not impose itself from without, as many cultural conservatives contended at the time. Rather, the spiritual desiccation or "desertification" of the West evidenced by a dearth of essential questioning springs directly from the self-refusal of the origin. Conversely, a conversational analysis that bears in mind such overdetermination by the origin will come to the conclusion that the conversation flows on subterraneously even when it appears to have dried up, much as the Ister — the Latin name for the upper reaches of the Danube, the river beside which the conversationalists pace in "Das abendländische Gespräch" — continues to course underground upon disappearing from view at the *Donauversickerungsstelle* near Möhringen. We *are* a conversation, Heidegger writes, hence unquenchable;[13] and in citing Hölderlin as his authority, he suggests that this "we" properly refers to those who become attentive to who they are by conversing *on* Hölderlin and *through* his word. "Das abendländische Gespräch" represents Heidegger's most concerted attempt to talk through the implications of this hypothesis.

The contestation of the matter of thinking in conversation occurs as the recovery, extrapolation, and re-presencing of its original and hitherto concealed possibilities, that is to say, as repetitive retrieval (*Wiederholung*).[14] In the conversation with which I am concerned here, "thinking" repeats the address of "poetry" (or "poetizing") without merely sending it back as an echo. Thinking and poetry speak (about) the same matter, but what they say is different and their manner of speaking distinct. Indeed, Heidegger suggests at times that their dialogue is bilingual: in order to communicate with each other, the language of poetry, *dichterisch*, and the language of thought, *denkerisch*, require the translational services of a meta-language that comprehends, and is comprehended by, both. This meta-language is language as such, understood as the defining trait of our being-in-the-world. "Language is the house of Being," Heidegger famously declares in his letter on humanism. "In its home man dwells. Those who think and those who create with words are the guardians of this home."[15] And in his 1936 speech on Hölderlin he proclaims: "Man's being is grounded in language; but this actually occurs only in *conversation*."[16] The particular conversation between thinking and poetry safeguards the dwelling in language that transpires in and as conversation in general. Heidegger, the no-longer-metaphysical thinker, and Hölderlin, the no-longer-metaphysical poet, together conspire to conserve the conversation that we ourselves are.

Everything depends upon thinking seizing the initiative to strike up a conversation with poetry. In itself, the abstract capacity to listen, and hence to make sense of what the other is saying, is not enough. The thinker must in addition already have decided to direct his ear to what the poet is saying. "Philosophy" fails to recognize poetry as a partner of equal standing because it mistakenly believes poetry has nothing to tell it, seeing in it at best a subaltern version of itself — ideas draped in verse — and at worst an indulgence in private feelings. Heidegger's task, as he understands it, is to put an end to this regrettable state of affairs by drawing philosophy into conversation with poetry, thereby causing it to metamorphose into something else, which he variously calls "incipient," "poetic," or "original thinking."[17] The most radical formulation of his mission statement is to be found in the final section of *Beiträge zur Philosophie* (Contributions to Philosophy, 1936–38), where he argues: "The historical destiny of philosophy culminates in the recognition of the necessity of making Hölderlin's word be heard."[18] *Beiträge zur Philosophie*, and by implication the contribution Heidegger will have made to philosophy, contribute to nothing less than the abdication of philosophy before the higher authority of (Hölderlin's) poetry.[19] Philosophy's traditional mission, the Socratic drive to self-knowledge, culminates and terminates in deixis, leaving behind an attentive, submissive, and participatory audience: the German expression used by Heidegger here, "Hölderlins Wort das Gehör zu schaffen," supports all three meanings. The figure of the attention-seeking thinker on the stage makes way for that of the awe-struck listener in the parterre. It is hardly surprising that Heidegger preferred to leave the publication of so audacious a claim until after his death.

The "knowledge" to which Heidegger refers does not represent the objectively ascertainable finding of any research program. It relies instead upon an act of recognition that no cognition can exhaust, an act that delineates the closure of philosophy even as it propels philosophy beyond and outside itself. This act has no need of predicative content apart from the proper name of the poet, which it thereby recognizes as the name proper to poetry: "*That Hölderlin!* The singularity of this 'that.' "[20] Recognition, observes Düttmann, simultaneously confirms and establishes the "unity of that which is to be recognized" and "the identity of the one who claims it."[21] In confirming Hölderlin as its historical purpose or determination, philosophy first establishes itself as that which was predestined to receive, and be received by, the poet's address. Hölderlin, in turn, comes to be established as the "poet's poet" through his ratification by philosophy.[22] Yet can philosophy overcome its initial reserve to make the first conversational move? Heidegger suggests not. On the one hand, the leap into conversation defies rational grounding and exceeds any possible justification, which is why philosophy's own conceptual resources are inadequate to the task. On the other, no external authority can compel philosophy to hearken unto Hölderlin's word except that word itself, which, however, philosophy only acknowledges to be authoritative once it has hearkened unto it. Because it does not yet know to need Hölderlin, philosophy claims not to need to know him. This aporia constitutes an irremovable obstacle blocking the path of philosophy to the summit where the parousia is scheduled to occur. Hölderlin's word remains both unheard and all-powerful, unheard because all-powerful, waiting in an ever-retreating future for an audience that never shows up.

Does Heidegger, the professor of philosophy who professes not to be a philosopher, escape this dilemma? Put differently, is *Beiträge zur Philosophie* still a work of philosophy, or does it call over to philosophy from the other side of the mountain? Heidegger's statements on the matter are marked by a curious ambivalence. While his thinking, which is a "thinking that is *underway*,"[23] a "way that itself goes,"[24] has *already* recognized Hölderlin's "ontohistorical uniqueness,"[25] and has thus begun conversing with poetry, Heidegger repeatedly makes clear that he by no means exempts himself from his judgment that we are *not yet* ready to converse with him. His first such caveat appears in the introduction to the 1934–35 lecture course, where he tells his students: "We must come to terms with the fact that the Germans needed a full hundred years before Hölderlin's work came before us in a form that compels us to confess that we still in no way measure up to his greatness and future power."[26] One is forced to conclude that the conversation begins at the very moment when Hölderlin extracts from us the confession that we are completely unfit to respond to him. Philosophy's path to Hölderlin is accordingly an endless one; or rather, it lies in the nature of this path to implicate its ending, to fold it back upon itself as a structural futurity, so that even when philosophy pricks up its ears, Hölderlin's word remains unheard, ever to come.

The result is a lopsided conversation indeed. One partner, hailed as the true dictator of the German people, does all the talking; the other prostrates himself before him, a sycophantic retainer who would gladly do his master's bidding if only he could ascertain what was being asked of him.

This immense and insurmountable disparity in the status of the interlocutors, driven to an extreme in the servile panegyrics of "Das abendländische Gespräch," helps explain the remarkable homogeneity of Heidegger's interpretations over the ensuing four decades. As we have seen, the belief that Hölderlin's voice had finally reached its proper audience was widespread among Nazi Germanists. Even Hyperion's *Scheltrede* found its way uncensored into wartime editions of Hölderlin's works on the grounds that his judgment about the barbarism of the Germans had been confuted by history. After over a century of neglect, the dream of the Fatherland pre-poetized by Hölderlin seemed to be on the verge of its realization. Heidegger never shared this belief. His reading of Hölderlin, notwithstanding the changes it underwent after 1945, could maintain its internal consistency because the poet's hour had not yet struck and could not be foretold. From the beginning, Heidegger's public reception of Hölderlin's poetry was stamped by this temporal disjunction.

Heidegger's Other Silence

In his short story "Lesebuchgeschichten" (Stories from a Primer, 1949) Wolfgang Borchert looks back upon a typical graduation ceremony at a German high school designed to boost the morale of the young men about to be sent off to war. His pared-down description of the address, delivered by a nameless authority figure, lists some of the most powerful and ubiquitous staples of Third Reich iconography: "Quoted Clausewitz. Gave 'em a few ideas: Honor, Fatherland. Had some Hölderlin read. Touched on Langemarck. Gripping ceremony, quite gripping."[27] The handbook of Prussian militarism, a by-product of the upsurge in nationalist sentiment that accompanied the Wars of Liberation; the hollow rhetoric of patriotic duty; the Battle of Langemarck from the Great War, which became a symbol of sacrifice for the Fatherland and in which 45,000 German volunteers, many of them students, were slaughtered; the stirring poetry of Hölderlin: all these number among the standard references being stockpiled as a kind of cultural arsenal to be deployed in support of the military effort in the East. They are the *Lesebuchgeschichten*, the textbook stories or hortatory tales of the new generation.

Although the speech described by Borchert takes place during the Second World War, all its motifs were already well established among petit bourgeois German nationalists at the time of the Nazi seizure of power. With a single exception, they can all be found in the speeches given by one such nationalist during his brief period as rector of Freiburg University, from April 1933 to April 1934. As if following Borchert's script, Heidegger cites Clausewitz to the students under his tutelage at the time;[28] in a speech delivered to the Institute for Pathological Anatomy he throws in the concepts of blood and soil;[29] at a matriculation ceremony held later the same year, he invites his audience to "place this festival in the reality and under the symbol of *Langemarck*."[30] Of the references listed by Borchert, Hölderlin's name alone fails to appear a single time in the speeches and public pronouncements made by Heidegger during this period. In a year in which, by the admission of even his most ardent apologists, Heidegger was wholly committed to the National Socialist cause, Hölderlin was passed over in silence.

This omission is puzzling for two reasons. First, we know that the intimate familiarity with Hölderlin's work demonstrated in the lecture series from the first semester after his resignation was the fruit of decades of prior reading and reflection. In 1953, in conversation with a visiting Japanese professor, Heidegger divulged that he had known Hölderlin's poetry since before the First World War,[31] and he describes elsewhere the enormous impact made by Hellingrath's edition upon students of his generation.[32] In April 1925 he writes to Hannah Arendt: "I live a great deal with Hölderlin"; in August of the same year he tells her that Hölderlin's *Hyperion* numbers among the few books on his writing desk.[33] On another occasion, he reveals that "Hölderlin's word, previously known alongside other poets, became fateful" for him in 1929/30, that is, at the onset of the *Kehre*.[34] By the time he was elected to the rectorship, then, Heidegger was not simply aware of Hölderlin's work; it had already assumed the central importance evident in the post-rectoral writings. It seems reasonable to expect that Heidegger would have cited him in support of the revolution in which, at the time, he so passionately believed.

Second, although the fascist consecration of Hölderlin was to culminate in 1943, the poet had been adopted (and adapted) for the revolution from the beginning. In March 1933 the Jewish cultural philosopher Eugen Rosenstock-Huessey expressed the — in retrospect tragic — opinion that "the National Socialist revolution is the Germans' attempt to realize Hölderlin's dream."[35] As early as 1934, Georg Lukács was alerting his fellow exiles to Hölderlin's increasing prominence in Nazi propaganda. In an article on *Hyperion* that provides one of the first formulations of the Jacobin thesis made famous over thirty years later by Bertaux, he complains how "the 'refinement' of the analysis through Dilthey and Gundolf, the eradication of all traces of social tragedy from Hölderlin's life and work, forms the basis for the coarsely demagogic, crassly mendacious desecration of his memory at the hands of the brownshirts of literary history."[36] Lukács goes on to quote articles from the *Nationalsozialistischer Monatsheft* (National Socialist Monthly), including one by the party philosopher Alfred Rosenberg, that adulate Hölderlin as a spiritual leader of the new Germany. Had he referred to Hölderlin in his speeches from the rectorate, Heidegger would thus have been following an established trend among the fascist cultural elite.

Under these circumstances, it seems pertinent to speak of a refusal to name Hölderlin rather than a mere omission. It seems appropriate to talk of a silence. The term "Heidegger's silence" is usually taken to refer to his unwillingness after the war to comment on, or express sorrow for, the extermination of European Jewry. As such, it is often used to denote his failure to acknowledge the guilt of the Germans and/or his own share in that guilt.[37] Heidegger's reticence with regard to Hölderlin offers a no less enigmatic counterpart to that notorious silence and partly explains, I believe, the political ambivalence of his interpretations of the poet both during and after the Third Reich.[38] Because information about the meaning of a silence can only be provided by examining its context, I will attempt to interpret this other silence from the moment of its public interruption. For now, I will pass over the lecture course on "Germanien" and "Der Rhein" that Heidegger began on 6 November 1934.[39] Although these lectures are indispensable for an understanding of his Hölderlin reception, they were intended for his students and lack the concision of a speech pitched at a wider public. I will turn, instead, to the first occasion on which Heidegger mentions the poet outside the lecture theater, a talk entitled "Die gegenwärtige Lage und die künftige Aufgabe der deutschen Philosophie" (The Current Situation and Future Task of German Philosophy), delivered on 30 November 1934 in Constance to the local branch of the German Society.

Heidegger begins by posing the perennial question: What is philosophy? and proceeds to dismiss two obvious answers. The first may be called the etymological: philosophy is the love of wisdom. Expanding on these terms, Heidegger draws the preliminary conclusion that philosophy is "the resolution to the essential questioning of the being and appearance of what is and what is not."[40] But he immediately qualifies this answer by remarking that, although it points toward where we have to look in order *really* to experience philosophy, it cannot substitute for that experience itself in which we first learn what philosophy is. Presumably, says Heidegger, real philosophy will only be found in the here and now, "in contemporary reality." The second answer, then, may be termed the actualist: philosophy is the cutting-edge of philosophical inquiry, the activities and research projects that currently go by that name. Proceeding from this definition, Heidegger ascertains that philosophy today is still grappling with the legacy of the three greatest thinkers of the nineteenth century, namely Hegel, Kierkegaard, and Nietzsche. But, again, this approach cannot tell us what philosophy is — on the contrary! It measures everything according to its timeliness, as "an *expression* or *achievement*" of a particular epoch, and thereby fails to recognize the untimeliness of all essential questioning.[41] Heidegger proceeds to explore this untimeliness, in a passage he will repeat almost verbatim the following year in *Einführung in die Metaphysik* (Introduction to Metaphysics).[42]

Here, on the threshold to Hölderlin, his clear allusion to Nietzsche hints at a conception of history that is irreconcilable with the historicist conversion of the past into a virtual museum, recalling the second untimely meditation on the advantages and disadvantages of history in relation to life. In his foreword to that text, Nietzsche defines the untimely as that which works "against the time and therefore upon the time and hopefully in favor of a coming time"[43] — quite in the spirit of a remark Heidegger makes a little later in the talk, which places history under the commissioning power of the future.[44] The reference to Nietzsche cuts both ways, however, insofar as it simultaneously dismisses as inadequate the conception of temporality that informs his vitalist historiography. The present from whose privileged vantage point Nietzsche evaluates the past is not to be confused with the ecstatic moment of authentic temporality, a point Heidegger had already rehearsed in *Sein und Zeit*.[45] In the second part of the speech, which is devoted to the question of history, Heidegger again explicitly draws on Nietzsche's text when he ponders and then rejects the notion that "the past only becomes 'directly relevant' history through its relation to the *respective present*."[46]

Heidegger's comments on the untimeliness of philosophy, which lead directly to the first appearance of Hölderlin's name, do not just allude to the second of the *Unzeitgemäße Betrachtungen* (Untimely Meditations). They also, and in a more subversive manner, recall the first, in which Nietzsche bitterly asks how "the magnificent Hölderlin" would have fared in the current "reality," whether he would have coped "in the present great time" ushered in by the unification of Germany over the groans of a defeated France.[47] At the moment in which they both turn to Hölderlin as to *the* untimely poet,[48] Heidegger's rejection of "contemporary reality" as the criterion for defining philosophy links up with Nietzsche's politically charged rejection of the reality of his own day. If all essential thinking is untimely, as both philosophers contend, if the immediate popularity of a thought necessarily serves as an index of its untruth, then the genealogy Hölderlin-Nietzsche-Heidegger testifies to a secret history that stands in opposition to the delusions of grandeur being entertained, in 1934 no less than in 1871, by the standard-bearers of the "present great time." The public acceptance of that history — the approval of the Constance branch of the German Society, for example — would deliver it over to superficiality; Heidegger would fall victim to his own publicistic success, calling forth a new wave of esotericism. It is in this doctrine of untimeliness that the function of Heidegger's jealously-guarded secret manuscripts, as well as the complex rites of initiation built around access to his lecture notes, is to be gauged.

Philosophy's untimeliness, however, need not damn it to permanent impotence. Heidegger continues: "Whatever is untimely can have its own time. Thus it is with philosophy. Thus it is with the two other fundamental powers through which an historical Dasein of a people is founded, with poetry and state-creation."[49] It would be wrong to read in "state-creation," as it appears here and in the parallel Hölderlin course, a groveling declaration of loyalty to Hitler, for the Nazi seizure of power was manifestly *not* untimely in the sense delineated by both Heidegger and Nietzsche, that is, it did not number among those genuinely historical occurrences "whose *fate* it remains never to find and never to be *allowed* to find an immediate resonance in its respective Today."[50] To remove any doubt about this, Heidegger adds: "If we ask about the present and future of German *philosophy*, then we mean *these times* [the times of philosophy, poetry, and state-creation] — not the coincidental today of current affairs. But do we know the authentic time, — the world-hour of our people? No one knows it. (cf. Hölderlin, "To the Germans" — the two last stanzas.)"[51] Heidegger goes on to quote these verses, in which the poet asks:

> Doch die Jahre der Völker,
> Sah ein sterbliches Auge sie?
>
> [But the years of the peoples,
> These what mortal's eye has seen?][52]

Beginning with the attempt to define philosophy, Heidegger reaches, via Hölderlin, the somewhat unexpected conclusion that "the world-hour of our people is hidden from us. And it *remains* hidden *so long* as we do not know *who we ourselves are*."[53] The question: What is philosophy? has thus given way to another: Who are we? — a question that, as Lacoue-Labarthe observes, inevitably slides into: Who are we, we Germans?[54] For Heidegger, philosophy is always already *our* philosophy, the philosophy of a given people; yet this givenness proves deceptive. For if, to use the language of *Sein und Zeit*, Dasein implies being-with-others in a historical world, and if the everyday appearance of inner-worldly beings presupposes that Dasein's worldliness remains unexpressed and unthematized, then the questioning of that worldliness can never pin it down to a set of characteristics: a horizon, by definition, withdraws from its objectification. The Germans are a people without qualities — or almost. For the question "Who are we (Germans)?" permits, at the same time, a single answer that manages to avoid the essentialist trap: we are the people who continuously ask ourselves who we are.

This answer, which cannot be detached from its question, introduces a radical difference between the Germans and every other people. Although the process of self-questioning that is constitutive of selfhood never *results* in selfhood as its precipitate, that restless search for an identity describes, in its incessant movement and prior to any empirical determination, the outlines of a German self that is beholden to become what it already is.[55] To the extent that other people question themselves, they partake of this identity. "Whenever they [the French] begin to think,"

Heidegger smugly observes in the *Spiegel* interview, "they speak German."[56] It is in this sense, I believe, that Heidegger refers to the Germans soon after the Constance address, in a highly charged turn of phrase, as "the metaphysical people."[57] Heidegger does not mean that the Germans are innately endowed with powers of reflection denied to other peoples, but that they accede to who they are by relentlessly questioning the meaning of being (German). Heidegger gives the name *Geschichte*, history, to this process of collective self-realization, in which the apparently solid givenness of a national identity explodes under the questioning gaze, allowing an open-ended selfhood to emerge from the rubble.[58] Germanness is thus not a birthmark or birthright but an ongoing struggle — a theme that marks Heidegger's distance from all forms of racist biologism and will come to dominate his wartime lectures on Hölderlin as the problem of the "free use of the national."[59] In the mid-1930s, however, Heidegger still believed that such a conception of Germanness could be both instituted and liberated from the fetters of legalism through a quasi-artistic act of state-creation.

Heidegger endorses this unorthodox nationalism in the other major reference to Hölderlin in his Constance speech, at its conclusion. Paraphrasing Hölderlin's great *Feiertagshymne*, he argues that philosophy can create an essential knowledge that

> alone creates the storm-space in whose realm — *if* at all — the lightnings of the gods will strike us and indicate the world-hour of the people. No one knows when that will happen. But we do know one thing, which Hölderlin, the most German of the Germans, says in a fragment of his late and authentic poetry: 'At one time I questioned the Muse, and she / Replied to me, / In the end you will find it. / About the Highest I will not speak. / But, like the laurel, forbidden fruit / Your country is, above all. To be tasted last / By any man.'[60]

The speech ends here, with an appeal to a strange nationalism indeed, one which apostrophizes Hölderlin as the most German of the Germans precisely in connection with a poem soberly renouncing all nationalist rhetoric — a juxtaposition the German Society must have found hard to swallow. The title *Deutscheste der Deutschen* hints at the crucial role Hölderlin comes to assume from this point onward in Heidegger's writing. Whereas the first citation in the speech arouses the impression that Hölderlin had been introduced merely to garnish a philosophical point, the second elevates him to the leadership of what one might call, following Hellingrath, "the secret Germany," the "people of Hölderlin."[61] Furthermore, the honorific tacitly contrasts Hölderlin with the world-citizen Goethe, whom Nietzsche had called "not a German, but a European event."[62] Here, too, Heidegger resurrects another central aspect of Hellingrath's interpretation.[63]

Heidegger's argument, as I have traced it so far, may be summarized as follows: philosophy is always that of an historical people; learning what philosophy is requires learning who we are; this, in turn, requires that we listen to the poet who, more than any other, questions who we are; this very questioning makes him quintessentially German. Both references to Hölderlin in Heidegger's speech brush up against the German question, the first by quoting from a poem addressed to the Germans, the second by addressing Hölderlin as the "most German of the Germans." Whereas the first citation leads Heidegger to the conclusion that a German identity is not something we can take for granted, the second intimates that we cannot even talk about the Fatherland in the face of Hölderlin's prohibition. The contrast between the probing self-interrogation of the Constance speech and the triumphal self-affirmation of the rectoral address could not be more pronounced. As late as August 1934, four months after his resignation, Heidegger still believed that Hitler had "raised and transfigured the new spirit of community into the formative power of a new order of the people."[64] By November, Heidegger had come to place all his hopes of political foundation in an unforeseeable and uncertain future, while Hölderlin had replaced Hitler as the "formative power" to which the Germans could look for leadership.

If Heidegger's turn to Hölderlin represents a turn away from Nazism, it nonetheless remains open to readings that find, in its continuing fixation upon the national as well as in its lofty indifference toward the politics of the day, an effective distraction from an ever-worsening political reality. This ambivalence can be brought into focus through a closer look at the speech's final reference to Hölderlin. As we have seen, Heidegger emphasizes that, although we cannot predict the world-hour of our people, "we do know one thing," which Hölderlin proceeds to tell us. Yet the relationship between Heidegger's introductory comment and the following citation is by no means as straightforward or reassuring as Heidegger makes out. What exactly is the one thing Heidegger says we *do* know, and which these lines reveal? What is the sole support Hölderlin offers us in a time of need?

Hölderlin's poem suggests two answers: we know, first, that the Fatherland is "forbidden fruit," hence that we should refrain from enlisting it for a cause (Nazism, for example) even if that cause seems to serve the interests of the Fatherland at the time; but we also know that we will "find it" (namely *das Höchste*, the Most High, which Hölderlin associates in this passage with *das Vaterland*) at the end, hence that history culminates in salvation, however such salvation is to be conceived. Consequently, the "one thing" of which, according to Heidegger, we may be absolutely certain is either that all talk of the Fatherland is premature and should be avoided at all cost, or that the patriotic *kairos* will come anyway; it may urge us to caution, or instill us with a quiet confidence. One answer does not preclude the other, because the poet's silence entails a fidelity to the Fatherland that will be amply rewarded at the moment of the latter's redemptive realization. The opportunity for talking about the Fatherland denied by the first answer thus finds refuge in the second, opening up a space in which one may still appeal to that which one forbids oneself. The poet's silence, that is, cannot be total if it is to assert itself *as* silence the moment it descends into the void: "Vom Höchsten will ich schweigen" (About the Highest I will not speak). This resolution should not be interpreted as a response to an injunction forced upon the poet from outside, as if the Most High were an imperious foreign power commanding its own concealment. The modal verb *will* expresses instead the *desire* for discretion, implying that the poet, more than any other, has a stake in the Fatherland's future. By allowing what he silences to mature undisturbed, the poet works in both their interests. The Fatherland is "forbidden fruit" not least because it has not yet ripened on the bough.

When Heidegger calls Hölderlin "the most German of the Germans" in relation to this poem, we should therefore understand the honorific as belonging to a patriotic discourse made possible by a turning away from patriotic discourse, as a faith in the future of the Fatherland derived from a lack of faith in what currently masquerades under that title. Heidegger means nothing less when, in a letter from 21 December 1934, he provides his friend Elisabeth Blochmann with a cryptic justification for his turn to Hölderlin: "I have set out from the innermost midst of the late poetry, with a provisional interpretation of "Germanien"; and precisely in order to repudiate any false timeliness."[65] The danger in such a strategy, of course, lies in its potential reversal: the choice of "Germanien," a text with obvious nationalist appeal, could just as easily awaken the impression Heidegger purports to repudiate. Gerhard Kurz, for example, argues that Heidegger's "identification of poetry, politics and struggle can be linked without difficulty to the National Socialist discourse."[66] This possibility is not an unfortunate side effect of Heidegger's conception of what it means to be German but its necessary corollary. No nationalism that seeks to rise above nationalism can immunize itself against such "misunderstandings" unless it submits to a silence more profound than Hölderlin's "About the Highest I will not speak," which is still a speaking of the Most High.[67] The ambiguity of Heidegger's patriotic speech lies in this tension between renunciation and annunciation at the heart of the "one thing" Hölderlin tells us.

Heidegger's negative determination of Germanness as an unsatisfied and potentially insatiable self-questioning entails a further political danger, in that it dismisses out of hand any praxis or political institution that seeks to put a halt to that process. In Constance, Heidegger argues that a people first attains to "freedom" and "true self-constancy" (*Selbständigkeit*) by engaging with other peoples in a dialectic of recognition, through which "the recognizers recognize each other as those who recognize themselves and thereby mutually push themselves to the highest unfolding of their essence."[68] As in the 1937 text "Wege zur Aussprache" (Paths to Expression), Heidegger warns here against isolating Germany or Germanness from neighboring peoples and cultures.[69] The word *Selbständigkeit* connotes for Heidegger the independence of a self that first comes to free standing through its agon with others.[70] The act of recognition essential to the establishment and confirmation of any identity calls, in turn, for recognition by others. In this second-order act of recognition, which can only come from outside, those who are recognized recognize themselves for the first time, that is, as a people whose selfhood always called for recognition and was not simply given. Freedom, for Heidegger, consists precisely in this recognition of one's own dependence on recognition.

Yet this conclusion, which could be used to challenge the narcissism and closed mimeticism of fascist self-representations, leads Heidegger instead to a statement all too complicit with such representations. He continues: "This true historical freedom as the self-constancy of recognition from people to people does not require the organized sham community of a 'League of Nations.'"[71] Heidegger supports the recent German withdrawal from the League — one of the decisive steps toward the destruction of the Wilsonian world order — on the grounds that any institutionalized delimitation of Germanness that is not an authentic act of state-creation can be written off without further ado. Goebbels would have found nothing objectionable in this. Heidegger's use of the word "organized," which can be read as an antonym of "founded," is revealing. The League of Nations is not the target of Heidegger's criticism insofar as it embodies certain ideals and goals with which he happens to disagree. Rather, the League merits its abolition qua organization, as a more or less arbitrary imposition upon the free movement of self-questioning and mutual recognition. When, on the same page, Heidegger calls Hölderlin the most German of the Germans, he thus presents him as an alternative to all such sham communities, regardless of their potential for conflict resolution or democratic legitimacy.

We are now in a better position to approach the enigmatic silence maintained by Heidegger toward Hölderlin during the rectorate and over the following months, a silence first broken before his students on 6 November 1934, and before a lay audience on 30 November. In Constance, Hölderlin emerges as the spokesperson for an untimely patriotism. He epitomizes a hesitant and indefatigable self-interrogation as far removed from the braggadocio of Hitler's nationalism as it is from the well-intended liberalism of Wilson's internationalism. Heidegger's silence prior to November anticipates the political ambiguities that would come to light in Constance. On the one hand, it suggests that, even at the height of his commitment to National Socialism, Heidegger kept in reserve the poet who meant more to him than any other. As such, his other silence can be understood as an unexpressed doubt or untimely residue dogging the revolution's "false timeliness":

> Denn es hasset
> Der sinnende Gott
> Unzeitiges Wachstum[72]
>
> [For the pensive god
> he hates
> Untimely growth].

Heidegger was able to salvage his Hölderlin interpretation after the war in large part because he had never used the poet to proselytize for Nazism. On the other hand, if the suppression of Hölderlin's name can be understood as a reservation, however marginal, about the "inner truth and greatness of the movement," then Heidegger's failure to heed this reservation — his temporary deafness to Hölderlin — means more than a simple omission. It implies an evasion of thought's responsibility toward what gives itself to be thought: an incursion of guilt.

Hölderlin on the Eastern Front

The decision for Hölderlin, once struck, became legislative for the subsequent development of Heidegger's thought. From 1934 on, there is scarcely a speech, lecture series, or essay of Heidegger's in which the poet is not cited as the partner and guarantor of Heidegger's struggle to overturn the legacy of metaphysical thinking. Hölderlin's achievement was for Heidegger nothing less than the poetic founding of Being, the establishment of a time-space in which to mourn the flight of the gods, to endure their absence, and to prepare the advent of the god to come. Understanding his influence on Heidegger during these years requires understanding why the rhetoric of influence fails to do it justice. That influence extended even to Heidegger's elaborate self-stylization following the failure of the rectorate: hence his obsession, in the writings of the mid-thirties, with an act of self-sacrifice that Being itself requires, the withdrawal to the hut at Todtnauberg corresponding to Empedocles' retreat to the slopes of Etna;[73] hence, too, his confidence that the ignorance and neglect to which he saw himself exposed on all sides ("no one understands what 'I' *think* here")[74] would be righted by a later generation. It is even possible that the habit he picked up in these years of composing manuscripts reserved for a posthumous readership was consciously modeled on the publication history of Hölderlin's late work. Just as the thinking poet had had to wait a hundred years to find Norbert von Hellingrath, whom Heidegger never ceases to praise in the most fulsome of terms, so the poetizing thinker is to entrust his own "secret masterpieces" to a faithful disciple, Friedrich-Wilhelm von Herrmann, who will administer them when he is gone.

One would nonetheless be mistaken to conclude that the same iron necessity governed every twist and turn in Heidegger's path of thinking after 1934. No logic immanent to that path ordained that the poet initially hailed as "the most German of the Germans" should one day evolve into a good European; and even if one accepts Heidegger's explanation that Hölderlin is the second by virtue of the first, the shift in emphasis is itself instructive and points to other, historical, factors. Throughout his long career, Heidegger's decision for Hölderlin sediments into different thematic strata depending upon the audience he was addressing at the time, the subject or text to which his attention was directed, and the particular historical and biographical context of each utterance, as well as the more general philosophical concerns that each stage of his thinking brought with it. The inner development of that thinking cannot alone account for the process by which some of these strata (that of the Occident, for instance, or the new mythology of the coming god) came to be deposited over others (the fixation upon the national, of course, but also the opposition of music and poetry drawn so forcefully in the first Nietzsche lectures). Rather, Heidegger's writings on the poet are characterized by a productive tension with the time in which they were written. Upon this assumption rests the basic argument of this chapter, namely, that the changes in Heidegger's Hölderlin interpretation after 1945 did not occur independently of 1945, whereby this date marks a caesura never explicitly acknowledged by Heidegger, but all the more legible for that.

Thus it is no coincidence that Heidegger's most intensive meditation upon Germanness came at a time when his countrymen were engaged in a murderous struggle to redefine exactly who was German and who not, with lethal consequences for the millions unfortunate enough to find themselves in the latter category. In the two wartime lecture series on Hölderlin, which engage with the poems "Andenken" and "Der Ister," Heidegger draws on the poet's first letter to Böhlendorff to construct his own philosophical model of the relationship between the native and the foreign. In essence, Heidegger argues that if the Germans are to learn "the free use of what is their own," they must first journey through what is strange or unhomely to them.[75] Heidegger has in mind the appropriation of a foreignness that is already proper to the Germans as their destinally interlinked other; a stringent necessity, rather than an idle curiosity, drives the Germans out into the open. Like Hölderlin, Heidegger identifies Germany's other as Greece. He borrows the poet's chiasmatic typology to formulate the relationship between the two peoples: the "heavenly fire" that is native to the Greeks is foreign to the Germans, while the "clarity of presentation" that is native to the Germans is foreign to the Greeks.[76] Just as the Greeks transcended their Asiatic origins by learning to present and control what is most proper to them (their "ownmost") in the "Junonian sobriety" of the Homeric epos, so the Germans will only truly become themselves by appropriating their foreign element, the heavenly fire that gives itself to be presented.[77] The respective ownmost of each people does not exist in isolation prior to the encounter with its other, nor does it emerge from that confrontation as its result or residue. Instead, the other already inheres in the proper as its symbiotic partner: "Precisely what is proper is always related to an other, the fire to the presentation, the presentation to the fire."[78]

At the same time, because "the free use of one's own is what is most difficult," the Germans may prove better able to imitate the inimitable ownmost of the Greeks than were the Greeks themselves.[79] The origin has become strange to the Germans, but this very distance gives them an advantage the Greeks never had: "Yet learning what is foreign, as standing in the service of such appropriation, is easier for precisely this reason."[80] The German "national" will be both the proper imitation of the Greek origin and the original imitation of the properly Greek.[81] The Greeks succeeded in appropriating what was strange to them, the clarity of presentation, and bequeathed it to the Germans as their native element, but the Greeks thereby migrated away from the searing heavenly flame and descended into the *Abendland*, the land of evening. The Germans are called upon to regenerate the *Abendland* by approaching the heavenly flame from out of their own element, completing the circle of history and returning to the hearth.[82] We must, argues Heidegger in the "Ister" lectures, "think more Greek than the Greeks themselves," but in doing so, "we ourselves must, in relation to ourselves, think more German than all Germans hitherto."[83] What E. M. Butler called "the tyranny of Greece over Germany" might finally be overcome through the invention or recuperation of a Greece that never was, and which comes to exist only in the course of its repetitive retrieval.[84]

The voyage through the foreign element is thus undertaken for the sake of the homely, and "this becoming homely in one's own," according to Heidegger, is the "sole concern" of Hölderlin's poetry.[85] Whether the "law of historicity" developed by Heidegger in these texts and their satellites (above all, the long essay on "Andenken" and the speech on "Heimkunft") proved compatible with the contemporaneous German military effort remains a matter of heated debate. His wartime account of German identity has been vilified by Adorno as an apologia for imperial conquest couched in the language of philosophy, and lauded by Fred Dallmayr as an act of civil courage;[86] striking a middle path, Christopher Fynsk finds the journey into the foreign element theorized by Heidegger "certainly less aggressive than a colonialism . . . but perhaps not more risky than a tourism."[87] Following Peter Szondi, several critics have offered alternative readings of the letter to Böhlendorff, which reveal the violence and insensitivity of Heidegger's interpretation.[88] Again, my goal is not to compare Heidegger's translation of Hölderlin with the original but to ground that translation in its historical and developmental context. How Hölderlin was used, and not what he may have intended, is the focus of my inquiry.

Heidegger held these lectures at a time when Hölderlin was becoming an increasingly important pawn in the cultural struggle that accompanied and mirrored the armed conflict. It was feared that the protracted and demoralizing struggle in Russia might result in the so-called *Veröstlichung* of German troops, that is, the erosion of the national virtues of rectitude, valor, and absolute obedience through their exposure to Slavic peoples and practices. Because Germanness entailed, above all, an unflinching willingness to fight and die for the Fatherland, the danger to the troops on the Eastern Front posed by *Veröstlichung* was seen to be as much military as cultural. Hölderlin's sublime and unmistakably German verses offered an effective antidote to this poison, which is why the Ministry of Propaganda saw fit to give its blessing to the field edition discussed in the introduction.

Heidegger's own *Erläuterungen zu Hölderlins Dichtung*, containing essays and speeches from 1936 to 1943, were published in the following year. Although they contained no direct criticism of the uses to which Hölderlin was being put at home and abroad, Heidegger took pains to distance himself in private from the prevailing tenor of the contemporary reception. As early as 1939 he deplored "the political misinterpretation of Hölderlin's 'Fatherland,'" adding that the Fatherland was not a good in itself but first received its meaning through the essential decision about the gods.[89] This statement also makes it clear that what Heidegger considered objectionable was not the focus upon the Fatherland as such but its distortion into a political category. His Hölderlin lectures from the 1940s are as full of patriotic topoi as the scribblings of Paul Kluckhohn and his ilk, but Heidegger believes his own nationalism to be situated on a loftier plane than politics. Whereas the 68ers located the political misinterpretation of Hölderlin's "Fatherland" in the travesty done to the poet's revolutionary convictions by the fascists, among whom they numbered Heidegger, for Heidegger *every* political interpretation was already a misinterpretation.

The blind spot of Heidegger's wartime nationalism, however — the moment at which it dovetails with the National Socialist reception of the poet — can be pinpointed through a comment Heidegger made shortly after the war, in the letter "Über den Humanismus" (On Humanism, 1947). His attempt there to disentangle his favorite poet from the web of Nazi propaganda avails itself of a strange argument indeed. "When confronted with death," he asserts, "those young Germans who knew about Hölderlin lived and thought something other than what the public held to be the typical German attitude."[90] Heidegger thereby suggests that familiarity with the works of Hölderlin sufficed, in itself and regardless of the level of critical sophistication or political awareness brought to the text by the individual reader, to immunize German soldiers against the lies of officialdom. "They died not for the Führer's Fatherland," comments Reinhard Mehring of this line, "but for Hölderlin's 'Germanien,' for a myth."[91]

Heidegger's statement is remarkable for three reasons. First, by treating Hölderlin's poetry as dangerous, dissident literature, Heidegger naïvely (or craftily) suppresses the fact that the fabricators of "the typical German attitude" quite clearly encouraged soldiers to read Hölderlin in the belief that it would strengthen their commitment to the total war. Heidegger would require a very persuasive argument indeed to demonstrate that Hölderlin's effect upon his readers was the opposite of that intended, but he never provides one. Second, this passage reprises the "Hölderlin on the Front" motif, which, as we have seen, had been a staple of Hölderlin literature since Hellingrath's death at the Battle of Verdun. Heidegger had himself already drawn upon this theme before the war, in *Der Ursprung des Kunstwerkes* (The Origin of the Work of Art, 1935), for instance, where he mentions how the hymns of Hölderlin "were packed into the knapsack during the campaign."[92] Moreover, as Anselm Haverkamp points out, his texts on Hölderlin continually circle around Verdun and the figure of the fallen philologist, as if afflicted by an inability to mourn.[93] Here, he goes a step further by directly opposing the soldiers' experience of Hölderlin to the war goals being pursued by the German government. In Heidegger's postwar account, the front was the place where the true Germany (which cannot be defeated) prevailed over Nazi attempts to appropriate it and pervert it for their own nefarious ends.

This move, which accords Hölderlin a national resonance and power otherwise denied him by Heidegger, leads to the third and most disturbing aspect of Heidegger's claim. It justifies the sacrifice demanded by warfare, and by implication the war itself, by charging it with a power of decision. Throughout the Third Reich, Heidegger had argued that it was not enough to read Hölderlin with the same attention one devotes to any other significant poet. Understanding Hölderlin meant accepting and acceding to his authority, abdicating the detached objectivity usually associated with the business of criticism. "To become acquainted with a poem, even in the most intimate detail," he warns in 1934, "does not yet mean *to stand in poetry's region of power*."[94] His texts over the next decade arouse the impression that there are in fact two Hölderlins: the "bearer of the name," whose poetry is the province of literary-historical investigation, and the "guardian of Being" known only to those who have submitted to his authority, the invisible church staffed by Heidegger and his acolytes.[95] In the letter, Heidegger suggests that this distinction was realized in the existential boundary situation into which the German troops had been thrown. The soldiers who knew of Hölderlin were automatically elevated above the "political misinterpretations" being produced by the German propaganda machine.

In *Sein und Zeit* Heidegger had identified the authentic accomplishment of human existence in being-unto-death: my acceptance of the finitude of my own being first leads me to shoulder full responsibility for how I think and live. Conscription activates being-unto-death in the proximity of sacrifice. Before experiencing armed combat, most young men would have contemplated their mortality as a mere idea, squandering their lives on the petty cares and blandishments of everydayness. In the thick of battle, they became aware of the abyss of nothingness upon which human existence is founded, and which civilian Dasein ordinarily chooses to ignore. Heidegger would certainly concede that a soldier might continue to exist inauthentically amidst the roaring cannonades; but for that very reason such a soldier would not truly have lived "in the face of death," *angesichts des Todes*. Those who did understood the poet with the heightened perceptiveness of one who teeters on the brink of oblivion. For Heidegger, warfare is the royal road to understanding Hölderlin.

Reading the statement in its broader context, it becomes clear that the knowledge of Hölderlin ascribed to these Germans extends to that of his ontohistorical significance:

> But the world's destiny is heralded in poetry, without yet becoming manifest as the history of Being. The world-historical thinking of Hölderlin that speaks out in the poem "Remembrance" is therefore essentially more primordial and thus more significant for the future than the mere cosmopolitanism of Goethe. For the same reason Hölderlin's relation to Greek civilization is something essentially other than humanism. When confronted with death, therefore, those young Germans who knew about Hölderlin lived and thought something other than what the public held to be the typical German attitude.[96]

The status of the "therefore" (*darum*) that introduces the last sentence warrants further consideration. What is the connection between the Greek-German relationship, as elaborated in Heidegger's dialectic of the native and the foreign, and the experience of reading Hölderlin under conditions of mortal danger?

The individual's acceptance of the possibility of imminent death need not, it seems to me, lead to any special insight into the process through which a people becomes homely in its historical being. Living in the face of death, whether on the battlefield or in the cancer ward, in a state of war or in times of peace, discloses my existence as ever-my-own, but does not of itself generate a sense of co-belonging — on the contrary, it could bring with it an awareness of absolute isolation. There is no compelling link between being-unto-death and the Greek-German relation poetized by Hölderlin, just as there is no compelling link between the *Daseinsanalytik* as a whole and Heidegger's historiography of Being. The grounds for Heidegger's "therefore" must be sought elsewhere. Perhaps the soldiers at the front experienced what it means to be German more profoundly than the civilian population through their shared camaraderie; perhaps spilling blood alongside other Germans engendered in them an awareness of historical groundedness that being-unto-death alone cannot furnish. Heidegger had argued along these lines in 1934, when he wrote about the Great War:

> The awakening of the front-spirit in the war and its consolidation after the war is nothing other than the creative transformation of that event into a formative power of future existence. The spirit of the front is the knowing will to a new community. . . . It is the kind of co-belonging in which everyone stands in unconditionally for everyone else in every situation.[97]

Yet this answer, too, does not reach far enough, for it still cannot explain how the soldiers so effortlessly understood the "world fate" inscribed by Hölderlin. It misses the dimension of the foreign or strange through which each historical Dasein must pass in order to find itself. In short, it overlooks the Greeks.

In the passage from the letter "Über den Humanismus" cited above, a series of connective particles ("therefore. . . for the same reason . . . therefore") establishes a causal chain linking the poet's world-historical thinking to the young Germans at war. Might not the *location* of these Germans in relation to the homeland, as well as their solidarity before death, afford them special insight into the geopolitics of Being? While Heidegger's remark could refer to any of the campaigns in which German soldiers fought, he was probably thinking of the Eastern Front in particular. Two sentences after describing the poet's effect upon the young Germans, Heidegger makes a rare favorable reference to Marx, which Anson Rabinbach interprets as an attempt to curry favor with the Soviet authorities: Heidegger's two sons were held in Russian captivity at the time.[98] Hölderlin was also more widely read on the Eastern Front than on any other. Above all, Heidegger had written, only a page before: "We have still scarcely begun to think of the mysterious relations to the East that found expression in Hölderlin's poetry."[99] Did these relations, which remained concealed to almost everyone else, dawn upon the young Germans who read Hölderlin while fighting in Russia? In the East, the birthplace of the cult of Dionysos and the origin of the Greek origin, did they perhaps "grasp the ungraspable," the "heavenly fire" of Being?[100] Was their violent *Auseinandersetzung* with the East the reason why they could better comprehend the dynamics of the Greek-German relationship, and hence see through the crudely racist nationalism of official German opinion? Realizing the wish expressed by the poet in "Die Wanderung" (The Journey), "Ich aber will dem Kaukasos zu!" (But I am bound for the Caucasus!), did they learn on the doorstep to Asia that most difficult of tasks, the free use of the national?[101] In short, did a "saving power" grow alongside the "danger" of *Veröstlichung*?[102]

Even if it cannot be proved that Heidegger's young Germans are the veterans of Stalingrad, even if Heidegger is referring in general terms to Hölderlin's readership within the *Wehrmacht*, his apparently anti-fascist remark betrays a deeper collusion with its target. The young Germans who knew of Hölderlin, and hence lived and thought something different in the face of death than the propaganda paraded as German opinion, were literally and figuratively not at home; they had ventured into foreign territory, albeit for the most part against their will. We are invited to conclude that this voyage into the unhomely prepared them to receive Hölderlin's poetry of homecoming, that this departure from Germany was undertaken in order that they might return to the more essential Germany of which Hölderlin is the prophet. Despite his distance from party dogma, the Heidegger of the war years shared with Hitler the belief that warfare was the ideal condition, if not the precondition, for learning who the Germans were, because it tested their mettle as no other experience could. The letter "Über den Humanismus" implies that a sedentary and peaceful people, one that is content to tarry in its native land, would not be able to understand Hölderlin (and hence the "world-historical thinking" stored up in his poetry) with the same keenness as a belligerent folk. This context illuminates Heidegger's horrifying comment from March 1940, a comment otherwise difficult to reconcile with his increasing coldness toward the Party at the time: "News reports are hard to come by, as always. But more important than the ever-vacillating news is the secure conviction that the Germans will not only 'win,' but will above all find their own essence and their spiritual-historical mission."[103] It is in this conflation of national self-discovery and military aggression, spiritual emigration and imperialist expansion, that Heidegger's own political misinterpretation of Hölderlin's "Fatherland" is to be found.

Into the Night

In May 1945 Germany's total war ended in total defeat. The nation's "zero hour" had struck, as if time itself had been razed to the ground by the phenomenon that Friedrich Meinecke, writing shortly after the unconditional surrender, christened the "German catastrophe."[104] In the following years, German writers and philosophers struggled to comprehend the enormity of what had happened. Karl Jaspers attempted to think through

the problem of German guilt; Thomas Mann saw the descent into barbarism anticipated in the avant-garde artist's Faustian quest to break
through the perceived decadence of liberal humanism; Theodor Adorno
declared the writing of poetry after Auschwitz to be barbaric; and a generation of young veterans eked out an impoverished language to convey
their sense of the senselessness and horror of the war. The collective
amnesia that accompanied the birth of the Bonn republic and grew apace
with the economic miracle did nothing to soothe the trauma, as the self-
flagellatory rituals of public apology and commemoration that thrive to
this day demonstrate all too well.

Heidegger's response to the German defeat received its most characteristic expression in the manuscript entitled "Das abendländische
Gespräch," begun in 1946 and abandoned unfinished two years and one
hundred and forty pages later. Composed in a Freiburg gutted by Allied
bombing raids, while its author was prohibited from teaching and on the
verge of a nervous breakdown, the dialogue shows not the slightest trace
of the conditions under which it was written. There is no mention of the
devastation unleashed by the Nazis, which had reached its traumatic climax
the previous spring, nor does Heidegger contemplate how the path to dictatorship might be avoided in future. Even the "current world-need"[105] or
"need of needlessness"[106] that Heidegger conjures elsewhere, to wit, the
delusional belief that the unlimited technical organization of the globe
leaves humanity nothing to want for, is missing from the dialogue. The valley of the upper Danube, which Hellingrath had called "the most German
of landscapes,"[107] sets the scene for a discussion of the poet Heidegger had
addressed twelve years before as "the most German of the Germans," yet
the conversationalists avoid talking about Germany. The balmy haze that
descends upon the countryside through which they wander appears, at the
same time, to shroud their remembrance of the recent past. Yet is this as
total a forgetting as it seems? Or does the repressed return, uninvited, to
haunt their sheltered and beneficent evening-land?

In the next section I will attempt to eavesdrop on "Das abendländische Gespräch" for what it leaves unsaid, interpreting it as Heidegger's subterranean conversation with the events of his own time. For now, I want
to explore the ways in which the dialogue intensifies and mythicizes
Heidegger's conversation with Hölderlin. I hope to show that the novelty
of "Das abendländische Gespräch" lies less in the development of new theses or angles of interpretation — for the dialogue largely recapitulates and
varies the arguments Heidegger had rehearsed about the poet since 1934 —
than in what one would be tempted to call its formal innovation, did not
this innovation challenge the legitimacy of formal analysis. The dialogue
breaks new ground by testing the boundaries between thinking, poetry,
and myth, and represents, I believe, Heidegger's most resolutely poetic
attempt to construct an arche-narrative of the West that would restore to

mythos and logos the unity rent asunder during the reign of metaphysics. In the final section of this chapter, I will argue that the failure of this attempt prepared the way for Heidegger's later meditations on the topology of Being.

Perhaps the quickest way of penetrating to the heart of "Das abendländische Gespräch" is through an elucidation of its title. Who are the conversational partners, and what are they conversing about? The first and most obvious response is that "Das abendländische Gespräch" is a postprandial chat on Hölderlin, conducted between two friends as they indulge in an evening stroll along the river Ister (the upper Danube). The word "occidental" (*abendländisch*) might refer to the object of their discussion, for at times they indeed come to talk about the fate of the West, or it might refer to the evening landscape (*Abendlandschaft*) against which the discussion unfolds. Either way, the title indisputably refers to a dialogue between two characters, simply named the Younger and the Elder, and hints at the weightiness of the stakes involved.

This answer, unsatisfying as it is, throws up a number of problems inherent to the dialogic form itself. "Das abendländische Gespräch" is Heidegger's only attempt to write a dialogue on Hölderlin, and an understanding of why he chose this medium, as opposed to the essay, speech, or monograph, is essential if its general significance is to be ascertained. Heidegger wrote a number of such dialogues in the mid- to late 1940s, the so-called *Feldweg-Gespräche* (Field-Path Dialogues), another of which I will have cause to examine later. "Das abendländische Gespräch" is the last and longest of these invented dialogues. The form may have functioned as a makeshift for the face-to-face teaching denied Heidegger at the time, first by the bombing of Freiburg, which disrupted his teaching schedule and forced him to flee with other staff and students to Castle Wildenstein near Beuron for six months, and then by the ban on teaching, which was finally lifted in 1950.[108] In the letter "Über den Humanismus," written at the same time as "Das abendländische Gespräch," Heidegger identifies this sort of direct communication with a like-minded audience — precisely what he lacked in the closing stages and aftermath of the war — as the element in which his thinking flourished. "Surely the questions raised in your letter," he writes to Beaufret, "would have been better answered in direct conversation. In written form thinking easily loses its flexibility. But in writing it is difficult above all to retain the multidimensionality of the realm peculiar to thinking."[109] In the paradoxical exercise of transcribing conversations that never took place, or that take place only in their transcription, Heidegger may have seen a means of keeping his thinking supple, responsive, and rich in the absence of an appropriate interlocutor.

However, the power relations established between the participants in these dialogues never mimic the master-disciple pattern characteristic of Heidegger's own pedagogical style. Nor are the dialogues *Streitgespräche,* texts that stage the contestation of opposed worldviews. The to and fro of banter remains unperturbed by the slightest trace of disagreement, creating the impression that these are not so much the documents of a process of mediation in the public sphere as they are the dictations of an obscure telepathic communion.[110] Reading them, one has the often cloying feeling that all the speakers are more or less stylized portraits of Heidegger himself. This holds particularly true of "Das abendländische Gespräch," in which one partner frequently concludes or rhapsodically supplements a sentence begun by the other, and in which the speaker's "I" occasionally drifts into an ecstatic first person plural. One could therefore hazard a psychoanalytic reading of "Das abendländische Gespräch" as the testament to a flight from reality: perhaps the isolation that Heidegger accepted as the fate of all great thinkers, and the resultant misunderstandings to which he saw himself exposed, drove him to invent the sympathetic companion he felt he lacked in the philosophical guild (particularly after Jaspers's "betrayal"). This would explain the text's claustrophobic hermeticism, its blithe indifference to the issues of the day, and its deafness to dissenting voices.

Such a reading, however suggestive it might prove in relating work to life, nonetheless falls short of the challenge posed by the dialogue form itself. Through his choice of genre, Heidegger locks into the foundational text of occidental philosophy, the Socratic dialogues, and formally registers his oft-expressed ambition to recuperate the Greek legacy upon German terrain. That Plato should figure as the silent partner in Heidegger's conversation on Hölderlin is hardly surprising, given that Heidegger is intent on uncovering and recovering for his people the abyssal ground of metaphysics occulted by the Platonic partition of Being into sensible and intelligible, transient and imperishable realms. At one stage, the Younger warns against a symbolic interpretation of the spiritual essence of the river, arguing that "only within metaphysics is there the physical and sensual in distinction to the non-physical and non-sensual. Indeed, metaphysics is the holding sway of this distinction."[111] By rescinding this distinction, Heidegger aims to reach behind Plato to the more original truth preserved in the fragments of the pre-Socratics, particularly in the poetic thinking of Heraclitus, Anaximander, and Parmenides explored in his wartime lectures.

Yet it would be overhasty to rank "Das abendländische Gespräch" alongside the confrontations with Plato from the 1930s, reading it as a poetic successor to the more stringent polemics found in the Nietzsche lectures and elsewhere. For the Plato with whom Heidegger converses in "Das abendländische Gespräch" is no longer the philosopher who fathered Platonism and who bears responsibility for Greece "fall[ing] out of the orbit of its essence,"[112] but rather the myth-maker who still attests, albeit in a fashion sullied by a nascent metaphysics, to the emergence from unconcealment that marks the authentic Greek experience of phenomenality: the

Plato of the *Phaedrus*. As such, Heidegger does not use "Das abendländis-che Gespräch" to pick a quarrel with Plato over his alleged nihilism, as he does elsewhere,[113] but enters into a dialogue with him similar to that with Hölderlin, a *Gespräch* in which each partner speaks from out of a deeper union. And the fact that this dialogue unfolds in the quintessentially Platonic genre *of* the dialogue heralds an unprecedented intimacy in their relationship, as a remark from Heidegger's 1944 course on Parmenides confirms: "From Plato's dialogue 'Phaedrus,' the conversation on 'the beautiful' (closing section), we learn moreover that Plato had a very clear understanding of the priority of the immediately spoken word over the written."[114]

For it is in the *Phaedrus*, as Heidegger argues in his 1943 lecture series on "Der Ister" — the poem discussed in "Das abendländische Gespräch" — that Plato still thinks pre-platonically, hence, from Heidegger's viewpoint, not yet (or not just) metaphysically.[115] The *Phaedrus* begins as Socrates and his young companion leave Athens for a walk along the banks of the Ilissus. As they search for a shady spot where they can sit down to chat, they praise the beauty of the river, and Phaedrus recounts a legendary tale with which it is associated. Socrates declines to submit an allegorical inter-pretation of the myth on the grounds that the Delphic injunction to self-knowledge is his primary concern.[116] A little later, however, he develops his own myth of the flight of the soul to a region "apprehensible only by intellect," "the abode of the reality with which true knowledge is con-cerned."[117] By reminding the lover of the sempiternal beauty in which his soul once bathed, the sight of earthly beauty helps him grow the pinions that will bear him aloft toward that celestial realm. The beautiful appear-ance, "that which shines forth most purely," provokes in the lover the remembrance or anamnesis of an original unity. It is the most powerful trace in the phenomenal world of the homeland from which the soul has suffered exile.[118] The beautiful being thus enjoys ontological priority over all other beings, for it partakes of that eternal Being that is every soul's birthright.

The fact that Heidegger never mentions Plato by name in "Das abendländische Gespräch" by no means invalidates my thesis that the dia-logue should be read as a response to the *Phaedrus;* indeed, it could hint that Plato's influence upon the text extends beyond approving citation or hostile reaction. The opening page adds weight to this suspicion. "Das abendländische Gespräch," like the *Phaedrus*, begins as a younger and an older man enjoy a summertime walk by a river. The organizing topic of conversation in "Das abendländische Gespräch," as in the *Phaedrus*, is the beautiful, with Hölderlin's line from "Der Ister," "Schön wohnt er" (Beautifully it dwells), providing the focal point of the discussion. The myth of the Occident developed in Heidegger's text, which thematizes the relationship between the spirit's destinal sending (*Geschick*), the beautiful, and human dwelling, recognizably responds to the paradigm established by Plato. Further, the slippage between thinking (*Denken*), remembrance (*Andenken*), reverence (*Andacht*), and thanks (*Dank*), which "Das abendländische Gespräch" shares with Heidegger's later Hölderlin interpretation as a whole, recalls the doctrine of anamnesis even as it displaces the object of remembrance from the transcendent source of all knowledge, the world of the Forms, to the gift of poetic saying.[119] Holger Schmid has demonstrated that the *Phaedrus* myth had an enormous significance for Heidegger in the 1940s and beyond, especially for his thinking of the four-fold.[120] Nowhere else, however, is its influence so profound and far-reaching. By transplanting Plato's riverine landscape to Swabia, by restaging the conversation between Socrates and Phaedrus on the banks of the upper Danube, Heidegger opens up his dialogue to the interpretation that every word is a response to his illustrious predecessor. At the same time, Heidegger's dislocating revisitation of Plato is mediated by Hölderlin's poem, not only because "Der Ister" is its topic and the Ister its topos, but also because "Der Ister" itself tells of a similar Greek-German translation that may have served Heidegger as a model. Borrowing from Pindar, Hölderlin tells how the river "invited" Hercules from Olympus (from the river Alpheus, adds Heidegger)[121] to seek shelter under its black spruce trees. Heidegger extends the invitation to Socrates and Phaedrus, who likewise transmigrate from a Greek to a German river, changed almost beyond recognition, as the older and younger man.

In order to understand why Heidegger enters into conversation with Plato's myth, and what the nature of this conversation might be, let us briefly turn to his most extensive discussion of the *Phaedrus*, found toward the end of the first lecture series on Nietzsche, "Der Wille zur Macht als Kunst" (The Will to Power as Art). In considering this text, it is important to note that Heidegger's remarks from 1936 cannot be transferred without further ado to his thinking a decade later. In particular, the combative rhetoric and heroic pathos typical of Heidegger's earlier encounters with the giants of occidental thinking yield, after the war, to a tacit refusal to reaffirm the destruction of Western metaphysics. Instead, Heidegger turns to the earliest Greek thinkers, in partnership with Hölderlin, to explore possibilities for restoring a non-exploitative relationship to the earth. "Das abendländische Gespräch" provides a striking image for this shift. In Heidegger's private mythology from the 1930s, the primal scene of essential thinking is the mountaintop. Throughout this period, Heidegger constantly envisages himself perched in glorious isolation upon a summit, towering above the hustle and bustle of the flatlands while calling over to the few other essential thinkers of the occidental tradition. In "Das abendländische Gespräch," Heidegger descends — like Zarathustra — from his lonely post into the valley of human habitation, never to leave it again. A downward movement from the bracing alpine heights to more temperate low-lying terrain complements the conversationalists' passage from Greece to Germany, resulting in a civilizing of Heidegger's conversation with Plato: once a titanic struggle, it now takes on a more amicable tone conditioned by the culture-bringing influence of the river. Heidegger's erstwhile effort to surmount (*überwinden*) metaphysics metamorphoses into the attempt to get over it (*verwinden*), to get along with its founding father, to walk together into the long twilight of the Occident without rancor or quarrel.

In 1936 the main thrust of Heidegger's argument consisted in demonstrating the mixed legacy of the *Phaedrus* myth for the thinking of being, and specifically for Nietzsche's "Platonism in reverse." On the one hand, Heidegger discovers in Plato's account of the beautiful the prototype of every determination of the artwork in occidental history up to and including Nietzsche's. The fatal move here, for Heidegger, is Plato's characterization of the artwork in terms of its appearance. Everything perceptible and tactile in an artwork — its material dimension or "earth" — comes to be regarded as the vehicle for its supratemporal idea. For Heidegger, the form-matter dichotomy that is at the heart of modern aesthetics has its origin in this separation.[122] The beautiful helps the lover to break free of the tyrannical hold exerted upon him by the physical world by denigrating the pleasures of the flesh. True or theoretical knowledge pertains to a sphere above and beyond the phenomenal, from which Being shines forth as the steadfast presence upon which the liberated soul comes to gaze. Against Plato, Heidegger insists that Being does not offer itself for showing, like an inextinguishable flame, but presents itself solely in its withdrawal. That is why the essence of truth — the transcendent source of Dasein's knowing relationship to its own being — is itself subject to (as well as the subject of) historical change.

On the other hand, the *Phaedrus* myth ascribes to beauty an ontological centrality negated in its later, Kantian determination as the reflective judgment of a disinterested aesthetic subject, and completely abandoned in its empiricist reduction to an emotional state induced by agreeable sensory impressions. The felicitous discordance of truth and beauty in the artwork, asserts Heidegger in his commentary on the myth, "tears us out of the forgetfulness of Being" that dominates our everyday lives. Seized by the beautiful, the lover is both moved (*berückt*) by its radiance and transported (*entrückt*) into a more essential relationship to Being.[123] As such, beauty is the nodal point at which the ontological difference becomes visible. For both Plato and Heidegger, the question of the beautiful belongs neither in a discussion of art's social function nor in a regional ontology but "in the circumference of the original question of the relationship of humanity to the existent as such."[124] Beauty, as Hölderlin declares in the foreword to the penultimate version of *Hyperion*, the key document of his aesthetic Platonism, is "being, in the sole sense of the word."[125] In the

1930s Heidegger finds confirmation for his belief that the artwork can be legislative for a historical epoch in the *Phaedrus* myth's identification of the beautiful with the truly existent, which accords the artwork a dignity and transfigurative power Plato was not always so willing to concede it.

Just as Plato's conversational partners adapt to the Ister landscape, so the postwar Heidegger reorients Plato's account of the beautiful to suit the occidental beauty of the Ister hymn. Heidegger's ambivalence regarding Socrates' myth emerges most strongly in the fundamental concept of the dialogue, that of beautiful dwelling. We usually think of dwelling as a specifically human capacity, but Heidegger expands its meaning to cover the relationship of place to humanity, as well as humanity's relationship to place. The power that organizes and founds their reciprocal relationship by "mak[ing] habitable the land" is the river.[126] Its course attunes and retunes the dwelling of those who build along its banks by determining how their livelihood is structured by the surrounding landscape. The beautiful, explains Heidegger in a footnote, gathers together and toward one another the inhabitants and their environs as their unifying middle or medium.[127] Yet while natural beauty's potential to reconfigure humanity's relationship with the world has its source in the beautiful's incalculable distance from innerworldly things (whether *vorhanden* or *zuhanden*, objectal or equipmental), its alterity also makes beauty only indirectly accessible to the beholding eye. Indeed, it is precisely this possibility of remaining unperceived and unappreciated that lends beauty its allure and power. We can all too easily dismiss Heidegger's idyllic river landscape with a cursory glance while speeding across a bridge, and even if we search for beauty's presence by visiting "nature reserves" — the term falls under the purview of the ubiquitous Heideggerian *Gestell* — it never lets itself be "found," like a lost hammer. Heidegger would reject the notion that his conversationalists are ecotourists *avant la lettre*. The river's beauty must first be coaxed out of its concealment, and it is here that the artwork steps in.

Heidegger emphasizes that the poem that names the river wants neither "to paint the natural beauty of the landscape," as if "Der Ister" were modeled upon the river of the same name, nor "to awaken and maintain a pleasure in nature," as if the response the poem engenders in the reader makes up the measure of its success.[128] Both the mimetic and the eudaemonic principles treat Hölderlin's poem as just another conditioned and conditioning being to which the quality of beauty happens to cling, and they thereby ignore the excess over against every standard of measurement that distinguishes the beautiful being from all other beings: " 'Beautiful,' simply beautiful; and for the beautiful that means always: beautiful beyond measure."[129] But if Heidegger and Socrates agree in positing an essential connection between beauty and being that is suppressed by the metaphysical identification of beauty with semblance, they part company in making sense of the role played by the artwork in revealing that connection.

Because Socrates makes eros, rather than *poiesis*, the privileged vehicle for the disclosure of the being of beings, he does not pay particular attention to the instantiation of artistic beauty. The *Phaedrus* provides no cause for believing that the babbling brook beside which Socrates and his companion recline appears to them as beautiful through the disclosive power of great art, even if one argues, following a line of reasoning suggested by *Der Ursprung des Kunstwerkes*, that the greatest Greek artwork is the polis itself. It would be even less plausible to read Plato's dialogue as an encomium to *Dichtung*. If anything, the beauty that sends the soul into heavenly raptures is a matter of what one might call a sensuously mediated intellectual intuition.

For Heidegger, by contrast, the conversationalists' understanding of the landscape through which they wander, and which the river defines, is codetermined by its poetic setting-into-truth. At the same time as Heidegger introduces a distinction between artistic and natural beauty, he makes their rigorous separation untenable. Both are sublimated into the artwork itself, for it is only the artwork that lends a voice to nature's ordinarily mute alterity.[130] The river in Heidegger's dialogue is both the Ister and "Der Ister," just as the measured pacing of the conversationalists by the riverside is both a summertime excursion and a peripatetic figure of the hermeneutic process: "How beautifully it dwells we learn . . . by walking along its bank and following it."[131] The conversationalists' meditation upon the landscape through which they wander will thus also and unavoidably retrace the contours of the hymn that names it. At the risk of distorting Heidegger's meaning, one could say that the poem commissions the river to beautify human dwelling, hence that the poet, even if he cannot *create* beauty, is the true architect of humanity's abode upon the earth.

Whereas the beautiful, for Socrates, serves as a guide to a place above the heavens, Heidegger's beautiful river directs his protagonists toward the earth, there to become homely in their historical being. Platonic beauty is other-worldly in origin, its refulgence ultimately a means to an end: having reached its destination, the soul has no need of the beautiful appearance that propelled its flight. Heideggerian beauty, by contrast, is this-worldly and abiding: "The beautiful that the verses name is the habitable inhabited by the inhabiting river."[132] The spur provided by the *Phaedrus* myth helps Heidegger overcome the problem of how Dasein can extricate itself from its customary strickenness in the existent without being driven to turn its back on an irredeemably fallen world. This problem had dogged his analysis, from *Sein und Zeit* onwards, of those attunements that disclose to Dasein its thrownness into an historical world. While the dreadful and the profoundly boring, the two privileged bearers of Dasein's self-understanding for Heidegger during the 1930s, cause everyday states of mind to be swallowed up in a vertiginous nothingness, the beautiful remains firmly rooted in the here and now: this river, these verses.[133] The beautiful opens up to the source of all presencing without becoming transparent or losing its stubborn thingness, its earthliness, in the process. Flight and grounding in one, it combines the transascendence of Plato's myth with a transdescendence that has since found favor among ecocritics.[134] Dread and boredom overcome Dasein in its withdrawal from the existent as such, temporarily engulfing the world in an abyss of alienation; beauty, by contrast, intensifies Dasein's sense of homeliness. Under the rubric of "beautiful dwelling," Heidegger brings Socrates' winged soul down to earth.

If the title "Das abendländische Gespräch" thus denotes, among other things, a conversation between Plato and Heidegger, and if it also suggests that this conversation hangs together, in an as yet unclarified manner, with the fate of the West, then the stakes of this conversation require further investigation. In Heidegger's opinion, Plato and Heidegger are more than two prominent names in a roll call of great philosophers; they are the first and last in a series whose parameters they define. One launches the project of metaphysics that the other interrogates and brings to term; they are the giants who stand at the beginning and end of the Occident and call to each other across the millennia. Both figures, however, are Janus-faced: Plato does not just anticipate the fateful transformation of the idea of truth into the certain knowledge of beings that culminates in the buttressing of the Cartesian self against the realm of deceptive appearances but also looks back, particularly in the *Phaedrus* and in the parable of the cave, to the original event and eventfulness of being; likewise, Heidegger does not just review the history of metaphysics after it has reached its conclusion in Nietzsche but also looks forward to the other beginning, itself the repetitive reinvention of the properly Greek. As such, "Das abendländische Gespräch" is an exchange with the Occident's other, the Orient, as well as an exchange about and of the Occident itself. Plato and Heidegger stand at the boundaries of the Occident, and it is at the boundaries, as Heidegger remarked in 1934, that the essential decisions fall.[135]

Heidegger is concerned, above all, to sketch the Occident's destinal dependence upon the East from which it sprang, "for Greece," as the Younger remarks, "is the world epoch in which not the first rising and beginning, but . . . the transition of the oriental to the occidental takes place."[136] The inner co-belonging of Orient and Occident had been misconstrued not only by the entire tradition of occidental philosophy but also by Heidegger himself, as he admits at one stage of the dialogue: "Thus, the spirit does not have two destinies, as we at first believed, an oriental and an occidental; rather, destiny is the sending from the Orient into the Occident."[137] "Das abendländische Gespräch" thus legitimates Heidegger's turning to Eastern (especially Taoist) thought at just this time[138] in a common world-destiny: if the voyage away from the Orient drives the spirit from the heavenly fire of Being — a supposition supported by the word *Abendland*, with its associations of twilight and decline — then the reappropriation of the flame, which is the prerequisite for the free use of the occidental ownmost, entails a movement toward the Orient or *Morgenland* that mirrors and undoes Plato's achievement. Whereas Plato, the great transitional figure in an age of transition, occidentalized the Orient, the task confronting post-metaphysical thinking is an Orientalization of the Occident. Socrates narrates his myth at high noon, the meridian separating morning(land) from evening(land); "Das abendländische Gespräch" begins "on the evening of a benign day in late summer," and trails off into darkness.[139] "The Evening-Land," says the Elder, "would then be the land of that evening that goes down into the night that rises to the morning from which the day springs forth that is purely reconciled with the night."[140] The circle of history closes upon its origin.

"Das abendländische Gespräch" attempts to go gently into the good night that precedes the redemptive dawn. Heidegger's ambition is to bring about the very process he describes, "the wandering of the heavenly flame from one side to the other," by repetitively re-orienting Plato's central myth from the *Phaedrus*.[141] He seeks not only to refashion that myth for modern times and a modern audience (for "we may not have anything *identical* with the Greeks," as Hölderlin acknowledges),[142] but in so doing to reverse the occidental trajectory and pass Plato in the opposite direction. Plato and Heidegger meet at the crossroads of the history of Being. At this stage, it is crucial to note that what I have called the Orientalization of Plato's myth cannot be effected merely through changing its content. Certainly "Das abendländische Gespräch" is underpinned by a grand narrative concerning the peregrinations of the world-spirit, one that is essentially identical to that developed in the wartime Hölderlin lectures, with the obvious exception that the Occident now stands in for Germany. However, the myth of the Occident that can be extracted from Heidegger's dialogue and propositionally expounded is still an *occidental* myth, in two respects. First, it can be clearly presented, and the "clarity of presentation," as both Hölderlin and Heidegger remind us, is the occidental trait *par excellence*. Second, it can be clearly presented *as a myth*, that is, as belonging to a discourse of an epistemic order that is different from scientifically verifiable truth. Yet this fundamental distinction is precisely what the process of Orientalization would revoke, by restoring to mythos and logos that originary indivision which, according to Heidegger, prevailed in the poetizing and thinking of the early Greeks.[143]

How does Heidegger overcome this problem? Clearly, the solution does not lie in abandoning the "clarity of presentation" in favor of a formless effusion or willful obscurity, for the poles of the native and the foreign are always already built into one another as their polar opposites. There is no getting around the fact that Heidegger's myth must *also* be clearly presentable, that the "ungraspable" flame of Being, if it is to lead the Occident to turn toward its other, forgotten destiny, must be grasped, appropriated, and controlled. The real, "oriental" myth in "Das abendländische Gespräch," however — and here the dialogue is unparalleled in Heidegger's output — is not a fable put forward by one or other of the conversationalists, which could then be excerpted from the dialogue and summarized in point form, but "Das abendländische Gespräch" itself. Herein lies its most important structural difference from the *Phaedrus*. Plato's myth about the liberation of the soul through beauty stands as a single episode, albeit the most important, in a much longer discussion. Socrates narrates the myth and then proceeds to talk about something else. The Attic landscape lends to the conversation the lyrical tone that distinguishes it from Socrates' civic disputations, but the bucolic setting is incidental to the myth itself, at most providing its occasion.

Heidegger's mythic intention, by contrast, informs every aspect of the dialogue, transcending the boundaries between foreground and background, discussion and setting, speakers and subject, idea and appearance. The landscape, which in the *Phaedrus* provides a pleasant backdrop to the discussion, assumes an integral, integrating role in Heidegger's text. Just as poem and river coalesce in the Hölderlinian river-spirit, so the land through which it meanders and which it makes habitable extends beyond the upper Danube valley to encompass the Occident itself. Those who follow its twists and turns with loving attention learn to dwell beautifully in occidental as well as Swabian responsibility. Indeed, the fact that the dialogue takes place over the course of a walk is by no means insignificant. Only as they stroll by the riverside do the conversationalists become attuned to the hidden connections between word and place founded by the poet, so that Hölderlin's poem comes to resonate "ever more abidingly" through their watchful presence.[144] "Das abendländische Gespräch" is quite literally a ramble on Hölderlin's poem, a thoughtful promenade that follows his word-traces and moves constantly in his spiritual and physical vicinity, an incessant being-underway to a language appropriate to the poet's.[145] Neither a journey (for it has no goal), nor a tour (for it does not return to its starting point), it is an *Erörterung* of "Der Ister": not so much an attempt to locate the river-poem on a map of the Occident as to transpose the reader to its site (*Ort*), whence the Occident takes its bearings.[146] Even when the conversation digresses from the poem, it never wanders away from it, "just as we are walking along its bank here and on all sidetracks . . . continually come back to it, because we cannot remove ourselves from it."[147] "Our conversations," notes the Younger, are "everywhere and always conversations of the evening-land."[148]

Because the Ister opens up to the conversationalists in and through "Der Ister" (and vice versa), because the Occident reveals its essence to them only inasmuch as they are already enframed by Hölderlin's evening-land,

Heidegger's painterly scene-setting is not indifferent to the matter of the dialogue but consubstantial with it. Hölderlin's poetics of place displaces poetry from the margins of cultural activity to the center of historical dwelling. The underlying unity of the conversation between the Elder and the Younger, the subject of that conversation, and the scenery against which it unfolds, indicate the extent to which every facet of the dialogue has been permeated by myth. We can see now how the differences between the accounts of beauty offered by Plato and Heidegger are formally instantiated in "Das abendländische Gespräch." The fully unified mythic being-in-the-world projected by and as the conversation has more in common with the Heraclitean *hen kai pan* (one and all), in which Hyperion saw the essence of beauty,[149] than with the lucid organization of the *Phaedrus*, which anticipates the divorce of mythos and logos by limiting myth to an interlude in an otherwise rational discourse. Heidegger's dialogue does not just thematize the mythic harmony of beautiful dwelling but itself aims to dwell beautifully in language, the "house of Being."[150] Its mythologemes, which can be extracted from it, clearly presented, and then demythologized,[151] are generated by a will to mythopoesis absent from his earlier texts. "Das abendländische Gespräch" represents Heidegger's most concerted endeavor to mythically temper the mythology of Being, which in his previous writings on Hölderlin still wore an occidental (Platonic) face. It is precisely in this constantly self-commenting interconnectedness of its elements that "Das abendländische Gespräch" comes closest to Hölderlin's late work, of which Walter Benjamin, in his important early essay on the poet, writes: "in this world every function of life is destiny. . . . That is the Oriental, mystical principle, overcoming limits, which . . . again and again so manifestly sublates the Greek shaping principle."[152]

Let us reexamine what I am calling the "oriental" dimension of Heidegger's text from another perspective. I have already discussed three of the conversations condensed in the dialogue's title, namely, those between the Younger and the Elder, Heidegger and Plato, and the Occident and the Orient. The title refers fourthly, of course, to the conversation between thinking and poetry discussed in the opening section of this chapter. When Heidegger first used the word *Gespräch* to describe his relationship to the poet, in the lecture course on "Germanien" and "Der Rhein" (1934–35), the word resonated with martial overtones. Hölderlin's poetry, more than any other, required *denkerische Eroberung*, thoughtful conquest and conquest by thought, just as thought, in turn, was mustered to march into poetry's *"region of power."*[153] The conversation between poetry and thinking was pitched to Heidegger's students as the loving strife of commensurate forces, a kind of *Auseinandersetzung* between friends.[154] By 1946 this conversation has undergone a radical metamorphosis. The aggressiveness of the earlier relation has been replaced by an almost obsequious fidelity. The conversation, if such it be, is no longer a contestation between equiprimordial partners, but thought's self-effacing correspondence to an antecedent and hallowed appellative power: "In interpreting we answer the sign by showing the sign again."[155]

Inasmuch as Heidegger's dialogue presupposes the absolute supremacy of the poetic word over its elucidation — he rejects the concept of criticism out of hand — the success of his perambulation along the Ister can be gauged solely by the extent to which it reverently repeats and tarries by every bend in Hölderlin's text. This idea receives its most concise formulation fairly late in the dialogue: "Denn Gespräch ist nur Gehör."[156] I translate, rather freely: "For the conversation that we ourselves are is only attentive obedience." The dialogue represents the thoughtful attempt to heed or hearken unto Hölderlin's poetry, and in this task lies for Heidegger, as we have seen, nothing less than the historical fulfilment of philosophy, and hence of occidental history. Yet can such a skewed relationship still be termed a conversation? Admittedly, "conversation" is a poor translation of *Gespräch*, which shares with the other *Ge-* words favored by Heidegger (*Gestell, Geschick, Geviert*, and so on) a grammatical indeterminacy better captured in the English gerund.[157] A conversing, in its Heideggerian inflection, is more than an exchange of complementary or contradictory constative utterances undertaken in the common search for truth. It is the reciprocal relationship that continually generates anew the shared identity of the conversational partners. As Derrida observes, the Heideggerian *Gespräch* is "the speech of the two who speak . . . who can receive their name only from *the very thing* that is said here, by the language or speech of this *Gespräch*."[158] If Derrida is right in saying that the conversationalists first emerge from out of the *Gespräch*, rather than the other way around, then the *Gespräch* entitled "Das abendländische Gespräch" makes it impossible to tell at what point a poetizing thinking stops talking and a thinking poetizing begins. The neighborhood Heidegger elsewhere proclaims between thinking and poetry spills into cohabitation, so monological has the dialogue become.[159]

Thinking is not only left without a stable position from which it might enter into a conversation with, let alone conquer, the poem under consideration; it is practically indistinguishable from its dialogic partner. Like the conversationalists hugging the riverside, thought clings so tightly to what gives itself to be thought that it appears to merge with it, as the Elder admits at one stage: "From time to time it seems to me that even our interpreting is already a poetizing."[160] The welcomed undifference of thinking and poetry to which such statements attest is strikingly characteristic of the dialogue's rhetorical style. Of course, Heidegger's vocabulary had long been saturated by Hölderlinian coinages, arousing the impression in some quarters that he had taken flight into the airy realm of poesy. Indeed, Gadamer identifies the poet's lasting importance to Heidegger in a "freeing of his tongue," which enabled him to adopt semi-poetic terms such as "gods," "heaven," "desert," and "earth," so abandoning the specialized philosophical terminology to which *Sein und Zeit* still partly adhered.[161] In "Das abendländische Gespräch" Heidegger goes still further by imitating the poet's speech at the basic level of syntax. The first sentence of the dialogue, for example, is recognizably modeled on the opening line of "Wie wenn am Feiertage" (As on a Holiday).[162] Even the dialogue's fragmentary state, far from indicating a dissatisfaction on the part of its author, may be a conscious imitation of the unfinished poem to which it is devoted. Heidegger quotes the poem's last two lines and has one of his protagonists say: "Thus ends the Ister song. No, thus it breaks off. . . . It is therefore no coincidence that this song is incomplete —." His partner continues: "Or is it completed precisely in this breaking off?"[163] When Heidegger's own text breaks off, quite abruptly, just two pages later, the possibility lies close to hand that this apparently premature ending is also "no coincidence."

Thought's thankful submission before the gift of the poetic word, and the mimetic obeisance that flows from it, repeal the strict separation of poetry and thinking upheld by philosophical discourse. The voices of poetry and thinking have become so intertwined as to be mistaken for a con-versing unison, as if Heidegger were obeying the imperative of the *Ältestes Systemprogramm* (Oldest System Program, 1797): "The philosopher must possess just as much aesthetical power as the poet."[164] Insofar as myth, understood in its originally Greek or pre-occidental meaning, embodies just such an inextricable unity of thinking and poetry, and insofar as the Occident signifies nothing less than their falling apart into "philosophy" and "art," this fourth conversation testifies more strikingly than the rest to Heidegger's attempted Orientalization of Plato's myth. Heidegger does not rest content with hanging a new mythology upon an old framework but aims to reorient what it means to think mythically, to orientalize the razor-sharp categories of Western thought, to prepare a time-space of beautiful dwelling for a massified and uprooted humanity.

Yet does "Das abendländische Gespräch," the ground and product of the four conversations packed into its title, fulfill this ambition? Can a change of such magnitude be talked into existence? Or is Heidegger's mythocentric attempt condemned to the bad mythologism it seeks to rise above? In order to answer these questions, I turn now to a fifth and final conversation: one between Heidegger and his time.

The Hidden Germany

On the few occasions after the war when Heidegger directed his attention to the events that culminated in Stalingrad and Auschwitz, it was to deny their deeper ("ontohistorical") import. The Second World War, despite its unprecedented human tragedy and millions of victims, "decided nothing"; the gas chambers, like the industrial methods of modern agriculture, were just another sign of the unbridled technologism contained embryonically in the thinking of Descartes;[165] fascism was merely a symptom of European nihilism. Long before the war broke out, it had become clear to Heidegger that the political movement from which he had once expected a radical cure for the cancer riddling the Occident could only prolong and exacerbate the agony. It was probably Hitler's Four-Year Plan, announced in 1936, that first led Heidegger to the conclusion that fascist Germany was of one essence with Bolshevik Russia and New Deal America, an insight confirmed by the "total mobilization" of German society during the war.[166] The nation's brilliant military successes during the first few years of armed conflict only obscured the fact that its defeat had already been decided upon metaphysical grounds, for it forgot, in its blind and self-aggrandizing pursuit of ever more material and territorial resources, that it could only be invincible as the nation of poets and thinkers.[167] Whether the Axis or the Allied powers "won" was a matter of relative indifference; either way, the Occident had long since fallen prey to a nihilism in whose black radiance the difference between torturer and tortured was effectively obscured. "The alliance between the masses and power," summarizes Niethammer, "on the historical basis of the technological domination of nature, was now supposed to have developed into a self-steering system which, with marginal differences of political expression, spanned virtually the whole world and constantly reproduced itself despite all wars and revolutionary changes."[168]

According to Heidegger's interpretation, then, the Second World War was a blip in the course of world history: distracting, destructive, but ultimately irrelevant. Nonetheless, as I began to demonstrate in the last section with regard to "Das abendländische Gespräch," a marked transformation occurs in Heidegger's thinking immediately after the war. The matter of thinking may remain constant throughout, but the earlier emphasis upon the voyage into the foreign element shifts to an enduring concern with beautiful or poetic dwelling. The Swabian *Heimatsidyll* of "Das abendländische Gespräch" rounds off the national *Bildungsroman* of the wartime lectures on Hölderlin, agonistic struggle subsides into an all-pervasive *Gelassenheit*, Germany submerges into the Occident, while pious thankfulness replaces questioning as the archetypal gesture of thought.

How can these changes be reconciled with Heidegger's dismissal of the events that accompanied their development? Toward the end of his life Heidegger maintained that his thinking could be divided most meaningfully into three stages. The questioning of the meaning of being (for Dasein), the dominant concern of *Sein und Zeit*, leads into the questioning of the truth of being as history. This change of tack, which takes place around 1930 and was not made public until several years later, coincides with the decision for Hölderlin. The third stage Heidegger designates as the questioning of the clearing or topology of being.[169] Through this tripartite narrative Heidegger implicitly criticizes the scholarly obsession with the *Kehre* on which his career is usually assumed to pivot. He also demands that his thinking be understood on its own terms, meaning that any contemporary historical occurrences it fails to endow with event-status are to be considered extrinsic to its development.

As a descriptive tool, I take Heidegger's retrospective schematization to be useful and convincing. Its explanatory power, however, is quickly exhausted as soon as one follows Heidegger in minimizing or denying the impact made upon his thinking by a war he regarded as epiphenomenal. Otto Pöggeler, for instance, correctly places the shift from the second to the third phase of Heidegger's thinking in the period just after the war; equally correctly, he argues that the encounter with Hölderlin belongs in the second phase, "and is taken up (transformed) into the third."[170] Yet because he accepts the spin Heidegger puts on his own intellectual development, Pöggeler is led to believe that the end of the Second World War only superficially affected Heidegger's thinking. Put simply, the emergence of Heidegger III is for Pöggeler not only irreducible to 1945 but almost irrelevant to it. Pöggeler acknowledges that Heidegger no longer addresses the Germans as the poet's chosen people; but by conceding this change, and this change alone, to the postwar, postnationalist *Zeitgeist*, he preserves the rest of Heidegger III from the influence of current affairs: "The poets who remain on track can, of course, no longer expect today to be able to pass the hints of the gods down to a 'people'; after the Second World War, Heidegger hears Hölderlin's poems from the echo they find in Trakl's lonely path into decline."[171] Why, one might ask, should it seem self-evident that the poets today be denied a national audience? If Heidegger had lost faith in the movement of national awakening long before war's end, why should he only abandon the rhetoric of *Volk* and *Vaterland* after 1945? And if he still thought a national renewal possible even after his disillusionment with Hitler had set in, why should this possibility be thwarted by Hitler's downfall? The glaring contradiction between Heidegger's self-interpretation, which Pöggeler follows, and his turn away from Germany, which Pöggeler treats as matter-of-fact, should have provoked a more thorough interrogation of the relationship between the genesis of Heidegger III and the moment of German defeat. The immanent reading demanded by Heidegger itself opens out onto the history he ignores.

The issue here is not whether Heidegger's thinking was historically determined, for he never claimed to be writing in a timeless bubble. On the contrary, we have seen how he continually stressed the untimeliness of essential questioning, which always feeds off its tension with the intellectual *mode du jour*, no summits without valleys. What is at stake, however, is the extent to which the history dismissed by Heidegger as inessential, small-h history (*Historie*) returns to haunt the scene of his thinking as it enters its third, most seemingly ahistorical, phase. Rephrased in terms of my core thesis, the reading of Hölderlin proffered in "Das abendländische Gespräch" is recognizably a *postwar* reading, despite the basic continuity of Heidegger's Hölderlin interpretation and despite his best efforts to ignore the German catastrophe or to downplay its significance. With the help of recently published documents we can now reconstruct Heidegger's response to the German defeat in the period leading up to the composition of "Das abendländische Gespräch" and so comprehend the dialogue as part of a process that may, with some justice, be regarded as Heidegger's own short-lived "working through of the past."

On the day the smoke cleared over the battlefields of Europe, Heidegger penned the final words to a dialogue entitled "Evening Conversation in a Prisoner of War Camp in Russia between a Younger and an Older Man," adding a note at the bottom of the page: "Castle Hausen in the Danube Valley, 8 May 1945. On the day when the world celebrated its victory and did not yet recognize that it has for centuries been the vanquished of its own rebellion."[172] The last third of the dialogue, in which Heidegger tries to account for the "leading into error of [his] own people," recapitulates much of what he had said and thought about the Germans' collective Dasein since 1934.[173] The poets and thinkers are "those who wait in the most noble manner," and "insofar as we become those who wait, we first become Germans"; the Germans, that is, are (originally and futurally) the people of poets and thinkers. This people, he continues, is also the most endangered, "not through threats from outside," but because it "tyrannized itself with its own unknowing impatience" in the belief "it had to wrest recognition from other peoples," whereas in fact — and here Heidegger adapts to the national calamity of 1945 the polemic against *Ausländerei* launched by Fichte after the national calamity of 1806[174] — "this overhasty sham essence remains only the eternally clumsy imitation of the foreign."[175] For Heidegger, the problem with the German special path or *Sonderweg* that led to the death camps was not that it veered too far away from the autobahn of Enlightenment but that it did not stray far enough. Entangled in a bad mimesis, the Germans succumbed to foreign influences and paid insufficient attention to their own historical essence. Like Adorno, Heidegger locates the source of the horror in a global malaise of which Nazism is only symptomatic; but by identifying the nazi tyranny with a slavish devotion to un-German ways of thinking, Heidegger, unlike Adorno, presupposes an original and uncontaminated Germanness still awaiting discovery. Far from being shaken by recent events, Heidegger's faith in Germany's unfulfilled mission has received the most emphatic confirmation, and he sees the steadfast pursuit of that mission as the only way out of the current misery: "And this quite unusable people would have to become the oldest people, since no one is concerned with it and no one makes use of its strange activity, which is a letting-be, and thus misuses it and prematurely uses it up."[176]

Barely a year prior to writing "Das abendländische Gespräch," from which Germany has vanished without a trace, Heidegger continues to avail himself of the old, now discredited trope of the Germany to come. The Nazi dictatorship, although sharply rebuked by Heidegger, comes to enjoy a certain posthumous solidarity with the people of poets and thinkers it so ruthlessly suppressed. Heidegger dissociates both Germanys, the Germany that could not wait and now lies vanquished as well as the Germany lying in wait for those who wait, from the "world" currently caught up in the throes of its delusional victory. Both Germanys embody, albeit in diametrically opposed ways, the truth of global nihilism to which the world remains blind, for they are at bottom one and the same: the "bad" foreign to which the Germans slavishly pandered is the negative image of the "good" foreign poetized by Hölderlin. The lesson Heidegger draws from the war is as logical as it is astounding. If the Germans once aped foreign manners in their impatient push for recognition, it is now (1945!) Germany's turn to teach the foreigners a thing or two: "That is why we must learn to know the necessity of the unnecessary and teach it, as learners, to the peoples."[177] This is a Heidegger who still wears his romantic nationalism on his sleeve.

At the same time the dialogue from 1945 clearly anticipates "Das abendländische Gespräch," which was almost certainly intended as its companion piece and sequel. Their titles alone suggest a common element: here an *Abendgespräch*, there an *abendländisches Gespräch*, both featuring the same dramatis personae, the Elder and the Younger, who appear in none of the other dialogues from the same period. The earlier dialogue concludes:

THE YOUNGER: Let us think of the poetizing.
THE ELDER: A good night to us both and to all in the camp.
THE YOUNGER: And to the homeland the blessing of its determination.[178]

In much the same manner as a television soap opera finishes with a preview of the coming episode, these parting words give an indication of what the reader can expect from Heidegger's next dialogue. They foreshadow both the topic of "Das abendländische Gespräch," the poetic saying of Hölderlin, and its topology, the homeland revisited by the protagonists in their thoughts as they go to bed.

Yet if "Das abendländische Gespräch" continues the "Abendgespräch," it also complements it, presupposing its diagnosis of the disease that afflicts Germany while proposing a holistic treatment in the form of beautiful dwelling, prescribed by the physician of the German soul, Hölderlin, and administered by his apothecary, Heidegger. The Germans exiled abroad in the first dialogue return in the second to the native land whose fate they ponder, but which they now no longer expressly discuss. The "Abendgespräch" provides the clue to its sequel's avoidance of patriotic speech. If no one is to "care about" the German people, and so exploit its "strange activity," if no one is to "prematurely use it up," as it was used up under the last regime, then it must efface itself for the sake of its eventual self-realization. By the end of the dialogue, the veil has already descended. That the entire "world" (not: the rest of the world) believes it has won the war implies not that Germany too has surreptitiously joined the victory party but that it has slipped off the map into the shadowy utopia where it will remain, virtually undisturbed, for the remainder of Heidegger's career. Thirteen years after cautioning the German Society in Constance with Hölderlin's self-imposed ban, "About the Highest I will not speak," Heidegger finally heeds it himself. Accordingly, and all appearances to the contrary, the Fatherland has not been abandoned in "Das abendländische Gespräch," to be replaced by a Swabian parochialism and/or good Europeanism, but hibernates within the Occident whose fate it has come to share, and whose rejuvenation (or Orientalization) it is entrusted with precipitating. In the valley of the upper Danube, Heidegger attempts to carry out the plan hatched in the Russian POW camp: that Germany *anonymously* become the teacher of peoples.

The "Abendgespräch" shows Heidegger trying to establish a safe distance between the conditions of his thinking about the German nation-state and the latter's exactly contemporaneous breakdown. This distance allows him, Cassandra-like, to expose the hollowness of the free world's triumph, but it also mitigates the unrelieved despair of German defeat. Heidegger focuses upon this second, more optimistic, consequence of his diagnosis of the age in an important letter to Rudolf Stadelmann dated 20 July 1945. "Everything now thinks of downfall," he observes, continuing: "We Germans cannot go under because we have not yet even gone up and must first see through the night."[179] At the end of the bloodiest conflict of modern times, Heidegger's insistence that Germany's rise and fall still stand before it may appear perverse, but the thinking behind it is entirely consistent with his earlier positions. Just as the rapid ascent and expansion of the Third Reich should not be confused with the advent of the true Germany — Hölderlin's Germany — so its disintegration, unforgettably metonymized in the images of the capital city reduced to rubble, need not foster the mood of apocalyptic despair that was endemic at the time. Indeed, if tragedy begins with the hero's downfall (*Untergang*), as Hölderlin speculates in the notes to *Empedokles*, then recent German history does not even deserve to be called tragic.[180] In Heidegger's account, the victims of the war fall silently into the cracks between the centuries-old rebellion of the Occident and the infinitely postponed dawning of the hidden Germany. What is needed, and what the Allied conquest and occupation of Germany could never deliver, is an authentic *Untergang*.[181]

In the last section I argued that "Das abendländische Gespräch" aims to navigate this descent with the guidance of Hölderlin. The opening lines of the same letter to Stadelmann, when read in conjunction with its comments on the future of Germany, provide the clearest available evidence of this ambition: "Your lines from Tübingen struck me like the voice of the poet from his tower by the native river. For the last half year I have sojourned in the land of my birth, at times in the most immediate stimulating proximity to the ancestral home of my forefathers in the upper Danube Valley below Castle Wildenstein. My thinking has gone far beyond mere interpretation to become a conversation with the poet, and his bodily proximity is the element of my thought."[182] Written just months before the composition of the dialogue, this extraordinary testament already encapsulates its essential features, and may rightly be regarded as its sketch in prose.[183] The ancestral home to which he refers here crops up again in the second sentence of the dialogue, when the Elder suggests that its proximity accounts for his partner's increasing receptiveness to Hölderlin's word. Heidegger had indulged in the same speculation, this time in an explicitly autobiographical context, in a preliminary comment to his course on "Der Ister" (a comment inexplicably omitted by the editors of the *Gesamtausgabe*): "Perhaps Hölderlin, the poet, had to become a determining fate for a thinker whose grandfather . . . was born in the sheep-stall of a dairy that lies in the upper Danube valley, close to the bank of the river under the rocks, while the 'Ister' hymn was being written."[184] What are we to make of these repeated attempts to interweave private genealogy and Occidental heritage, physical proximity and spiritual affinity, biographical coincidence and historical fate, Hölderlin's poetry and Heidegger's thinking, against the background of a shared topography? Why did Heidegger write again to Stadelmann on 1 September, obviously alluding to his conversation with Hölderlin (and perhaps specifically to "Das abendländische Gespräch"): "As far as the rest is concerned, I am of the conviction that the occidental spirit will awaken from out of our Swabian land"?[185]

We have seen that Heidegger always associated Hölderlin with the other, true, Germany, which opened up a perspective from which the Germany of the present could be criticized. Two Germanys thus came to coexist in Heidegger's thinking, which the "Abendgespräch" designates the impatient Germany, identified with the Nazi tyranny, and the Germany of those who wait, the people of poets and thinkers. Yet just as each Germany has its spiritual figurehead or leader — Hitler on the one hand, Hölderlin on the other — so each is tied to a particular auratic place from which they draw their symbolic (and not just symbolic) power. In the case of Hitler's Germany, this is the administrative and political center of the Reich, Berlin.[186] In 1945, as the Nazi *Götterdämmerung* descended upon the

Prussian seat of government, as Hitler shot himself in his bunker underneath the Chancellory Building, and as Soviet troops unfurled a Soviet flag over a Berlin devastated by Soviet shells, one could be forgiven for entertaining apocalyptic visions. Everyone thought of *Untergang* — everyone, that is, who conflated Germany's fortunes with those of its capital.

Yet Hölderlin's Germany has a heartland of its own that no bombs can destroy, one whose unassuming appearance belies its history-forming power. It makes its first entrance in 1933, when Heidegger still believed he could swabianize Berlin or "lead the leader." Declining the second offer of a prestigious professorship at Humboldt University, perhaps the highest recognition the state could bestow upon his work, Heidegger wrote to a local Party journal to explain why he had decided to remain in the provinces. The determining factor in his decision, he revealed, was "the inner belonging of my own work to the Black Forest and its people," which derived "from a centuries-old, irreplaceable Alemannian-Swabian rootedness in the native soil."[187] Heidegger's organic metaphor betrays his archconservative distaste for cities as places without tradition (and ciphers of modernity in general); by extension, his thinking would wilt and perish were it to be transplanted from its fertile indigenous soil to the smoggy, alien climate of Berlin. Like the upper Danube valley of "Das abendländische Gespräch" and the correspondence with Stadelmann, the Black Forest figures for the Heidegger of 1933 as a "creative landscape," in the double sense that it stimulates his philosophical creativity and creates the conditions for his philosophizing in the first place. At this stage, however, there is no indication that Heidegger's predilection for rural south-west Germany over the nation's single metropolis brings with it a conception of national renewal to rival Hitler's, nor that Hölderlin stands at its vanguard. These elements would first fall into place with the failure of Heidegger's ambitious plan to establish a national training center for university teachers in the city, and his subsequent transference of allegiance from the statesman to the poet.

By war's end, the Berlin-Swabia dichotomy already evident in 1933 had hardened into an intractable opposition. Seen in this light, Heidegger's letter to Stadelmann from July 1945 reads like a manifesto for a Germany that only now, at this precise moment in history, emerges from the rubble of the Reich, before quickly being consigned (by 1946) to the second oblivion presaged in the "Abendgespräch." Heidegger's fusion of horizons envisages the creation of a Greater Swabia whose spiritual axes extend from Nürtingen to Meßkirch, from Tübingen to Freiburg, and which is obliquely proposed as an alternative, indestructible seat of German power following the literal and symbolic obliteration of Berlin. Accordingly, the letter's repudiation of the German catastrophe should be given the following emphasis: Everyone and everything now thinks of *Untergang*, (but) *we* Germans cannot go under . . .

My survey of Heidegger's writings on Germany from May 1945 to 1946 has argued for a revision of two widespread assumptions about his postwar philosophy. The first, put forward by Pöggeler, maintains that he relinquished all hope of a popular or *völkisch* response to Hölderlin's poetry once the war helped him perceive that the people could only act inauthentically, as a manipulable mass, at the current historical nadir. While it is true that overtly nationalist tropes all but disappear from his vocabulary within six months of the unconditional surrender, his later thinking does not abandon the presumption that Germany can lead, and not merely participate in, the project of occidental renewal upon which he would ruminate for the rest of his life. The revised Hölderlin may seem more palatable, if also rather more bland, than the patriotic icon of yesteryear, but he is still the most German of the Germans.

Yet to conclude that the shift consists solely in a change in rhetorical strategy pressed upon Heidegger by political exigency and personal expediency, and hence to validate what Dieter Thomä calls his "fiercely maintained claim of lifelong, only marginally damaged consistency," would be to ignore my second, equally important, finding.[188] In the letters and dialogues I have examined, Heidegger behaves as if the end of the war had in fact ushered in a new era for Germany by making it possible for the long dormant occidental spirit to "awaken from out of our Swabian land." Heidegger varies the comforting platitude that hope is at its greatest when all hope seems lost by intimating that the false *Untergang* of 1945 opens up a window of opportunity for the genuine *Untergang* envisaged by Hölderlin to break over a chastened people, spreading from the heartland of the hidden Germany to envelop the world in its beneficent pall. From this perspective, it becomes apparent why "Das abendländische Gespräch" fails to meet its mythopoetic objective. Heidegger's refusal to recognize the caesura that makes his postwar thinking on Hölderlin possible means that he is unable to reflect upon the changed conditions under which Hölderlin is now to be read. Rather than revise his one-sided historiography to accommodate the lessons of the war, Heidegger takes his leave of history altogether. The Swabian landscape he conjures up so lovingly is a sterilized and depopulated fiction, a bunker disguised as a paradise. The war disappears into this unblemished, virginal landscape as if it had never happened. There is no room here for the hundreds of thousands of displaced persons trudging across German territory at the time, nor for the millions of dead and those who mourn them. Heidegger's earlier writings on the poet could likewise be reproached with ignoring the realities of the day,[189] but the crucial difference lies in the later interpretation's de-worlded and tensionless atemporality, its unrelenting, often vertiginous sense of stasis. Whereas once the process of reading Hölderlin opened out onto another history, the other of history (*Historie*), which was nonetheless the only history worthy of the name (*Geschichte*), it now provides an exit from history onto a virtual homeland where nothing ever happens. Stranded by the outcome of the events he had hoped to steer, Heidegger is left to repeat a single plaintive mantra to anyone willing to listen: read in reverence, dwell in beauty, wait in hope. The Younger and the Elder are the sacerdotal, faintly ridiculous cousins of Beckett's Vladimir and Estragon, their slow-paced *Untergang* the basic figure of the "decline into profundity" common to all of Heidegger's postwar writings.[190]

I noted earlier that their parting words in the "Abendgespräch," exchanged just before they go to bed, invite us to read "Das abendländische Gespräch" as its sequel. Can one not construe the later dialogue as a kind of dream script that picks up the "Abendgespräch" where it left off, as the two friends fall asleep under a Siberian sky, evocations of *Dichtung* and *Heimat* still ringing in their ears, kindling their memories and firing their imaginations? The dream is a pleasant one, for it allows them to forget both the privations suffered by their loved ones in the distant homeland and their own harsh plight in the camp. "Not completed," *nicht abgeschlossen*, Heidegger wrote at the foot of the manuscript, as if he too wanted the dream to continue indefinitely, as if his long and blissful walk into the twilight of the Occident should never come to an end.[191] But the morning broke at last, and if Heidegger continued to wander somnambulistically through Hölderlin's evening-land, it was because the new day dawned upon a world he thought already to have put behind him.

Epilogue: To Be Continued

"*The poetic character of thinking is still concealed,*" writes Heidegger in a short text from 1947. "*Where it does show itself, for a long time it resembles the utopia of a half-poetic understanding. But thinking poetizing is in truth the topology of Being.*"[192] Heidegger defends the dialogue he was writing at the time by appealing to the riper discernment of later generations. If "Das abendländische Gespräch" resembles "the utopia of a half-poetic understanding," if its interlocutors appear to indulge in "a stroll in a pleasant imaginary world,"[193] it is because, even in the new millennium, it falls upon an Occident not yet ready for it. Only after a "long time" has elapsed will the no-place of Hölderlin's *Abendland* reveal itself to be the place dictated by Being wherein thinking becomes homely. Heidegger was fond of quoting the poet's line from "Mnemosyne":

> Lang ist
> Die Zeit, es ereignet sich aber
> Das Wahre[194]
>
> [Long is
> the time, but what is true
> will take place].

In mathematics, topology denotes the study of "those properties of figures and surfaces which are independent of size and shape and are unchanged by any deformation that is continuous" (OED). The topology of Being designates a thinking approach to Being liberated from the perspectival distortions inherent to the Cartesian subject and its successor, the super- and pseudo-subject of modern technology; or rather, a thinking that apprehends the true contours of Being even when they are subject to such distortions. Thinking corresponds to the topology of Being in the same way that the protagonists of "Das abendländische Gespräch" correspond to their native land. In both cases, poetry allows the topographical forms that bewilder or distract the untrained eye to be seen for what they are, the gift of Being. In this sense, the poems of Hölderlin function for the late Heidegger much as they did for the teenaged Martin Walser, who traipsed around the countryside near Lake Constance using them as a kind of Baedeker.[195] More emphatically, what poetry lets appear cannot be said to have existed prior to its poetic naming and measuring. As Heidegger comments in his next major text on Hölderlin: "Poetizing first lets dwelling become a dwelling. . . . Poetizing is, as letting-dwell, a building."[196] Poetic thinking thereby exposes itself to the charge that its figures are the constructs of an overactive imagination.

"Das abendländische Gespräch" is the first and only text of Heidegger in which the poetic character of thinking is not just shown (presented or argued), but seeks to show itself. The conversation, I have argued, was intended to guide the Occident toward the free use of its ownmost by leading it into and through its foreign element. Did Heidegger believe he had succeeded? Neither the dialogue's posthumous publication nor its fragmentary form necessarily indicate his dissatisfaction with it. The former may indicate that the dialogue was conceived, like the *Beiträge zur Philosophie*, as his legacy to a yet unborn readership; the latter, I have argued, in all likelihood responds to Hölderlin's unfinished "Ister" hymn.

The evidence of his later writings is equally ambivalent. On the one hand, although he continued to scrutinize the topology of being, he was never driven to repeat the attempt to realize it poetically. The dialogue's unified, fully integrated mythic world splintered into quasi-autonomous, quasi-metaphorical figures of thought like the four-fold or the Occident of the essays on Trakl. His texts came to resemble the surviving, barely legible scraps of an ancient map, and it was up to the individual reader to decide whether her inability to find her way into the lost kingdom was due to her own shortcomings or the absence of a crucial hieroglyph. Pöggeler phrases it nicely: "One could summarize the many lectures, treatises and letters Heidegger published in his last decades as *fragments* to a topology of being."[197] The search for the one true beginning still evident in the dialogue's rather muted eschatology, which led Heidegger to the Orient and to "the mysterious relations to the East which in Hölderlin's poetry have become word," yields to a vision of multiple inceptions, none of which is said to articulate the definitive experience of Being.[198] After "Das abendländische Gespräch," Heidegger follows unmarked forest paths that take him away from the centering homeliness of the riverbank in pursuit of fugitive "signs" and "hints." That he might lose his way in the undergrowth was a risk he willingly accepted.[199] Certainly, he never again voiced the conviction that the Occident would rise from its torpor, expressing instead the increasingly forlorn and formulaic hope that homo faber might one day be brought to his senses.

On the other hand, these subsequent developments are not inconsistent with the project of "Das abendländische Gespräch." Perhaps Heidegger jettisoned the heavy teleological ballast of his earlier thinking after writing the dialogue because it was no longer needed. By this I do not mean that, having reached the end of history, all one could do was twiddle one's thumbs while awaiting the event of Being. On the contrary, the journey away from the Occident (and, it should be added, from occidental myth-making) made available to Heidegger a bricolage of hitherto unheeded traditions and voices: the paintings of Cézanne, the gnomic wisdom of the Chinese sages, and the verses of a local Alemannian poetess, to name a few. Furthermore, the dialogue's emphasis upon Dasein's earthliness — conceived, against Plato, as original to spiritual existence — entails an abandonment of the chiliastic expectations to which the *Beiträge* had given rise. In his later years, Heidegger takes pains to avoid the misunderstanding that the advent of the gods is a possible, indeed hoped-for historical event. In the second *Griechenlandreise* (1967), he comments on a variant of "Der Archipelagus" (The Archipelago): "For the poet, the present gods are so closely present, so pressing, that precisely their proximity prevents him from approaching them qua poet, that is, saying them. The poet must step back from this proximity such that it becomes a distance that protects him from overhastily naming the ones who are present."[200] The contrast with the 1934 interpretation of "Germanien" is striking. Whereas once the absence of the gods was to be endured, and their return awaited, in a mood of resolute mourning, Heidegger now reveals that stance to be a self-protective measure. Mourning is the function of an excess, not a lack, and the teleological trajectory of the god to come, which pushes the redemptive goal of history into an inscrutable future, helps keep the presence of the divine at a safe distance. To dwell beautifully means to accept the undesirability of mystic fusion with the divine while remaining receptive to the holy, the dimension wherein the absent gods draw close in their absence. Accordingly, the "other inception" is not some ecstatic encounter with the divine to which poetic thinking points the way but poetic thinking itself.[201] Insofar as the poetic character of thinking shows itself in "Das abendländische Gespräch" in a way Heidegger did not subsequently attempt to realize, it makes sense to think of the dialogue as an "other inception" in Heidegger's own thinking, and to read the later texts, particularly those on dwelling and poetry, in its light.

The dialogue demands to be read as a key transitional text between Heideggers II and III. While its ambitious theorization of the spirit's migration from the Orient to the Occident via Greece recalls and augments the ontohistories of the 1930s and early 40s, its thorough-going poeticization of that mythology, condensed in the ethos of beautiful dwelling, gestures toward the topological studies of the 1950s and beyond. Politically, too, the dialogue marks a watershed, for it represents the exact point at which Heidegger drops the previously omnipresent reference to Germany. Heidegger's nationalism goes to ground in "Das abendländische Gespräch"; he no longer dares or cares to speak its name.

Heidegger continued to write and publish on Hölderlin in the following years, albeit rather less prolifically and without the same sense of urgency that characterized his earlier engagement, but he only hinted twice at the poet's ongoing leadership of the secret Germany. Significantly, both occasions came to light within days of his death, putting an end to the long silence that had befallen the Fatherland ever since "Das abendländische Gespräch"; both vividly convey the stakes involved in his lifelong dialogue with the poet. The first is to be found in the *Spiegel* interview, conducted in 1966 and first published a decade later. "Do you attribute a particular role to the Germans?" asked one interviewer, doubtless alluding to Heidegger's controversial statements on national destiny from the 1930s. The answer was succinct: "Yes, in this sense: in conversation with Hölderlin."[202] The second occasion fell in early 1976, when Heidegger's remains were interred in his native Meßkirch. Heidegger had requested that an excerpt from the same poem he had quoted in Constance over forty years previously, "An die Deutschen," be recited over his grave. In 1934 he had used the last two stanzas to warn his audience that there was no way of foretelling the "world-hour" of the German people. This time he cited the first two stanzas, and the message differed accordingly. Evoking the gnawing doubts as well as the undiminished hopes of his encounter with the poet, they represent his last, still unheeded, address to the German nation and provide a fitting epitaph to his life's work.

> Spottet nimmer des Kinds, wenn noch das alberne,
> Auf dem Rosse von Holz herrlich und viel sich dünkt,
> O ihr Guten! auch wir sind
> Thatenarm und gedankenvoll!
>
> Aber kommt, wie der Stral aus dem Gewölke kommt,
> Aus Gedanken vielleicht, geistig und reif die That?
> Folgt die Frucht, wie des Haines
> Dunklem Blatte, der stillen Schrift?[203]

[Never laugh at the child, seeing the silly one
Feel important and great up on his rocking-horse;
O my brothers, we too are
Poor in deeds though we've thoughts enough!

But as lightning from clouds, out of mere thoughts perhaps
Will the deed in the end, lucid, mature, leap out?
As from dark orchard leaves, from
Quiet scripts does the fruit ensue?][204]

Notes

[1] "noch zeit-raum-loses Werk unser historisches Getue schon überwunden und den Anfang einer anderen Geschichte gegründet hat, jener Geschichte, die anhebt mit dem Kampf um die Entscheidung über Ankunft oder Flucht des Gottes." Heidegger, *GA* 39:1.

[2] "steht in einem unumgänglichen Bezug zur Dichtung Hölderlins." Heidegger, *GA* 16:678.

[3] Heidegger's wish that the *Gesamtausgabe* be entitled *Wege*, Paths, was not shared by the publisher. *Wege, nicht Werke* nonetheless stands inscribed over volume 1 of the edition.

[4] "Das Hörenkönnen ist nicht erst eine Folge des Miteinandersprechens, sondern eher umgekehrt die Voraussetzung dafür." Heidegger, *GA* 4:39; English translation from Heidegger, *Elucidations to Hölderlin's Poetry*, trans. Keith Hoeller (New York: Humanity Books, 2000), 57.

[5] Heidegger, *GA* 4:159–60; *Elucidations*, 184. See also Jacques Derrida, "Heidegger's Ear: Philopolemology (*Geschlecht* IV)" in *Reading Heidegger: Commemorations*, ed. John Sallis (Bloomington: Indiana UP, 1993), 160–217.

[6] Paul de Man, *Blindness and Insight: Essays in the Rhetoric of Contemporary Criticism* (Minneapolis: U of Minnesota P, 1983), 254. In basic agreement with de Man are Reinold Schmücker, "Monologisches Gespräch: Heideggers Vorlesung über Hölderlins Hymne 'Andenken,'" *Zeitschrift für Germanistik* 2.3 (1992): 550–68; and A. W. Prins, "Heideggers 'Andenken': Zwiesprache und Gewalt," in *Poesie und Philosophie in einer Tragischen Kultur*, ed. Heinz Kammerle (Würzburg: Königshausen & Neumann, 1995), 73–86. Maurice Blanchot, on the other hand, writes of the *Erläuterungen;* "So we do not have to fear that the commentary adds to the text. We can say that anything lent to it had been borrowed from it." Blanchot, *The Work of Fire*, trans. Charlotte Mandell (Stanford, CA: Stanford UP, 1995), 113. See also Robert Savage, "Between Heidegger and Hölderlin: The 'Sacred' Speech of Maurice Blanchot," in *After Blanchot: Literature, Criticism, Philosophy*, ed. Leslie Hill, Brian Nelson, and Dimitris Vardoulakis (Newark: U of Delaware P, 2005), 149–67.

[7] "Wo *ein* Gespräch sein soll, muß das wesentliche Wort auf das Eine und Selbe bezogen bleiben. Ohne diesen Bezug ist auch und gerade ein Streitgespräch unmöglich." Heidegger, *GA* 4:39; *Elucidations*, 57.

[8] "Stimme des Freunds." Heidegger, *GA* 2:217.

[9] Heidegger's difference from Wittgenstein on this point may be summarized thus: that whereof one cannot speak, thereof one must converse.

[10] The *Kehre* generally designates the turning in Heidegger's thought from the question of the meaning of Being (for Dasein) to that of its epochal truth and eventfulness. On Hölderlin's role in the *Kehre*, see Otto Pöggeler, "Heideggers Begegnung mit Hölderlin," *Man and World* 10 (1977): 15.

[11] "Das Gespräch und seine Einheit trägt unser Dasein." Heidegger, *GA* 4:39; *Elucidations*, 57.

[12] "der Bund mit der Sache selbst, die eine und dieselbe ist von Parmenides bis zu Hegel." Heidegger, *GA* 32:19.

[13] Heidegger, *GA* 4:38; *Elucidations*, 57.

[14] On the relationship between *Wiederholung* and *Zwiesprache*, see Beda Allemann, *Hölderlin und Heidegger* (Zurich: Atlantis Verlag, 1954), 97–102.

[15] "Sprache ist das Haus des Seins. In ihrer Behausung wohnt der Mensch. Die Denkenden und die Dichtenden sind die Wächter dieser Behausung." Heidegger, *GA* 9:313; English translation from Heidegger, *Basic Writings*, trans. David Farrell Krell (San Francisco: Harper, 1993), 217.

[16] "Das Sein des Menschen gründet in der Sprache; aber diese geschieht erst eigentlich im *Gespräch*." Heidegger, *GA* 4:38.

[17] Poetry is conceived by Heidegger as the postal service between Dasein and Being that directs their correspondence by establishing their interrelationship, even if that relationship be one of (the remembrance of) loss and abandonment. See Heidegger, "Vom Ursprung des Kunstwerks: Erste Ausarbeitung," *Heidegger Studies* 5 (1989): 20. See also Friedrich-Wilhelm von Herrmann, *Heideggers Philosophie der Kunst: Eine systematische Interpretation der Holzwege-Abhandlung "Der Ursprung des Kunstwerkes"* (Frankfurt am Main: Klostermann, 1994), 10.

[18] "Die geschichtliche Bestimmung der Philosophie gipfelt in der Erkenntnis der Notwendigkeit, Hölderlins Wort das Gehör zu schaffen." Heidegger, *GA* 65:422; English translation from Heidegger, *Contributions to Philosophy (from Enowning)*, trans. Parvis Emad and Kenneth Maly (Bloomington: Indiana UP, 1999), 297.

[19] See Otto Pöggeler, *Der Denkweg Martin Heideggers* (Pfullingen: Neske, 1963), 51.

[20] "*Daß Hölderlin!* Die Einzigkeit dieses 'daß.'" Heidegger, *GA* 75:371. On Hölderlin's name, see Marc Froment-Meurice, *That Is to Say: Heidegger's Poetics*, trans. Jan Plug (Stanford, CA: Stanford UP, 1998), 82–83. Froment-Meurice argues that what makes Hölderlin synonymous with the essence of *Dichtung*, but not (yet) anonymous in the essence of *Dichtung*, what prevents the fusion of two names into a single essence, is also what allows Heidegger to name Hölderlin (in the strongest, performative sense of the word) the "poet of the poet."

[21] Alexander García Düttmann, *Between Cultures: Tensions in the Struggle for Recognition* (London: Verso, 2000), 24.

[22] Heidegger, *GA* 39:30.

[23] "ein Denken, das *unterwegs* ist." Heidegger, *GA* 65:4; *Contributions*, 3.

[24] "ein Weg, der selber geht." Heidegger, *GA* 65:83; *Contributions*, 57.

[25] "seynsgeschichtliche Einzigkeit." Heidegger, *GA* 75:371.

[26] "Wir müssen mit der Tatsache fertig werden, daß die Deutschen volle hundert Jahre Zeit brauchten, bis überhaupt das Werk Hölderlins in jener Gestalt vor uns kam, die uns zwingt einzugestehen, daß wir seiner Größe und zukünftigen Macht heute noch in keiner Weise gewachsen sind." Heidegger, *GA* 39:7.

[27] Wolfgang Borchert, *Das Gesamtwerk* (Hamburg: Rowohlt, 1949), 341; English translation from *The Man Outside: The Prose Works of Wolfgang Borchert*, trans. David Porter (London: Calder & Boyars, 1966), 252.

[28] Heidegger, *GA* 16:116.

[29] "Jedes Volk hat die erste Gewähr seiner Echtheit und Größe in seinem Blut, seinem Boden und seinem leiblichen Wachstum." Heidegger, *GA* 16:151.

[30] "so daß wir künftig diese Feier in die Wirklichkeit und unter das Sinnbild von *Langemarck* stellen." Heidegger, *GA* 16:199.

[31] Heidegger, *GA* 12:88.

[32] Heidegger, *GA* 12:172.

[33] "Ich lebe viel mit Hölderlin." Martin Heidegger and Hannah Arendt, ed. Ursula Ludz, *Briefe, 1925 bis 1975* (Frankfurt am Main: Klostermann, 1998), 20 and 46. Muñoz discerns the influence of *Hyperion* in Heidegger's thinking of negativity in the late 1920s and early 1930s, above all in the speeches "Was ist Metaphysik?" (What is Metaphysics?) and "Vom Wesen der Wahrheit" (On the Essence of Truth). Breno Onetto Muñoz, *Überschritt ins Unumgängliche: Heideggers dichterische Wende jenseits der Metaphysik* (Frankfurt am Main: Peter Lang, 1997), 55–69. See also Manfred Riedel, "Seinserfahrung in der Dichtung: Heideggers Weg zu Hölderlin," in *"Voll Verdienst, doch dichterisch wohnet / Der Mensch auf dieser Erde": Heidegger und Hölderlin*, ed. Peter Trawny (Frankfurt am Main: Klostermann, 2000), 19–49.

[34] "wurde Hölderlins Wort, zuvor schon wie andere Dichter zunächst bekannt, zum Geschick." The treatise from which this comment is taken, *Das Ereignis* (The Event), remains unpublished. Otto Pöggeler, who was granted access to Heidegger's manuscripts, cites it in his *Der Denkweg Martin Heideggers*, 218.

[35] Cited by Picht in "Die Macht des Denkens," in *Erinnerung an Martin Heidegger*, ed. Günther Neske (Pfullingen: Neske, 1977), 199.

[36] Georg Lukács, "Hölderlins Hyperion," in *Der andere Hölderlin: Materialen zum "Hölderlin"-Stück von Peter Weiss*, ed. Thomas Beckermann and Volker Canaris (Frankfurt am Main: Suhrkamp, 1972), 19–47; here, 33.

[37] See Berel Lang, *Heidegger's Silence* (Ithaca, NY: Cornell UP, 1996).

[38] Ever since Pöggeler argued that "one cannot talk about Heidegger and Hölderlin without touching on Heidegger's relationship to National Socialism," increasing attention has been drawn to the connection between Heidegger's turn to Hölderlin and his turn from Hitler. The best work on the theme remains Annemarie Gethmann-Siefert's vigorously critical "Heidegger und Hölderlin: Die Überforderung des 'Dichters in dürftiger Zeit,'" in *Heidegger und die praktische Philosophie*, ed. Gethmann-Siefert and Pöggeler (Frankfurt am Main.: Suhrkamp,

1988): 191–227. The chapters on the Hölderlin lectures in Fred Dallmayr's *The Other Heidegger* (Ithaca, NY: Cornell UP, 1993) offer a far more sympathetic reading. Somewhat surprisingly, none of the essays in the collection edited by Peter Trawny, "*Voll Verdienst, doch dichterisch wohnet / Der Mensch auf dieser Erde*": *Heidegger und Hölderlin*, pursues the political implications of Heidegger's turn to the poet.

[39] See Heidegger, *GA* 16:335.

[40] "die Entschlossenheit zum wesentlichen Fragen nach dem Sein und Schein dessen, was ist und nicht ist." Heidegger, *GA* 16:316.

[41] "als einen *Ausdruck* oder als eine *Leistung* der jeweiligen Zeit." Heidegger, *GA* 16:318.

[42] Heidegger, *GA* 40:10–11.

[43] Friedrich Nietzsche, "Unzeitgemäße Betrachtungen," *Werke*, vol. 3.1 (Berlin: Walter de Gruyter, 1972), 243.

[44] Heidegger, *GA* 16:324.

[45] Heidegger, *GA* 2:523.

[46] "so daß die Vergangenheit erst durch den Bezug auf die *jeweilige Gegenwart* 'lebensnahe' Geschichte wird." Heidegger, *GA* 16:322.

[47] Nietzsche, "Unzeitgemäße Betrachtungen," 168.

[48] See Gunter Martens, "Hölderlin-Rezeption in der Nachfolge Nietzsches: Stationen der Aneignung eines Dichters," *HJb* 23 (1982/83): 57. Martens argues that Heidegger's reception of Hölderlin was strongly influenced by Nietzsche's presentation of Hölderlin as a critic and victim of his time.

[49] "Was unzeitgemäß ist, kann seine eigene Zeit haben. So ist es mit der Philosophie. So ist es mit den beiden anderen Grundmächten, durch die ein geschichtliches Dasein eines Volkes gestiftet wird, mit der Dichtung und der Tat der Staatsschöpfung." Heidegger, *GA* 16:318.

[50] "deren *Schicksal* es bleibt, nie einen unmittelbaren Widerklang in ihrem jeweiligen Heute finden zu können, und nie finden zu *dürfen*." Heidegger, *GA* 16:318.

[51] "Wenn wir nach der Gegenwart und Zukunft der Deutschen *Philosophie* fragen, dann meinen wir *diese Zeiten* — nicht ein zufälliges Heutiges. Aber wissen wir die eigentliche Zeit, — die Weltstunde unseres Volks? Keiner weiß sie. (vgl. Hölderlin, An die Deutschen — die zwei letzten Strophen.)" Heidegger, *GA* 16:319.

[52] Hölderlin, *StA* 2.1:10: *Poems and Fragments*, trans. Michael Hamburger (London: Routledge & Kegan Paul, 1966), 125; translation modified.

[53] "die Weltzeit unseres Volkes ist uns verborgen. Und sie *bleibt so lange* verborgen, als wir nicht wissen, *wer wir selbst sind*." Heidegger, *GA* 16:319.

[54] Philippe Lacoue-Labarthe, "Poetry's Courage," in *The Solid Letter: Readings of Friedrich Hölderlin*, ed. Aris Fioretos (Stanford, CA: Stanford UP, 1999), 78.

[55] See Françoise Dastur, "Europa und der 'andere Anfang,'" in *Europa und die Philosophie*, ed. Hans-Helmuth Gander (Frankfurt am Main: Klostermann, 1993), 185–96; here, 189.

[56] "Wenn sie zu denken anfangen, sprechen sie deutsch." Heidegger, *GA* 1:679.

[57] "das metaphysische Volk." Heidegger, *GA* 40:41.

[58] See Heidegger, *GA* 40:152.

[59] See James Phillips, *Heidegger's Volk: Between National Socialism and Poetry* (Stanford, CA: Stanford UP, 2005).

[60] "allein schafft den Gewitterraum, in dessen Bereich — *wenn* überhaupt — die Blitze der Götter uns treffen und die Weltstunden des Volkes ansagen. Keiner weiß, wann das geschieht. Aber eines wissen wir, was Hölderlin, der Deutscheste der Deutschen in einem Bruchstück seiner späten und eigentlichen Dichtung sagt: 'Einst hab ich die Muse gefragt, und sie / Antwortete mir / Am Ende wirst du es finden. / Vom Höchsten will ich schweigen. / Verbotene Frucht, wie der Lorbeer, ist aber / Am meisten das Vaterland. Die aber kost' / Ein jeder zuletzt.'" Heidegger, *GA* 16:333–4; English translation from Hölderlin, *Poems and Fragments*, 537.

[61] Norbert von Hellingrath, *Hölderlin-Vermächtnis*, ed. Ludwig von Pigenot (Munich: Brockmann, 1936), 124 and 148. By suggesting that Hölderlin is the *Deutscheste der Deutschen* not despite, but because of, his mantic distance from nationalistic blather and party politics, Heidegger betrays his debt to the Hölderlin reception among the George Circle — not only to Hellingrath, whom Heidegger acknowledged as his precursor and guide, but also to Gundolf and Komerell, whose writings on Hölderlin he is known to have studied.

[62] Friedrich Nietzsche, "Götzendämmerung," *Werke*, vol. 6.3 (Berlin: Walter de Gruyter, 1969), 145. In the first part of his book on Nietzsche, based on a 1936–37 lecture course, Heidegger declares that Goethe, who misrecognized the uniqueness of the Greek inception, is a "catastrophe" (*Verhängnis*); Hölderlin, on the other hand, is a "fate" (*Schicksal*). Heidegger, *GA* 6.1:146.

[63] See Hellingrath, *Hölderlin-Vermächtnis*, 124–25: Hölderlin's "richness of poverty" makes us aware of the "poverty of the richness" Goethe has to offer. Carl Schmitt recalled: " 'Youth without Goethe' (Max Kommerell), that was for us after 1910 *in concreto* youth with Hölderlin, that is, the transition from an optimistic-ironic-neutralizing genialism to a pessimistic-active-tragic genialism." Note from 18 May 1948, in Schmitt, *Glossarium*, 152.

[64] "daß Adolf Hitler jenen neuen Geist der Gemeinschaft zur gestaltenden Macht einer neuen Ordnung des Volkes erhöht und durchgesetzt hat." Heidegger, *GA* 16:302. Gerhard Ritter, a former student, argues that Heidegger was "from June 30, 1934 secretly an embittered opponent of the Nazi regime and had also fully lost . . . his belief in Hitler." Heidegger's lectures in August, which glowingly praise the *Führer*, seem to contradict this opinion. Bernd Martin, ed. *Martin Heidegger und das dritte Reich* (Darmstadt: Wissenschaftliche Buchgesellschaft, 1989), 160.

[65] "Ich habe ganz aus der innersten Mitte der Spätdichtung angesetzt, mit einer vorläufigen Auslegung von 'Germanien'; und zwar gerade, um jede falsche Zeitgemäßheit abzuwehren." Heidegger, *GA* 16:335.

[66] Gerhard Kurz, "Hölderlin 1943" in *Hölderlin und Nürtingen*, ed. Peter Härtling and Gerhard Kurz (Stuttgart: J. B. Metzler, 1994), 103–28; here, 109.

[67] Thus the very lines Heidegger cites here to distance Hölderlin from premature nationalist appropriations are quoted, directly beneath the swastika, on the title

page of the program for the festivities in Tübingen marking the 100th anniversary of the poet's death. Zeller, *Klassiker in finsterer Zeit, 1933–1945*, 2 vols. (Marbach: Schiller-Nationalmuseum, 1983), 2:89.

[68] "daß die Anerkennenden sich als die sich Anerkennenden anerkennen und damit sich gegenseitig in die höchste Entfaltung ihres Wesens hinaufsteigern." Heidegger, *GA* 16:333.

[69] See Heidegger, *GA* 13:15–22.

[70] Heidegger implicitly authorizes this interpretation of *Selbständigkeit* as the free standing (*Stehen*) of the self (*Selbst*) in Heidegger, *GA* 40:152.

[71] "Diese wahre geschichtliche Freiheit als die Selbständigkeit des Anerkennens von Volk zu Volk bedarf nicht der organisierten Scheingemeinschaft einer 'Liga der Nationen.'" Heidegger, *GA* 16:333.

[72] Quoted by Heidegger in Heidegger, *GA* 39:110, and again in *GA* 40:215.

[73] Curd Ochwadt notes that Heidegger had by 1939 (in fact probably much earlier) written a 92-page manuscript on Empedocles, which he subsequently destroyed. Heidegger, *GA* 75:404.

[74] "Niemand versteht, was 'ich' hier *denke*." Heidegger, *GA* 65:8; *Contributions*, 6.

[75] "der freie Gebrauch des eigenen." Hölderlin, *StA* 6:425.

[76] "das feuer vom Himmel," "die Klarheit der Darstellung." Hölderlin, *StA* 6:425–26.

[77] "Junonische Nüchternheit," "das Eigene." Hölderlin, *StA* 6:426.

[78] "Das Eigene gerade ist je auf ein Anderes bezogen, das Feuer auf die Darstellung, die Darstellung auf das Feuer." Heidegger, *GA* 52:131.

[79] "der freie Gebrauch des Eigenen das Schwerste ist." Hölderlin, *StA* 6:426.

[80] "das Lernen des Fremden aber, das im Dienste dieser Aneignung steht, ist eben deshalb leichter." Heidegger, *GA* 53:154; English translation from Heidegger, *Hölderlin's Hymn "The Ister,"* trans. William McNeill and Julia Davis (Bloomington: Indiana UP, 1996), 124.

[81] On original imitation, see Peter Murphy and David Roberts, *Dialectic of Romanticism* (London: Continuum, 2004), ch. 4.

[82] Heidegger, *GA* 53:156; *Hölderlin's Hymn "The Ister,"* 125.

[83] "griechischer denken als die Griechen selbst"; "wir selbst müssen in bezug auf uns selbst künftighin deutscher denken als alle bisherigen Deutschen." Heidegger, *GA* 53:100; *Hölderlin's Hymn "The Ister,"* 81.

[84] See E. M. Butler, *The Tyranny of Greece over Germany: A Study of the Influence Exercised by Greek Art and Poetry over the Great German Writers* (Cambridge: Cambridge UP, 1935).

[85] "die einzige Sorge." Heidegger, *GA* 53:60; *Hölderlin's Hymn "The Ister,"* 49.

[86] Fred Dallmayr, *The Other Heidegger*, 176.

[87] Christopher Fynsk, *Heidegger, Thought and Historicity* (Ithaca, NY: Cornell UP, 1986), 204.

[88] Beda Allemann, the author of the first full-length study on this topic, *Hölderlin und Heidegger*, ventures a partial criticism of Heidegger's interpretation when he argues that Hölderlin's word "colony" (found in a late variant of "Brod und Wein" and identified by Heidegger with the foreign element through which the "own" must pass) refers to the relationship of the divine to the worldly, not of Greece to Hesperia (172). Szondi's beautiful reading of the letter, "Überwindung des Klassizismus," is reprinted in *Hölderlin-Studien: Mit einem Traktat über philologische Erkenntnis* (Frankfurt am Main: Insel, 1967). Andrzej Warminiski's ingenious interpretation explores the "Egyptian" element in Hölderlin's thinking neglected by Heidegger; see Warminski, *Readings in Interpretation: Hölderlin, Hegel, Heidegger* (Minneapolis: U of Minnesota P, 1986) and, more recently, "Monstrous History: Heidegger reading Hölderlin" in *The Solid Letter: Readings of Friedrich Hölderlin*, ed. Aris Fioretos (Stanford: Stanford UP, 1999): 201–15. Several of the essayists in Fioretos's collection, especially Edgar Pankow, Rainer Nägele, and Fioretos himself, provide fresh readings of this seminal text, readings that diverge from Heidegger's.

[89] "politische Mißdeutung des 'Vaterlands' bei Hölderlin." Heidegger, *GA* 75:277.

[90] "Die jungen Deutschen, die von Hölderlin wußten, [haben] angesichts des Todes Anderes gedacht und gelebt als das, was die Öffentlichkeit als deutsche Meinung ausgab." Heidegger, *GA* 9:339; *Basic Writings*, 243. Heidegger must be referring to soldiers here, and not civilians, because although millions of ordinary Germans "lived and thought" "in the face of death" under the threat of Allied bombing, they were not predominantly "young Germans."

[91] Reinhard Mehring, *Heideggers Überlieferungsgeschick: Eine dionysische Selbstinszenierung* (Würzburg: Königshausen & Neumann, 1992), 75.

[92] "während des Feldzugs im Tornister mitverpackt." Heidegger, *GA* 5:3.

[93] Anselm Haverkamp, *"Laub voll Trauer": Hölderlins späte Allegorie* (Munich: Wilhelm Fink, 1991), 77. In English, *Leaves of Mourning: Hölderlin's Late Work — with an Essay on Keats and Melancholy*, trans. Vernon Chadwick (Albany, NY: SUNY P, 1996).

[94] "Ein Gedicht kennenlernen, das heißt noch nicht: *im Machtbereich der Dichtung stehen*." Heidegger, *GA* 39:19.

[95] "Träger des Namens," "Wächter des Seyns." Heidegger, *GA* 65:464; *Contributions*, 326 (translation modified).

[96] "Aber das Weltgeschick kündigt sich in der Dichtung an, ohne daß es schon als Geschichte des Seins offenbar wird. Das weltgeschichtliche Denken Hölderlins, das im Gedicht 'Andenken' zum Wort kommt, ist darum wesentlich anfänglicher und deshalb zukünftiger als der bloße Weltbürgertum Goethes. Darum haben die jungen Deutschen, die von Hölderlin wußten, angesichts des Todes Anderes gedacht und gelebt als das, was die Öffentlichkeit als deutsche Meinung ausgab." Heidegger, *GA* 9:339; *Basic Writings*, 242–43.

[97] "Das Erwachen des Frontgeistes im Kriege und seine Verfestigung nach dem Kriege ist nichts anderes als die schöpferische Verwandlung dieses Ereignisses zu einer gestaltenden Kraft des künftigen Daseins. Der Frontgeist ist der wissende

Wille zu einer neuen Gemeinschaft. . . . Das ist jene Art des Zueinandergehörens, in der jeder unbedingt für jeden anderen in jeder Lage einsteht." Heidegger, *GA* 16:299.

[98] Heidegger, *GA* 9:339; *Basic Writings*, 243. See Anson Rabinbach, *In the Shadow of Catastrophe: German Intellectuals between Apocalypse and Enlightenment* (Berkeley: U of California P, 1997), 113.

[99] "Wir haben noch kaum begonnen, die geheimnisvollen Bezüge zum Osten zu denken, die in Hölderlins Dichtung Wort geworden sind." Heidegger, *GA* 9:338; *Basic Writings*, 241. The vagueness of this concept of East-West relations is surely deliberate: it is broad enough to encompass Jünger's (or Lukács's) admiration of the Soviet experiment as a counter to Western decadence, Hesse's magical mystery tour of the Orient, and Nietzsche's opposition of Dionysian revelry and Apollonian dream-vision, all subsumed under Hölderlin's dialectic of the native and the foreign.

[100] Heidegger, *GA* 4:88; Hölderlin, *StA* 6:426.

[101] Hölderlin, *StA* 2.1:138; *Poems and Fragments*, 393.

[102] Cf. Hölderlin, *StA* 2.1:165.

[103] "Die Nachrichten sind stets knapp. Aber wesentlicher als die immer schwankenden Neuigkeiten ist die feste Zuversicht, daß die Deutschen nicht nur 'siegen,' sondern vor allem ihre geistige-geschichtliche Bestimmung finden." Heidegger, *GA* 16:357.

[104] Friedrich Meinecke, *The German Catastrophe*, trans. Sidney B. Fay (Boston: Beacon, 1963).

[105] "die jetzige Weltnot." Heidegger, *GA* 9:364.

[106] "Not der Notlosigkeit." For example, Heidegger, *GA* 16:335.

[107] Hellingrath, *Hölderlin-Vermächtnis*, 135.

[108] Rüdiger Safranski, *Ein Meister aus Deutschland: Heidegger und seine Zeit* (Munich: Hanser, 1994), 385.

[109] "Diese Fragen Ihres Briefes ließen sich wohl im unmittelbaren Gespräch eher klären. Im Schriftlichen büßt das Denken leicht seine Beweglichkeit ein. Vor allem aber kann es da nur schwer die ihm eigene Mehrdimensionalität seines Bereiches innehalten." Heidegger, *GA* 9:315; *Basic Writings*, 219.

[110] Reinhold Mehring comments of one such dialogue: "In the course of this conversation, there is no place for contradiction. The participants are typecast through their roles in the conversation and are without individual characteristics. . . . The *Feldweggespräch* is not a dialectical experiment, but a didactic translation." Mehring, *Heideggers Überlieferungsgeschick: Eine dionysische Selbstinszenierung*, 145.

[111] "Nur innerhalb der Metaphysik gibt es das Physische und das Sinnliche im Unterschied zum Nicht-Physischen und Nicht-Sinnlichen. Die Metaphysik ist sogar das Walten dieses Unterschieds." Heidegger, *GA* 75:166; see also 180.

[112] "fällt das Griechentum aus der Bahn seines Wesens heraus." Heidegger, *GA* 53:95; *Hölderlin's Hymn "The Ister,"* 77.

[113] See Heidegger, *GA* 6.2:309.

[114] "Aus Platons Dialog 'Phaidros,' dem Gespräch über 'das Schöne' (Schlußstück) erfahren wir überdies, daß Platon ein sehr klares Wissen vom Vorrang des unmittelbar gesprochenen Wortes vor dem nur geschriebenen hatte." Heidegger, *GA* 54:132.

[115] Heidegger, *GA* 53:110; *Hölderlin's Hymn "The Ister,"* 88.

[116] Plato, *Phaedrus & Letters VII and VIII*, trans. Walter Hamilton (Harmondsworth, UK: Penguin, 1973), 24–25.

[117] Plato, *Phaedrus*, 52.

[118] Plato, *Phaedrus*, 56–57.

[119] See Heidegger, *GA* 75:307.

[120] Holger Schmid, "Geschick und Verhältnis des Lebendigen: Die griechische Sphäre zwischen Heidegger und Hölderlin," in Trawny, *"Voll Verdienst, doch dichterisch wohnet / Der Mensch auf dieser Erde": Heidegger und Hölderlin*, 163–80.

[121] Heidegger, *GA* 75:172.

[122] Heidegger, *GA* 6.1:78.

[123] "aus der Vergessenheit des Seins herausreißt." Heidegger, *GA* 6.1:199.

[124] "im Umkreis der ursprünglichen Frage des Verhältnisses des Menschen zum Seienden als solchem." Heidegger, *GA* 6.1:195. As Lacoue-Labarthe points out, Heidegger reads the theory of mimesis proposed in book 3 of the *Republic*, which imposes stringent didactic and moral constraints upon the artwork, through the parable of the cave in book 10, taking pains to demonstrate how the former flows from the latter despite preceding it in the dialogue. Philippe Lacoue-Labarthe, *Typography: Mimesis, Philosophy, Politics*, trans. Christopher Fynsk, (Stanford: Stanford UP, 1998), 76–77.

[125] "Seyn, im einzigen Sinne des Worts." Hölderlin, *StA* 3:236–37.

[126] "machen urbar das Land." Heidegger, *GA* 75:192.

[127] Heidegger, *GA* 75:175; see also 177.

[128] "die Naturschönheit dieser Landschaft malen," "den Naturgenuß erwecken und rege halten." Heidegger, *GA* 75:175.

[129] " 'Schön,' einfach schön; und das heißt doch für das Schöne stets: Über die Maßen schön." Heidegger, *GA* 75:174.

[130] See J. M. Bernstein, *The Fate of Art: Aesthetic Alienation from Kant to Derrida and Adorno* (Cambridge: Polity, 1993), 122.

[131] "Wie schön er wohnt, lernen wir . . . indem wir an seinem Ufer gehen und ihm folgen." Heidegger, *GA* 75:177.

[132] "Das Schöne, das die Verse nennen, ist das Wohnliche, worin der wohnende Strom wohnt." Heidegger, *GA* 75:176.

[133] On boredom, see Heidegger, *GA* 29/30:117–249.

[134] See Johnathan Bate, *The Song of the Earth* (London: Picador, 2001), 205–83; Kate Rigby, *Topographies of the Sacred* (Richmond: U of Virginia P, 2005).

[135] Heidegger, *GA* 39:170.

[136] "denn das Griechenland ist das Weltalter, in dem nicht der erste Aufgang und Anfang, sondern . . . der Übergang des Morgenländischen zum Abendländischen stattfindet." Heidegger, *GA* 75:141.

[137] "Der Geist hat also nicht, wie wir zuerst meinten, zwei Geschicke, ein morgenländisches und ein abendländisches, sondern das Geschick ist die Schickung aus dem Orient in den Okzident." Heidegger, *GA* 75:146.

[138] In 1946–47 — while writing "Das abendländische Gespräch" — Heidegger attempted to translate the calligraphy of Lao Tse. See Otto Pöggeler, *Neue Wege mit Heidegger* (Freiburg: Alber, 1992), 318.

[139] "am Abend eines gütigen Tages im sich neigenden Sommer." Heidegger, *GA* 75:59.

[140] "Das Abendland wäre dann jenes Land jenes Abends, der untergeht in jene Nacht, die aufgeht zu jenem Morgen, dem jener Tag entspringt, der rein versöhnt ist mit der Nacht." Heidegger, *GA* 75:146.

[141] "der Wanderung des himmlischen Feuers von der einen auf der anderen Seite." Heidegger, *GA* 75:173.

[142] "wir nicht wohl etwas *gleich* mit ihnen haben dürfen." Hölderlin, *StA* 6:426.

[143] Heidegger, *GA* 54:104.

[144] "immer bleibender." Heidegger, *GA* 75:59.

[145] Anke Bennholdt-Thomsen has investigated the poetics of place in Hölderlin, examining his revisitation of the memory sites at which the "traces and voices of the past" are preserved (304). According to Bennholdt-Thomsen, this procedure derives from antique mnemonic techniques that sought to bridge the gulf between present and past (300). Heidegger's retreading of the textual and physical space associated with Hölderlin's name can likewise be understood as the presentation or presencing of an auratic site. Anke Bennholdt-Thomsen, "Das topographische Verfahren bei Hölderlin und in der Lyrik nach 1945," in *Hölderlin und die Moderne: Eine Bestandaufnahme*, ed. Gerhard Kurz, Valerie Lawitschka and Jürgen Wertheimer (Tübingen: Attempto, 1995): 300–322.

[146] See Heidegger's comments on *Erörterung* in his Trakl intepretation in Heidegger, *GA* 12, esp. 73–78.

[147] "so wie wir hier an seinem Ufer gehen und auf allen Seitenpfaden . . . stets zu ihm zurückkehren, weil wir uns nicht entfernen können." Heidegger, *GA* 75:143.

[148] "Unsere Gespräche . . . überall und immer Gespräche vom Abendland." Heidegger, *GA* 75:157–58. See also Heidegger, *GA* 54:219.

[149] Hölderlin, *StA* 3:85.

[150] "das Haus des Seins." Heidegger, *GA* 9:313.

[151] I allude here to John Caputo's *Demythologizing Heidegger* (Bloomington: Indiana UP, 1993), which attempts to jettison Heidegger's *grand récit* of the Greek-German heritage, and so come up with a new, leaner Heidegger, one who has learned from Levinas and Derrida, a Heidegger whose exclusionary myth of Being Caputo would like to see replaced with an inclusive, misceginated, "jew-greek" myth of justice. From the perspective of "Das abendländische Gespräch," the fundamental problem in Caputo's approach is that it brings to Heidegger's text

an exclusively occidental conception of myth-making. Caputo sidesteps the fact that Heidegger is trying, not merely to impose his own dubious myth about the Occident upon the Occident, but to radically change (to orientalize) what it means to think mythically.

[152] Walter Benjamin, "Zwei Gedichte von Friedrich Hölderlin," in *Gesammelte Schriften*, vol. 2.1, ed. Rolf Tiedemann and Hermann Schweppenhäuser (Frankfurt am Main: Suhrkamp, 1977), 124–25; English translation from *Selected Writings*, trans. Stanley Corngold, ed. Michael W. Jennings et al., 4 vols. (Cambridge MA: Harvard UP, 1996–2003), 1.34.

[153] "Machtbereich." Heidegger, *GA* 39:5, 19.

[154] See Heidegger, *GA* 39:6, 69; *GA* 6.1:409–10.

[155] "Im Deuten antworten wir, das Zeichen wiederzeigend, dem Zeichen." Heidegger, *GA* 75:63.

[156] Heidegger, *GA* 75:190.

[157] Heidegger's employment of this word in "Das abendländische Gespräch" is itself of Hölderlinian origin. The poet's line *Seit ein Gespräch wir sind, und hören können voneinander* ("Since we are a conversation, and can hear from one another"), which Heidegger had interpreted at some length in the mid-1930s, resounds unmistakably in *Denn Gespräch ist nur Gehör*. However, the ideal of universal brotherhood that animates Hölderlin's line is entirely missing from Heidegger's.

[158] Jacques Derrida, *Of Spirit: Heidegger and the Question*, trans. Geoff Bennington and Rachel Bowlby (Chicago: U of Chicago P, 1989), 83.

[159] See Reinold Schmücker, "Monologisches Gespräch: Heideggers Vorlesung über Hölderlins Hymne 'Andenken,'" 550–68; Heidegger, *GA* 13:80.

[160] "Bisweilen ist mir, als sei sogar unser Deuten schon ein Dichten." Heidegger, *GA* 75:95.

[161] Hans-Georg Gadamer, *Heidegger's Ways*, trans. John W. Stanley (Albany, NY: SUNY P, 1994), 164–65, 179.

[162] Heidegger, *GA* 75:59.

[163] "So endet der Ister-Gesang. Nein, so bricht er ab. . . . Darum ist es kein Zufall, daß dieser Gesang unvollendet ist —," "Oder ist er gerade vollendet in diesem Abbrechen?" Heidegger, *GA* 75:194.

[164] G. W. F. Hegel, "Das älteste Systemprogramm des deutschen Idealismus," in *Mythologie der Vernunft. Hegels "ältestes Systemprogramm" des deutschen Idealismus*, ed. Christoph Jamme and Helmut Schneider (Frankfurt am Main: Suhrkamp, 1984), 12.

[165] Heidegger makes this "scandalously inadequate" (Lacoue-Labarthe) comparison in an unpublished version of the lectures on technology he delivered in Bremen in 1949. See Philippe Lacoue-Labarthe, *Heidegger, Art and Politics*, trans. Chris Turner (Oxford: Blackwell, 1990), 34.

[166] See Theodor Kisiel, "Heidegger's Philosophical Geopolitics in the Third Reich," in *A Companion to Heidegger's Introduction to Metaphysics*, ed. Richard Polt and Gregory Fried (New Haven, CT: Yale UP, 2001), 242–43.

[167] Heidegger, *GA* 54:114.

[168] Lutz Niethammer, *Posthistoire: Has History Come to an End?*, trans. Patrick Camiller (London: Verso, 1992), 142.

[169] Pöggeler, "Heideggers Begegnung mit Hölderlin," 15.

[170] Pöggeler, "Heideggers Begegnung mit Hölderlin," 15.

[171] Pöggeler, *Neue Wege mit Heidegger*, 328.

[172] "Schloß Hausen im Donautal, am 8. Mai 1945. Am Tage, da die Welt ihren Sieg feierte und noch nicht erkannte, daß sie seit Jahrhunderten schon die Besiegte ihres eigenen Aufstandes ist." Heidegger, *GA* 77:240.

[173] "eine verblendete Irreführung des eigenen Volkes." Heidegger, *GA* 77:206.

[174] See Johann Fichte, "Reden an die deutsche Nation," in *Werke VII* (Berlin: Veit, 1846): 259–499, esp. 325–26, 374–75, and 465.

[175] "die in der edelsten Weise wartenden," "indem wir Wartende werden, werden wir erst Deutsche," "nicht durch Bedrohungen von außen, sondern dadurch, daß es sich selbst mit der eigenen unwissenden Ungeduld tyrannisierte," "sich endlich die Anerkennung von seiten der anderen Völker erkämpfen müsse," "dieses voreilige Scheinwesen doch nur die ewig unbeholfene Nachahmung des Fremden bleibt." Heidegger, *GA* 77:232–35.

[176] "Und dieses ganz unbrauchbare Volk müßte das älteste Volk werden, da niemand sich um es kümmert und keiner sein seltsames Tun, das ein Lassen ist, in Gebrauch nimmt und so vernutzt und vorzeitig verbraucht." Heidegger, *GA* 77:234.

[177] "Darum müssen wir die Notwendigkeit des Unnötigen wissen lernen und sie als Lernende den Völkern lehren." Heidegger, *GA* 77:237.

[178] "DER JÜNGERE: Lass uns an das Dichtende denken. / DER ÄLTERE: Eine gute Nacht uns beiden und allen im Lager. / DER JÜNGERE: Und der Heimat den Segen ihrer Bestimmung." Heidegger, *GA* 77:240.

[179] "Alles denkt jetzt den Untergang. Wir Deutschen können deshalb nicht untergehen, weil wir noch gar nicht aufgegangen sind und erst durch die Nacht hindurchmüssen." Heidegger, *GA* 16:371.

[180] See Hölderlin, *StA* 4:149.

[181] Although the *Untergang des Abendlandes* motif is of Spenglerian provenance, Heidegger holds against Spengler (whom he labelled a mere writer, a *Schriftsteller*, not a *Denker*), that the origin of the problems facing Western civilization is not to be sought in the terminal decline of the Occident, but, on the contrary, in the delay or self-refusal of that decline. From *Einführung in die Metaphysik* on, Heidegger uses the word *Untergang* in a positive sense. See, for example, Heidegger, *GA* 65:7, 225, and 397; *GA* 12:73. For a comparison of Heidegger and Spengler, see Michael Zimmerman, "The Ontological Decline of the West," in *A Companion to Heidegger's Introduction to Metaphysics*, ed. Polt and Fried (New Haven, CT: Yale UP, 2001), 185–204.

[182] "Ihre Zeilen aus Tübingen trafen mich wie die Stimme des Dichters aus seinem Turm am heimatlichen Strom. Das letzte halbe Jahr weilte ich im Geburtsland und zeitweise in der nächsten erregenden Nähe des Stammhauses meiner Väter im

oberen Donautal unterhalb der Burg Wildenstein. Mein Denken ist weit über bloße Interpretation hinaus zu einem Gespräch mit dem Dichter geworden, und seine leibhafte Nähe ist das Element meines Denkens." Heidegger, *GA* 16:370.

[183] It also licenses an autobiographical reading of "Das abendländische Gespräch," which was presumably written in a mood of wistful retrospection after Heidegger had returned to Freiburg to find his professional life in tatters and his home overrun by billeted French soldiers.

[184] "Vielleicht mußte Hölderlin, der Dichter, zum bestimmenden Geschick der Auseinandersetzung werden für einen Denkenden, dessen Großvater um dieselbe Zeit der Entstehung der 'Isterhymne' . . . in ovili (im Schafstall einer Meierei) geboren wurde, die im oberen Donautal nahe dem Ufer des Stromes unter den Felsen liegt." Pöggeler, "Heideggers politisches Selbstverständnis," in *Heidegger und die praktische Philosophie,* ed. Gethmann-Siefert and Pöggeler, 41. Safranski explains: "From Castle Wildenstein [to which the University of Freiburg relocated during the bombing of the city] one can see the old Danube house, to which belonged the sheep-stall where Heidegger's grandfather was born." Heidegger continued to lecture on Hölderlin, and particularly the "Ister" hymn, during his sojourn there. Years later, the inhabitants of the house at the time still recalled the frequent visits of the philosophy professor. Safranski, *Ein Meister aus Deutschland,* 17 and 386.

[185] "Im übrigen bin ich der Überzeugung, daß aus unserem schwäbischen Land der abendländische Geist erwachen wird." Heidegger, *GA* 16:396.

[186] Despite the fact that Hitler was an Austrian, that National Socialism had its power base in Bavaria, and that Prussia had been a Social Democratic stronghold throughout the Weimar years, Heidegger viewed Nazism as a Prussian phenomenon. Shortly after Hitler's accession to power he asks: "Will we show ourselves equal, in this south-western border region, to the shift of the political will of the Germans toward the north-east?" Heidegger, *GA* 16:240.

[187] "die innere Zugehörigkeit der eigenen Arbeit zum Schwarzwald und seinen Menschen," "aus einer jahrhundertelangen, durch nichts ersetzbaren alemannisch-schwäbischen Bodenständigkeit." Heidegger, *GA* 13:10–11. See Robert Savage, "My Own Private Swabia: On the Idiocy of Heidegger's Nationalism," *Thesis Eleven* 87 (2006): 112–21.

[188] Dieter Thomä, "The Name on the Edge of Language: A Complication in Heidegger's Theory of Language and Its Consequences," in *A Companion to Heidegger's Introduction to Metaphysics,* ed. Polt and Fried, 105.

[189] See Pöggeler, "Heideggers Begegnung mit Hölderlin," 61.

[190] Niethammer, *Posthistoire,* 3 and 79.

[191] Heidegger, *GA* 75:196.

[192] *"Der Dichtungscharakter des Denkens ist noch verhüllt. Wo er sich zeigt, gleicht er für lange Zeit der Utopie eines halbpoetischen Verstandes. Aber das denkende Dichten ist in der Wahrheit die Topologie des Seyns."* Heidegger, *GA* 13:84.

[193] Bernstein, *The Fate of Art,* 133.

[194] Hölderlin, *StA* 2.1:193.

[195] Martin Walser, *Leseerfahrungen, Liebeserklärungen: Aufsätze zur Literatur* (Frankfurt am Main: Suhrkamp, 1997), 172.

[196] "Das Dichten läßt das Wohnen allererst ein Wohnen sein. . . . Dichten ist, als Wohnenlassen, ein Bauen." Heidegger, *GA* 7:193.

[197] Pöggeler, *Philosophie und Politik bei Heidegger* (Freiburg: Alber, 1974), 71; my emphasis.

[198] See the comments in "Hölderlins Erde und Himmel," Heidegger, *GA* 4:177. See also Caputo, *Demythologizing Heidegger*, 97.

[199] See Heidegger, *GA* 4:160.

[200] "Die gegenwärtigen Götter sind für den Dichter so genau anwesend, so bedrängend, daß ihre Nähe gerade ihm verwehrt, als Dichter, d.h. sie sagend, ihnen zu nahen. Der Dichter muß noch vor dieser Nähe zurücktreten, daß sie zur Ferne wird, die ihn davor schützt, übereilt die Gegenwärtigen zu nennen." Heidegger, *GA* 75:266.

[201] See Clare Pearson Geiman, "Heidegger's *Antigones*," in Polt and Fried, *A Companion to Heidegger's Introduction to Metaphysics*, 181.

[202] "Sie messen speziell den Deutschen eine besondere Rolle zu?," "Ja, in dem Sinne, im Gespräch mit Hölderlin." Heidegger, *GA* 16:679.

[203] Heidegger, *GA* 16:750.

[204] Hölderlin, *StA* 2.1:9; *Poems and Fragments*, 123.

2: Polemic: Adorno, "Parataxis"

Doch als sich ihre Gewande berührt,
Und keiner vernehmen konnte
Die eigene Rede des andern, wäre wohl
Entstanden ein Zwist, wenn nicht aus Zweigen herunter
Gekommen wäre die Kühlung.

[But when their garments had touched
And none could comprehend
The other's peculiar speech, a quarrel
Might well have begun, if coolness had not fallen
Upon them from the boughs.]
— Hölderlin, "Die Wanderung" (The Journey)

T HEODOR W. ADORNO'S SPEECH had been announced under the title "Parataxis: Zur philosophischen Interpretation der späten Lyrik Hölderlins" (Parataxis. On the Philosophical Interpretation of Hölderlin's Late Poetry). The renowned social theorist was scheduled to deliver the keynote address at the 1963 convention of the Hölderlin Society, held for the first time in a divided Berlin, before an audience that included some of the finest literary critics in the German-speaking world. Although Adorno was not known as a Hölderlin specialist, it was hoped that he might be able to open up a fresh perspective on familiar terrain, to illuminate some of those aspects of the poet's work that tended otherwise to escape the philologist's blinkered gaze. Similar considerations had motivated the Society to invite Martin Heidegger, likewise something of an outsider in relation to the guild, to address the convention four years earlier; and while the resulting meditation on "Hölderlins Erde und Himmel" (Hölderlin's Earth and Sky) had not been to everyone's taste, it was generally agreed that the establishment of lines of communication between the narrow circle of Hölderlin scholarship and the most influential philosophical movements of the day could only further the society's goal of awakening the interest of a broader public in the poet in whose service it stood. Adorno's title promised just such a dialogue, suggesting a philosophical discussion of the interpretations to which Hölderlin's late poetry had given rise, a reflection upon the inherent philosophical problems to which they responded, and thus, at least implicitly, the outline of his own philosophical interpretation of that poetry, presumably centered around the suspension of subordinating and coordinating particles in Hölderlin's lyric work after 1800. It all depended on how one construed the relationship, itself paratactic, between the word "parataxis" and the following clause. When he came to publish the revised version of the speech in the following year, Adorno would simplify the title to "Parataxis: Zur späten Lyrik Hölderlins" (Parataxis. On Hölderlin's Late Poetry), confirming that his philosophical interpretation of philosophical interpretation was a roundabout way of approaching the poetry itself.

Roundabout indeed. For it soon became apparent that for Adorno the development of a philosophical *dialogue* with the assembled philologists first necessitated a massive *polemic* against Heidegger's own Hölderlin interpretation, which Adorno spent most of the first half of the address attacking.[1] "Good titles," he once wrote, "are so close to the work that they respect its hiddenness; the intentional titles violate it."[2] Even allowing for his sense of discretion, the original title chosen by Adorno seems excessively indirect for a speech that might just as well have been called "Adorno contra Heidegger." Nothing less than the latter's ritual expulsion from the community of the initiated was the price demanded by Adorno for an undistorted conversation about Hölderlin. Adorno made a "refusal of communication" (Mörchen)[3] with Heidegger his condition *sine qua non* for communicating on Hölderlin. Needless to say, many of his listeners were unwilling to enter into a dialogue on such terms. What began as an attempt to build a bridge between philosophy and philology — for unlike his opponent, Adorno stressed their interreliance — ended in a minor scandal. "Scarcely another lecture stimulated such a lively discussion as this one," read the euphemistic report in the 1963–64 yearbook, in which the speech, contrary to the society's custom of publishing all the lectures from that year's convention, was conspicuously absent.[4]

There is some disagreement about what actually came to pass on that summer day in Berlin. The *eminence grise* of German literary criticism, Emil Staiger, come down from Zurich to speak on Empedocles, recalled his version of events years later. Almost alone among his colleagues, Staiger had sought to make Heidegger's eccentric ideas on poetry fruitful for his discipline, corresponding with the philosopher on a verse from Mörike and arranging for the publication of his student Beda Allemann's dissertation on Heidegger and Hölderlin. No friend of Adorno's, he was not amused by the twenty-minute-long "polemical tirade against Heidegger" that thundered from the podium. "Adorno had to be rapped over the knuckles," he told an interviewer in 1975. "Someone in the audience — he could no longer remember whom — got up in protest and interrupted the lecturer with the words: it was an unbelievable impudence to attack someone who was not there and had no opportunity to defend himself. [Peter] Szondi [the speech's eventual dedicatee] then made the unnecessary comment: Heidegger might not be there in person, but he had been cited at length; this was a legitimate and unobjectionable method of criticism."[5] The Hölderlin scholar Jochen Schmidt, considerably younger than Staiger and by no means so well-disposed toward the "language of Meßkirch,"[6] takes up the story from a different angle: "In the middle of a fulminating speech . . . the Heidegger faction stood up, led by a highly regarded Hölderlin scholar, and quit the hall in protest, as up on the podium an irritated Adorno briefly peered over the gleaming edges of his spectacles into the lecture theater of the Berlin Academy of Arts." For Schmidt, the speech contained little of value on its ostensible topic, but it was brutally successful in its demolition of Heidegger, breaking the hold of the existentialist reading once and for all.[7] As if in symbolic affirmation of the break, Heidegger canceled his membership in the Society soon afterwards, furious that it had granted "that man," as he was wont to call Adorno, a forum at which to speak against him.

Adorno failed to turn up as planned to the general discussion of the three main lectures on the following afternoon: "it [was] reported that he was unexpectedly called away and had to excuse himself at the last minute."[8] One suspects that Binder's lapidary comment in the yearbook may be deliberately vague: "Unfortunately Mr. Theodor Adorno was prevented from attending the plenary session, so his lecture could not be formally discussed."[9] For according to Schmidt, the respected scholar who had led the exodus of Heideggerians on the previous day, and who was now entrusted with chairing the discussion of Adorno's talk (most of which he had not even heard), was none other than Binder himself![10] Seen in this light, Adorno's decision to leave Berlin prematurely does not seem surprising at all. Binder, who had dedicated one of his most important monographs "in grateful esteem" to Heidegger,[11] opened the sitting in Adorno's absence by citing the verse, "Seit ein Gespräch wir sind und hören können voneinander" (Since we are a conversation and can hear from one another), one of the five "ominous *Leitworte*"[12] elucidated by Heidegger in "Hölderlin und das Wesen der Dichtung" — in the context perhaps a snub at the guest speaker who had so flagrantly refused to converse with Heidegger and then made off without hearing what his audience had to say in response.[13] The protocol of the discussion gives a fair idea of what he might have expected had he stayed: "The discussion turns to the concept of demythologization used by Mr. Adorno. . . . The suggestion that sacrificial death be understood as a sign of demythologization finds no approval. It is instead recommended that the concepts of sacrifice and tragedy not be combined with the problems of myth and demythologization. . . . This discussion concludes with the finding that the plethora of myth concepts has served rather to confuse than to advance Hölderlin scholarship."[14]

Bernhard Böschenstein, meanwhile, insists that the address met with neither heckling nor a spontaneous walkout, and that the heated exchange to which Staiger refers in fact took place in Adorno's absence, during the discussion session the following day.[15] Böschenstein stood on good terms

with both Heidegger, who had summoned him a few years before to consult him on Hölderlin, and Szondi, whom he had befriended when they
were both undergraduates in Zurich, so there is no reason to suspect him
of partisanship.[16] If what he says is true, then Staiger and Schmidt's conflation of two separate incidents — the speech and the objections raised
against it in response — into a single fictitious primal scene testifies all the
more tellingly to the enduring impact the speech made upon its audience:
for Staiger, its "unbelievable impudence" was still provoking his indigna-
tion a dozen years after the event; for Schmidt, its significance as a
"caesura" in the history of postwar Hölderlin reception perhaps led him to
fantasize evidence to corroborate his well-founded impression that Adorno
had purged the society of Heideggerian elements.[17] Precisely because of
their empirical unreliability, both eyewitness reports accurately reflect the
lived reality of the occasion, and both thereby attest to the speech's effectiveness as an *intervention* in the previously well-regulated, somewhat
sleepy field of Hölderlin scholarship. "Parataxis" was a scandal, regardless
of whether it can be shown to have caused one. Adorno's own account of
the speech, to be found in a letter to Herbert Marcuse written shortly
thereafter, only adds to the confusion on this point. According to Adorno,
the address was interrupted at one stage, not by an irate Heideggerian, but
by a deranged "Megaera"[18] who took him to task for changing his sur-
name from "Wiesengrund" to the less Jewish-sounding "Adorno" while in
American exile.[19] Suffice it to conclude that where so much smoke clouds
the latecomer's vision, a fire must once have raged.

I have gone in some detail into the fracas that accompanied the lecture
because I believe it to be anything but tangential to the views advanced in
the lecture itself. If we are to take seriously Adorno's claim that his philosophical statements represent a form of praxis, indeed the only legitimate
form at a time when meaningful political change is blocked on all sides,
then the fate that befalls them in the world needs to be understood as a calculated effect of their argumentative content. Adorno's polemic against
Heidegger demands dissent and would have missed its target had it been
greeted with polite applause. Furthermore, the provocative intention
underlying that polemic extends to the interpretation of Hölderlin
advanced in its wake, disallowing any hard and fast distinction between
Adorno the incendiary publicist and Adorno the sober hermeneut. This
interpretation sets out to release the "critical and utopian"[20] energies in
Hölderlin's poetry supposedly stifled by Heidegger's elucidations, that is,
to rehabilitate that poetry *as itself polemical*, directed against an existing
society in view of a better one. For Adorno, "Hölderlin did not play
along,"[21] and on the 120th anniversary of his death and 20th anniversary
of his consecration by the Nazis, it is high time his intransigence toward all
ideological appropriations attract the attention it deserves. Assuming
Adorno is right, how is one to account for the fact that until 1963 those

who busied themselves with the poet had all but unanimously chosen to ignore the polemical tenor of his work? The O.E.D. defines polemic as "controversial argument or discussion; argumentation against some opinion, doctrine, etc.; aggressive controversy," making clear that a non-controversial polemic, a polemic with which everyone heartily agrees, is a thing of impossibility. Adorno can only refashion Hölderlin into a polemical author, therefore, by smashing the broad consensus that had hitherto prevailed on his poetry and had made possible his institutionalization in a society bearing his name. The controversy fanned by the polemic against Heidegger provides a practical demonstration of another polemic, Hölderlin's own: "Asserted too soon [by Heidegger], the reality of the poetic undermines the tension between Hölderlin's poetry and reality and neutralizes his work into something in league with fate."[22]

Polemics have fallen into disrepute since their heyday in the age of Voltaire. The historical project of Enlightenment was marked from the beginning by an ambivalence toward polemics, which derived from the necessity of establishing and maintaining, if necessary through violent means, a space in which only the non-coercive force of the better argument would hold sway. Once this forum for the free exchange of ideas had been secured against those who threatened it from outside — "obscurantists" was the insult of choice — the shock troops of Enlightenment found that their services were no longer in demand. Today, those who engage in polemics are commonly viewed as individuals of questionable moral character who choose to vent their spleen upon their victims without the least regard for decorum or academic nicety. Michel Foucault echoed a widespread sentiment when he justified his own aversion to the practice by pointing out that the polemicist

> proceeds encased in privileges that he possesses in advance and will never agree to question. . . . His final objective will be not to come as close as possible to a difficult truth but to bring about the triumph of the just cause he has been manifestly upholding from the beginning. The polemicist relies on a legitimacy that his adversary is by definition denied.[23]

The polemicist violates, in other words, the very norms of communicative rationality he had once fought tooth and nail to defend.

No philosopher since Nietzsche polemicized more persistently, with such obvious relish, and to deadlier effect, than Adorno; at the same time, none espoused the legacy and unfulfilled potential of the Enlightenment with greater passion. These two moments in his thought need to be understood in their relation to each other. From what source did Adorno derive the legitimacy he denied his adversary? How, to misquote the title of a novel by Trollope, did he know he was right? The category of the polemic(al) will accordingly stand at the center of my interpretation. Unlike previous commentators, I do not intend to test the strength of the arguments ranged against Heidegger in the course of the speech, and so determine whether or not the polemic was justified: no polemic ever is. Nor will I cast judgment on the persuasiveness of Adorno's reading of Hölderlin's late poetry, which fell on unsympathetic ears at the time and has since been found wanting by a number of Hölderlin specialists.[24] Forty-five years after the essay's publication, critical interest in it can no longer stand or fall on the plausibility of its individual claims. Instead, I hope to show how a highly idiosyncratic thinking of the polemic(al) informs both sections of the essay, founding their inner unity as well as their articulated disjunction. Drawing on this concept, I will reconstruct what is perhaps the essay's key interpretative gambit, its antimythological rescue of myth, and consider the inflection of salvation (*Rettung*) and polemic that is the hallmark of what Adorno calls "late style." Finally, I will endeavor to work through some of the unspoken presuppositions underlying the "philopolemology" (Derrida)[25] shared by both Adorno and Heidegger, and so locate one source of the disagreement that exploded so memorably in Berlin.

The Strange Case of Dr. Wiesengrund and Mr. Rottweiler

Before considering the status of the polemic in "Parataxis," it might prove useful to examine other instances of the term in Adorno's work, if only to indicate that the significance I attribute to it in the Hölderlin speech is neither unprecedented nor inconsistent with comparable thematizations. Although the term does not crop up very often — it is not even listed in the index to *Ästhetische Theorie* (Aesthetic Theory), for example — the strategic weight and semantic density that accrue to it when it does appear, causing it to pull surrounding tropes and figures into its gravitational field, belie its sparse deployment. Symptomatically, the term stands watch over both the entry- and exit points to Adorno's oeuvre, taking up a conspicuous position in his lecture on "Die Aktualität der Philosophie" (The Actuality of Philosophy) from 1932, his first as a professional philosopher, and in the introduction to *Stichworte* (Catchwords), the last text he was to complete before his death in 1969. While its deployment elsewhere would repay critical attention, notably in the monograph on Kierkegaard, I will restrict myself to examining its meaning and function in these two liminal texts.

As its title suggests, "Die Aktualität der Philosophie" is concerned with justifying the philosophical enterprise in the face of mounting doubts as to its relevance and even possibility. These doubts may come from outside philosophy, from those who believe it to be an idle or meaningless pursuit, but they also gnaw at philosophy from within, as Adorno's opening statement makes clear: "Whoever chooses philosophy as a profession today must first reject the illusion that earlier philosophical enterprises began with: that the power of thought is sufficient to grasp the totality of the real."[26] What is at stake here is precisely the relationship between the "within" and the "without," the system and the environment of philosophy: between the operational effectiveness of the conceptual weaponry philosophy develops in its ever more sophisticated attempts to "grasp" (*ergreifen*, closely related to *angreifen*, attack) the real, conceived here as the world in its totality, and the continuing recalcitrance of the real to submit to its authority. Because philosophy cannot regulate its traffic with its outside in an internally consistent manner, the crisis of philosophical system engenders a crisis in the system of philosophy. Adorno's response to this impasse, however, is not to reject the "totality of the real" as a pseudo-problem thrown up by the very sort of thinking that seeks to capture it in its conceptual net, as would a later generation of philosophers, nor to replace it as the goal of philosophical activity with a more modest proposal, such as the analytic effort to clarify language use. Adorno manages instead to maintain philosophy's traditional objective, while at the same time recognizing the futility of its ever being achieved, with the help of an unlikely ally: the polemic. For it is the polemic that emerges as philosophy's *ultima ratio* once the ultimacy of ratio presumed by the great metaphysical edifices has been revealed to be wishful thinking: "No justifying reason could rediscover itself in a reality whose order and form suppresses every claim to reason; only polemically does it present itself to the knower as total reality."[27]

These programmatic lines, not rescinded by anything Adorno would write later, invest the polemic with a quite extraordinary epistemological importance. The vigor with which an irrational reality repudiates the advances of reason, far from driving the philosopher into an all-engulfing skepticism, itself gives rise to philosophical knowledge. Moreover, because Adorno continues to insist on defining philosophy in terms of a totality with which it is never identical, but which it is nonetheless called upon to identify, this insurmountable resistance becomes the *only* possible source of such knowledge. The gravest danger to philosophy is equally its saving power. While reason still proves capable of learning about the world, it does so solely insofar as its attempts to rediscover itself in a regular and universal lawfulness, whether construed as world-spirit, divine plan or Great Chain of Being, are perpetually thwarted.

Two consequences can be drawn from Adorno's reformulation of his own job description. First, the polemic compels the philosopher to *interpret* reality rather than schematize it. Whereas the philosopher's task had once been to refine his instrumentarium of concepts until he had removed all the obstacles that stood in the way of the rational reconstruction of the world, that is, the reconstruction of the world as a rational one, it now consists in accepting that these obstacles are actually the ineliminable symptoms or traces of a whole that does not yield to direct interrogation. The philosophical habitus changes accordingly: the "strong" subject bent on tailoring the world to his system makes way for a "weak" subject to whom totality offers itself *ex negativo*, in the fractures and opacities with which it taunts the concept; Adorno speaks of "exact imagination" as the requirement for this new type of philosopher.[28] Second, and correlatively, the polemical refusal of the real to comply with his categories must still be *provoked* by the philosopher,[29] who in this sense acts no differently than his idealist counterpart. In other words, the fundamental difference between the two conceptions of philosophy outlined at the beginning of "Die Aktualität der Philosophie" does not lie so much in how they operate — both share the same horizon, use the same tools, and are frustrated in the same way — as in how they make sense of their inevitable failure: in the first case, as a temporary and rectifiable setback; in the second, as evidence of a polemic that flares up whenever reason tests its strength against its indomitable other (which, as *Dialektik der Aufklärung* [Dialectic of Enlightenment, 1947] will argue, is also the other *of* reason: the irrational whole that evades the grasp of reason is itself weirdly rational). Both philosophers bear the brunt of the polemic, but only the second recognizes it as such.

Such a polemic can end neither in victory for the philosopher — this was the self-deception to which the metaphysician succumbed — nor in defeat, which would mean renouncing the possibility of philosophical knowledge altogether. In fact, it cannot end at all; this is doubtless why Adorno almost always refers to the polemic in its adverbial form. The polemic figures instead as the field of tension maintained between its constitutive poles, a productive friction that would rigidify into simple opposition did not philosophy shuttle back and forth between them in its struggle to translate the inconceivable into the medium of thought. The polemic is the inhospitable element in which philosophy, understood by Adorno (via Novalis and the early Lukács) as a transcendental homesickness, takes up provisional quarters. We can already discern here the tentative outline of what, thirty years later, will go by the name of negative dialectics, which likewise seeks to make fruitful for philosophy the very incommensurability (or "non-identity") of concept and conceptualized. And is not the "revocation of synthesis in the movement of the spirit itself" which Adorno perceives in Hölderlin's poetry also anticipated in the notion of a cognition that becomes possible once reason, painfully made aware of its own finitude, has been cured of its hybris?[30] For now, I retain Adorno's characterization of the polemic as a disproportionate relation in which philosophy finds itself destroyed and redeemed in one and the same gesture.

The second incidence of the term mentioned above appears much more conventional, at least to a cursory reading. It strikes a note of defiance in the final sentence of the introduction to *Stichworte*, a collection of occasional essays and radio addresses translated into English as *Catchwords;*

> The title *Catchwords* alludes to the encyclopaedic form that, unsystematically, discontinuously, presents what the unity of experience crystallizes into a constellation. This technique used in a small volume with somewhat arbitrarily chosen catchwords could conceivably be used in creating a new *Dictionnaire philosophique*. The association with polemics that the title conveys is a welcome one to the author.[31]

What is the polemical association to which Adorno refers? The word *Stichworte* derives from the verb *stechen*, to cut, scratch or stab. Accordingly, *Stichworte* are words intended to draw blood, just as the title of Adorno's previous collection of critical models, *Eingriffe*, evokes the flash of the surgeon's scalpel laying bare the object with a few deft strokes. At a time when Adorno found himself under fierce attack from his critics on both right and left — the former for allegedly encouraging the student protests, the latter for not encouraging them enough — his introductory words to the last book he would prepare for publication[32] announce his refusal to retire wounded from the fray. The pugnacious self-image they project seems diametrically opposed to that sketched in "Die Aktualität der Philosophie." There the polemic dealt the philosopher a salutary shock that rocked his claims to mastery; here it is the philosopher who flaunts his mastery of the polemic. Teddie Wiesengrund, the pampered philosopher-aesthete, has transmogrified into Hektor Rottweiler,[33] the feared and fearful "theory- and man-eating dialectical monster."[34]

As the English translation correctly suggests, the primary meaning of *Stichworte* has nothing to do with polemics, and the word's violent connotations usually go unheard in German. The first definition listed in Grimm under the *Stichwort* "Stichwort" is "an injurious, generally malicious and secretly apposite . . . word, sometimes also meant to be gently teasing," but the entry goes on to note that this meaning died out around the middle of the nineteenth century. Ever since, the term has denoted first and foremost a word in a reference work, a keyword or heading; hence Adorno's allusion to the *dictionnaire philosophique*. When Adorno draws attention to its polemical association, he is thus playing off the long-submerged original meaning of the term against its more familiar modern usage: his catchwords are long-range missiles, not harmless captions. The introduction expressly invites us to read the essays that follow in the light of these polemical *Stichworte*. Taking up the invitation, one notices that if there is a common thread binding together the pieces that make up the book, if there is a single concern unifying Adorno's treatment of such diverse topics as "Education after Auschwitz," "On Subject and Object," "Experiences of a European Scientist in America," and "On the Question: What Is German?" then it has to do with fighting the type of reified consciousness that automatically subsumes its material under catchwords, so excluding or forcefully assimilating whatever crosses its path.[35] *Stichworte* is a sustained polemic against thinking in *Stichworte* (in the customary meaning), and as such, it designates as much the enemy as the means of attack.

Retrospectively, the title assumes a radicality to which the closing words of the introduction provide the decisive clue. For we can see now how Adorno has used the word *Stichworte* as a *Stichwort* in the precise sense of the term given by Grimm, that is, as an "injurious, generally malicious and secretly apposite . . . word." Only on this occasion, instead of being used to stab a foreign body, the *Stichwort* has been turned upon itself. From this self-inflicted gash, this *Stichwunde*, bleed the words that congeal into Adorno's philosophical dictionary. As was the case in "Die Aktualität der Philosophie," the polemic both indicated and demonstrated in the title marks a productive tension structurally incapable of reaching a conclusion, inasmuch as the destructive force of the *Stichwort* remains parasitically dependent upon its target. Once again, the polemic is heralded, with a quasi-Heraclitean claim to universality, as the element in which the philosopher is most at home. The polemical association welcomed by Adorno, far from contradicting his earlier adumbration of the polemic, thus proves entirely consistent with it.

Nevertheless, there can be no doubt that a shift in emphasis has taken place between the two texts from what one might call a theoretical to an applied polemology, a shift that mirrors a dramatic change in Adorno's standing as a public philosopher in Germany during the same period. In 1932, Adorno was interested in the polemic to the extent that it threatened the age-old philosophical dream of penetrating appearances to apprehend the "totality of the real." Almost four decades later, he is its avowed practitioner, and his polemics in the intervening years against such epiphenomena of modern life as jazz, horoscopes, and Hollywood, and against such figures as Lukács, Stravinsky, and of course Heidegger, had become the stuff of legend. Upon being told that one of the epigonic Heideggerians he had savaged in *Jargon der Eigentlichkeit* (Jargon of Authenticity, 1964) had suffered a nervous breakdown as a result, Adorno reportedly snarled that it served him right. This ferocious, divisive Adorno is very much on display in "Parataxis" — one thinks of his splendidly contemptuous dismissal of Heidegger's language as "high-faluting gobbledegook"[36] — but as we will see, in the course of the essay's second half, which is devoted to exploring the polemic that is Hölderlin's late poetry, Adorno also revisits the terrain first charted in "Die Aktualität der Philosophie." Almost alone among his writings,[37] "Parataxis" allows us to observe Teddie Wiesengrund and Hektor Rottweiler side by side, paratactically cohabiting the same textual space. The extremes touch, the extremities of Adorno's career as well as the extremes of his public persona, in the faultline that runs down the middle of his performance in Berlin.

Understanding Polemically

The polemic surfaces from its anonymity on a single occasion in "Parataxis." It follows a discussion of Hölderlin's formal, stylistic, and syntactic innovations focused on the paratactic scars that furrow the late work. Adorno is concerned to relate the peculiarities of Hölderlin's linguistic technique to what he calls the "truth content"of his poetry. I will cite and analyze this crucial passage at some length:

> The linguistic technique coincides with the antisubjectivism of the content. It revises the deceptive middle-of-the-road synthesis from the extreme point — from the point of view of language; it provides a corrective to the primacy of the subject as an organon of such synthesis. Hölderlin's procedure takes into account the fact that the subject, which mistakes itself for something immediate and ultimate, is something utterly mediated. *This incalculably portentous change in the linguistic gesture must, however, be understood polemically and not ontologically* [my italics]; not as if language, strengthened by the sacrifice of subjective intention, were simply something beyond the subject. In cutting the ties that bind it to the subject, language speaks for the subject, which — and Hölderlin was probably the first whose art intimated this — can no longer speak for itself.[38]

What does it mean to understand something polemically, not ontologically? Before examining the explanation subsequently offered by Adorno, let us first consider this injunction on "how one is to read" at its most basic semantic level.[39] The italicized sentence can be construed in one of two ways. Either the change ascribed to Hölderlin in the relation between language and subject — better, in the linguistic constitution of subjectivity — is to be understood as being of a polemical, rather than an ontological nature; or this change is to be understood in a polemical, rather than an ontological fashion. In the first case, the statement makes an objective claim about Hölderlin's poetry, namely, that it leaves the attentive reader no choice but to understand the change as a polemical one. Whoever understands it otherwise has simply misunderstood it, disregarding the implied imperative (the change *should* or *must* be understood so) dictated by the poetry itself. In the second case, the statement concerns the position the reader is to take up in relation to that change, and hence in relation to Hölderlin's work as a whole. It prescribes not *as what* it is to be understood, but *how* we are to understand it, and thus problematizes the act of interpretation, which the first variant treats as straightforward. While the imperative force of Adorno's dictum may still emanate from Hölderlin's poetry, in a manner that will have to be explored further, it may also come from outside that poetry, from a hermeneutics that brings certain methodological presuppositions to the analysis of a poem.

One might be tempted to dismiss the second proposed reading on the grounds that Adorno could not possibly mean that we should read Hölderlin in a polemical fashion. Does not his interpretation purport, on the contrary, to free Hölderlin from a hermeneutics of violence? Does he not claim, as a self-declared advocate of the "immanent analysis of literary works," to break through the monadic self-sufficiency of a poem by patiently immersing himself in it?[40] How then can he seriously suggest that we adopt a polemical attitude toward a central aspect of Hölderlin's work — and this at the very moment when he most directly contrasts his own interpretation to Heidegger's, just pages after warning: "One should not set up an abstract contrast between Heidegger's method and some other method"?[41]

Three factors speak against this objection. The first is that if Adorno had wanted to preclude the latter reading, he would have written: "This change is to be understood as a polemical one." As it stands, the grammatical construction favors the conclusion that the polemical relation holds sway between reader and text, rather than within the text itself. If I were to recommend that a set of instructions be read carefully, for instance, I would not mean that the instructions themselves were careful. The problem lies here in an ambiguity in the concept of understanding, which in this instance can imply both a correct or adequate grasp of the meaning of Hölderlin's words and, more broadly, a particular view of those words which need not coincide with any objectively ascertainable meaning. Second, the contention that something is of a polemical rather than an ontological nature is itself an ontological one, hence contradictory. Furthermore, the phrase of an "ontological nature" is tautologous, since every statement about the being or essence of a thing is by definition ontological. The third factor to bear in mind is that to understand something in a polemical fashion is not the same as to polemicize against it. Adorno is clearly not arguing that the change by which the subject comes to recognize itself as utterly mediated should be denounced by the reader, as if the reader hoped thereby to regain that immediacy and ultimacy which Hölderlin has already revealed to be delusional. What understanding polemically *does* mean will have to be clarified by examining the context of Adorno's remark. Provisionally, one can say that the prejudice that sees in the polemic little more than a form of willful misunderstanding is one not shared by Adorno.

The first transcription ventured above can therefore be ruled out in favor of the second. What still requires explaining is how this distinction between polemical and ontological ways of understanding relates to its referent, the anti-subjectivism whose effects Adorno describes at the beginning of the passage.[42] In texts by Adorno, the word "however" usually betrays something other than the chronic scrupulousness with which the conscientious scholar hastens to qualify his every generalization. It serves instead to signpost a dialectical turning point, the moment at which a necessarily one-sided line of argument, pursued with sufficient rigor, brings forth its own corrective. When Adorno maintains that the change that strips the subject of the semblance of spontaneity "must, *however*, be understood polemically and not ontologically," he thus hints that this change stands no less in need of critical revision than the ideology it unmasks. Just as the anti-subjective impulse animating Hölderlin's poetry "corrects" the preponderance of the subject, so a polemical understanding will correct that very correction, whereas an ontological understanding will enshrine or hypostatize it. The ontologist accepts the "death sentence" pronounced by Hölderlin; the polemicist contests the verdict.[43]

Adorno now expands upon how Hölderlin is not to be understood, clearing the ground for the positive determination of polemical understanding to come: "not as if language, strengthened by the sacrifice of subjective intention, were simply something beyond the subject." This is an obvious shot at Heidegger's view that Hölderlin has left behind the modern subject-object dichotomy, together with the scientific approach to nature that is its corollary, to found a more originary relation to Being; a jibe, too, at the mysticism that would transfigure Hölderlin into an empty vessel through which language itself comes to speak.[44] Adorno believes that Heidegger confuses the sacrifice of subjective intention in a poem with the obliteration (Heidegger would say: *Überwindung*) of subjectivity as such, failing to realize that even the most devastating demonstration of the subject's nugatoriness must still be subjectively articulated. The ontologist's denigration of the subject negatively mirrors the celebration of the subject indulged in by many of Hölderlin's contemporaries. For just as the bourgeois ideology of autonomous subjectivity neglects the constitutive role of language in subject-formation, so Heidegger ignores the equally important counter-truth that language would dissolve into the empyrean without a concrete subject to speak it. While recognizing, indeed greedily seizing upon the genuinely anti-subjective dimension of Hölderlin's poetry, Heidegger distorts its philosophical meaning by taking it *at its word*.

Under the catchword "de-aestheticization" (*Entästhetisierung*) this reproach formed the ground bass to Adorno's polemic at the beginning of the essay: "What is true and possible as poetry cannot be so, literally and unrefractedly, as philosophy."[45] Here, it further complicates the binary opposition "polemical/ontological understanding" that is gradually taking shape as perhaps the most important conceptual distinction in "Parataxis." For Heidegger, the *pólemos* launched by language against the subject actually results in the latter's destruction. If a polemical understanding, by contrast, holds that the subject survives this assault; if it insists that the interdependence of language and subjectivity prevents the acknowledged supremacy of language from ever being converted into absolute victory; if it refuses to take the anti-subjectivism of Hölderlin's poetry at face value; and if it consequently emphasizes what one might call the anti-anti-subjective aspect of Hölderlin's critique of language (which is not to be confused with the restoration of the autonomous subject), then to understand the language-subject relation polemically means to understand *that it is* a polemical relation, in the precise sense Adorno gave the term in "Die Aktualität der Philosophie." The philosopher's repudiation of the subject's demise corresponds to, and releases, a polemic *in Hölderlin* prematurely foreclosed by Heidegger.

Adorno's next sentence, the culmination of his argument, leaves no room for doubt on this: "In cutting the ties that bind it to the subject, language speaks for the subject, which . . . can no longer speak for itself." The subject has taken the place of reason, language that of a hostile reality, but otherwise the narrative schema has barely changed since 1932. At first, the subject imagines it can use language to authenticate its expressive ideal, the Wordsworthian spontaneous overflow of powerful feelings, much as the traditional philosopher hoped to fathom the world through the exercise of reason alone. The subject's inability to infuse language with the quick of individual feeling, manifested in the drab "conformity"[46] of conventional lyric poetry, leads it to relinquish this ambition. "In this process the illusion that language would be consonant with the subject or that the truth manifested in language would be identical with a subjectivity manifesting itself disintegrates."[47] Oddly foreshadowing Hölderlin's fate in the tower, language declares the subject henceforth to be *unmündig*, unauthorized to speak for itself; Adorno goes so far as to speculate that it might be possible to derive Hölderlin's madness from his poetry, much as the musicologist Groddeck once attempted to derive Beethoven's deafness from his late compositions.[48] As if in mimicry of Hölderlin's capitulation before language, the very syntax of Adorno's passage twice concedes the subject-position (in both senses of the term) to its usurper: "*language* speaks for the subject"; "Hölderlin was probably the first *whose art* intimated this." Hölderlin will have marked, then, that point in the history of literature at which the expressive paradigm of early romanticism first becomes a problem,[49] and if this change is described as "incalculably portentous," then in part because it represents, years before Baudelaire or Rimbaud, the opening move in the endless endgame of artistic modernity in which we are still caught up: "The idealistic Hölderlin inaugurates the process that leads to Beckett's protocol sentences, empty of meaning."[50]

Just as, in "Die Aktualität der Philosophie," the antagonism met with by reason proved its unexpected comrade-in-arms, so the polemic that once prevented the subject from speaking now helps it find its voice. No longer purporting to control meaning, the subject discovers, without actively searching for it, a new language commensurate to its experience of the incommensurability of language and subjectivity. To borrow the reflexive verb used by Adorno in 1932, language "offers itself" (*bietet sich . . . dar*) as a lifeboat to the subject set adrift from its transcendental moorings.[51]

Hölderlin's "sacrifice of subjective intention" is undertaken "out of subjective freedom,"[52] for the sake of what it apparently condemns to silence, just as Adorno had earlier held fast to philosophy's millennial goal of cognizing totality by abandoning it. Here as there, the polemic designates an unequal relation in which one term of the dyad finds itself simultaneously destroyed and redeemed by the antagonist it had originally sought to bring under its dominion.

Every polemic must satisfy two essential requirements: it must involve a refusal of communication (for example, Adorno's in relation to Heidegger), and a communication of that refusal of communication to a third party (for example, the Hölderlin Society). The target of a polemic is never the same as its addressee. That is why Horkheimer and Adorno, having written a polemic so wide-ranging that it seemed to set every conceivable readership in its sights, were forced to address it as a "message in a bottle" to an unknown posterity. Though it may bristle with all manner of invectives, exaggerations, and deliberate distortions, no strictly private correspondence may be deemed to be polemical. The open letter, on the other hand, is suited to polemical speech because it is pitched not so much at the target of the polemic, its ostensible addressee, as at the public peering over his or her shoulder; this detour enables it to communicate the non-communication indispensable to the functioning of the polemic. The polemic thus appears to its target as the communication, via an addressee with which it is not identical, of a refusal of communication. The polemic sketched with incomparable density in "Parataxis" represents a limit case insofar as the agent that refuses to communicate with the subject is language itself, the very means of communication. This refusal of language (*genitivus obiectivus* as well as *subiectivus*) gives rise to the following difficulty: if the cutting of communicative threads adduced by Adorno is to be taken seriously, if language's self-refusal is absolute, how is its polemic against the subject to be recognized *as* polemical, that is, as a *communicable* refusal of communication? To whom can language communicate its refusal to speak, if not to the subject with which it has broken all communicative ties?

Adorno has already given us the answer. To whom else but the reader who understands Hölderlin's poetry in a polemical rather than an ontological fashion? Whereas Adorno's ontological reader must grasp the refusal of language as an imperious silence that banishes the subject to oblivion, leaving language to unfold unperturbed in an impossibly rarefied, subject-free space, only the reader who refuses this refusal can recognize it as polemical — and as such, despite everything, as a means of communicating with the subject. Against Heidegger, Adorno presses home both the rhetoricity of Hölderlin's performance, which mitigates its anti-subjectivism, and its efficacy *as* a rhetorical performance, which empowers it to speak for the subject. The polemic unleashed in Hölderlin's late work relies upon the active resistance of its addressee (the philosophically qualified reader, that is, Adorno) in order to reach, and redeem, its target (the subject); or rather, this resistance first transforms what would otherwise be a purely destructive relation, and hence no relation at all, into a properly polemical one.

We are now in a better position to make sense of one of the passage's most puzzling aspects. Adorno seems to digress in the course of the argument from specifying *how* the portentous change inaugurated by Hölderlin is to be understood, namely polemically, not ontologically, to detailing *what* manner of change it might be, namely a polemical, not an ontological one. He seems in so doing to repeat the misconstrual of polemical understanding identified earlier, which proved guilty of smudging just that distinction. Yet we can see now why this slippage was both legitimate and necessary. Just as the "linguistic technique" and "content" of Hölderlin's poetry converge in their shared anti-subjectivism, so the reader's technique ultimately joins up with an objective "truth content" in the polemical structure that they have in common, but that only a polemical interpretative procedure can bring to light. The methodological comments that preface the essay state nothing less: "The path of the determinate negation of meaning is the path to the truth content."[53] Determinate negation in "Parataxis" is the polemical resistance to the surface meaning of Hölderlin's poetry that leads straight to its polemical heart, philosophy's response to the dilemma "that every work wants to be understood purely on its own terms but none can in fact be so understood."[54] To understand Hölderlin's work *polemically* is thus to *understand* it polemically, not to strike an arbitrary pose that leaves the reader blind or insensitive to it. And of course, the abstract confrontation of polemical and ontological understandings by means of which Adorno denies any point of contact between his approach and Heidegger's is itself a polemical move, the local effect of a polemologic that underwrites his entire argument.

If one were searching for confirmation of this, one need look no further than *Negative Dialektik* (Negative Dialectics, 1966). "Nothing," Adorno announces there in a fortissimo passage, "nothing on earth and nothing in the empty sky can be saved by being defended. . . . Nothing can be saved unchanged, nothing that has not passed through the portal of its death."[55] Whether one applies these apocalyptic lines to Adorno's rescue of Hölderlin or to Hölderlin's rescue of the subject, the same holds true: salvation lies, if anywhere, in the polemic.

Polemical Semblance

Polemic and salvation are the twin poles between which "Parataxis" oscillates, and they delimit its field of argumentation. Their relationship generates a ferment in which each term passes imperceptibly into the other. On the one hand, the polemic figures a kind of loving hate that mortifies in order to save: no resurrection without the stench of death. The subject finds its voice in losing it, philosophy comes through its defeat to know reality, and so on. As a gnostic category, the polemic affords a glimpse of divine truth through its absolute negation of the fallen world of the demiurge, anticipating the salvation of the particular in the universal envisaged by Adorno's regulative "utopia of knowledge."[56] On the other hand, as an unrelieved negativity that resists being swept into the speculative movement of sublation, the polemic equally designates the salvation of the particular *from* the universal. Adorno explains how in his *Philosophie der neuen Musik* (Philosophy of New Music, 1949): "The absolute liberation of the particular from the universal makes it, through its polemical and principled relation to the latter, itself into something general."[57] The polemic becomes the marginalized placeholder for a good universality through the intransigence of its opposition to a bad one. It permits Adorno to think reconciliation without giving up on contingency, and to uphold the claims of the non-identical without saturating it in the light of the idea. Yet because a refusal of communication is also a refusal of media(tiza)tion, Adorno's theoretical domestication of the polemic, while allowing it to be perceived as such, also threatens to downgrade it into just another discursive turn. The challenge lies in enduring the tension of polemic and salvation without dissolving it in favor of one or the other. Three interrelated questions need to be posed here. First, how do polemic and salvation belong together in Adorno's reading of Hölderlin's late work? By what law can something fallen, attacked, negated, and repudiated be simultaneously raised, transcended, affirmed, and fulfilled? Second, how is their co-belonging structurally articulated in the essay? What does the form of "Parataxis," as "sedimented content," reveal about the polemic?[58] And third, what is the relationship between this oxymoronic polemic, this salvation without armistice or amnesty, and the polemic as it is commonly understood, which certainly does not intend the salvation of its target? I will address these questions in reverse order over the next three sections, moving from a consideration of Adorno's decidedly non-redemptive polemic against Heidegger in the context of his Hölderlin interpretation to a discussion of "late style" as the self-reflection of the polemic in the medium of art.

To ground these questions, however, a brief recapitulation of Adorno's concept of aesthetic redemption is called for. This concept receives its most comprehensive treatment in *Ästhetische Theorie*, in which Adorno decrees "the redemption of semblance" to be "central to aesthetics," adding that "the emphatic right of art, the legitimation of its truth, depends on this redemption."[59] For Adorno, art requires the intervention of philosophy in order to transform its semblance character, the stigma inflicted upon it by a bad social totality and the mark of its impotence, into utopian *Vor-Schein* or pre-semblance, the source of its minimal discrepancy from the realm of means-ends rationality and the sole guarantor of its truth. While an artwork is the product of human activity, hence something subjectively willed, it can only instantiate a form of cognition to be found nowhere else if its truth content transcends volition. Art justifies itself as art, rather than as a sugar coating to make otherwise unpalatable religious, political, or philosophical messages easier to swallow, when it reflects upon its semblance character, the agent of its categorial distinction from all other spheres of a fully rationalized, disenchanted society. By virtue of its semblance character, the autonomous artwork appears as a thing in and for itself, obeying none but its own formal law and supremely indifferent to the onlooker; yet its production, reception, and artifactuality all tie it back to the universe of consumption and exchange. Adorno therefore writes: "The question of the truth of something made is indeed none other than the question of semblance and the rescue of semblance as the semblance of the true."[60] The salvation of semblance does not imply its overcoming as *dissemblance* or *illusion*, nor the discursive explication of a truth content for which the artwork would be the mere *appearance*, but the demonstration of a discursively inexhaustible truth-claim bound up with the modality of aesthetic *appearing*.[61]

Adorno's rationale for a philosophical engagement with art can be linked to the analysis of the polemic ventured so far. Accordingly, the salvation of semblance undertaken in and as "Parataxis" maintains a twofold relation to the polemic. Firstly, it releases in Hölderlin an implacable antagonism toward the status quo, which has been left unheeded by philology and transmuted by Heidegger into the myth of the founder-poet. This antagonism, however, is void of any determinable political content: it directly concerns neither the repressive regime of Hölderlin's day nor that of Adorno's own. The semblance character of art makes it the refuge for a form of cognition — mimetic, non-subsumptive, and sensuous — that has otherwise been banished from modern life. Consequently, although Adorno has a clear eye for Hölderlin's philosophical and affective attachment to the ideals of the French Revolution, he holds that the politicization of art, expressed in the demand that its always particular truth-claims become legislative for a community, amounts to its false sublation. As J. M. Bernstein comments, "to politicize art is to employ the rationality it refuses for the sake of the rationality it enjoins."[62] Adorno's adamant aestheticism, which marks his distance from the post-1968 reception of Hölderlin on the Left, makes it difficult to say wherein the specific polemical thrust of Hölderlin's poetry lies, beyond the mere fact of its being art. A number of passages in *Ästhetische Theorie* do indeed suggest that art is polemical a priori, insofar as it formally constitutes itself through the determinate negation or cancellation of social reality.[63] Philosophy's task would then be to recognize that art's refusal of communication, its monadic imperviousness to external demands, is itself a form of communication, and so to realize it *as* polemical. This is exactly what Adorno sets out to do in "Parataxis." Second, as we have seen, this polemicization of Hölderlin's work follows from an interpretative comportment that itself operates polemically. The difference between polemical and ontological understandings would thus be that between an approach that locates art's latent critical force in its constitutive distance from other domains of the social, and one that attempts to abolish that distance by interpretative fiat: "Heidegger glorifies the poet supra-aesthetically, as a founder, without reflecting concretely on the agency of form."[64]

A further, equally intimate, connection between salvation and polemic in "Parataxis" becomes apparent once the historical dynamic discerned by Adorno in the afterlife or *Nachgeschichte* of an artwork is taken into account. For Adorno, the truth content of an artwork has a temporal core. Among other things, this means that the truth of a poem depends upon its bearing witness, in however mediated a fashion, to the time of its creation: as an "historical-philosophical sundial" refracting the beam of light shot out by critique.[65] Adorno takes Heidegger to task for violating this maxim through his obsession with the poet's heroic individuality, which allegedly leads the philosopher, "all his perorations about historicity notwithstanding," to catapult Hölderlin into the timeless firmament of genius.[66] The "historical core of the truth content itself" dictates that no poem has a guarantee of immortality.[67] Once-celebrated works shed meaning as they age, grow silent, and sink into the footnotes of literary history. Others, all but ignored at the time of their appearance, patiently await a posterity equipped to unlock their secrets; like Heidegger, Adorno reckons Hölderlin to this latter category.[68] In "Parataxis," the relationship between a poem and its afterlife is described as a process of self-realization, almost of revelation: "What unfolds and becomes visible in the works, the source of their authority, is none other than the truth manifested objectively in them."[69] But this confident claim, which makes history the final arbiter of aesthetic value, is in fact ambiguous. It is compromised by a further postulate, according to which the changes undergone by an artwork over the course of its evolution invest it with meanings that were not merely concealed at its conception, lying ready to be stumbled upon by future generations, but that cannot even be said to have existed before the moment of their belated discovery. Thus Adorno argues in the *Einleitung in die Musiksoziologie* (Introduction to the Sociology of Music, 1962) that a "history of the critique of Beethoven could demonstrate how with every new layer of critical consciousness, new layers of his work itself were uncovered, *in a certain sense first constituted themselves through that process* [my italics]."[70]

Once history is no longer conceived of as the stage upon which the truth content of an artwork comes to blossom before an ever more discriminating audience, once it is conceded the power to precipitate changes in the artwork's inner development, such that work and temporal reception reciprocally condition one another, the discomforting possibility arises that even a misinterpretation may cause a previously unknown stratum in Hölderlin's poetry to crystallize, demonstrating a potential for misuse that will haunt each subsequent reading. Adorno moves to limit the damage by insisting that only a particular form of reception he calls "critique" is of any consequence for a poem's truth content. Critique registers, as upon a seismograph, the tremors issuing from the artwork as it grows older, using knowledge of the most "advanced" compositional techniques of the day to pick up reverberations too faint for the ordinary ear. Yet if "history has retroactive force," as Adorno insists against the historicist endeavor to know the past "as it actually happened," does not the exoteric, one is tempted to say "inauthentic" reception of a poet — in this case, the sinister popularity whipped up for Hölderlin during the Second World War — also prove relevant for critique, as the index and catalyst of a subcutaneous transformation?[71] And if that is correct, might not the scandalous violence with which Adorno takes to Heidegger, whose interpretation he explicitly (and controversially) assimilates to the nationalist orgy of 1943,[72] betray a residual doubt as to the purity of the poet for whose sake he was fighting? From this angle, Adorno's offensive public relations campaign is to be understood as a defensive reflex designed to prevent his self-implicating theory of interpretation from sliding into self-incrimination.

The problem may be clarified by means of a detour to another speech delivered by Adorno in the same year, 1963, on a similarly solemn commemorative occasion, that of the 150th anniversary of Kierkegaard's birth. While the speech rehearses many of the arguments from his *Habilitationsschrift*, the tone is much sharper than thirty years earlier, and for reasons not unrelated to the catastrophe that had transpired in the interim. Adorno begins by drawing attention to a contradiction between Kierkegaard's distrust for the worldly success of a doctrine and the dubious influence exerted by his writings upon the theological seminaries and philosophical seminars of the early twentieth century. "By the measure of his own writing, Kierkegaard cannot be victorious,"[73] yet the same uncompromising individualism that drove him into isolation during his lifetime and harried him to an early grave has since degenerated into an intellectual fad: "From that individual has arisen the mendacious chatter that proclaims the others to be inauthentic and themselves fallen to chatter. That was sealed in Germany when, before 1933, the Nazi Emanuel Hirsch took out a general lease on him: victory as defeat." Adorno leaves no doubt that Kierkegaard would have recoiled in horror from his posthumous fame. Nonetheless: "The trajectory of such a victory is that of a self-unfolding untruth of Kierkegaard's doctrine."[74] The parallel to his interpretative strategy in "Parataxis," which likewise uses a review of its subject's afterlife as a point of entry into the work, only underscores the startling divergence in Adorno's evaluation of the evidence. The travesty suffered by Hölderlin at the hands of Heidegger reflects nothing more than the latter's philistinism, that inflicted upon Kierkegaard by Hirsch nothing less than the former's involuntary complicity. On what grounds, then, does Kierkegaard's misappropriation by the Nazis cast a retroactive judgment upon his work, whereas Hölderlin, whose writings proved incomparably more amenable to their evil ends, escapes scot free from the tribunal of history? Why do Heidegger's commentaries, which Adorno rightly or wrongly makes representative for the entire National Socialist reception, take hold of Hölderlin as their helpless prey, rather than revealing a potential in his poetry that can now be seen to have inhered in it from the first? Why was Kierkegaard partially responsible for his historical fate, Hölderlin the victim of a crude falsification that leaves the truth content of his poetry intact?

However convincing the arguments leveled against Heidegger in "Parataxis" may be, in themselves they cannot suffice to answer such questions, just as the most compelling textual refutation of Hirsch's claims does nothing to alter the fact that they were in some sense authorized by Kierkegaard. This is where the polemic comes to the rescue. The opening line of "Parataxis" drops the hint: "There is no question that understanding of Hölderlin's work has grown along with his fame since the school of Stefan George demolished the conception of him as a quiet, refined minor poet with a touching life story."[75] Tellingly, Adorno recasts the George Circle's messianically tinged "discovery" of Hölderlin in polemical terms, reminding his audience — whose stated aim, after all, was to further the poet's fame und understanding — that a moment of radical discontinuity or violence is sometimes required to set in motion the tranquil dialectic of scholarly progress. In retrospect, Adorno's words read like a veiled apology for the bad manners that would soon have Staiger gasping for breath. But they also offer a way out of the cul-de-sac into which Adorno's thinking of the historicity of artworks had led him. The conventions of academic debate notionally adhered to by the Hölderlin Society, as by every other such organization, presuppose both the reasonableness of the participants and the respectability of their positions. Regardless of whether they are actually observed in day-to-day practice, such conventions operate under the normative assumption that consensus can be reached through the non-coercive force of the better argument. Once an interlocutor has shown himself to be immune to reason, however, they become an encumbrance rather than an aid to the common search for truth; Adorno probably had something like this in mind when he remarked that it is not possible to have a conversation with a fascist.[76] From the perspective of a theory of discourse, the polemicist violates the rules of the game for the sake of the outcome, his principal objective being to ostracize a member of the language community who had misused the rights of speech he had enjoyed hitherto. "Ideology critique," Peter Sloterdijk writes with reference to Adorno, "designates the polemical continuation of a broken-down dialogue with other means."[77] The opening words of "Parataxis" justify the coming attack on Heidegger, whose philosophy Adorno branded in the same year as being "fascist to its innermost cells,"[78] by presenting it, against all appearances, as an indispensable moment in the process of enlightenment. Heidegger's obscurantist arguments may prove to be irrefutable, but they can nonetheless be *disabled* by creating discursive conditions under which they will no longer be given a hearing.[79]

For all its rhetorical force, Adorno's war of words ultimately depends for its effectiveness upon the (polemical) salvation of (polemical) semblance that follows and informs it. Only such salvation can show that the fight will have been worthwhile. Without it, any argument about Hölderlin descends into a puerile and meaningless squabble for possession of one of the countless scraps on the trash-heap of culture "after Auschwitz." The salvation of semblance undertaken in "Parataxis" offers Hölderlin the chance, refused to Kierkegaard, of a precarious sanctuary from the vicissitudes of his reception. Not by exempting his poetry from history — art's semblance character is historical through and through — but by polemically intervening in history, and demonstrating through that event of interpretation what Adorno's own theory of reception could not: that Hölderlin's poetry is not what Heidegger has made it to be. The appropriate theoretical response to "the right-wing German cult of Hölderlin" is an eminently practical one.[80]

The Sundered Whole

I pointed out earlier that "Parataxis" is divided into roughly equal halves — in the printed version, they take up twenty-one and twenty-three pages, respectively — the first of which corresponds to Adorno's polemic against Heidegger, and the second to his interpretation of Hölderlin (or, as we can now specify, to the salvation of semblance in Hölderlin's late work). Of course, this schematic division cannot be taken as absolute, given that Adorno's sense of how Hölderlin is to be read inevitably colors the polemic against Heidegger; given, too, that the shots discharged there continue to ricochet in the immanent reading that ensues. Each half of "Parataxis" maintains numerous connections with its counterpart, not least through the vindication of the polemic in "polemical understanding" sketched above. Yet the bar of white space that juts between them should not be bridged too hastily in our eagerness to apprehend the essay as a whole. The unity of the essay is the product, not the encompassing ground of its inner dislocation. If indeed the first half stands under the sign of the polemic, the second under that of salvation, and if, as I have been arguing, polemic and salvation name two aspects of the same state of affairs, then we have reason to suppose that an X-ray picture of "Parataxis" might provide the clearest possible indication of the difference *and* identity of these terms.

This suspicion is confirmed by a comment Adorno made toward the end of his life. Rolf Tiedemann and Gretel Adorno, as reliable witnesses as any, report it in their afterword to *Ästhetische Theorie:* "he noted of his own method that it had the closest affinities with the aesthetic texts of the late Hölderlin."[81] The editors cite the remark in drawing attention to the paratactic organization of Adorno's posthumous work, which eschews the linearity of expository argument to circle, in ever varying approaches, around the same central aporias of art. Applied to "Parataxis," the only text he devoted to the poet,[82] Adorno's admission effectively collapses the distinction between what he says about Hölderlin's late work, the essay's thematic content, and how he says it, its form. Not unlike Heidegger's mimesis of the poetic word in "Das abendländische Gespräch," the proximity acknowledged by Adorno substitutes the intimacy of communion for the sense of detachment with which the professional critic usually approaches the literary object. As the convergence point of Adorno's late philosophical method and Hölderlin's late work, "Parataxis" stages the critical confluence of interpretation and self-description.

Thus emboldened to search "Parataxis" for statements that communicate subterraneously with Adorno's own formal procedure, one comes across the following reading of "Hälfte des Lebens" (Half of Life), Hölderlin's best-known paratactic structure:

> In a manner reminiscent of Hegel, mediation of the vulgar kind, a middle element standing outside the moments it is to connect, is eliminated as being external and inessential, something that occurs frequently in Beethoven's late style; this not least of all gives Hölderlin's late poetry its anticlassicistic quality, its rebellion against harmony. What is lined up in sequence, unconnected, is as harsh as it is flowing. The mediation is set within what is mediated instead of bridging it. As Beißner and more recently Szondi have emphasized, each of the two stanzas of "Hälfte des Lebens" has an inherent need for its opposite. In this regard as well, content and form are demonstrably one. In order to become expression, the antithesis of sensuous love and being cast out, an antithesis of content, breaks the stanzas apart, just as conversely it is only the paratactical form itself that produced the caesura between the halves of life.[83]

Adorno's observation that each stanza in "Hälfte des Lebens" requires its opposite holds just as true for the two massive discursive blocks that make up "Parataxis," whose architecture he may well have modeled on this very poem. The relation between the idyllic landscape of the first stanza and the wintry world of the second mirrors in reverse that between polemic and salvation in "Parataxis." Salvation is the unspoken yearning of the polemic, which in turn acts as the plenipotentiary and executor of salvation, yet their solidarity demands absolute discretion if it is to avoid betrayal. Were polemic and salvation to declare their union through the good offices of "a middle element standing outside the moments it is to connect" — one is reminded here of the marriage-meddling Mittler in Goethe's *Wahlverwandtschaften* (Elective Affinities)[84] — then they would fall victim to the same extorted reconciliation from which the polemic had resiled in the first place.

According to Adorno, Hölderlin exposes such mediation as the logical equivalent to the subjugation of nature, insofar as he demonstrates that the copula through which synthesis is effected remains indifferent to whatever it happens to be synthesizing.[85] Rather than forcing the halves of life into the Procrustean bed of identity (A=B), Hölderlin leaves them juxtaposed without commentary (A/B), such that their "harsh jointure"[86] insinuates synthesis in the painful absence of synthesis. The abrupt cry of "Weh mir"[87] (Alas) at the beginning of the second stanza, which shatters the blissful image evoked by its predecessor, advertises and exacerbates the wound in life that a hypotactic transition, be it even a *doch* (yet) or *aber* (but), would presume to suture. Like the antithetical moods to which each stanza gives voice, the opposition of polemic and salvation in Adorno's essay is to be overcome not by flattening them into synonymity but by driving their contrast to an extreme. Their relationship is itself polemical. "Parataxis" (and parataxis, the formal correlate of this process of distension and dissociation) may accordingly be characterized as the (dis)union of polemic and salvation under the preponderance of the polemic. Just as Hölderlin's poem rends a mythic wholeness of life into disconnected halves, so Adorno's aptly-named essay submits to paratactic diremption the virtual unity of polemic and salvation that can only be inferred, never posited as such: here the brutally insensitive Hektor Rottweiler, there the hyper-sensitive Teddie Wiesengrund; here a refusal of communication, there a communion that has no need of it; here the sound and the fury of the polemic, there the redemptive calm of Hölderlin's "intention to cast aside synthesis and trust to pure passivity in order to completely fill the present."[88] What nonetheless allows one to speak of dissociation and diremption, rather than an insignificant side-by-side of unrelated elements, is the fact that in both cases the burden of mediation comes to be transposed from the suspended copula to "within what is mediated." As we have seen, the polemic against Heidegger generates of itself the need for the salvation of semblance, while that salvation, far from leaving the polemic behind as its mere prelude, bestows upon it the greatest possible epistemological dignity.

The striking parallels between the subject matter of "Parataxis" and its formal constitution — "in this regard as well, content and form are demonstrably one" — by no means end there. In "Hälfte des Lebens," the structural *symmetry* of the two stanzas is offset by the *dissymmetry* of the stylistic principles that organize them. The language of the first half flows in a continuous movement over the course of a single sentence, beginning with the description of the yellow pears, rising to the apostrophe to the lovely swans that occupies the middle line of the stanza, before subsiding at the end, along with the swans' drunken heads, into the holy-sober water. The form reproduces the ripple effect on the surface of the lake that emanates from "Ihr holden Schwäne" (You lovely swans), from both the line and the swans themselves. The next stanza, by contrast, is broken into two sentences, the first a despairing question, the second not so much its answer as a paratactic recognition that no answer will be forthcoming:

> Die Mauern stehn
> Sprachlos und kalt, im Winde
> Klirren die Fahnen[89]

> [The walls stand
> Speechless and cold, in the wind
> Weathercocks clatter].

The form seems to buckle and collapse here under the weight placed upon the suffering, isolated subject, which only now makes itself heard in a series of strongly alliterative, staccato-like phrases:

> Weh mir, wo nehm' ich, wenn
> Es Winter ist, die Blumen . . . ?[90]

> [Alas, where shall I find when
> Winter comes, flowers . . . ?]

What Adorno calls the "antithesis in content of sensuous love and being cast out" in "Hälfte des Lebens" is thus matched *and* unbalanced by a formal antithesis of smooth hypotaxis and disturbed parataxis within a paratactic (always already sundered) whole.

Similarly, a crude overview of the structure of "Parataxis" reveals that each of its halves entails a different mode of presentation, which militates against their synthesis in an overarching whole. The first half is composed of eight enormous paragraphs. The opening pair, recognizably the introductory section of the essay, establish philosophy's prerogative to concern itself with Hölderlin, while the remaining six are taken up with showing how Heidegger has abused that right. The first sentence of the third paragraph ensures an unruffled transition: "While Hölderlin's poetry, like everything that is poetry in the emphatic sense, needs philosophy as the medium that brings its truth content to light," — this the result of the argument so far — "this need is not fulfilled through recourse to a philosophy that in any way seizes possession of the poetry" — this the omen of things to come.[91] Each of the following four paragraphs then sets out to denounce a particular weakness of Heidegger's reading: its anti-aesthetic celebration of the poet (§3); its fixation on the late work's gnomic sayings at the expense of their contextual significance (§4); its barely concealed allegiance to certain fascistic topoi (§5); and its willful disregard for the collective historical experience from which Hölderlin's poetry draws (§6). The penultimate paragraph preempts the obvious retort — if Heidegger got it so wrong, how is one to explain Hölderlin's attractiveness to him? — with reference to the role of abstractions in the hymnic work. There follows a last, emphatic, attempt to liberate Hölderlin once and for all from the clutches of ontology: "[Hölderlin's] distant phantasmata of the nearby cannot be hoarded up in the treasury of *Heimatkunst.*"[92] The well-defined tripartite structure of this essay within the essay — the preparation, execution, and *coup de grâce* of the polemic, as it were — articulates the relentless momentum driving the argument toward its goal. This is, essentially, that of "smashing Heidegger," a plan hatched out decades earlier by Benjamin and Brecht,[93] but first carried out by Adorno during the early 1960s.[94]

The second half consists of nine paragraphs, again of colossal dimensions. The first (§9) proposes that the corrective to Heidegger's procedure be sought in the relationship of form and content in Hölderlin's late work: "What philosophy can hope for in poetry is constituted only in this relationship; only here can it be grasped without violence."[95] §10 to §13 go on to view this relationship through the prism of form, paying especial attention to Hölderlin's paratactic technique and his use of correspondences; §14 to §17 discuss the content, thematizing the poetry's explicit critique of synthesis. The unity of form and content in the "poetized" (*Gedichtete*), a term Adorno borrows from Benjamin's early essay on Hölderlin,[96] makes their disentanglement a consciously heuristic measure. To study one in isolation from the other is justified only if their partition annuls itself over the course of the interpretation, which is what Adorno's approach evidently intends. Yet he also insists that the unity of form and content does not precede its critical elaboration: "But there is scarcely any aesthetic object that demonstrates more forcefully than Hölderlin's work that the assertion of an unarticulated unity of form and content is no longer adequate. Such a unity can be conceived only as a unity across its moments; the moments must be distinguished from one another if they are to harmonize with the content and be neither merely separate nor passively identical."[97] Each paragraph in the second half must therefore be understood as performing a function that is at once analytic and synthetic; each examines an integral part of a whole that first emerges through its reconstruction; each explicates the same matter of thinking from a different vantage point; and each refers, by virtue of its fragmentariness, to the aggregate of the parts. Benjamin's description of the tractate in his *Ursprung des deutschen Trauerspiels* (Origin of the German Play of Mourning, 1928) is apposite to that book's most avid reader: "Tirelessly the process of thinking makes new beginnings, returning in a roundabout way to its original object. This continual pausing for breath is the mode most proper to the process of contemplation."[98] The moments when Adorno's argument snatches breath before taking another tilt at Hölderlin — and what else is signified by a paragraph break? — stand in the same relation to the form of the essay's second half as does parataxis to a compound sentence.

The pronounced contrast between the polemical, progressive ductus of the first half and the constellative, cyclical procedure of the second finds its strict analogy, and perhaps its model, in the stylistic dissymmetry of "Hälfte des Lebens." What is the import of this split between polemical and redemptive presentation, and how does it further our understanding of "Parataxis" as a (paratactic) whole? A letter from Benjamin to Adorno, dated 19 June 1938, provides the germ of an answer. Adorno had invited him to comment on his recently completed manuscript on Wagner. In accord with later critical opinion,[99] Benjamin identified what he took to be a polemical motivation behind the book, and went on to contrast the polemic qua literary form with salvation:

> A polemical engagement with Wagner by no means has to exclude illumination of the progressive elements in his work, as you yourself show, and especially if these cannot simply be separated from the regressive ones like the sheep from the goats. But yet — and here, dear Teddie, you might surprise me in body and soul with your own favorite image from Indian Joe about unearthing the hatchet and provoking a fight[100] — it seems to me that any such salvation, undertaken from the perspective of the philosophy of history, is incompatible with one undertaken from a critical perspective that is focused upon progress and regress. . . . I hardly imagine you will wish to contradict me if I say that the philosophical project of such salvation requires a form of writing which. . . has a particular affinity with musical form itself. Salvation is a cyclical form, polemic a progressive one. . . . The decisive element in such salvation — am I not right? — is never simply something progressive; it can resemble the regressive as much as it resembles the ultimate goal, which is what Karl Kraus calls the origin.[101]

It is impossible not to recall here the fourteenth of the theses on the concept of history, committed to paper shortly afterwards, which takes as its epigraph the same Karl Kraus dictum cited by Benjamin at the end of his critique. Thesis XIV opposes the "empty, homogenous time" of progress, which is also the time of social democracy, to the "now-time" of revolutionary upheaval.[102] The latter bursts open the "continuum of history" to redeem possibilities that had been neglected by the inexorable march of progress (which, as Benjamin's letter makes clear, is equally that of regress; expressed in the language of the "Theses," there is no document of civilization that is not also one of barbarism).[103] Accordingly, polemic and salvation are the concomitant formal principles to the historico-philosophical perspectives of progress and messianic rupture. They are irreconcilable because the rhythm and manner of their unfolding are dictated by radically different temporalities. The polemic operates within the unilinear time of history, deriving its legitimacy from a telos that makes possible the identification, if not the segregation, of pro- and regressive tendencies. The literary form of salvation, on the other hand, interrupts history to present its object in the undiminished actuality of the day of creation. Benjamin's reference to music makes clear that this process is not to be conceived as the abstract negation of transitoriness — music, after all, is the art form most closely wedded to time — but as the fulfillment of the transitory in recurrence, the renewed coming to be of what had long since passed away and had apparently missed its moment; I will return to this figure in the next chapter in the course of my discussion of the Brechtian paradigm of citation. For Benjamin, whereas the polemic occupies the profane time-space of evolution, salvation anticipates the *kairos* of revolution (the indifference of origin and goal in "cyclical form"), and there can be no congress between the two.[104]

As Benjamin foresaw, Adorno showed no inclination to contest his insightful comments on the musical technique proper to *Rettung*. He also conceded the justness of Benjamin's central criticism regarding the monograph's polemical conception.[105] Citing an "attenuating circumstance," however, he insisted that he "did not relate the idea of 'saving' Wagner solely and unconditionally to the progressive features of his work, but rather attempted everywhere to emphasize the entanglement of the progressive and the regressive moments."[106] While this somewhat muted defense might seem merely to reiterate the inseparability of progressive and regressive elements already acknowledged in Benjamin's original letter, it actually points to a key divergence in their respective philosophies of history. For in relating his attempted salvation of Wagner to the "entanglement of the progressive and the regressive moments" accentuated throughout the book, Adorno commits what Benjamin must have regarded as an illegitimate incursion into the exclusive province of the polemic. Between the lines, Adorno is arguing that polemic and salvation can no more be separated than progress and regress. To be sure, his assent to Benjamin's comments on the literary form appropriate to each indicates that he does not dispute their opposition. But whereas Benjamin withdraws that opposition from mediation, so proclaiming it to be absolute, Adorno sees it as the polarized function of a *single* historico-philosophical perspective, just as he grasps the antithesis of "Hälfte des Lebens" as the diremption of a life that must at least be thinkable in an undirempted state. In other words, the non-communication of salvation and polemic correctly identified by Benjamin is to be understood as being polemical in nature, hence tenuously communicative. The circumstance referred to by Adorno is "attenuating" in the precise sense that it qualifies the finality of their severance: "And perhaps it is also indicative of this fact that the work possesses more of a cyclical form in your own sense than you are ready to credit."[107]

The debate played out between Benjamin and Adorno in 1938 repeats itself exactly twenty-five years later as an immanent conflict between the stylistic opposition of polemic and salvation on the one hand, and their operative entwinement and speculative identity on the other. This conflict cannot be resolved in "Parataxis," nor is such a resolution attempted; instead, the essay bears out and dramatizes: it *is* this conflict. Or to paraphrase Adorno: in order to become expression, the antithesis of salvation and polemic breaks apart the essay, just as, conversely, it is only the paratactic form itself that brings about their scission. Paradoxically, this cut in the text is the stitch that holds it together, the binding that prevents it splitting down the middle into Benjamin's utterly disparate spheres. It is to this *Schnittstelle*, this empty yet perilously fraught caesura, that we must now turn.

The End of the Polemic

Adorno's concept of the caesura has its prehistory. From its humble origins in prosody, where it designates a division in a metrical foot indicating a pause in delivery, the caesura first rises to theoretical prominence in Hölderlin's poetological reinscription of a poetics of tragic effect. The basic problem Hölderlin addressed in the notes to *Oedipus* displays a marked resemblance to the constitutive dilemma of "Parataxis": through what technique can the violently conflicting drives that constitute the proper subject of tragedy — Hölderlin names them the boundless copulation and boundless separation of man and god — be brought together, bounded, in a beautiful work of art?[108] Hölderlin's answer is audaciously speculative: "Thereby, in the rhythmic sequence of the representations wherein the *transport* presents itself, there becomes necessary *what in poetic meter is called caesura*, the pure word, the counter-rhythmic rupture; namely, in order to meet the onrushing change of representations at its highest point in such a manner that very soon there does not appear the change of representation but the representation itself."[109] Two points need to be noted here, however briefly. Firstly, the caesura delimits and protects the work by bringing to a halt the catastrophic oscillation that threatens to derange the presentation. It *takes the measure* of the tragedy; that is to say, it moderates the work's excessive drives by determining their proportions and relative weighting within the tragic poem as a whole. It thereby guarantees the continuing relatedness of the opposing poles that are flung apart, with tremendous velocity, at the height of the tragic transport.[110] Second, as a pure word eviscerated of meaning, the caesura marks the hiatus around which the entire play is structured. It is an absence — nothing happens at the caesura; it is not the peripeteia[111] — but it is an absence that reveals the conditions of presence and presencing in the play, and as such is "the liberation by default — but a non-negative default — of meaning itself or of the truth of the work."[112]

We can already surmise that the caesura of "Parataxis" functions in much the same way, and it comes as no surprise that Adorno twice introduces the concept into his interpretation. Yet although Adorno was familiar with Hölderlin's theory of tragedy,[113] neither of these references makes mention of it, just as the essay in general shows little interest in the poet's protracted meditations on the genre. Of more immediate relevance to Adorno's use of the term is Benjamin's study on *Die Wahlverwandtschaften*. In that text, thought by Adorno to be the finest he ever wrote, Benjamin extends the range of the caesura far beyond the bounds of tragedy by bringing it into connection with what he calls "the expressionless," which is "a category of language and art and not of the work or of the genres." The expressionless "is the critical violence that, while unable to separate semblance from essence in art, prevents them from mingling."[114] For Benjamin, the expressionless power of language cannot be translated without remainder into appearance — it does not tarry in the medium of language, awaiting release from the poet — nor does it transcend appearance, floating in a languageless ether accessible only to mystic intuition. Rather, the expressionless communicates itself in the caesura as the spiritual form of an artwork, which otherwise lies submerged in the means of its expression. That "occidental Junonian sobriety," which Hölderlin considered the greatest achievement of Greek art, "is only another name for the caesura, in which, along with harmony, every expression simultaneously comes to a standstill, in order to give free reign to an expressionless power inside all artistic media."[115] The organic flux of the harmonious work of art must momentarily be transfixed in order that the expressionless, punctuating appearance, appear as such; for caesuras, as Winfried Menninghaus points out, are "partitioning cuts, which, precisely as lacunae, . . . indicate the position of the knife itself."[116] The Benjaminian caesura brings the expressionless to expression without delivering it over to language, pointing the way to the truth content of the work, that region in which the distinction between appearance and essence is both articulated and resolved into a higher unity.

Much more could be said about the caesura in both Hölderlin and Benjamin. Its significance for Adorno, however, will clearly lie in his own elaboration of the concept. To convey a sense of how he refashions it, I cite the first and more extended of the two references in "Parataxis."[117] The context is a discussion of "Friedensfeier," the great hymn discovered and published only a few years before Adorno delivered his speech: "The fact that the keyword [*Stichwort*] 'thanks' follows the word 'fate' at the end of these lines, mediated by the word 'but,' establishes a caesura in the poem; the linguistic configuration defines gratitude as the antithesis of fate, or, in Hegelian terms, as the qualitative leap that in responding to fate leads out of it."[118] Because a caesura is, literally, an incision (from the Latin *caedere*, to cut up), one might expect it to manifest itself as a tear in the close-knit fabric of the poem. Yet unlike the caesura of "Hälfte des Lebens," which coincides with the unmediated break between the stanzas, the cut that disrupts Hölderlin's celebration of peace is not paratactic; on the contrary, it follows upon a mediating particle, a "but." Adorno locates the caesura instead in a *Stichwort*, a word whose polemical associations he has already taught us not to ignore: "the keyword 'thanks,'" which cuts itself free from its antithesis in cutting into it. Rephrased in the discourse-theoretical terms suggested by the rhetoric of the passage, thanks represents a conversational counter-turn — a response to fate — that in the same stroke cuts short the conversation. Its *Antwort* or answer to fate, a constative utterance, can only prevent fate having the last word because it is equally a *Stichwort*, a performative utterance. Thanksgiving is the polemical riposte to fate, the cutting rejoinder that leaves fate speechless.

Adorno now attempts to explain how thanks, this most improbable of combatants, overcomes its almighty adversary: "In its content, gratitude is purely and simply antimythological; it is what is expressed at the moment when eternal variance is suspended. While the poet praises fate, the poetry, on the basis of its own momentum, opposes gratitude to fate, without the poet having necessarily intended this."[119] If "myth is catastrophe in permanence,"[120] as Adorno remarks in a speech on Wagner from the same year, then thanks is antimythological because it signals that the catastrophe has been averted or brought to a (provisional) close: Hölderlin composed "Friedensfeier" upon receiving news of the Treaty of Lunéville, which promised to put a stop to the bloodshed in Europe. As the eternal return of the same, the catastrophe of history stands for the attack that never fails to draw a counterattack, the crime interminably perpetuated through its punishment. Thanksgiving is premature unless all arms have been laid to rest. The immobilization of myth therefore seems to require that one refrain from aggression, even when incited by an enemy. At times, notably whenever he comments on the "docility" or "supreme passivity" characteristic of Hölderlin's spiritual bearing,[121] Adorno holds out the prospect of such a general ceasefire, envisaged in idealist terms as a peace with nature: "Metaphysical passivity as the substance of Hölderlin's poetry is allied, in opposition to myth, with the hope for a reality in which humanity would be free of the spell of its own entanglement in nature, an entanglement that was reflected in the conception of absolute spirit."[122] But because the caesura that leads out of mythic fate is a *Stichwort*, because the counter-rhythmic interruption that suspends the cycle of violence is itself violently polemical, salvation assumes the guise of a catastrophe to end the state of permanent catastrophe. In an irredeemably fallen world, all hope gravitates toward the apocalypse, the ultimate circuit-breaker.

The harbinger of the apocalypse in which it would come to term, the polemic stands for — and stands in the way of — the universal amnesty invoked by Hölderlin. The polemic works toward a state in which it would become superfluous, a state whose advent it thereby indefinitely postpones. Its fate replicates the historical fate of art, whose polemical effectiveness against instrumental rationality hinges upon its social effectlessness, the fact that it changes nothing; this is why the work of art becomes the privileged locus and agent of the polemic in Adorno's thought. In the same book on Wagner whose polemical conception had been criticized by Benjamin, Adorno detects a conventional happy ending lurking behind the Schopenhauerian facade of the world conflagration that engulfs the stage at the end of the *Ring*. The negation of the bourgeois world celebrated by Wagner, transfigured too quickly into the positive, forfeits its negativity and results in a false "redemption" (*Erlösung*).[123] The conclusion is unavoidable that for an authentic salvation, for a rigorously polemical *Rettung*, Wagner's catastrophe is *not catastrophic enough*.[124] In the smooth roundedness of its construction, in the perfect arc with which it falls back upon its origin, the *Ring* lacks a caesura to rupture and complete it.[125] Through its destruction of aesthetic totality, the caesura transforms the "bad" catastrophe of history — fate — into the "good" catastrophe of (the truth content of) art. Catastrophe is the ineluctable remnant of myth in salvation, which is always salvation from myth. Like the subject in Hölderlin's poetry, myth thus survives its own demise: "There is a mythic layer inherent in the substance of Hölderlin's work, as in any genuine demythologization."[126]

While the Benjaminian provenance of this concept of the caesura is unmistakeable, I want to argue that it owes its specific inflection in "Parataxis" to its affiliation with "late style." The caesura in "Friedensfeier" is not just one example among others, such that the analysis of a different caesura might have yielded an entirely different interpretative conclusion. Rather, what Adorno says of the *Stichwort* "thanks" holds true of the caesura in general: it is "purely and simply antimythological." Adorno calls works that are scored by a caesura "late works." The late work is intrinsically antimythological because it is self-reflexively polemical, that is, it polemicizes against, and strives to redeem, that which constitutes it as a work of art: its semblance character. For Adorno, the caesura, itself semblance because itself an aesthetic category, is the redemptive (catastrophic) cut in semblance that refers art to what would be more or other than semblance. To demonstrate this, I will turn to Adorno's writings on Beethoven, which contain his most detailed accounts of late style. This move is justified, indeed necessitated, by the frequent comparisons of Hölderlin's late work to Beethoven's drawn in "Parataxis" and elsewhere, for which the concept of late style serves as the *tertium comparationis*.[127]

This concept requires some preliminary clarification. The term resonates with the mellow wisdom of a ripe old age, yet the poetry analyzed in "Parataxis" is that of a man barely over thirty, with half his life still before him. (Hölderlin philology has had to resort to the clumsy epithet "very late work" to deal with the poems of madness.) At the very least, "late style" suggests the final stage in a process of maturation through early and middle styles, yet Adorno denies Beethoven's ninth symphony the title of a late work, which he nonetheless accords to much of the chamber music composed before it. Late style is thus a qualitative ascription, not a chronological one. We come a little closer to Adorno's meaning when we recall that lateness also carries overtones of tardiness, of the *too* late, and hence of dis-appointment. The late work misses the moment when the creative will fused part and whole, particular and universal into the harmonious work of art, intruding instead upon a scene of abandonment: a heap of lifeless, used-up material on the one hand; an insubstantial, listless subjectivity on the other.[128] The word "style" is also problematic in this context, given that it ordinarily designates the signature of an irreducible individuality, that indefinable, unreproducible X that permeates every phrase and stamps it as belonging to Beethoven and no other — the mark, that is, of an authentic and sovereign subject. How, then, can Adorno claim that Hölderlin and Beethoven, but also such wildly dissimilar artists as Rembrandt, Michelangelo, Goethe, and El Greco, have a style *in common*?[129]

This is the point at which Adorno takes up his analysis. For Adorno, the subject that has attained an absolute mastery of its craft is precisely what the late work deconstructs; late style is the autocritique of the concept of style. I quote from the 1937 essay "Spätstil Beethovens" (Beethoven's Late Style), Adorno's most compressed statement on the matter: "The usual view explains [the dissonance peculiar to late works] with the argument that they are products of an uninhibited subjectivity, or, better yet, 'personality,' which breaks through the envelope of form to better express itself."[130] Adorno proposes instead that the proximity to death that the late work radiates so powerfully, far from reflecting the experience of the composer, lies in its incommensurability with the category of individual experience. The brittle hollowness that pertains to the fragmentary hymns of Hölderlin or the last quartets of Beethoven is legible as the shell of an evacuated interiority, the anorganic residue of an organic middle period. Such texts are the barren site from which the expressive subject has taken leave, a process sketched by Adorno in the notes to his unfinished monograph on Beethoven: "Whereas the 'classical' style sublates [the individual element] within the totality and gives it the *semblance* of significance . . ., now the insignificance of the individual element emerges as such and makes it the 'accidental' bearer of the universal. In other words, late style is the self-consciousness of the nugatoriness of the individual, the existent. Therein lies the relationship of late style to *death*."[131] And in "Spätstil Beethovens" he asserts: "The power of subjectivity in late works of art is the irascible gesture with which it takes leave of the works themselves. It breaks their bonds, not in order to express itself, but in order, expressionless, to cast off the semblance of art."[132]

Late style's expressive affinity to death derives from art's struggle to transcend expression, to cast aside its semblance character and become knowledge. This task is Sisyphean, because art's knowledge of itself in the late work confronts it with the impossibility of its self-transcendence into knowledge: "Late style would mean that the music becomes aware of the *limit* of this movement — the impossibility of canceling its premises by force of its own logic."[133] Much as the thoughts of the inmate desperate to escape come to be dominated by the bars of his prison cell, so the late work's effort to overcome its semblance character throws it all the more forcefully upon semblance, which is now revealed to be the fatal admixture to *all* art. The appearance of vitality with which the classical work captivates its audience was just that: appearance, and the late work exposes such appearance as ideological. Arriving *post festum*, the late work retroactively ruins the party. But because it cannot claim exemption from its polemic against semblance, it also attacks its own foundations. When Adorno, once again adopting a terroristic vocabulary, calls Hölderlin's poetry an "assassination attempt on the harmonious work of art," the image of a suicide bombing aimed at the explosion of appearance is more pertinent than that of a sniper's bullet aimed at its liquidation.[134] As art and anti-art alike, the late work foreshadows the achievement and predicament of the European avant-gardes since around 1910, rehearsing the same aporetic scenario laboriously played out in *Ästhetische Theorie*, defined by the exhaustion of latency and the liberation of dissonance.[135] Adorno's somewhat forced coupling of Hölderlin and Beethoven to Beckett and Schönberg, respectively, establishes late style as the ontogenetic prefiguration of art's phylogenesis in modernity — a genealogy of modernism that permits him to salvage a tradition of, and from, the irreversible dissolution of tradition.

What role does the caesura play in the late work? The concluding lines of "Spätstil Beethovens" provide a cryptic answer:

> [Beethoven] no longer gathers the landscape, deserted now and alienated, into an image. He lights it with rays from the fire that is ignited by subjectivity, which breaks out and throws itself against the walls of the work, true to the idea of its dynamism. . . . It is subjectivity that forcibly brings the extremes together in the moment. . . . The caesuras, the sudden discontinuities that more than anything else characterise the very late Beethoven, are those moments of breaking away; the work is silent at the instant when it is left behind, and turns its emptiness outward. Not until

then does the next fragment attach itself, transfixed by the spell of subjectivity breaking loose and conjoined for better or worse with whatever
preceded it; for the mystery is between them, and it cannot be invoked
otherwise than in the figure they create together. This sheds light on the
Widersinn that the very late Beethoven is called both subjective and
objective. Objective is the fractured landscape, subjective the light in
which — alone — it glows into life. He does not bring about their harmonious synthesis. As the power of dissociation, he tears them apart in
time, in order, perhaps, to preserve them for the eternal. In the history of
art late works are the catastrophes.[136]

I will not endeavor to undertake an exhaustive analysis of this passage,
which gathers together all the central motifs of the much later essay on
Hölderlin. The key term is perhaps *Widersinn*. Susan H. Gillespie offers
the following translation of the sentence in which it appears: "This sheds
light on the nonsensical fact that the very late Beethoven is called
both subjective and objective."[137] According to this rendering, Adorno's
enlightening explanation enforces the hermeneutic directive that where
nonsense was, there sense shall be. In translating Adorno's *Widersinn* into
prospective meaning, however, Gillespie misses the polemical thrust of the
passage. For according to a distinction that Adorno may have picked up
from Husserl,[138] *Widersinn* is not *Unsinn*, a complete absence of meaning
to be dispelled in the light of interpretation, nor is it *Gegensinn*, an alternative meaning that could exist peaceably alongside its counterpart, as if
the subjectivity and objectivity ascribed to late Beethoven were two sides
of the same coin. Rather, *Widersinn* is meaning inimical to meaning:
polemical meaning. The question as to whether *Widersinn* polemicizes
against meaning as such, and is itself meaningless, or whether it polemicizes against particular meaning, and is itself meaningful, is not to be
decided one way or the other. In the first case, *Widersinn* would be converted into a privative form of meaning and then ignored; in the second,
it would be neutralized into a potential source of meaning and then interrogated. Either way, the polemic, which feeds off the tension between its
overtly totalizing hostility to meaning-making and its covert meaning
as salvation, would be silenced through its redirection into a semantic
economy.[139]

Adorno's interpretation of late style is caught in the same dilemma.
How is one to understand polemical meaning without betraying it to the
enemy? And if polemical meaning repels every attempt to understand it,
where does that leave the interpreter? In "Spätstil Beethovens," Adorno's
solution is to *shed light on* Widersinn, that is, to make the recognition that
the late work is contra-sensical, *widersinnig*, the spur to further interpretation rather than its defeat. The critic's task, like the philosopher's in
"Die Aktualität der Philosophie," is to embrace this resistance to meaning
without trying to circumvent or surmount it. I take this to be the strategy

common to all of Adorno's writings on late style, including "Parataxis."
In the opening pages of that essay, Adorno admiringly enumerates
Beißner's philological elucidations to Hölderlin's "Winkel von Hardt" —
"Beißner's explanation of the mention of something 'übrig,' 'left over,' as
the place that remained is illuminating"[140] — but goes on to argue that
philology is ill-equipped to fathom the poem's "disturbed character": "It
will be understood only by someone who not only ascertains the prag-
matic content, the content which has its locus outside the poem and
which is manifested in its language, but also continues to feel the shock
of the unexpected name Ulrich, someone who will be troubled by the 'far
from mute' . . . ."[141] To understand "Winkel von Hardt," in other words,
is to learn through the experiences of shock and irritation that it withdraws from our attempts to understand it, however illuminating such
attempts may be. Hölderlin's residual site, which Beißner neatly relocates
outside the poem, remains within the poem itself as the unidentified,
unidentifiable no man's land from which it launches its campaign against
meaning. Indeed, Wolfgang Binder inadvertently corroborates Adorno's
respectful critique of Beißner when he proposes that the line "an übrigem
Ort" (at the place left over) be read as meaning "not here or there, but
somewhere as such."[142] By seeking to assign to poetry a clearly delimited
space determined by a set of externally imposed coordinates, Beißner's
topographical reading leaves no room in the poem *übrig*, that is, unaccounted for. Like Heidegger, Adorno suggests that Hölderlin's poetry
founds its own place; but for Adorno, that place is unsettled, unsettling,
and completely unsuited to "beautiful dwelling." It is the desolate,
uninhabitable, and apocalyptic landscape of the late work, and if
Adorno remarks that Beethoven no longer gathers this landscape into an
image, then this is because he well knows that no map could possibly
accommodate it.

As the site of *Widersinn*, the caesura is the reader's portal to that hostile landscape, the interface beween art's narrowly circumscribed social,
historical, and institutional situation and a utopia that is neither here nor
there, "but somewhere as such." The caesura precipitates the catastrophe
of meaning in the late work while promising salvation as the meaning of
catastrophe. This promise is of course *widersinnig*, and from the outside
must even appear to be nonsensical. Common sense tells us that it is
absurd to hope for salvation from destruction. But such is the price and
risk of the caesura, which has nothing more than a *perhaps* to justify its
attack on semblance: "As the power of dissociation, it tears them apart in
time, in order, perhaps, to preserve them for the eternal." The grammatical subject of this sentence is late Beethoven. Its true subject is the caesura,
that same caesura that Adorno elsewhere calls "the contra-sensical caesura,
which places hope in existence through its decay."[143] Polemic would be its
other name.

Epilogue: Being Polemical

"Polemic is not simply a stylistic means," writes Thorsten Bonacker in his essay "Culture Industry and Adorno's Polemic," one of few to broach the topic. "It takes culture in its protection because it is itself culture, without reifying culture."[144] Throughout this chapter I have argued that the scope of Adorno's polemic extends well beyond the list of his declared enemies to encompass those authors and texts he thought most worth protecting. Adorno believed that the assiduous preservation and maintenance of cultural artefacts practiced by organizations such as the Hölderlin Society was not enough to guarantee their continued actuality. In his mission to release such works from the formaldehyde of their canonization, Adorno did not shirk from using polemical means. In the case of "Parataxis," this not only meant polemicizing against those who stood in his way; it also entailed employing an interpretative approach he called "polemical understanding" to activate a hitherto dormant polemic in Hölderlin's poetry, one directed against instrumental rationality, the expressive subject, the semblance character of art, and even meaning itself. Adorno's post-catastrophic Hölderlin — and of all the figures discussed in this study, Adorno's thinking was most indelibly marked by the catastrophe — evades the fate that befalls art after Auschwitz, and legitimates the polemics waged in his name, by staging the catastrophe *as art*.

The polemic that raised tempers in Berlin to such a pitch that Adorno, writing to Peter Szondi to offer him the dedication of the essay, felt obliged to warn him that the honor might endanger his chances of securing a professorship, has long since faded into history.[145] As the dust settles on the battlefield, the sense of irreconcilable antagonism that once attached to the names of Adorno and Heidegger has come to seem ever more questionable. The personal and ideological opposition that stood in the way of any *rapprochement* in their lifetime has given way to a more nuanced understanding of the two thinkers' historical contemporaneity and philosophical proximity. Not without reason was the first full-length study devoted to the topic subtitled "investigation of a philosophical refusal of communication."[146] According to its author, a *disinclination* to communicate, a politically overdetermined *unwillingness* to perceive the other's position served to hamper dialogue, rather than any inherent incapacity. Shared thematic interests — a similar valuation of the artistic sublime,[147] a tendency to think in gnostic categories,[148] an obsession with catastrophe,[149] a fascination with the unsayable,[150] a lack of interest in the question of justified power and domination,[151] an ambivalence toward myth,[152] an ahistorical substructure underlying and belying their respective philosophies of history[153] — have become much more obvious over time. The possibility cannot be dismissed out of hand that such commonalities, which Adorno was clear-sighted enough to admit in private,[154] might inform even the public performance of their abnegation. Adorno's vituperative confrontation of polemical and ontological understandings in "Parataxis" may serve both to mask and to indicate a deeper consensus concerning the polemic itself.

Heidegger's most sustained reflection on the polemic is to be found in his 1934/35 lecture series on Hölderlin, in which he attributes a different "fundamental mood" or *Grundstimmung* to each of the two poems he examines. Taking his cue from the Heraclitean fragment on the strife that engenders and commands the universe, Heidegger defines the *Grundstimmung* in terms of the reciprocal relationality of conflictual powers, neither of which precedes its attunement in the *Stimmung*. The agonistic tension of these powers determines their essence and sets limits on their freedom; better, it decides in the first place what they are free to do, and it is thus properly productive of the poem in which their struggle is fought out.[155] Heidegger gives the name "Feind-seligkeit" — philopolemology, following Derrida's coinage — to the *Grundstimmung* of "Der Rhein," the second poem analyzed in the lecture course. The conflict here holds sway between *der Ursprung*, the origin seeking to hold back the impetuous young Rhine, and *das Entsprungene*, the river-spirit surging forth from the origin to cut its way toward the sea. Although the river succeeds in breaking free of its bondage, it will never be able to rid itself of its origin, which instead secretly determines every one of its later bends and narrows. In departing from the origin, the river only confirms its supremacy; but in order to demonstrate that supremacy, the origin must already have been broken with, left behind, even forgotten. The origin, that is to say, requires *history*, which for Heidegger is always that of the removal from, and potential repetitive recuperation of, an origin so overwhelming it first had to be put at a distance. At the source of history, as the source of history, stands the *pólemos:*

> In this chiasmatic reciprocity there reigns an original hostility [*Feindschaft*], which, however, because it is not a breaking apart of opposites, but rather their originary unity, has the character of a blissfulness [*Seligkeit*] — *Feind-seligkeit* — if we can give to this word this countervailing meaning [*widerwendigen Sinn*] of opposition and inclination.[156]

Heidegger does not hesitate to identify this "blissfulness [*Seligkeit*], which is nonetheless only and authentically the blissfulness of hostility [*Feindseligkeit*]" with "inwardness itself, Being."[157] Being (is) polemical.

The gap separating Heidegger's *widerwendingen Sinn*, which is not to be explained, only understood,[158] from Adorno's *Widersinn*, which is to be understood only insofar as it resists explanation, is at once infinitely vast and infinitesimally small. On the one hand, an untraversable void opens up between the origin that spews forth history and the catastrophe that devours it, between the anaphora of the great beginning and the prolepsis of the apocalyptic end, between "Germania" and "Auschwitz."[159] The events marked by these epochal names feature on different calendars, accord Hölderlin incompatible positions in the story of art, and give rise to mutually exclusive accounts of the world-historical significance of the Nazi dictatorship; to that extent one may speak of non-communication. Adorno is also right to suggest that Heidegger understands the polemic ontologically. Adorno's complaint would be that in conflating polemic and origin, Heidegger seeks to appropriate for idealism the greatest threat to idealism, transforming the last refuge of the non-identical into the generative principle of identity.[160] On the other hand, the fact that Heidegger's polemic is poles apart from Adorno's indicates that their non-communication may itself be polemical, that is, that their conflictual bipolarity reproduces externally the internal structure of the polemic described by both in near-identical terms. Both polemics have as their corollary the caesura of history, leaving the diagnostician of modernity stranded in an entropic post-histoire in which nothing new can ever happen. Adorno and Heidegger would then be communicating on the polemic, and thus on Hölderlin, precisely through their refusal to communicate; the refusal dis/closes communication.

This hypothesis may be tested by reexamining the concept that has shadowed the polemic from the beginning, the concept of salvation. "Only a god can save us," Heidegger famously intoned in the *Spiegel* interview from 1966. Less well known is a remark made by Adorno at the height of the student unrest three years later, likewise in conversation with *Der Spiegel:* "There's a sentence in Grabbe that reads: 'For nothing but despair alone can save us.' That is provocative, but not at all stupid."[161] What is the difference, if any, between these uncannily similar attempts to envisage an uncertain escape from a state of damnation assumed to be both certain and inescapable? Although Heidegger's oracular saying has been the subject of much speculation, his numerous other comments on the matter leave little doubt that he conceives salvation in terms of the destinal sending of Being. In the *Beiträge*, for instance, he asserts that "a *salvation* of beings" is not to be brought about through an act of will, collective or otherwise, but is possible "*only out of the deepest* ground of Being itself."[162] Because Hölderlin is the founder of Being in a time of need, the lone voice whose song fills with holy mourning the distended interval between the departure of the gods and the arrival of the god to come, a vigilant preparedness for the grace of Being goes hand in hand with an attentiveness to Hölderlin's poetry. And if the deepest ground of Being is polemical, as Heidegger's early lectures on Hölderlin maintain, then Heidegger's savior, far from bearing the Christian insignia of the prince of peace, gifts the recovery of the bliss (*Seligkeit*) of an originary hostility (*Feindseligkeit*) that has descended, over the course of Occidental history, into the current twilight of nihilism, total war, and unbridled technologism. Heidegger's salvation designates just such a destinal turning from a destructive to a productive polemology.[163]

The adage cited by Adorno likewise establishes an intimate connection between polemic and salvation. Despair, Adorno observes in *Negative Dialektik*, requires its opposite in order to be thought in the first place: "The disturbed and damaged course of the world . . . resists all attempts of a desperate consciousness to posit despair as an absolute."[164] Despair is never "nothing but despair alone," as Grabbe wrote, for were it entirely trapped in hellish immanence, it would prove incapable of recognizing itself as despair, and hence as needful of salvation. In order to posit the present situation as one of objective despair, Adorno must already have gleaned from it signs of hope for something better. Any statement that we find ourselves in such a situation thus tends intrinsically to overstatement, qualifying despair in the moment of its unqualified ascertainment. Two premises can be culled from the above: First, only unmitigated despair can save us; and second, unmitigated despair is impossible. The logician would be forced to complete the syllogism by concluding that nothing can save us, that we are beyond salvation. From this viewpoint, Grabbe's doubly emphatic demand must appear untenable, if not downright absurd. Adorno nonetheless stands by it, insisting it is "not at all stupid," because the failed attempt to think nothing-but-despair, coupled with an insight into the necessity of that failure, leads to the empowering realization that the present, no matter how desperately bad it may be, must contain concealed within it the seeds of its salvation. Driven to an extreme, despair turns into its own antidote, vindicating the hyperbolic pessimism for which Adorno was often reproached.[165] Herein lies the philosophical legitimation for Adorno's legitimation of philosophy in the closing section of *Minima Moralia*: "The only philosophy which can be responsibly practiced in face of despair is the attempt to contemplate all things as they would present themselves from the standpoint of redemption."[166] Grabbe's aphorism epitomizes the *Widersinn* of a matter that makes sense in making no sense at all, a hope nourished through the renunciation of hope, a salvation made possible through the impossibility of salvation — a state of affairs we have learned to regard as being typically polemical. In the context of the interview, the quotation is also polemical in the more obvious sense that it represents a retort to the student movement whose revolutionary élan Adorno could not share, whose actionist methods he greeted with skepticism, and whose leaders were accusing him at the time of betraying their cause.

Both Heidegger's and Adorno's recipes for salvation can be read as glosses on Hölderlin's formula:

Wo aber Gefahr ist, wächst
Das Rettende auch

[But where danger threatens
That which saves from it also grows].[167]

For both, the danger lies above all in the forgetting of the danger, in the need of needlessness (Heidegger) or denial of despair (Adorno) of a postwar West Germany more preoccupied with the profane goals of affluence and political stability than with its own redemption. Once the danger has been recognized and accepted, the saving power that grows alongside it will also reveal itself: in the *pólemos* of the origin on the one hand, in the contra-sensical polemic on the other. But while Heidegger and Adorno may be saying much the same thing here, they are not saying it in the same way, and that makes all the difference. Whereas Heidegger's statement bespeaks a resigned mysticism, Adorno adopts a self-consciously provocative pose; whereas Heidegger relieves his readers of responsibility for their spiritual convalescence, Adorno prescribes them a grueling course of homeopathic treatment; whereas Heidegger encourages complacency, Adorno expressly forbids it. Taken together, their professions of faith succinctly indicate why these in many respects so like-minded thinkers found it impossible to communicate with each other, and why this non-communication nonetheless represents a form of communication. With good reason enemies during their lifetime, Heidegger and Adorno now appear to be polemicizing from out of the same *Grundstimmung*. Their disembodied, antagonistic voices rise and commingle in the interminable mourning of modernity.

Notes

[1] On the immediate background to this attack, see Adorno's letter to Gershom Sholem from 17 April 1963, in Scholem, *Briefe II: 1948–1970*, ed. Thomas Sparr (Munich: C. H. Beck, 1995), 269.

[2] "Die guten Titel sind so nahe an der Sache, daß sie deren Verborgenheit achten; daran freveln die intentionierten." Adorno, *GS* 11:327.

[3] Herrmann Mörchen, *Adorno und Heidegger: Untersuchung einer philosophischen Kommunikationsverweigerung* (Stuttgart: Klett-Cotta, 1981).

[4] Wolfgang Binder, "Bericht über die Diskussion," *HJb* 13 (1963–64): 178.

[5] Gerhard van den Bergh, *Adornos philosophisches Deuten von Dichtung. Ästhetische Theorie und Praxis der Interpretation: Der Hölderlin-Essay als Modell* (Bonn: Bouvier, 1989), 233. In his 1968 introductory lectures on sociology, Adorno remarked that his differences with Staiger were so extreme that the possibility of discussion was ruled out in advance. Adorno, *Einleitung in die Soziologie*, ed. Christoph Gödde (Frankfurt am Main: Suhrkamp, 1993), 257.

[6] See Robert Minder, "Heidegger und Hebbel oder die Sprache von Meßkirch," in Minder, *"Holderlin unter den Deutschen" und andere Aufsätze zur deutschen Literatur* (Frankfurt am Main: Suhrkamp, 1968), 86–153.

[7] Jochen Schmidt, "Stellungnahme," *Deutsche Vierteljahresschrift* 63 (1989): 684.

8 Van den Bergh, *Adornos philosophisches Deuten von Dichtung,* 145.

9 Binder, "Bericht über die Diskussion," 185.

10 Personal E-mail from Prof. Jochen Schmidt, 18 April 2001.

11 Wolfgang Binder, "Hölderlins Namenssymbolik," *HJb* 11 (1958–60): 95–204.

12 Adorno, *GS* 11:452–53; *Notes to Literature,* trans. Shierry Weber Nicholsen, 2 vols. (New York: Columbia UP, 1992), 2:114.

13 Benzler, "Bericht über die Jahresversammlung in Berlin," *HJb* 13 (1963/64): 172–84.

14 Binder, "Bericht über die Diskussion," 186.

15 Conversation with Prof. Bernhard Böschenstein, Sept. 2003.

16 See Bernhard Böschenstein, "Arbeit an Hölderlins Griechenland. Zwei Tage im März 1959 am Rötebuckweg," in *"Voll Verdienst, doch dichterisch wohnet / Der Mensch auf dieser Erde": Heidegger und Hölderlin,* ed. Peter Trawny (Frankfurt am Main: Klostermann, 2000), 221–26.

17 Jochen Schmidt, "Stellungnahme," 684.

18 One of the Furies.

19 Quoted in Stefan Müller-Doohm, *Adorno: Eine Biographie* (Frankfurt am Main: Suhrkamp, 2003), 548.

20 "kritische und utopische." Adorno, *GS* 11:454; Adorno, *Notes to Literature,* 2:115.

21 "Hölderlin hat nicht mitgespielt." Adorno, *GS* 11:467; *Notes to Literature* 2:127.

22 "Die allzu früh [von Heidegger] behauptete Wirklichkeit des Dichterischen unterschlägt die Spannung von Hölderlins Dichtung zur Wirklichkeit und neutralisiert sein Werk zum Einverständnis mit dem Schicksal." Adorno, *GS* 11:454; *Notes to Literature* 2:115.

23 Michel Foucault, "Polemics, Politics, and Problematizations," in *Ethics: Subjectivity and Truth,* ed. Paul Rabinow (London: Penguin, 2000), 112.

24 Even Szondi, the essay's dedicatee, expressed reservations, criticizing in particular its analysis of the relationship, central in Hölderlin's late work, between antiquity and Christianity. See Peter Szondi, *Briefe,* ed. Christoph König and Thomas Sparr (Frankfurt am Main: Suhrkamp, 1993), 135–36. Peter Fenves is probably right to argue that Adorno commits exactly the same blunders he criticizes in his opponent: "discovering in the poetry what had already been given out as philosophy; making the poet into the exponent of the very same philosophical theses. . . that the philosopher elsewhere lays down; turning the poet into a witness for philosophy. Adorno becomes the specular double of the Heidegger whom he attacks." Peter Fenves, "Measure for Measure: Hölderlin and the Place of Philosophy," in *The Solid Letter: Readings of Friedrich Hölderlin,* ed. Aris Fioretos (Stanford: Stanford UP, 1999), 30. Similarly, Dieter Henrich maintains that "Adorno uses Hölderlin as no more than an occasion for the pure employment of aesthetic categories, which, unlike the elements in Heidegger's thought, are forged directly from Hegelian material. . . . Adorno's notes on Hölderlin are based on nothing more than scattered

observations. Adorno never seriously considers the structural form of a single one of the poems." Dieter Henrich, *The Course of Remembrance and Other Essays on Hölderlin*, ed. Eckart Förster (Stanford: Stanford UP, 1997), 300–301.

[25] Jacques Derrida, "Heidegger's Ear: Philopolemology (*Geschlecht* IV)," trans. John P. Leavey, in *Reading Heidegger: Commemorations*, ed. John Sallis (Bloomington: Indiana UP, 1993): 160–217.

[26] "Wer heute philosophische Arbeit als Beruf wählt, muß von Anfang an auf die Illusion verzichten, mit der früher die philosophischen Entwürfe einsetzten: daß es möglich sei, in Kraft des Denkens die Totalität des Wirklichen zu ergreifen." Adorno, *GS* 1:325; Adorno, "The Actuality of Philosophy," trans. Benjamin Snow, in *The Adorno Reader*, ed. Brian O'Connor (Oxford: Blackwell, 2000), 24.

[27] "Keine rechtfertigende Vernunft könnte sich selbst in einer Wirklichkeit wiederfinden, deren Ordnung und Gehalt jeden Anspruch der Vernunft niederschlägt; allein polemisch bietet sie dem Erkennenden als ganze Wirklichkeit sich dar." Adorno, *GS* 1:325; "The Actuality of Philosophy," 24; translation modified.

[28] "exakte Fantasie." Adorno, *GS* 1:342. For a useful discussion of the term, see Shierry Weber Nicholsen, *Exact Imagination, Late Work: Adorno's Aesthetics* (Cambridge, MA: MIT P, 1997), 4–5.

[29] In the lectures entitled "Philosophical Terminology" held around the same time as the "Parataxis" speech, Adorno defined philosophy as "die Anstrengung des Begriffs, die Wunden zu heilen, die der Begriff notwendig schlägt" (the straining of the concept to heal the wounds it has of necessity itself inflicted). Adorno, *Philosophische Terminologie*, vol. 1 (Frankfurt am Main: Suhrkamp, 1973), 55–56. Adorno is paraphrasing Hegel here.

[30] "Widerruf der Synthesis aus der Bewegung des Geistes selber." *GS* 11:486–87; *Notes to Literature* 2:144.

[31] "Der Titel 'Stichworte' mahnt an die enzyklopädische Form als jene, die systemlos, diskontinuierlich darstellt, was durch Einheit der Erfahrung zur Konstellation zusammenschießt. So wie in dem kleinen Band mit einigermaßen willkürlich ausgewählten Stichworten verfahren wird, wäre allenfalls ein neues Dictionnaire philosophique denkbar. Die Assoziationen mit Polemik, die der Titel mit sich führt, sind dem Autor willkommen." Adorno, *GS* 10.2:598; Adorno, *Critical Models: Interventions and Catchwords*, trans. Henry W. Pickford (New York: Columbia UP, 1998), 126; translation modified.

[32] The book appeared in bookshops immediately after his death; see the editorial afterword in Adorno, *GS* 10.2:838.

[33] Hektor Rottweiler was a pseudonym mostly used by Adorno in articles from the 1920s, which he also briefly revived in the 1950s.

[34] Ludger Lütkehaus, "Mangel an Güte, objektive Solidarität," *Die Zeit* 16 (10 Apr. 2003), 17.

[35] *GS* 10.2:684; *Critical Models*, 199. In the cited passage, Adorno makes such thinking partially responsible for "Auschwitz."

[36] "hochtrabende Kalauer." Adorno, *GS* 11:453; *Notes to Literature* 2:114; translation modified.

[37] His *Philosophie der neuen Musik* (Philosophy of the New Music, 1949) is the only other text that bears comparison in this respect.

[38] "Die sprachliche Verfahrungsweise findet sich mit dem Antisubjektivismus des Gehalts zusammen. Sie revidiert die trügende mittlere Synthesis vom Extrem, von der Sprache her; korrigiert den Vorrang des Subjekts als des Organons solcher Synthesis. Hölderlins Vorgehen legt Rechenschaft davon ab, daß das Subjekt, das sich als Unmittelbares und Letztes verkennt, durchaus ein Vermitteltes sei. Diese unabsehbar folgenreiche Veränderung ist jedoch polemisch zu verstehen, nicht ontologisch; nicht so, als ob die im Opfer der subjektiven Intention bekräftigte Sprache an sich, schlechterdings jenseits des Subjekts wäre. Indem die Sprache die Fäden zum Subjekt durchschneidet, redet sie für das Subjekt, das von sich aus — Hölderlin war wohl der erste, dessen Kunst das ahnte — nicht mehr reden kann." Adorno, *GS* 11:478; *Notes to Literature* 2:137; translation modified.

[39] "Wie zu lesen sei." Adorno, *GS* 5:326.

[40] "immanente Analyse von Dichtung." Adorno, *GS* 11:450–51; *Notes to Literature* 2:112.

[41] "Der Heideggerschen Methode wäre keine andere abstrakt zu kontrastieren." Adorno, *GS* 11:468; *Notes to Literature* 2:128.

[42] This distinction, it might be added, was already implicit to "Die Aktualität der Philosophie," a text provoked by Adorno's critical reception of *Daseinsphilosophie.*

[43] "Todesurteil." Adorno, *GS* 11:463; *Notes to Literature* 2:122.

[44] For example, Heidegger, *GA* 10:143.

[45] "Was wahr und möglich ist als Dichtung, kann es nicht buchstäblich und unge- brochen als Philosophie sein." Adorno, *GS* 11:453; *Notes to Literature* 2:114.

[46] "Konformismus." Adorno, *GS* 11:478; *Notes to Literature* 2:37.

[47] "Damit zergeht der Schein, die Sprache wäre schon dem Subjekt angemessen, oder es wäre die sprachlich erscheinende Wahrheit identisch mit der erscheinenden Subjektivität." Adorno, *GS* 11:478; *Notes to Literature* 2:137.

[48] Adorno, *GS* 11:480n; *Notes to Literature* 2:340n.

[49] On the "expressivist turn," see Charles Taylor, *Sources of the Self: The Making of the Modern Identity* (Cambridge MA: Harvard UP, 1989), 368–90.

[50] "Der idealische Hölderlin inauguriert jenen Prozeß, der in die sinnleeren Protokollsätze Becketts mündet." Adorno, *GS* 11:478–79; *Notes to Literature* 2:137.

[51] "What fascinates Adorno in Hölderlin's paratactic poetry," remarks Brunkhorst, "are the aesthetic extensions of the autonomy of the modern subject." Hauke Brunkhorst, *Theodor W. Adorno: Dialektik der Moderne* (Munich: Piper, 1990), 204.

[52] "aus subjektiver Freiheit." Adorno, *GS* 11:478.

[53] "Die Bahn von dessen bestimmter Negation ist . . . die zum Wahrheitsgehalt"; "Stoffschicht." Adorno, *GS* 11:451; *Notes to Literature* 2:112.

[54] "daß jegliches Werk rein aus sich verstanden werden will, aber keines rein aus sich verstanden werden kann." Adorno, *GS* 11:451; *Notes to Literature* 2:112.

[55] "nichts auf der Erde und nichts im leeren Himmel ist dadurch zu retten, daß man es verteidigt. . . . Nichts kann unverwandelt gerettet werden, nichts, das nicht

das Tor seines Todes durchschritten hätte." Adorno, *GS* 6:384; in English, Adorno, *Negative Dialectics*, trans. E. B. Ashton (New York: Seabury, 1973), 391–92; translation modified.

[56] Cf. Rolf Tiedemann, "Concept, Image, Name: On Adorno's Utopia of Knowledge," in *The Semblance of Subjectivity: Essays in Adorno's Aesthetic Theory*, ed. Tom Huhn and Lambert Zuidevaart (Cambridge, MA: MIT P, 1997), 123–45.

[57] "Die absolute Befreiung des Besonderen von der Allgemeinheit macht es durch die polemische und prinzipielle Beziehung auf diese selber zu einem Allgemeinen." Adorno, *GS* 12:53.

[58] "sedimentierter Inhalt." Adorno, *GS* 11:469; *Notes to Literature* 2:128.

[59] "die Rettung des Scheins"; "das Zentrum von Ästhetik"; "das emphatische Recht der Kunst, die Legitimation ihrer Wahrheit, hängt von jener Rettung ab." Adorno, *GS* 7:164; English translation from Adorno, *Aesthetic Theory*, trans. Robert Hullot-Kentor (London: Athlone, 1997), 107.

[60] "Die Frage nach der Wahrheit eines Gemachten ist . . . keine andere als die nach dem Schein und nach seiner Errettung als des Scheins von Wahrem." Adorno, *GS* 7:198; *Aesthetic Theory*, 131. See also J. M. Bernstein, *The Fate of Art: Aesthetic Alienation from Kant to Derrida and Adorno* (Cambridge: Polity, 1992), 252.

[61] These distinctions are unfolded in Martin Seel, *Aesthetics of Appearing*, trans. John Farrell (Stanford, CA: Stanford UP, 2005).

[62] Bernstein, *The Fate of Art*, 269. See also J. M. Bernstein, "Why Rescue Semblance? Metaphysical Experience and the Possibility of Ethics," in *The Semblance of Subjectivity: Essays in Adorno's Aesthetic Theory*, ed. Tom Huhn and Lambert Zuidevaart. (Cambridge MA: MIT P, 1997), 177–212.

[63] Albrecht Wellmer writes of the "polemical relationship of art to reality" in Adorno's thought. Albrecht Wellmer, "Wahrheit, Schein, Versöhnung: Adornos ästhetische Rettung der Modernität," in *Adorno-Konferenz 1983*, ed. Ludwig von Friedeburg and Jürgen Habermas (Frankfurt am Main: Suhrkamp, 1983), 143. Moreover, Adorno holds that each individual artwork polemicizes against the institution of art. Asked to name the ten greatest novels of German literature, Adorno replies: "Ein Kunstwerk ist der Todfeind des anderen und möchte kein anderes neben sich haben" (Every work of art is the deadly enemy of every other and cannot stand to have any other near it; Adorno, *GS* 20:736).

[64] "Er verherrlicht den Dichter, überästhetisch, als Stifter, ohne das Agens der Form konkret zu reflektieren." Adorno, *GS* 11:452; *Notes to Literature* 2:114.

[65] "geschichtsphilosophische Sonnenuhr." Adorno, *GS* 11:60. The image is taken from Lukács's *Theorie des Romans* (Theory of the Novel). The following passage of the book, which influenced Adorno greatly, may also have spurred his thoughts on the polemical nature of modern art: "A totality that can be simply accepted is no longer given to the forms of art: therefore they must either narrow down and volatilise whatever has to be given form to the point where they can encompass it, or else they must show polemically the impossibility of achieving their necessary object and the inner nullity of their own means." Lukács, *The Theory of the Novel*, trans. Anna Bostock (London: Merlin, 1971), 38–39.

[66] "allen Perorationen über die Geschichtlichkeit zum Trotz." Adorno, *GS* 11:461; *Notes to Literature* 2:121.

[67] "geschichtliche[r] Kern des Wahrheitsgehalts selber" Adorno, *GS* 11:461; *Notes to Literature* 2:121; translation modified.

[68] See Adorno, *GS* 11:447; *Notes to Literature* 2:109. "Die großen Werke warten" (The great works wait) Adorno writes in *Ästhetische Theorie*. Adorno, *GS* 7:67.

[69] "Was in den Werken sich entfaltet und sichtbar wird, wodurch sie an Autorität gewinnen, ist nichts anderes als die objektiv in ihnen erscheinende Wahrheit." Adorno, *GS* 11:449; *Notes to Literature* 2:110.

[70] "Eine Geschichte der Kritik Beethovens könnte dartun, wie mit jeder neuen Schicht des kritischen Bewußtseins von ihm auch neue Schichten seines Werks selbst sich enthüllten, in gewissem Sinn durch jenen Prozeß überhaupt erst sich konstituierten." Adorno, *Einleitung in die Musiksoziologie* (Frankfurt am Main: Suhrkamp, 1975), 179. The metaphor applies quite literally in the case of Hölderlin. A comparative study of editions of his late work from Hellingrath to Burdorf could demonstrate how differing conceptions of the poetized rebound upon the material constitution of the poem. In Beißner the textual layers discarded by Hellingrath as inessential find their way into the critical apparatus; in Sattler they are superimposed upon the "final version." In each case an underlying interpretation produces the poem that inspired it.

[71] "hat Geschichte rückwirkende Kraft." Adorno, *GS* 11:432. Compare Freud: "Whenever someone gives an account of a past event . . . we must take into account what he unintentionally puts back into the past from the present or from some intermediate time, *thus falsifying his picture of it* [my italics]. In the case of a neurotic it is even a question whether this putting back is an entirely unintentional one." Sigmund Freud, *Introductory Lectures on Psychoanalysis*, trans. James Strachey (Harmondsworth, UK: Penguin, 1973), 379.

[72] See Fred Dallmayr, *The Other Heidegger* (Ithaca, NY: Cornell UP, 1993), 176; Christopher Fynsk, *Heidegger: Thought and Historicity* (Ithaca, NY: Cornell UP, 1986), 204; Marc Froment-Meurice, *That Is to Say: Heidegger's Poetics*, trans. Jan Plug (Stanford, CA: Stanford UP, 1998), chap. 5.

[73] "Nach dem Maß seiner eigenen Schriftstellerei darf Kierkegaard nicht siegen." Adorno, *GS* 2:239.

[74] "Aus jenem Einzelnen ist das verlogene Gerede geworden, das damit sich brüstet, die anderen seien uneigentlich und dem Gerede verfallen. Besiegelt wurde das, als ihn in Deutschland vor 1933 der Nationalsozialist Emanuel Hirsch in Generalpacht nahm: Sieg als Niederlage"; "Die Bahn solchen Sieges ist die einer sich entfaltenden Unwahrheit von Kierkegaards Lehrgehalt." Adorno, *GS* 2:244.

[75] "Seitdem die Georgeschule die Ansicht von Hölderlin als einem stillen und feinen Nebenpoeten mit rührender vita zerstört hat, wuchs fraglos wie der Ruhm auch das Verständnis sehr an." Adorno, *GS* 11:447; *Notes to Literature* 2:109.

[76] Adorno, *GS* 3:236. Similarly, Benjamin argues that fascism's chance "consists not least in the fact that in the name of progress its opponents treat it as an historical norm." Benjamin, *Gesammelte Schriften*, ed. Rolf Tiedemann und Herrmann Schweppenhäuser (1974), 1.2:697.

77 Peter Sloterdijk, *Kritik der zynischen Vernunft* (Frankfurt am Main: Suhrkamp, 1983), 1:53.

78 "bis in ihre innersten Zellen faschistisch." Adorno, *GS* 19:638. For a detailed discussion of this reproach, see Philippe Lacoue-Labarthe, *Heidegger: Art and Politics*, trans. Chris Turner (Oxford: Blackwell, 1990).

79 On other occasions, Adorno compares his role in relation to Heidegger to that of the little boy in Andersen's tale of the Emperor's new clothes. See, for example, Adorno, *Ontologie und Dialektik*, ed. Rolf Tiedemann (Frankfurt am Main: Suhrkamp, 2002), 232. In both cases, an outsider breaks the spell cast by a figure who until then had unquestioningly been granted an audience, by bringing that audience to see reason. The allusion to the court ceremony of Todtnauberg, to the nimbus of regal dignity cultivated by Heidegger and his followers, should also not be ignored.

80 "Der Hölderlin-Kultus der deutschen Rechten." Adorno, *GS* 11:458; *Notes to Literature* 2:119.

81 Adorno, *GS* 7:541; *Aesthetic Theory*, 364.

82 I disregard Adorno's early musical setting of Hölderlin's poem "An Zimmern."

83 "Auf eine an Hegel mahnende Weise sind Vermittlungen des vulgären Typus, ein Mittleres außerhalb der Momente, die es verbinden soll, als äußerlich und unwesentlich eliminiert, wie vielfach in Beethovens Spätstil; nicht zuletzt das verleiht Hölderlins später Dichtung ihr Antiklassizistisches, gegen Harmonie sich Sträubendes. Das Gereihte ist als Unverbundenes schroff nicht weniger denn gleitend. Vermittlung wird ins Vermittelte selbst gelegt anstatt zu überbrücken. Jede der beiden Strophen der 'Hälfte des Lebens' bedarf, wie Beißner und neuerdings Szondi betont haben, in sich ihres Gegenteils. Auch darin erweist Inhalt und Form bestimmbar sich als eines; die inhaltliche Antithese von sinnhafter Liebe und Geschlagenheit bricht, um Ausdruck zu werden, ebenso die Strophen auseinander, wie umgekehrt die parataktische Form den Schnitt zwischen den Hälften des Lebens selbst erst vollzieht." Adorno, *GS* 11:473; *Notes to Literature* 2:132–33.

84 See Benjamin, *Gesammelte Schriften*, 1.1:129.

85 See in particular Adorno's reading of the ode "Natur und Kunst," Adorno, *GS* 11:482; *Notes to Literature* 2:140–41.

86 Hellingrath's term "harte Fügung" is apposite here; Adorno cites it approvingly in a footnote. See Adorno, *GS* 11: 474n; *Notes to Literature* 2:340n.

87 Hölderlin, *StA* 2:117.

88 "Vorsatz, der Synthesis sich zu entschlagen, der reinen Passivität sich anzuvertrauen, um Gegenwart ganz zu erfüllen." Adorno, *GS* 11:487; *Notes to Literature* 2:142.

89 Hölderlin, *StA* 2:117.

90 Hölderlin, *StA* 2:117.

91 "Während indessen die Hölderlinsche Dichtung, gleich jeder nachdrücklichen, der Philosophie als des Mediums bedarf, das ihren Wahrheitsgehalt zutage fördert, taugt dazu ebensowenig der Rekurs auf eine wie immer auch ihn beschlagnahmende." Adorno, *GS* 11:452; *Notes to Literature* 2:113.

[92] "Seine fernen Phatasmata des Nahen lassen sich nicht in der Schatzkammer von Heimatkunst sich horten." Adorno, *GS* 11:467; *Notes to Literature* 2:126.

[93] See Walter Benjamin, *Gesammelte Briefe III*, ed. Christoph Gödde and Henri Lonitz (Frankfurt am Main: Suhrkamp, 1996), 522.

[94] The opening salvo was launched in 1960/61 with a lecture course, "Ontology and Dialectics"; the barrage culminated in 1966 with the appearance of Adorno's philosophical magnum opus, *Negative Dialectics*, petering out to the occasional potshot in the works that followed. The corpus of anti-Heideggeriana that emerged from Frankfurt during this period also included a series of talks held in Paris and Rome in early 1961 that set out "to unmask Heidegger once and for all" ("Merleau-Ponty shocked," Adorno noted in his diary afterwards), and the influential *Jargon der Eigentlichkeit*, published in 1964 and conceived as a pamphlet against the rhetoric of the German existentialists and their epigones. While the broad acceptance met with by his efforts doubtless testified to Adorno's polemical talent, the apparent ease of his victory showed that the assault may have come too late. The wave of popularity enjoyed by Heidegger during the 1950s was already beginning to ebb by the time Adorno embarked upon his crusade, while the productive reception taking place across the Rhine remained deaf to his warnings, notwithstanding his personal appearance in Paris. Certainly, to maintain, as he did in "Parataxis," that contemporary Hölderlin interpretation clung heteronomously "in large measure . . . upon the unquestioned authority of a thought that sought out Hölderlin's of its own accord" (Adorno, *GS* 11:452; *Notes to Literature* 2:114) was to indulge in a wild and potentially insulting exaggeration of Heidegger's hold upon his audience. Even those few scholars who stood close to Heidegger, such as Binder and Staiger, were by no means willing to believe his every word.

[95] "Nur in diesem Verhältnis konstituiert sich, was Philosophie an Dichtung hoffen darf, ohne Gewalt zu ergreifen." Adorno, *GS* 11:469; *Notes to Literature* 2:128.

[96] The poetized is defined there as the "synthetic unity of the intellectual and perceptual orders" of the poem, which, as *synthetic* unity, forms as much the "product" as the "subject of the investigation." Benjamin, *Werke*, 2.1:105–6; *Selected Writings*, trans. Stanley Corngold, ed. Michael W. Jennings et al., 4 vols. (Cambridge, MA: Harvard UP, 1996–2003), 1:18–19. On this essay and its influence on "Parataxis," see especially Alexander Honold, *Der Leser Walter Benjamin: Bruchstücke einer deutschen Literaturgeschichte* (Berlin: Verlag Vorwerk 8, 2000), chap. 2; Peter-André Alt, "Das Problem der inneren Form: Zur Hölderlin-Rezeption Benjamins und Adornos," *Deutsche Vierteljahresschrift* 61.3 (1987): 531–63.

[97] "Daß aber auch die Beteuerung unartikulierter Einheit von Form und Inhalt nicht länger zureicht, zeigt kaum an einem ästhetischen Gegenstand sich eindringlicher als an Hölderlin. Nur als gespannter zwischen ihren Momenten ist solche Einheit zu denken; sie sind zu unterscheiden, wenn sie im Gehalt zusammenstimmen sollen, schlechthin Getrenntes weder noch indifferent Identisches." Adorno, *GS* 11:469; *Notes to Literature* 2:128.

[98] Benjamin, *The Origin of German Tragic Drama*, trans. John Osborne (London: New Left Books, 1977), 28.

⁹⁹ The manuscript was published upon Adorno's return from exile as *Versuch über Wagner*. See Carl Dahlhaus, *Richard Wagners Musikdramen* (Stuttgart: Philip Reclam, 1996), 7: "And even today, those who write on Wagner still tend to extremes: to polemic or to apology (it may suffice to recall the books of Theodor W. Adorno, on the one hand, and Curt von Westernhagen, on the other)."

¹⁰⁰ An allusion to Adorno's libretto *Der Schatz des Indianer Joe* (The Treasure of Indian Joe), but also, no doubt, to his already virulent philopolemology.

¹⁰¹ "Eine polemische Befassung mit Wagner schließt in keiner Weise die Durchleuchtung der progressiven Elemente seines Werkes, die Sie vornehmen, aus, zumal diese sich von den regressiven sowenig wie die Schafe von den Böcken scheiden lassen. Wohl aber — und hier, lieber Teddie, dürften Sie mich mit Leib und Seele bei *Ihrem* Lieblings- und Indianerspiel, dem Ausgraben des Kriegsbeils, überraschen — erweist sich die geschichtsphilosophische Perspektive der Rettung, wie mir scheinen will, mit der kritischen der Pro- und Regressionen als unvereinbar. . . . Sie sind gewiß nicht willens, mir zu widersprechen wenn ich sage, daß die Rettung als philosophische Tendenz eine schriftstellerische Form bedingt, die . . . mit der musikalischen besondere Verwandtschaft hat. Die Rettung ist eine zyklische Form, die polemische eine progressive. . . . Das Bestimmende in der Rettung — nicht wahr? — ist niemals ein Progressives, es kann dem Regressiven so ähnlich sehen wie das Ziel, das bei Karl Kraus Ursprung heißt." Adorno and Benjamin, *Briefwechsel*, 336–37; in English, *The Complete Correspondence 1928–1940*, trans. Nicholas Walker (Cambridge, MA: Harvard UP, 1999), 258–59; translation modified. In the commentary he devotes to this passage, Richard Leppert claims that Benjamin is "essentially" accusing Adorno of a "lack of mediation": "The progressive aspects of Wagner, though acknowledged by Adorno, are insufficiently set in tension with the regressive tendencies that principally define the study." Richard Leppert, "Commentary" in *Essays on Music*, by Adorno, trans. Susan Gillespie et al., ed. Leppert (Berkeley: U of California P, 2002), 528–31. One must insist, on the contrary, that for Benjamin, the inadequacy of Adorno's polemic against Wagner does not lie in any one-sided, Beckmesserish preoccupation with his blatantly regressive tendencies, nor, correspondingly, in its insufficient illumination of the progressive aspect of Wagner's achievement, but in its continuing indebtedness to a conception of history that operates with precisely these categories. Benjamin's letter makes clear that the *Rettung* he has in mind is to be identified with neither progress nor regress, *both* of which it assigns to the purview of the polemic. As we will see, it is *Adorno* who is essentially (if indirectly) accusing *Benjamin* of a "lack of mediation" — much as he would five months later, this time with all desirable explicitness, in his critique of Benjamin's essay on Baudelaire.

¹⁰² "Jetztzeit." Benjamin, *Gesammelte Schriften*, 1.2:701.

¹⁰³ Benjamin, *Gesammelte Schriften*, 1.2:696.

¹⁰⁴ "This way of looking at things . . . is trying to give a concept of how much it costs our usual way of thinking to come to an idea of history that avoids *any* complicity with the one that these politicians [that is, the social-democratic and liberal politicians who proved powerless to prevent the rise of fascism] continue to hold on to." Benjamin, *Gesammelte Schriften*, 1.2:698; my italics.

¹⁰⁵ Adorno and Benjamin, *Briefwechsel*, 344; *Complete Correspondence*, 265.

[106] "mildernde Umstand"; "daß ich die Motive der Rettung Wagners keineswegs umstandslos auf seine progressiven Züge bezog, sondern überall das Ineins von Progressiv und Regressiv akzentuiert habe." Adorno and Benjamin, *Briefwechsel*, 345; *Complete Correspondence*, 265. See also Adorno's letter to Horkheimer from 29 Nov. 1937, in Adorno and Horkheimer, *Briefwechsel, 1927–1969*, vol. 1: *1927–1937* ed. Christoph Gödde and Henri Lonitz (Frankfurt am Main: Suhrkamp, 2003), 492.

[107] Adorno and Benjamin, *Briefwechsel*, 345; *Complete Correspondence*, 265.

[108] Hölderlin, *StA* 5:195 and 201; *Essays and Letters on Theory*, trans. Thomas Pfau (Albany: State U of New York P, 1988), 101 and 107.

[109] "Dadurch wird in der rhythmischen Aufeinanderfolge der Vorstellungen, worin der Transport sich darstellt, das, was man im Silbenmaße Zäsur heißt, das reine Wort, die gegenrhythmische Unterbrechung notwendig, um nämlich dem reißenden Wechsel der Vorstellungen, auf seinem Summum, so zu begegnen, daß alsdann nicht mehr der Wechsel der Vorstellung, sondern die Vorstellung selber erscheint." Hölderlin, *StA* 5:196; *Essays and Letters on Theory*, 102.

[110] See Hölderlin, *StA* 5:196; *Essays and Letters on Theory*, 101.

[111] In both the Sophoclean plays he translated, Hölderlin located the caesura in the speeches of the prophet Tiresias.

[112] Philippe Lacoue-Labarthe, *Musica Ficta (Figures of Wagner)*, trans. Felicia McCarren (Stanford, CA: Stanford UP, 1994), 141. See also Lacoue-Labarthe, "The Caesura of the Speculative," trans. Christopher Fynsk, in *Typography* (Stanford, CA: Stanford UP, 1998): 208–35.

[113] See Adorno, *Beethoven: Philosophie der Musik*, 102: "Hölderlin hat vom kalkulablen Gesetz der Tragödie gesprochen. Der vorbestimmte Gegenstand dieser Theorie dürfte die Beethovensche Durchführung des symphonischen Typus sein. . . . Darauf ereignet sich das Analogon zum Hölderlinschen Begriff der Zäsur. Es ist der Augenblick des Eingriffs der Subjektivität in die Form" (Hölderlin spoke of the calculable law of tragedy. The predetermined object of this theory was probably the Beethovenian exposition of the symphonic type. . . . From this follows the analogy to Hölderlin's concept of the caesura. It is the moment when subjectivity intervenes in the form).

[114] "das Ausdruckslose"; "eine Kategorie der Sprache und Kunst, nicht des Werkes oder der Gattungen"; "die kritische Gewalt, welche Schein vom Wesen in der Kunst zwar zu trennen nicht vermag, aber ihnen verwehrt, sich zu mischen." Benjamin, *Werke*, 1.1:181–82; *Selected Writings*, 1:340.

[115] "abendländische Junonische Nüchternheit . . . ist nur eine andere Bezeichnung jener Cäsur, in der mit der Harmonie zugleich jeder Ausdruck sich legt, um einer innerhalb aller Kunstmittel ausdruckslosen Gewalt Raum zu geben." Benjamin, *Werke*, 1.1:182; *Selected Writings*, 1:341.

[116] Winfried Menninghaus, *Ekel: Theorie und Geschichte einer starken Empfindung* (Frankfurt am Main: Suhrkamp, 2002), 436.

[117] The other reference is in Adorno, *GS* 11:472; *Notes to Literature* 2:132.

[118] "Dadurch, daß am Ende dieser Zeilen, vermittelt durch ein Aber, auf Schicksal das Stichwort Dank folgt, wird eine Zäsur gesetzt, die sprachliche Konfiguration

bestimmt den Dank als Antithesis zum Schicksal oder, in Hegelscher Sprache, als den qualitativen Sprung, der aus Schicksal, auf es antwortend, herausführt." Adorno, *GS* 11:451–52; *Notes to Literature* 2:113.

[119] "Dem Gehalt nach ist Dank antimythologisch schlechthin, das, was laut wird im Augenblick der Suspension des Immergleichen. Lobt der Dichter das Schicksal, so setzt diesem die Dichtung den Dank entgegen, aus dem eigenen Momentum, ohne daß er es gemeint haben muß." Adorno, *GS* 11:452; *Notes to Literature* 2:113.

[120] "Der Mythos ist die Katastrophe in Permanenz." Adorno, *GS* 16:561; Adorno, "Wagner's Relevance for Today," trans. Susan H. Gillespie, in *Essays on Music*, ed. Richard Leppert, 599.

[121] "Fügsamkeit"; "oberste Passivität." Adorno, *GS* 11:475; *Notes to Literature* 2:134–35.

[122] "Die metaphysische Passivität als Gehalt der Hölderlinschen Dichtung verschränkt sich wider den Mythos mit der Hoffnung auf eine Realität, in welcher die Menschheit jenes Bannes der eigenen Naturbefangenheit ledig wäre, der in ihrer Vorstellung vom absoluten Geiste sich spiegelte." Adorno, *GS* 11:491; *Notes to Literature* 2:149.

[123] Adorno, *GS* 13:139.

[124] See Adorno, *GS* 16:560; "Wagner's Relevance for Today," 598: "Wagner gewährt keine Weltuntergangmusik, wie er sie verheißt; sie fällt ab, löst die Erwartung der obersten Katastrophe nicht ein, die daran sich knüpft" (Wagner conceives no music of world destruction adequate to the one he prophesies. It falls off, fails to fulfill the expectation of the maximal catastrophe that it has aroused).

[125] For Benjamin, the caesura is the force that "completes the work, by shattering it into a thing of shards." *Gesammelte Schriften*, 1.1:181; *Selected Writings*, 1:340.

[126] "Wie jeglicher genuinen Entmythologisierung wohnt dem Gehalt Hölderlins eine mythische Schichte inne." Adorno, *GS* 11:455; *Notes to Literature* 2:116. On modern art as an anticipation of the apocalypse, see also Adorno, *GS* 7:131.

[127] In Adorno, "Parataxis," *GS* 11:456, 473, 477, and 480; elsewhere: Adorno, *Beethoven*, 102 and 268.

[128] See Benjamin's distinction between symbol and allegory in *The Origin of German Tragic Drama*. On Adorno's concept of allegory, see Britta Scholze, *Kunst als Kritik: Adornos Weg aus der Dialektik* (Würzburg: Königshausen & Neumann, 2000), 209–86.

[129] See Adorno, *GS* 7:168.

[130] "Die übliche Ansicht pflegt das damit zu erklären, daß sie Produkte der rücksichtslos sich bekundenden Subjektivität oder lieber noch 'Persönlichkeit' seien, die da um des Ausdrucks ihrer selbst willen das Rund der Form durchbreche." Adorno, *GS* 17:13. On "Spätstil Beethovens," see also Edward Said, "Adorno as Lateness Itself," in *Adorno: A Critical Reader*, ed. Nigel Gibson and Andrew Rubin (Oxford: Blackwell, 2002), 193–208.

[131] "während der 'klassische' Stil es in der Totalität aufhebt und ihm den Schein des Bedeutenden verleiht . . ., tritt jetzt die Nichtigkeit des Individuellen als solche

hervor und macht es zum 'zufälligen' Träger des Allgemeinen. Mit anderen Worten, der Spätstil ist das Selbstbewußtsein von der Nichtigkeit des Individuellen, Daseienden. Darin beruht das Verhältnis des Spätstils zum *Tode.*" Adorno, *Beethoven*, 232–33.

[132] "Die Gewalt der Subjektivität in den späten Kunstwerken ist die auffahrende Geste, mit welcher sie die Kunstwerke verläßt. Sie sprengt sie, nicht um sich auszudrücken, sondern um ausdrucklos den Schein der Kunst abzuwerfen." Adorno, *GS* 17:15.

[133] "Der Spätstil würde bedeuten, daß die Musik der *Grenze* dieser Bewegung innewird — der Unmöglichkeit, kraft der eigenen Logik die Prämisse aufzuheben." Adorno, *Beethoven*, 26.

[134] "Attentat aufs harmonische Kunstwerk." Adorno, *GS* 11:480; *Notes to Literature* 2:139. Adorno held fireworks to be the epitome of aesthetic semblance; see Adorno, *GS* 7:125–26.

[135] On the problem of latency and contingency, see David Roberts, *Art and Enlightenment: Aesthetic Theory after Adorno* (Lincoln: U of Nebraska P, 1991).

[136] "Er sammelt nicht mehr die Landschaft, verlassen jetzt und entfremdet, zum Bilde. Er überstrahlt sie mit dem Feuer, das Subjektivität entzündet, indem sie ausbrechend auf die Wände des Werkes aufprallt, treu der Idee ihrer Dynamik. . . . Subjektivität ist es, welche die Extreme im Augenblick zusammenzwingt. . . . Die Zäsuren aber, das jähe Abbrechen, das mehr als alles andere den letzten Beethoven bezeichnet, sind jene Augenblicke des Ausbruchs; das Werk schweigt, wenn es verlassen wird, und kehrt seine Höhlung nach außen. Dann erst fügt das nächste Bruchstück sich an, vom Befehl der ausbrechenden Subjektivität an seine Stelle gebannt und dem voraufgehenden auf Gedeih und Verderb verschworen; denn das Geheimnis ist zwischen ihnen, und anders läßt es sich nicht beschwören als in der Figur, die sie mitsammen bilden. Das erhellt den Widersinn, daß der letzte Beethoven zugleich subjektiv und objektiv genannt wird. Objektiv ist die brüchige Landschaft, subjektiv das Licht, worin einzig sie erglüht. Er bewirkt nicht deren harmonische Synthese. Er reißt sie, als Macht der Dissoziation, in der Zeit auseinander, um vielleicht fürs Ewige sie zu bewahren. In der Geschichte von Kunst sind Spätwerke die Katastrophen." Adorno, *GS* 17:16–17.

[137] Adorno, "Late Style in Beethoven," trans. Susan H. Gillespie, in Adorno, *Essays on Music*, 564–68; here, 567.

[138] Husserl's example of a nonsensical sentence (*Unsinn*) is "king but or similar and," which, although intelligible in its component parts, cannot be understood as a whole. His example of a contrasensical sentence (*Widersinn*), "A square is round," makes perfect sense as a grammatical construction but suffers from the apriori impossibility of its implied object. Edmund Husserl, *Logische Untersuchungen*, ed. Ursula Panzer (The Hague: Martinus Nijihoff, 1984), 2:342–43.

[139] For an excellent account of Adorno's theory of the (perpetually frustrated) constitution of meaning in aesthetic texts, an account that nonetheless skirts the problem of *Widersinn* (and thus the problem of the polemic), see Christoph Menke, *Die Souveränität der Kunst: Ästhetische Erfahrung nach Adorno und Derrida* (Frankfurt am Main: Suhrkamp, 1991).

[140] "einleuchtend Beißners Erklärung der Rede vom 'übrigen' als dem übrig gebliebenen Ort." Adorno, *GS* 11:449; *Notes to Literature* 2:111.

[141] "Charakter von Verstörtheit"; "Verstehen wird es, wer nicht nur des pragmatischen Gehalts rational sich versichert, der außerhalb des im Gedicht und seiner Sprache Manifesten seinen Ort hat, sondern wer stets noch den Schock des unvermuteten Namens Ulrich fühlt; wer sich ärgert an dem 'nicht gar unmündig.'" Adorno, *GS* 11:450; *Notes to Literature*, 2:111.

[142] Wolfgang Binder, *Hölderlin-Aufsätze* (Frankfurt am Main: Insel, 1970), 353.

[143] "die widersinnige Zäsur, die Hoffnung in Existenz legt durch deren Zerfall." Adorno, *GS* 1:189. A few pages earlier: "Es [das Bilderreich] ist nicht scheinlose Wahrheit, sondern verspricht widersinnig die unerreichbare in der Opposition ihres Scheins" (It [the realm of images] is not truth without semblance; on the contrary, it promises, contradictorily, the unattainable [truth] in the opposition of its appearance). Adorno, *GS* 1:181.

[144] Thorsten Bonacker, "Dabei sein ist alles. Kulturindustrie und die Polemik Adornos." I wish to thank Dr. Bonacker for permission to quote from his unpublished manuscript.

[145] See Adorno's letter to Szondi from 28 November 1963: "I am immodest enough to imagine that you will be delighted by the dedication; but I know the ways of the academic world too well not to know that a dedication from me, and precisely that of this text, and precisely at this time, when an appointment must soon become acutely important for you, could harm you under certain circumstances." Cited in Szondi, *Briefe*, 141.

[146] Herrmann Mörchen, *Adorno und Heidegger*.

[147] See Jan Rosiek, *Maintaining the Sublime: Heidegger and Adorno* (Bern: Peter Lang, 2000).

[148] See Peter Sloterdijk, *Nicht gerettet: Versuche nach Heidegger* (Frankfurt am Main: Suhrkamp, 2002), 235–74.

[149] See Rüdiger Safranski, *Ein Meister aus Deutschland: Heidegger und seine Zeit* (Munich: Hanser, 1994), 469.

[150] See Sabine Wilke, *Zur Dialektik von Exposition und Darstellung: Ansätze zu einer Kritik der Arbeiten Martin Heideggers, Theodor W. Adornos und Jacques Derridas* (New York: Peter Lang, 1988), 192; Rüdiger Bubner, "Kann Theorie ästhetisch werden? Zum Hauptmotiv der Philosophie Adornos." In *Materialien zur ästhetischen Theorie: Th. W. Adornos Konstruktion der Moderne*, ed. Burkhardt Lindner and W. Martin Lüdke (Frankfurt am Main: Suhrkamp, 1980), 112.

[151] Hermann Mörchen, *Macht und Herrschaft im Denken von Heidegger und Adorno* (Stuttgart: Klett-Cotta, 1980), 176.

[152] See David Roberts, "Art and Myth: Adorno and Heidegger," *Thesis Eleven* 58 (1999): 19–34, esp. 22.

[153] See Herbert Schnädelbach, *Philosophie in Deutschland, 1831–1933* (Frankfurt am Main: Suhrkamp, 1983), 87.

[154] See Rolf Wiggershaus, *Die Frankfurter Schule: Geschichte — Theoretische Entwicklung — Politische Bedeutung* (Munich: Hanser, 1986), 658.

155 Heidegger, *GA* 39:82–83, 125–26.

156 "In dieser sich überkreuzenden Gegenstrebigkeit waltet die ursprüngliche Feindschaft, die aber, weil sie kein Auseinanderbrechen der Gegensätze ist, sondern vielmehr ursprüngliche Einigkeit, den Charakter einer Seligkeit hat — 'Feindseligkeit' —, wenn wie diesem Wort diesen widerwendigen Sinn des Gegen- und Zueinander zuweisen dürfen." Heidegger, *GA* 39:245.

157 "Seligkeit, die dich nur und eigentlich Feindseligkeit ist"; "die Innigkeit selbst, das Seyn." Heidegger, *GA* 39:256.

158 "das Verstehen ist eigentlich . . . das Wissen des Unerklärbaren . . . das Verstehen läßt gerade das Unerklärbare als ein solches stehen." Heidegger, *GA* 39:247.

159 See Alexander García Düttmann, *Das Gedächtnis des Denkens: Versuch über Heidegger und Adorno* (Frankfurt am Main: Suhrkamp, 1991), 9.

160 See Adorno's early lectures "Die Aktualität der Philosophie" and "Die Idee der Naturgeschichte," in which he charges Heidegger with resorting to a surrogate idealism. Adorno, *GS* 1:325–65.

161 "Nur noch ein Gott kann uns retten"; "Es gibt einen Satz von Grabbe, der lautet: 'Denn nichts als nur Verzweiflung kann uns retten.' Das ist provokativ, aber gar nicht dumm." Adorno, *GS* 20.1:405. Adorno again cites Grabbe's dictum in a radio talk with Arnold Gehlen.

162 "eine *Rettung* des Seienden"; "*nur noch aus dem tiefsten* Grund des Seyns selbst." Heidegger, *GA* 65:100; *Contributions to Philosophy (from Enowning)*, trans. Parvis Emad and Kenneth Maly (Bloomington: Indiana UP, 1999), 69 (translation modified).

163 See Gregory Fried, *Heidegger's Polemos: From Being to Politics* (New Haven, CT: Yale UP, 2000).

164 "Der verstörte und beschädigte Weltlauf . . . wiederstreitet dem Versuch verzweifelten Bewußtseins, Verzweiflung als Absolutes zu setzen." Adorno, *GS* 6:395–96; *Negative Dialectics*, trans. E. B. Ashton (New York: Seabury P, 1973).

165 See Lukács's famous taunt about the "Grand Hotel Abyss," in *Theory of the Novel*, 22. See also Ernst Bloch, *Atheismus im Christentum* (Frankfurt am Main: Suhrkamp, 1968), 324.

166 "Philosophie, wie sie im Angesicht der Verzweiflung einzig noch zu verantworten ist, wäre der Versuch, alle Dinge so zu betrachten, wie sie vom Standpunkt der Erlösung aus sich darstellten." Adorno, *GS* 4:281; *Minima Moralia*, trans. E. F. N. Jephcott (London: New Left Books, 1974), 247.

167 Hölderlin, *StA* 2:165; *Poems and Fragments*, trans. Michael Hamburger (London: Routledge & Kegan Paul, 1966), 463.

3: Citation: Brecht, *Die Antigone des Sophokles*

Wir träumen von Originalität und Selbstständigkeit, wir glauben lauter Neues zu sagen, und alles dies ist doch Reaktion, eine milde Rache gegen die Knechtschaft, womit wir uns verhalten gegen das Altertum.

[We dream of originality and autonomy; we believe we are saying all kinds of new things and, still, all this is reaction, a mild revenge against the slavery with which we have behaved toward antiquity.]

— Hölderlin, "Der Gesichtspunkt aus dem wir das Altertum anzusehen haben" (The Perspective from Which We Have to Look at Antiquity)

O N 31 OCTOBER 1947, WHILE HEIDEGGER was still laboring on his "Abendländisches Gespräch," Bertolt Brecht boarded a plane from New York bound for Paris, never to set foot on American soil again. He was glad to be leaving. The six years he had spent there had been lean ones, embittered first by the sense of impotence and frustration shared by every exile, then by the wave of anti-Communist hysteria that followed upon the euphoria of Allied victory. On the day before his flight he had been summoned to Washington by the House Committee for Un-American Activities to face questions about his political affiliations and those of his friends. One journalist described his testimony as a "smokescreen," claiming his thick accent and evasive answers had mystified his interrogators. Brecht cut out the article and pasted it proudly in his work journal.[1] The experience convinced him that he had long outstayed his welcome, and he resolved to leave immediately, despite not yet having been granted authorization to enter occupied Germany. "The flight was pleasant," he reported to Ruth Berlau upon his arrival, "and it was pleasant to fly away."[2]

From Paris, Brecht made his way to Zurich, where he hoped to find work at the Schauspielhaus, one of few European theaters to have continued staging his plays during the war. While strolling the city streets he bumped into Hans Curjel, with whom he had collaborated on the premiere of *Mahagonny* some twenty years earlier. Curjel, now manager of the provincial theater at Chur, invited him on the spot to direct a play for the coming season, offering him the choice between *Macbeth, Phaedra, Mutter Courage* (Mother Courage), *Die heilige Johanna der Schlachthöfe* (Saint Joan of the Stockyards), and *Antigone*. Brecht settled upon the last, insisting he be given the freedom to adapt it as he saw fit. He selected the translation by Hölderlin, "which is played rarely or not at all, because it is reputed to be too dark," on the advice of his set designer and old friend Caspar Neher, who had produced it in Hamburg the previous year.³ Berlau recalls seeing Brecht examining several translations of the play when she visited him in early January: "I even saw a text in Greek, for Brecht had found someone who knew a bit of Greek."⁴ His decision to use the most user-unfriendly *Antigone* on the German market was thus not made for want of an alternative, although it met with objections from critics and contributed, along with the rapid delivery he demanded of his actors, to the bewilderment of the general public.⁵ Brecht completed work on the text in the space of little more than a fortnight; rehearsals began in January, and the first performance took place on 11 February. While a few reviewers voiced lukewarm praise — one heralded an "interesting, noteworthy attempt to strike out on new paths," another a "theatrical event"⁶ — the critical reception was generally subdued. The production was not a popular success, surviving only five performances, including a Sunday matinee in Zurich, before being taken off the boards.

A few revivals of *Die Antigone des Sophokles* (The Antigone of Sophocles) in the former GDR did little to halt its slide into oblivion. Today the play is as good as dead. Brecht himself referred to it dismissively as "a routine piece of work" (*Fleißarbeit*),⁷ and later commentators have tended to agree with him: a product of convenience, a work of transition, a kind of team training camp in the provinces undertaken in preparation for Berlin (so the recollection of Helene Weigel, who performed in the title role),⁸ but hardly a masterpiece to rank alongside *Mutter Courage* or *Galileo*. Hölderlin's challenging translation appealed to Brecht because it gave him and his wife the opportunity to feel their way back into German-language theater after an enforced hiatus of well over a decade. "Presumably it's my return to the German-speaking world that's driving me into this project," Brecht notes in his work journal on 16 December, the construction suggesting that he had little control over the matter.⁹ In a similar vein, he writes around the same time of having "fallen into a new job."¹⁰ All the signs point to a relatively insignificant by-product of a lifetime devoted to theatrical experimentation.

On the face of it, there also seems little point expending much energy examining *Die Antigone des Sophokles* in terms of the postwar Hölderlin reception. Even if Brecht's choice of translation was not as arbitrary as his remarks at the time suggest — there are indications that his friend Hanns Eisler had sparked in him a flicker of enthusiasm for the poet while they were smoldering together in the "hell" of Hollywood¹¹ —, it seems self-evident that that translation served him primarily as a window on to Sophocles' fable rather than as an end in itself. His prior interest in Hölderlin had been desultory, his rare comments disparaging. In the late 1920s he had found him fit only for parody;¹² in 1940 he had viewed him as the founder of the "fully pontifical" line of German poetry that had culminated in George and necessitated a general "laundering of the language" (*Sprachwaschung*);[13] a few years later he had privately denounced the nationalist panegyrics through which Johannes Becher had sought to reclaim Hölderlin for the exiled Left.[14] Now he showed scant regard for the philosophical and political program that underwrote Hölderlin's translation, in which, according to Walter Benjamin, "meaning plunges from abyss to abyss until it threatens to become lost in the bottomless depths of language."[15] While perceptive enough to recognize its "astonishing radicality," Brecht also noted that it was "fairly faithful," a comment that flies in the face of the hundreds of errors in translation that have since been identified by philologists.[16] (I will consider later, on the basis of the changes he made to the translation, what kind of fidelity he may have had in mind.) Unlike Heidegger and Adorno, Brecht had no ambitions to redeem Hölderlin for Germany, nor did he aspire to redeem Germany through Hölderlin. He was pursuing the more modest, but also more presumptuous, objective of using this translation as a template to articulate his own revision of the play: "Even if one felt obliged to do something for a work like 'Antigone,' we can only do so by letting it do something for us."[17]

This narrow focus on the translation's "material value" makes *Die Antigone des Sophokles* something more and less, at any rate something other than an "elucidation" (Heidegger) or "critique" (Adorno) of Hölderlin. For both Heidegger and Adorno, the mysteries of the poet's work are accessible only to a select few, whether these be imagined as the addressees of his prophetic calling or the coterie of late modernists sensitive enough to recognize him as one of their own. "Das abendländische Gespräch" was not destined for publication during its author's lifetime, while Adorno, for all his ostentatious animosity toward Heidegger, joins him in seeking succor for the ailments of postwar Germany in the most densely rebarbative products of the poet's maturity. Brecht's refunctioning of Hölderlin after and in view of the catastrophe, by contrast, remains ever heedful of the reminder hanging around the neck of the donkey that stood on his window-sill: "Even I must understand it."[18] *Die Antigone des Sophokles* represents a public expression of interest in the question of the poet's efficacy today — the question, that is, as to *what Hölderlin is still good for*. My main concern in this chapter will therefore lie in exploring the implications and consequences of Brecht's decision to use Hölderlin's words as the medium of the adaptation, that is, to stage *Antigone* as the re-citation (albeit by no means verbatim) of a classical German author's translation of a classical Greek tragedy.[19] I take to my reading the basic media-theoretical insight that the medium does not exhaust its function in conveying a preexisting message to the receiver but is in each case indissociable from the message itself. In other words — and "other words" will be at stake here: words of an other recited as if they were Brecht's own; Brecht's own words recited as if they belonged to an other; own and other words intermingling in the adaptation to the point of their indistinguishability — *what* is selected for citation in *Die Antigone des Sophokles* must be thought together with the fact that there is citation *in the first place*, whereby this "in the first place" marks the logical and temporal precedence of quotation over invention, the reported over the freshly minted word. Through his transformative reinscription of the play into a discourse that is constitutively open-ended and non-totalizing, Brecht demonstrates that the practice of citation need not entail an attitude of pious obeisance before the cited text, as it does in "Das abendländische Gespräch," nor imply the consummation of that text in the process of its philosophical exegesis, as it does in "Parataxis." Whereas philosophers had hitherto contented themselves with interpreting Hölderlin's words in various ways, in *Die Antigone des Sophokles* Brecht sets out to change them.

Whose Antigone?

In the beginning was the citation: *Die Antigone des Sophokles: Nach der Hölderlinschen Übertragung für die Bühne bearbeitet* (The Antigone of Sophocles. Adapted for the stage from Hölderlin's translation). By attributing Antigone to a single author, the title encloses every word that follows within a pair of invisible quotation marks. Even Brecht's interpolations, those amendments and sections of newly added dialogue that allow one to speak of "Brecht's *Antigone*" as a play in its own right,[20] will have been indirect quotations from the master script, paraphrastic marginalia to an urtext twice removed. The title thus disables in advance the charge of plagiarism (the illicit denial of citation) that had been leveled against him in the past on account of his self-professed laxness in matters of intellectual property.[21] To this day, *Die Antigone des Sophokles* has never found its way into the Brecht canon, even though the case could be made that it is no more derivative, no less authentically Brechtian a production than, say, *Die Dreigroschenoper* (The Threepenny Opera).[22] One need look no further than the title to understand why. It defines Brecht's task not as one of *rewriting* Antigone, in a manner akin to Jean Anouilh's famous wartime production in Paris, but of *reciting* it for the modern stage. Anouilh had retold the story in a racy, colloquial speech that paid little heed to the letter of Sophocles' drama, preferring to treat the text of the tragedy as the dispensable vehicle for the mythic narrative at its core.[23] Brecht's title, by contrast, announces his intention to decontextualize and recontextualize — to resite — words that already have a history of their own, and so to establish, through that act of selective translation, a continuity with the time and place of recital. Before any particular content, *Die Antigone des Sophokles* affirms a line of tradition (and not just *any* line, either, but the most redolent imaginable, that of the "tyranny of Greece over Germany"), and it affirms tradition as such, if by "tradition" we mean the present-day citability of texts that belong to a bygone era. This should make us wary of placing undue emphasis on Brecht's denial, made shortly before he set to work on Hölderlin's translation, that "something like a German literature" had survived Hitler's war.[24]

Brecht's self-effacing nod to Sophocles is nonetheless ambiguous: it can equally be read as a distancing gesture. A cited textual tradition or traditional text is, by definition, not one's own, and it therefore never simply goes without saying. Drawing upon a vast stockpile of endlessly recyclable (re)sources, the recitalist enjoys a certain liberty with regard to the material he chooses to cite, material for which he knows someone else to be accountable. Pushed to insouciance, the citation avails itself as a self-disavowing comic device, as witnessed by its rise to prominence in the German novel since Wieland.[25] At the same time, the recitalist shoulders the responsibility of inventing tradition each time anew by striking a distinction between what is still citable, and by that measure canonic, and what is out-of-date or better reserved for later use. Like Mr. Peachum from *Die Dreigroschenoper*, he recognizes that the same phrases that yesterday moved an audience to tears may have become jaded and utterly ineffective overnight: "What's the use of the finest and most stirring sayings painted on the most enticing boards if they get used up so quickly?"[26] And he draws from this the conclusion that sometimes a citation needs to be tampered with in order to prolong its shelf life.

Any decision to cite one text over another demonstrates that the so-called *Erbe* or national literary heritage, which the likes of Becher and Lukács had defended during the war and now thought to administer as its sole legitimate heirs,[27] was never theirs to begin with. The choice of a citation, unlike the bequest of an inheritance, is contingent and non-binding. Why is Brecht citing Sophocles' play here, and not one of the alternatives offered him by Curjel? Under what conditions is he citing it, and to what ends? Why cite at all? Such questions are not extrinsic to the title, which Adorno rightly regards as the microcosm of the work.[28] In the space opened up between citation (*énoncé*) and recital (*énonciation*), between the play by Sophocles and the play that cites the play by Sophocles, the person who is reciting wins the freedom to reflect upon, criticize, or reject what she is saying. To recite lines that are not one's own is to act. The title thus draws attention to the play's status as a *performance* of *Antigone*, counteracting the theatrical illusion that for the course of the presentation suspends the ontological difference between an actor and the role she occupies. One cannot take at face value the convictions, feelings, or intentions expressed in someone's words if it is simultaneously made clear that that person has borrowed those words from someone else.

Further, the elevation of an author's name to the title of a production vacates the space ordinarily reserved for acknowledging his entitlement to the play. If Sophocles owns *Antigone*, who owns *Die Antigone des Sophokles?* Not Brecht, surely, otherwise the title would be meaningless or disingenuous; but not Sophocles, either, for then the authorship of the title would still remain unaccounted for. By invoking what Brecht once called "the question of ownership, which in the bourgeoisie, even as far as spiritual matters are concerned, plays a (quite bizarre) role," the citation of ownership in the title problematizes the ownership of citation.[29] The cited word, like the loan-word, has been removed from its native context without yet settling in to its new environment. Its strangeness, marked by the typographical, verbal, or gestural acknowledgement that it belongs elsewhere, is never absolute: the citation is required here and now, in this passage, to help secure my argument or to plug a gap created by the inadequacy of my powers of expression, and it is therefore always *on the way* to becoming my own.[30] Split between its original and present contexts, the citation belongs nowhere, too, since it can in principle be transplanted to any other setting. In his adaptation of the first stasimon (*pollà tà deinà* . . .), Brecht introduces an excursus on property relations that suggests a radical solution to the titular aporia. Man, the Chorus of Elders proclaims, cannot fill his belly by himself, "but the wall / He erects around his property, and the wall / Must be torn down!"[31] Do these lines, which resituate *Antigone* through the indirect citation of Rousseau and Marx, invite us to tear down the wall erected in the title? Could and should the *Antigone* of Sophocles be collectivized into *our Antigone* (and who might this collective include — the audience, the Germans, the "workers of the world," *das Volk*)? Or does the inappropriability of the citation — no matter how much I identify with them, the words I quote will always bear the trace of another — make such questions inappropriate? In short, is it possible to continue a tradition without first taking possession of it?

The problems of citation raised in the title become particularly acute, and acutely political, once it is considered that the Antigone ascribed to Sophocles refers as much to the eponymous heroine as to the play in which she stars. In 1948, the year of the production, Antigone was being refashioned in Germany as a paragon of those civic and moral virtues that had been sorely wanting under the Third Reich and would need to be inculcated in the next generation were the disasters of the past not to be repeated. Educational authorities on both sides of the newly hung Iron Curtain seized upon the tragedy as a relatively non-controversial, potentially cathartic contribution to the process of denazification. In the wake of the dictatorship, Creon's insistence on patriotic duty over private scruple no longer seemed, as it still had for Hegel, a position just as defensible as Antigone's appeal to the unwritten laws of heaven.[32] For many it stirred up instead fresh memories of the man who had overseen the execution of millions in the name of a national exigency that brooked no opposition. In part 3 of his epic novel of exile *November 1918*, written during the siege of

Stalingrad, Alfred Döblin had seen the spirit of Antigone incarnated in the communist revolutionary and martyr Rosa Luxemburg.[33] His friend Brecht went a step further, depicting the ruler of Thebes as a tyrant and clown addressed by his lackeys as "Mein Führer" (changed from "My King").[34] Perhaps unwittingly, he was following the example furnished by Hölderlin, for whom Antigone embodies a "form of reason" that is resolutely "political, and republican at that."[35]

At stake in the title, then, is the possibility of adopting Antigone as the figurehead of a new Germany, "Antigone" now understood as a citable character type instantiating the values of anti-fascist resistance. Brecht raises this possibility in his foreword to the *Antigonemodell 1948* — the very title of the book in which he published the play seems to recommend her as a role model — but he dismisses it just as quickly: "The drama of Antigone was selected for the following theatrical enterprise because its content ensured it a certain actuality and because it imposed interesting formal tasks. As far as the political content is concerned, the analogies to the present, which after the thoroughgoing rationalization [of the fable] had become surprisingly powerful, proved disadvantageous on the whole: the great figure of resistance in the ancient drama does not represent the fighters of the German resistance, who must appear most important to us."[36] This exclusion of Antigone from the elaborate system of correspondences established in the adaptation comes as something of a surprise and goes some way to explaining why the play failed to resonate with contemporary audiences. For Brecht, Antigone was a scion of the Theban ruling elite, driven by conscience, insight, and religious custom to betray her class interest, but she was not the true representative of her people. That part, which would eventually be cast in *Die Tage der Commune* (The Days of the Commune, 1956), is still missing from the ancient drama: "*Antigone's* deed can only consist in helping the enemy [that is, Argos, the city against which Creon is waging an imperialist war], which is her moral contribution; she, too, has eaten all too long of the bread that was baked in the dark."[37] The quotation marks have hardened here into scare quotes: Antigone, still shackled to the mind-forged manacles of her time and class, is better left to Sophocles after all.

Yet this passage, which seems to bring her closer to Count Stauffenberg than to Red Rosa, needs to be read in conjunction with a short poem appended by Brecht to the program booklet:

Antigone

Komm aus dem Dämmer und geh
Vor uns her eine Zeit
Freundliche, mit dem leichten Schritt
Der ganz Bestimmten, schrecklich
Den Schrecklichen.

Abgewandte, ich weiß
Wie du den Tod gefürchtet hast, aber
Mehr noch fürchtest du
Unwürdig Leben.

Und ließest den Mächtigen
Nichts durch, und glichst dich
Mit den Verwirrern nicht aus, noch je
Vergassest du Schimpf und über der Untat wuchs
Ihnen kein Gras.
Salut!³⁸

[Come out of the twilight
And walk before us a while,
Kind one, with the light step
Of one whose mind is fully made up, terrible
To the terrible.

You who turn away, I know
How you feared death, but
Still more you fear
Unworthy life.

And you let the powerful get away
With nothing, and did not reconcile yourself
With the obfuscators, nor did you ever
Forget affront and let the dust settle
On their misdeeds.
I salute you!]

The sober disavowal of Antigone in the foreword and the enthusiastic avowal of Antigone in the poem reflect the double nature of the citation as estrangement and repetitive renewal. For whereas Brecht maintains in the foreword that the "historical remoteness" of the play forbids an "identification with the main character," hence that Antigone is citable *only* as belonging to Sophocles and cannot be translated without remainder into the present, in the poem he lends her story a perennial topicality bordering on the timeless.³⁹ The citation distances, but it can also bridge that distance through the recurrence of the once-said in the now-time of the speaker; it demythologizes by confining a legend or saying (*Sage*) to the moment and agent of its fixation in writing, and it preserves myth by representing it to an audience that may yet recognize, in its fading letters, the refracted image of its own condition. Brecht's vacillation between emphasizing Antigone's exemplariness for the revolution and her unsuitability for exemplification, which Jan Knopf puts down to a change of heart, in truth expresses a tension in the citation itself.⁴⁰

This tension is already apparent in the poem, which dispenses with the detour of a byline to call Antigone directly by name, addressing her as a free agent whom no man is entitled to call his own. For what exactly is the twilight from which she is invited to emerge? Is it the barbaric dawn of the West? The haze of interpretations and mystifications that had gathered around her over the centuries, shrouding what Brecht calls the "highly realistic popular legend" at the core of the play?[41] Or simply the sepulchral gloom to which Creon had banished her? Should we join Bernard Knox in reading the appeal to Antigone as a lament for the failure of ordinary Germans under Hitler to step onto the political stage, forsaking the everyday anonymity in which they hoped to escape detection?[42] Or is she called forth instead to illuminate the crepuscular entr'acte in which the Germans found themselves at the time of the production, three years after the collapse of the Third Reich and twenty months before the foundation of the GDR — to "go before us" in this obscure state as a beacon of light, blazing with the same fierce spirit that once brought a tyrant to his knees? The technique of citation resolves the hermeneutic dilemma, not by making the shadow of the past disappear, but by causing it to appear as such; it trains the spotlight on Antigone, not that she may communicate with us face to face, but that we may see and salute her in her inimitable aversion. It is no accident that the poem whose title summons her to unmediated presence should go on to apostrophize her as "Abgewandte," literally "the averted one" (and it should be remembered that in Antigone's mother tongue, an apostrophe is, literally, a turning away). Does not every citation likewise turn toward a figure that is turned away from it? Might not the citation be the figure of this deviant form of address, as Sibylle Benninghof-Lühl has suggested?[43]

The O.E.D. reminds us that to cite is not only "to quote (a passage, book, or author); gen. with implication of adducing as an authority"; it is also, and in the first place, "to summon officially to appear in court of law."[44] The relationship between poem and play is accordingly that between Antigone's initial citation from backstage and her subsequent testimony before the tribunal of posterity. Like Brecht's earlier drama *Das Verhör des Lukullus* (The Trial of Lucullus, 1938), *Die Antigone des Sophokles* restages the trial (or stages the retrial) of the title character.[45] Illuminated from this angle, the poem's opening injunction can be seen to bring into focus the essential difference between Brecht's and Lacan's recension of the myth. For Lacan, Antigone places herself outside the symbolic network that structures and organizes the everyday life of the polis. She incarnates the death drive at its purest and most destructive, the suicidal impulse to transgress all socio-symbolic limits that carries her to an impossible zero-position beyond the reach of the law;[46] or as Creon puts it in Anouilh's production: "What matters for her is to refuse and to die."[47] For Brecht, the obverse is true: Try as she might to tarry in the shadowy realm of *atè*, Antigone cannot avoid interpellation by the symbolic order. Her situation is not that of someone who is already dead while still alive, as Lacan maintains; rather, some two and a half millennia after being removed from sight, she still finds herself prevented from dying by the fascinated gaze of the big Other, the invisible public that commands her to perform in a space of absolute visibility. Her attempt to escape through suicide the punishment imposed by Creon is thus undertaken in vain: she is in truth condemned to a fate worse than death, that of a "buried life with a good roof for shelter," as the tyrant puts it; that is to say, a life in the theater.[48] In Brecht's production, Antigone endures her time of trial with the listlessness of an actress worn down by umpteen performances of the role that made her famous. Brecht's instruction to Weigel that she speak her lines as if citing them, coupled with the fact that she was, at forty-seven, conspicuously far too old for a part intended for a girl, captures exactly this sense of wearying routine. Exiled to a provincial theater and in the twilight phase of her career, Antigone is now simply going through the motions. After taking her final curtain call, she withdraws to the twilight zone whence she came, there to languish in silence until her next citation.

What could break her out of the loop in which she is caught, which is, precisely, that of mythic repetition? At the height of her cross-examination by Creon, already sensing the crypt looming before her, Antigone cries out (to the Elders, who are refusing to listen? or to the audience, which is powerless to intervene?): "But I call upon you to help me in distress / And so also to help yourselves."[49] On the level of the citation, her plea registers the forlornness of her plight to the same extent that it is doomed to ineffectuality. If her fate is already scripted, as textual authority and the laws of the polis join Creon in stipulating, if recourse to an appellate court is out of the question, then her petition loses all sense of urgency and becomes susceptible to its transfiguration unto innocuousness. Like the deathbed speech of St Joan of the Stockyards, it can be brushed aside by being made to signify nothing more threatening than the last sigh of a beautiful soul. This is of course the (non-)reaction of the Elders, for whom Antigone is simply playing her preordained part in a spectacle that will culminate in her immurement, when they will be relieved of the obligation to lend her an ear. Their recognition of the *theatricality* of her cry for help entrenches them in their position as voyeurs at the very moment she is demanding that they abandon it. In this respect, the Elders function as stand-ins for the theatergoers in front of them, whose response to the desperate entreaties of the heroine is to remain motionless in their seats, looking on in silence as she is dragged off by the palace guards.[50] On the level of the recital, however, which is that of a theatricality to the second degree (the performance of a performance), her words exert a more subversive influence. They remind the audience, long since inured to the inexorability of tragedy, of the individual and collective responsibility it bears for the perpetuance of the conditions under which tragedy is still possible. We, the people, are shown to be no less implicated in the show trial we are witnessing than is Antigone herself. At this moment, the contemplative attitude with which we have drawn pleasure from her impending sacrifice becomes tendentially (and tendentiously!) inseparable from the culpability incurred by those who stood by while the horror unfolded. The roles of spectator and accused have undergone a dramatic reversal. Antigone, once cited, cites us in return, and against her damning indictment there can, in 1948, be no appeal: "So you let it happen. And hold your tongues before him. / Let it not be forgotten!"[51]

Prologue in Hell

Brecht's ambivalence regarding the appropriability of Antigone after the catastrophe is already thematized in the prelude (*Vorspiel*) to the play, set in Berlin during the last month of the war. Returning to their flat after a night spent in an air-raid shelter, two nameless sisters notice that someone has paid a visit while they were out: the door stands ajar, fresh footprints disturb the dust, and in the corner of the room they find a knapsack, with ham and bread inside. The second sister, who will soon step into the role of Antigone, realizes that their brother must have returned from the front: "And we hugged and were glad / For our brother was in the war and he was well."[52] Suddenly they hear a blood-curdling scream from outside. The second sister wants to investigate, but is held back with the warning: "Whoever wants to see will be seen."[53] As they get ready for their day shift in a local factory, the first sister, later Ismene, sees her brother's military overcoat hanging in the cupboard. She concludes that he must have deserted from the army: "And we laughed and were glad: / Our brother was out of the war. He was well."[54] Once again a terrifying cry interrupts their celebrations. This time the second sister ignores her sibling's advice and leaves the flat to find her brother strung up outside, apparently lifeless: "Sister, they have hanged him, / That's why he cried out for us."[55] The second sister is about to cut him down and try to resuscitate him when an SS man appears and accuses them of consorting with the "traitor" he has just executed. The first sister replies — and the echoes of the passion play, of Peter's denial of Christ and of the two Marys weeping at the foot of the cross, are too strong to be missed —"Dear sir, do not punish us / For we do not know this man."[56] The *Vorspiel* ends with a question mark: will the second sister risk her life in a foolhardy attempt to free her brother, who is probably dead anyway, or will she follow her sister's example in acquiescing to his murder?

The function of this prelude, according to Brecht, is "to set a point of topicality and to sketch the subjective problem."[57] (One might add that it does so in adapting the conventions of Greek tragedy to a modern setting. The reversal of fortune in the *Vorspiel*, the dashing of the sisters' expectant happiness at its height, the cruel irony that their brother is being executed at precisely the moment when, for the first time since he left for the front, they believe him to be safe from harm, their lack of understanding [*diánoia*], which at the same time is an ethical failing — all these motifs accord surprisingly well with the Aristotelian account of tragedy from which Brecht was polemically distancing himself at the time.)[58] It is not difficult to trace the parallels between the wartime drama in Berlin and the tragedy about to transpire in Thebes, especially when we learn in the next scene that the traitor Polynices, like the brother in the prelude, has deserted from the front. In Brecht's version, Creon has conscripted the young men of Thebes to invade the distant city of Argos — "a Stalingrad of today"[59] — and rob it of its mineral wealth. Fleeing the battlefield after seeing his brother fall in combat, Polynices returns to his home town, only to be hacked to pieces outside the city gates on Creon's orders. Antigone's decision to bury his mangled corpse in defiance of Creon's edict is thus as much a symbolic protest against the latter's gross mismanagement of the state as it is an act of familial piety. In the prelude, the second sister stands on the threshold of an analogous decision. All the other players in the scene have already slipped into their later roles; she alone is poised to become her future self, contemplating the step into open rebellion but not yet prepared to take it. This is presumably the subjective problem to which Brecht refers.

But is her translation into Antigone at all possible? As Brecht was well aware, the similarities between the sister's situation and that of Antigone break down upon closer inspection. Were she to disobey the SS thug, her likely reward would be a bullet in the back of the head, not a public forum at which to speak out against Hitler's tyranny. The suffering inflicted upon an individual in Greek tragedy has the potential to inaugurate a turning in the historical destiny of his or her people; that unleashed by the German catastrophe merely adds to the statistics. Dürrenmatt's remark that today Creon would get his secretary to dispose of Antigone is apposite here.[60] The woman's complicity in her brother's murder, subjectively indicated by her initial heedlessness to his cries for help and objectively corroborated by her daily service to the total war economy, means that a failure to act now would be no less disastrous than rash defiance. Yet because the self-sacrifice demanded by her situation will have been not tragic but utterly meaningless, her best efforts to emulate Antigone are doomed to fall short of their target. As that illustrious proper name recedes ever deeper into the pluperfect, the anonymous "Second Sister" is left stranded in a traumatic present, bereft of any precedent to guide her conduct. Brecht has no choice but to discontinue the scene here: to show her assuming the mantle of Antigone would be to forfeit credibility; to show her refusing it would be to abandon hope. The freeze frame at the moment of (in)decision, followed by the cut to ancient Thebes, offers the protagonist an escape from a predicament that admits of no individual solution.[61] The stalled actualization of the Antigone myth makes way for its distanced repetition qua citation: "The Antigone drama then unfurls the whole narrative objectively, on the foreign level of the ruling class."[62]

If the last lines of the *Vorspiel* cast into doubt the project of updating *Antigone* for the new Germanys that have emerged, rather by default than by design, from out of the ruins of fascist dictatorship, its first lines shed light on the considerations that motivated Brecht to recite this particular play at this time and at this stage in his career. The opening quatrain introduces two motifs that will be of cardinal importance, those of homecoming and daybreak:

> *Tagesanbruch. Zwei Schwestern kommen aus dem*
> *Luftschutzkeller zurück in ihre Wohnung.*
> DIE ERSTE   Und als wir kamen aus dem Luftschutzkeller
> Und es war unversehrt das Haus und heller
> Als von der Früh, vom Feuer gegenüber, da
> War es meine Schwester, die zuerst es sah. (*BFA* 8:195)

> [*Daybreak.   Two sisters return from the air-raid shelter to their flat.*
> SISTER ONE   And as we came from out of the air-raid shelter
> And the house was unscathed and brighter
> From the fire opposite than from the daybreak, then
> It was my sister who saw it first.]

The long night of terror appears to be over, a new day is dawning, both sisters have survived their ordeal, and their house stands intact. Yet the catastrophe that is about to befall them, dimly foreshadowed in the proleptic "it" of line four, takes place on the level of syntax in the very sentence expressing the hope that the perils and dangers of the night have been put behind them. In the context of the first couplet, the word "brighter" (*heller*) stands in contrast to an earlier, darker time: the house is brighter than when the sisters left it for the air-raid shelter. The comparative first emerges in its true, sinister meaning in the enjambement connecting lines two and three. The word that suggested a fresh start is now revealed to be the very opposite, for the brighter light bathing the house has been spent by the conflagration across the street caused by the nighttime bombing, not by the morning sun. The Nazi *Götterdämmerung*, which reached its hellish apotheosis at just this time, "*April 1945*," and in just this city, overpowers the false dawn of a new era, dragging the optimistic first couplet back into the nightmare from which its speaker thought herself provisionally secure.

Brecht had sketched this apocalyptic scenario once before, in a diary entry from August 1943: "One's heart stops beating when one reads about the air bombardments on Berlin. Because they are not connected with any military operations, one sees no end to the war, only an end to Germany."[63] The theme of inauthentic daybreak added to the 1948 version preempts one of the most important changes made to Sophocles' fable in the adaptation. In the *Antigone* of Sophocles the war against Argos is already won, and the war-weary citizens of Thebes would like nothing better than to forget about the bloodshed and return to their everyday lives. The first choral ode begins with the image of the rising sun banishing the specters of the foregoing night: "Glory! — great beam of the sun, brightest of all / that ever rose on the seven gates of Thebes, / you burn through night at last!"[64] Only against this background is the chorus's initial support of Creon comprehensible, even sympathetic. Antigone threatens to reignite the internecine strife that had almost destroyed Thebes, which is why Creon is entirely within his rights when he orders her to be buried alive for refusing to accede to his demands. In Brecht's version, by contrast, the war is not yet over; *it merely appears to be so.* Upon his first entrance, Creon orchestrates a triumphal procession to divert attention from the fact that his campaign against Argos is consuming ever more material and human resources, with no end to the hostilities in sight. While Creon crows his success before the chorus of old men, Tiresias, despite his blindness, is perceptive enough to realize that the metal lacquer coating the victory columns is "thin indeed."[65] Like the sisters, whose premature rejoicing drowns out the cries for help coming from outside, the elders are as much the authors as the victims of their delusion. Tiresias's clear-sighted analysis of the city's plight indicates that they accept Creon's lies only because they do not *want* to open their eyes. This crucial change to Sophocles' conception is already prefigured in the opening lines of the *Vorspiel*. The night in the air-raid shelter that the sisters have survived can be read as a symbol of Hitler's suicidal war, the brighter light that greets them as they emerge from the bunker as the sign that it has finally come to an end. That this sign proves in line three to be deceptive, that the war has in fact entered its most desperate and dangerous stage, shows clearly enough the *Vorspiel*'s function as a harbinger of events to come.

The theme of daybreak needs to be read in conjunction with its counterpart. The precarious situation outlined in the quatrain — namely, one of coming home to find the destructive legacy of fascism (the rampant fire) still virulently active in the guise of a fresh start (the morning light) — corresponds exactly to Brecht's view of his own situation in returning to the German theater scene in 1948; both motifs, that of homecoming and that of an illusory (literally *scheinhaft*) beginning, are to be found in neither of his pre-texts. It might be recalled that his return to the German-speaking world had, by his own admission, "driven" him to undertake the play, his first since the end of the war. The opening lines of the *Vorspiel* can accordingly be understood not just as a coded anticipation of the adaptation's plot but equally as a meta-commentary on the conditions of its reception as they were perceived by Brecht at the time of writing. Brecht expands upon these conditions at the beginning of his foreword to the *Antigonemodell 1948*, in a passage that could almost be taken for an explication of the sister's parable:

> The total material and spiritual breakdown has doubtless created a vague thirst for the new in our unhappy, hapless-making land, and as far as art is concerned, it is . . . gearing up to try out new things here and there. But because there seems to be a lot of confusion about what is old and what new, and because fear of the return of the old is mixed up with fear of the advent of the new, and because, furthermore, the defeated are in many places being instructed to overcome solely the mental and spiritual aspects of Nazism, artists would do well not blindly to place their trust in the assertion that the new is welcome. . . . Thus it may prove difficult, precisely in the time of reconstruction, to make progressive art. This should spur us on.[66]

Brecht is arguing here neither for a return to the discredited old, nor for a cult of the new under whose auspices the old will continue to flourish, but for a new relationship between old and new.[67] While the foreword does not go into this relationship in any detail, *Die Antigone des Sophokles* is evidently meant to represent just such a progressive dramaturgy, one that steers a course between artistic recidivism and innovation for innovation's sake; hence the need for citation as a self-conscious deportment toward a national repertory that, while deeply compromised by thirteen years of "Göring-theater," still contains too much of value to warrant its outright rejection.[68]

The *Vorspiel* ends as it began, with a demonstration of the supremacy of old over new, night over day, hellfire over regenerative light. The second sister, like art after the catastrophe, is left paralysed by her inability to find a reliable point of orientation. "Nonetheless, art can only orient itself by progressing, and it must . . . emerge from the state of waiting for action to that of action itself, and in the general decay set to work at some place or other."[69] By the next scene, she is suddenly at this "someplace," which could be any place, even "*in front of Creon's palace*," urging to rebellion a woman who, just minutes before, was wringing her hands in despair, addressing her by name in a strange and archaic tongue: "Sister, Ismene, twinned sprig / of Oedipus' bough . . . ."[70] The act of citation makes it possible.

The Precedence of Citation

The paradigm of citation briefly sketched by Brecht in the foreword, and ushered in by the frustrated attempt at mythic reenactment in the *Vorspiel*, determines the changes made to Hölderlin's translation in the adaptation itself. This, my central claim regarding *Die Antigone des Sophokles*, may strike the reader as contradictory. After all, what sense does it make to talk of citation when, as Hans Bunge has calculated, Brecht left only 19.5% of Hölderlin's verses untouched, adopting a further 32.3% almost unchanged? What of the remaining 48.2%, which Brecht either subjected to substantial revision or dropped altogether, not to mention the numerous new verses he penned for the production?[71] It is certainly true that if one defines citation as the exact replication of a given wording, the concept will be of limited value in understanding the play. Then one would also be forced to dismiss Brecht's title as a fraudulent attempt to pass off as Sophocles' the caprices of his own dramaturgical fancy. But my point is that the play draws attention to the fact that no citation, be it even the most fastidious or comprehensive, takes place without an element of distortion (or interpretation, depending on one's perspective). The risk of being quoted out of context is not only inherent to every utterance, it is the condition of its being quoted at all. By citing Hölderlin *in other words*, Brecht brings to the surface of the text the ordinarily inconspicuous process of transformation that a source undergoes whenever it is deployed in a different context, whereby the original context is acknowledged to be the more or less speculative hypostasis of later citations. "(Re-)translation" might seem to describe more fittingly what Brecht is doing here, but it is too broad a term to account for the distancing effects he aims at in the production, nor does it capture the performativity specific to the citation, its inseparability from the here and now of its recital.

Brecht discusses the relationship between his citation and the source from which it derives its authority, but whose "solid letter"[72] it repeatedly violates, in a letter sent from the workshop to his son Stefan. "The changes that compelled me to write entirely new sections," he explains there, "are done in order to cut out the Greek 'moira' (the fateful); that is to say, I am attempting to push through to the underlying folktale."[73] Far from superimposing the image of his own time on events of long ago, as some critics argue,[74] Brecht maintains that his alterations and expurgations are derived from — are literally dictated by — an antecedent recitation. In breaking the spell cast by myth, his rationalization of the fable lays bare its long-concealed substrate. (Needless to say, this conflation of terminus ad quem with terminus a quo is itself a mythic, indeed typically Romantic, move). Like Hölderlin before him, Brecht thus refuses to concede that he may have distorted the substance of the play through his interventions. All appearances to the contrary, the process of citation continues unabated, indeed with a greater degree of fidelity than ever before. Both Hölderlin and Brecht purport to have liberated the quintessence of the tragedy, the one through a translational procedure aimed at rekindling the primordial, heavenly fire that barely flickers through Sophocles' verse, the other through a citational procedure aimed at recurring to its more fundamental hypotext.[75] Both see themselves pursuing an archaeological, although by no means antiquarian, agenda. The tale of Antigone, they insist, was already partially occluded in the Sophoclean "original," itself the first surviving deposit in a textual palimpsest covering a foundation that is anonymous, authorless, and long since effaced — if indeed it ever existed. For in the absence of hard documentary evidence, who can vouch for this autochthonous prehistory,[76] or refute Hellmut Flashar's suspicion that we are dealing here with another of Brecht's tall stories?[77] Who can tell the difference between citation and confabulation once the cited source has gone irretrievably missing?

When adaptation is equated with adequation to a legendary urtext, origin is the goal. Benjamin chose this Karl Kraus quote as the motto for his fourteenth thesis on the philosophy of history, in which the act of citation is likened to a "tiger's leap" that seizes hold of the "actual present, no matter where it moves in the thickets of long ago."[78] Brecht was probably familiar with Thesis XIV, either through his conversations with Benjamin in the late 1930s, when it was first put to paper, or through its posthumous publication in 1944. At any rate, the concepts developed there aptly summarize his practice in *Die Antigone des Sophokles*. The tiger's leap is dramatized in the sudden transition from Berlin to Thebes at the end of the *Vorspiel*. It disrupts the continuity of linear narrative (in Benjamin's words: it blasts open the continuum of history) by ripping out of context the material upon which it pounces, in this case the *Antigone* of Sophocles, and arranging it in a new, unforeseen constellation.[79] In the now-time of citation, which is also the time of the stage, disparate temporalities are juxtaposed in a configuration that is one of neither simple supersession nor simple retrogression. Taking up the metaphor of the public spectacle, Benjamin adds that the leap lands "in an arena in which the ruling class gives the commands." In the production in Chur, this is the space in which Creon and his cast(e) hold sway, symbolically demarcated by a row of four totem-poles crested with horses' skulls; the populace remains silent and invisible throughout. Atavism and actualization, like derivation and innovation, are fused together in the sign of an immutable barbarism, "given that we still have the idolized state of class warfare!"[80] The doctrine of progress, enshrined as socialist orthodoxy in the state Brecht would shortly make his own, has been relinquished in this, his last production of exile — without, as we will see, having been replaced by the platitude that there can be nothing new under the sun.

It would nonetheless be a mistake to confuse Brecht's mission to excavate the popular legend with the putative recuperation of some great and insurpassable origin. What lies at the beginning, before Antigone embarks upon her remarkable literary and philosophical career, is not the singularity of an epochal event (and be it ever so ripe with futurity), but the plurality of folktale, with its plethora of minimal variations and embellishments; not Antigone as she appears for the first time on stage, resplendent in the afterglow of creation, but Antigone in the obscurity from which Sophocles plucked her. The origin of the origin is lost in common speech, dispersed in the breath of a thousand retellings that are coeval, immemorial, and equally (in)authentic. The origin of the origin, that is to say, is *itself a citation*, the scene of an infinite regress rather than of ultimate referential certainty. The radicality of this position becomes apparent once its corollary is taken into account: if the origin is secondary, the secondary is original. Citation is therewith freed from a slavish adherence to scripture and elevated to an art form in its own right: the *Antigone* ascribed to Sophocles is *also* a play by Brecht. In order to keep functioning, however, the act of citation still requires the regulative idea of an urtext. Without such an idea, it risks lapsing into the bourgeois ideology of creative genius against which it was directed in the first place. When there is nothing outside the citation, there is no such thing as citation, all distinctions based on text-genetic priority having faded into equiprimordiality. This is why Brecht is compelled to rewrite the origin under erasure, holding fast to the goal of a return to the source while all but admitting that this source is the figment of the citations to which it gives rise.

In the same letter to his son, Brecht remarks: "I have used the Hölderlinian (fairly faithful) translation from the Greek; it has something Hegelian about it that you'll probably recognize, and a Swabian popular gestus that you probably won't (the 'people's grammar' extends right into the highly artistic choruses!)."[81] Around the same time, he transcribed several of Hölderlin's more pungent swabianisms into his work journal, all of which he retained in the adaptation itself, notwithstanding his audience's potential unfamiliarity with the idiom.[82] To a certain extent, his enthusiasm may be attributed to his fierce and lifelong attachment to his native Swabia,[83] doubtless consolidated by his reunion in Chur with his boyhood friend Neher.[84] Brecht felt "right at home" in the translation, as he noted in his journal, in part because he was able to hear the distant echo of his youth in its unusual mix of "Swabian intonations and high-school Latin constructions."[85] Of greater significance than any affinity based on the accident of birth, however, was his professional interest in exploiting such colloquial turns of phrase for the pseudo-ethnographic, anti-classicistic tendency that characterized the production as a whole (as well as, behind it, the broader project of epic theater schematized a few months later in the *Short Organon*). By leavening high tragedy with south German dialect, practically an example of the V-Effect before the letter, Hölderlin succeeded in recapturing something of that earthy, vernacular quality that had suffered from the folktale's transformation into Literature, a quality that had gone entirely missing from the polished translations that had since established themselves in the repertoire. Hölderlin's erratic, frequently erroneous version struck Brecht as being "fairly faithful," then, not because it accurately rendered the nuances of Sophocles' Greek into modern

German — Brecht lacked the philological acumen to ascertain whether this was the case, and the pedantry to care — but because he thought it best approximated to the rough-hewn, archaic, and specifically oral linguistic gestus proper to its hypotext.[86]

Brecht's citation may accordingly be read alongside Heidegger's conversation as an attempt to rehabilitate the *Heimatdichter* Hölderlin in the wake of the latter's nationalist appropriation during the Second World War. Both Brecht and Heidegger sensed the regenerative potential of a language steeped in an ordinarily suppressed and silenced regional culture; both rejected the smoothly sublime High German brought to the height of its expressive power by Hölderlin's contemporaries.[87] Again, however, their differences in this regard should not be passed over too quickly. Brecht's attitude of "grateful malice" (to borrow Walter Jens' suggestive phrase)[88] toward his place of birth is irreconcilable with what Peter Sloterdijk calls Heidegger's "will to tarry in his natal space,"[89] not least because bitter experience had taught him what it was like to have his countrymen turn against him. In the first scene of the adaptation, Ismene tries to dissuade her grief-stricken sister from breaking Creon's prohibition on burial by appealing to her sense of civic belonging, which she insists will prove to be stronger, and more enduring, than the anger she currently feels about the infamy done to their brother. Antigone's place, she pleads, is in Thebes and among the living; "the old / homely elms and rooftops" will soon reemerge through her "veil of tears" to assuage her pain.[90] The wistful image evoked by these words, to be found nowhere in Sophocles, is not that of an ancient cityscape but the remembered Augsburg of Brecht's youth, with its lovely baroque skyline and tree-lined river. It is as if Brecht, poised on the brink of return from exile, were allowing himself a brief retrospective glance at the life that might have been his had he followed Ismene's advice, the snug security he might have enjoyed had he chosen, like his compatriot from Meßkirch, to stay put in the provinces. But Ismene is cast in the role of the temptress here, and Antigone's response — "I hate you" — is unparalleled in its bluntness (compare Hölderlin: "For saying such a thing, I would hate you").[91] This is as close as we will ever come to a real-life dialogue between Heidegger and Brecht, whom we must imagine standing in front of Hitler's palace, circa 1934, as they deliver these lines: the former justifying his decision to spend the years of national awakening ensconced in "Alemanian-Swabian rootedness in the native soil," as he put it in the same year;[92] the latter refusing to heed the call of his origin if it means falling silent before a political regime he knows to be abhorrent. At the end of the conversation, Heidegger retreats upriver to stage his fantasy of beautiful dwelling along the sanitized, sanctified, and de-urbanized banks of the Danube. Brecht, meanwhile, locates his Marxist play firmly within the walls of the polis, amid a bloody power struggle being waged between a proto-fascist military oligarchy and a dissident splinter faction that has aligned itself with the enemy. Viewed from the gates of Thebes, the conversationalists' riverside excursion resembles a controlled flight from the injustice being perpetrated, behind their backs and out of earshot, by the Creons of this world. Their perambulatory meditation on the need of needlessness brings them to a site where they can build their poetic dwellings undisturbed by the cries of the needy.

All the changes made to Hölderlin's translation in the name of its rationalization serve to accentuate this political dimension. I will restrict myself to outlining the most significant. Following Brecht's operation to excise the Greek *moira* from the play, the blind augur Tiresias employs his reason alone, rather than his prophetic gifts, to divine that something is rotten in the state of Thebes. The populace is reported to be aghast less at the severity of the punishment meted out by Creon — this is a side issue for Brecht — than at the more comprehensive failure of his rule, which has left them blighted with poverty and burdened with an unwinnable war. Creon's attempt to intimidate the populace by making an example of Antigone is both the sign and consequence of that failure, not its root cause. Haimon informs his father in Hölderlin's version "how the city is full of mourning for the virgin";[93] this is generalized and sharpened by Brecht to "Know that the city is full of inner disquiet."[94] The chorus of elders undergoes a similar "transmotivation" in Brecht's hypertext, revealing itself to be far more interested in the material gains it expects from the sack of Argos than in any martial glory.[95] Hölderlin's chorus proclaims with patriotic pride: "But illustrious Victory has arrived, / Favorable to Thebes, rich in wagons."[96] Brecht has at the same point: "But lucrative Victory has arrived, / Favorable to Thebans rich in wagons."[97] Whereas victory was once perceived to benefit the entire polis, it now only adds to the coffers of those who are wealthy enough as it is: the elders themselves. Brazenly identifying their particular interests with the greater good of Thebes, the big property owners confirm Marx's maxim that the leading ideas of a given age are ever the ideas of the ruling class. To concentrate the audience's attention still further on the political drama, and to prevent its sympathies from gravitating toward Creon at the end, Brecht also jettisons the figure of Euridyce, the tyrant's wife. Antigone's parting words to the chorus make explicit the lesson he hopes to communicate by eliminating the metaphysical backdrop from the play (or rather, as Werner Frick comments, substituting for it a Marxist *moira*):[98] "Do not, I beg you, speak of fate. / That I know. Speak of / Him who condemns me, innocent; weave / Him a fate!"[99] The infernal machine of tragedy has not been set in motion for the amusement of the gods, as Jean Cocteau would have it, but by a human hand, and for all-too-human purposes.[100]

Although such emendations to the plot are motivated by the impulse to show that man is the author of his own destiny,[101] their cumulative effect is to minimize the influence of individual actions upon the affairs of state.

Asked why she seems so intent on stirring up trouble, Brecht's Antigone volunteers the lapidary response: "Just for an example."[102] By her own admission, her rebellion is a symbolic gesture that serves at best to illustrate and bring into focus the broader tensions that riddle the body politic; in itself, it changes nothing. Creon's fate has long since been decided by forces beyond her control, as Tiresias is the first to grasp. By the end of the play, the Elders who had backed Creon to power, distant relatives of the Chicago cauliflower moguls of *Arturo Ui*, have deserted their man as the resurgent army of Argos nears the city gates. Thebes faces absolute ruin: "The city is finished for us, used to reins and / Without reins."[103] The parallels to Germany's own "zero hour" hardly need stressing.

It is important that this dress rehearsal for the apocalypse be read in the proper light. If the meaning of any citation is determined as much by the manner of its deployment as by its propositional content, then the semi-permeable borders that separate it from the discourse in which it is embedded — the margins between proper and borrowed speech, as it were — deserve particular attention. They provide instruction on the speaker's comportment toward the cited material, as well as on how he expects an audience to receive it: with approval or skepticism, in deference or disdain, as confirmation or provocation. The prelude that precedes and prepares the citation ends, as we have seen, with a crisis of indecision. More specifically, it sets up a double-bind situation in which the second sister is confronted with the necessity and impossibility of becoming Antigone. A choice has to be made; a choice cannot be made; *incipit citatio*. *Die Antigone des Sophokles* is thus introduced as a *citation of precedent*. A precedent case is cited whenever a decision has to be reached for which normative guidelines are lacking. It operates on the assumption of a structural homology between past and present situations, without which the precedent would prove incapable of providing useful counsel: the sister's dilemma (and, behind it, that of the audience of 1948) is to be construed as comparable to Antigone's. At the same time, the current situation must be experienced in its historical discontinuity, as a genuine predicament, for the need for a precedent to arise in the first place: her dilemma, along with that of the audience, is also unlike Antigone's. Were the horizon of possibilities already circumscribed by the ever-same, were we able to discern, in the infinite variety of human endeavor, nothing other than the permutations of mythic invariance, there would be no point in ransacking the archives of cultural memory in search of cases similar in kind to help guide our conduct, for we would have no alternative but to act the way we do. Brecht's citation of *Antigone* as a precedent for postwar Germany, far from forcing the conclusion that things are predestined to remain much the way they always have been (the cynical *plus ça change* muttered by the onlooker to the tragedy of history), necessarily implies that the future still stands wide open.

We should bear this in mind when making sense of the last lines of the play, spoken by the Elders as the city comes crashing down around them: "For time is short / Catastrophe is all around, and there is never enough time / to live on, unthinking and easy, / From connivance to sacrilege and / To grow wise in old age."[104] Hölderlin ends on the exactly opposite note, offering the consolation that while the blows dealt by the gods may have destroyed the ruling family, "they have taught us in old age to think."[105] By denying his chorus the benefit of such hindsight, Brecht ensures that the "great disorder" that set the city on its course to self-destruction will survive right down to the present day. The cuts he made to the fable point to the existence of underlying laws of history that will continue to demand the sacrifice of countless unnamed Antigones, including the second sister, so long as Creon and his ilk remain in charge. We still have tragedy, Brecht seems to be saying, because those who bear witness to it — the theater-going public no less than the chorus of ancients — fail to grow wise after the event. Through their tacit consent, the metaphorical devastation of the house of Thebes comes full circle in the literal devastation of the houses of Berlin. Crucially, however, the catastrophe posited as inescapable from within the immanence of the citation appears as the result of a choice when viewed from the standpoint of the recitalist. The fact that the Elders' fatalistic credo is given the final word in the play challenges the audience to see to it that it not have the final word elsewhere, thereby overturning the precedent of myth cited in (and as) the (genre of) tragedy. The selfsame time of eternal return, which the old men of Thebes believe to be too fleeting to permit reflection, provides the essential counterpart and foil to the revolutionary project of a "great order," whose realization depends upon our learning from the mistakes of the past.[106] So regarded, the playwright's innermost concern is to issue a caveat powerful enough to abolish the need for subsequent recitals of the trial of Antigone: " . . ." — *end of citation.*

Coming Home

The paradigm of citation developed in *Die Antigone des Sophokles* has been examined under its three constitutive aspects. These may be summarized as follows. First, conceived in spatial terms, citation, like translation, enacts a process of *decontextualizing recontextualization,* such that the very givenness of the chosen text is revealed to be the after-effect of its originary dislocation (a dis-location at, and of, the origin). "Quotation," writes Edward Said, "is a constant reminder that writing is a form of displacement."[107] He might well have cited *Die Antigone des Sophokles* in support of this claim. The site proper to the play is neither Thebes, its point of departure, nor Berlin, its provisional destination, but a habitable inbetween called Chur.

The matter of citation constantly finds itself held up at such way stations, where its transit from terminal to terminal is both frustrated and impelled by the impossibility of its assimilation without remainder into a new setting. This indwelling itineracy, at once the condition and index of its citability, makes its every sojourn a stopover from the start. As a rhetorical topos, the citation is as far removed from a free-floating utopianism as from the nativist dream of rootedness to a privileged place. It is an émigré much like Brecht, forced to set up house amid strangers while waiting with half-unpacked bags for the next train out of town. After paying a visit to Brecht's apartment in Zurich around the time of the adaptation, Max Frisch noted in his diary: "Everything is set up so that he could leave within forty-eight hours; unhomely."[108] Citation, the portmanteau tradition of the intellectual in exile, belongs at the heart of this scene of non-belonging.

Second, considered in its temporal dimension the act of citation brings about the *estrangement in repetition* of its signified. The multiple versions of the play that jostle together in the "final" performance script — a script that eschews precisely the historical-philosophical category of finality — are fused into a single horizon during the recital, resulting in a virtual simultaneity of *Antigones* past and present. Citation advertises the secondarity of tradition, in contrast to the romantic originality of Heidegger and the tragic originality of Adorno. At the same time, and in the same time, we have seen how Brecht reiterates the play in such a manner as to distance it from the immediate concerns of his audience — not because such concerns were a matter of indifference to him, but because he thought they could best be addressed by avoiding the false actualization of the myth. Antigone is cited, not as the heroine of the current historical moment (as Wagner had cited her exactly a century before, at another turning point in German and European history), but as the heroine of a bygone historical moment, and she is to be treated with due caution.[109]

Third, in legal parlance citation designates a *summons to adjudication.* Brecht's citation of *Antigone* transforms the stage into a brightly lit courtroom, the actors into witnesses called forth from the "twilight" to read aloud from their age-old affidavits, and the public into jurors charged with determining the pertinence of the myth to postwar Germany. Such a concept of citation stands at odds with the idealist doctrine that holds the autonomy of art and the disinterestedness of aesthetic judgment to be sacrosanct. The evidence presented in the theater subserves a verdict that lies outside the domain of art and beyond the jurisdiction of the playwright. It falls in the sphere of social praxis: the (re)actions of the public will decide whether the catastrophic precedent cited by Brecht is to be upheld in future. Consequently, the meaning of the citation qua speech act will depend upon the response it elicits from those for whom it is recited. Brecht's task is confined to precipitating the decision by heightening their awareness of the stakes involved.

We are now in a position to compare this paradigm of citation with the two others discussed in earlier chapters. My aim so far has been to approach all three paradigms as exemplary responses to the German catastrophe, responses that employ the key figure of Hölderlin to reconnect with the tradition and begin again after the caesura of 1945. To recapitulate: Heidegger, who had invested the most in the poet, resumed and relocated the *conversation* in which they had been engaged since well before the war; Adorno sought by means of a self-implicating *polemic* to redeem him as the forefather of aesthetic modernism; Brecht used him as the pretext for his *citation* of tragedy. Notwithstanding the massive differences in philosophical style, political belief, and biographical trajectory, which at times give rise to the impression that these three thinkers inhabited parallel universes, they shared a fundamental insight that led them to spurn the philological methodology in vogue at the time, monumentalized in the Stuttgart edition of Hölderlin's works. Belonging to a generation stamped by the experience of epochal rupture — their birth dates span the years between 1889 and 1903 — they recognized that the discipline of philology could no longer be relied upon to secure the transmission of culture that had hitherto provided it with its rationale. The severed link between old and new was not to be reconstituted through the painstaking reproduction and exegesis of sacred texts. Indeed, the industry expended upon such ventures was itself a symptom of the de-essentialization (Heidegger), commodification (Adorno) or "plastering over" (Brecht) of the work of art.[110] Each thinker was moved by this insight to set up Hölderlin as a test case for the im/possibility of reception after the catastrophe. In this final section, I want therefore to interpret conversation, polemic, and citation as *radical philologies*, that is, as strategies of textual engagement that take Hölderlin as the occasion to get to the root of a breakdown in the transmissibility of tradition — the *tradere* of *traditio* — as such.

Benjamin's concept of the "now-time" (*Jetztzeit*), which has already been raised in connection with Adorno and Brecht, will serve me as my guiding thread. This concept may well have been elaborated in response to the notion of repetitive retrieval (*Wiederholung*) first put forward by Heidegger in *Sein und Zeit*. In the lecture courses Heidegger had given in the 1930s, repetition had denoted the confrontation with, and dismantling of, the fundamental metaphysical positions of the philosophical tradition from Plato to Nietzsche, undertaken in readiness for the "other inception" of the event of Being. By 1946, it had mutated into an explicative dialogue (*Zwiesprache*) or conversation (*Gespräch*) between thinking and poetry from which Heidegger had come to expect nothing less than a reawakening of the Occidental spirit. For the Heidegger of "Das abendländische Gespräch," now-time is light years away from the instant of messianic interruption theorized by Benjamin. It is the eerily distended, absolutely uneventful time of the conversation itself. The ontological metronome

that sets the pace for the conversationalists' slow walk along the banks of
the Ister brings the anteriority of founding and the futurity of advent into
a single measure, a collected presence-of-mind marked by its serene obliv-
iousness to the distractions of fallen history. This ecstatic present is dis-
pensed by the poetic word upon which they meditate underway:

THE YOUNGER:	The measure of the middle determines the ability to tarry, which neither lapses into hesitation nor flees to overhastiness.
THE ELDER:	This measure concerns time in the sense of the right time, that time at which it is always time to . . .
T. Y.	That time that we name when we specifically say and even call out "Now."
T. E.	As the Ister hymn sets off at the beginning: "Now come, fire!"
T. Y.	"Now" — we only say this first word of the hymn when we allow it to sound and resound in a tarrying in which a long waiting has gathered . . .
T. E.	and now comes to completion.[111]

The "now" uttered at the beginning of the Ister hymn, and repetitively retrieved over the course of the conversation, is not the called-for
moment of sunrise but the moment of calling; not the coming dawn but
the gathering dusk of the evening land. This now-time, in which is con-
summated the protracted waiting that is Occidental history, nonetheless
wants for nothing, for the daybreak that has yet to take place is already co-
present in the call as the response rising to meet it. The time whiled away
co-responding to Hölderlin's verse in anticipation of the event, a time in
which nothing happens and history has ground to a halt, *is itself that event.*
Absence and arrival coincide in the poetic annunciation of Being, quelling
the impetus for action and replacing it with the much-vaunted *Gelassenheit*
that pervades Heidegger's postwar philosophy. The very poverty of the
poet's "time of need" is the index of an inexhaustible richness, as
Heidegger points out in his elucidation of the same passage in the 1942
lecture series on "Der Ister": "This distinctive significance of the 'Now'
demands that in this temporal word of time we also come to hear something distinctly significant and await a concealed fullness of poetic time and
of its truth. . . . The 'now' names an appropriative event."[112]

The poet's "now" stands in the same relationship to the time of sunrise as does the conversationalists' "now" to the time of the poem.
Heidegger will never cease admonishing his listeners that they (we) have
still to hearken unto Hölderlin's poetry, nor will he ever claim to have
brought that poetry into the light of its actuality through his tireless
interpretative, pedagogic, and publicistic activity. What lies in the way of
its appropriate reception is not simply the inattentiveness of its readership,
and certainly not the inadequate illumination of its historical background,

but an essential untimeliness proper to the poetry itself, which for that reason lies in wait for the German people as their national task and destiny. This is not to say that for Heidegger our appointment with Hölderlin has been postponed until a later date, presumably to be determined at the discretion of Being. On the contrary, the poet's now-time is dawning even as we speak: in 1936, when excerpts from the conversation were first released for publication; in 1946–48, when the conversation was briefly intensified following the collapse of the Hitler regime; and from this time forth, whenever two or three are gathered in his name to dwell upon his word. It is the continuous present in which his poetry reveals itself to us *as not yet having dawned upon us.* Hölderlin appears in his full radiance as a barely discernible glimmering in the east, an inkling of light still too much one with the darkness to merit the title of sunrise. His is a daybreak prior to daybreak, its aubade sung by the watchful few who have their eyes already trained on the horizon. Small wonder, then, that Heidegger should compare "this 'now' " — that is, the 'now' of "Now come, fire!," issuing from the ongoing night — to "a star that has suddenly risen and that shines over everything."[113] Hölderlin's "now" *is* the sun whose advent it invokes, and its invisible rays warm the conversationalists as they descend ever deeper into the gloom of what they alone know to be the coming dawn.[114]

It is instructive to turn at this point to the now-time peculiar to the polemic, which shimmers through it as its other time and the time of its other: the time of salvation. This is at once the negative truth of the catastrophe of history, within which the polemicist continues to operate, and the negation of historical consciousness as such, which vitiates the now by tethering it to a before and after.[115] Its image is that supine animal happiness glimpsed by Adorno whenever he lifts the veil on the good life (something that happens less infrequently than his self-imposed *Bilderverbot* would lead one to expect).[116] He does so on a single occasion in "Parataxis," in his gloss on the lines: "Vorwärts aber und rückwärts wollen wir / Nicht sehn. Uns wiegen lassen, wie / Auf schwankem Kahne der See"[117] (But forward and backward we will / Not look. Be rocked as / On swaying skiff the sea.) The decision, comments the philosopher, "is like an intention to cast aside synthesis and trust to pure passivity in order to completely fill the present. For all synthesis — no one knew that better than Kant — occurs in opposition to the pure present, as a relationship to the past and the future, the backwards and forwards that falls under Hölderlin's taboo."[118] The ensuing side-thrust directed against "the chimera of origin" cannot quite conceal the equally chimerical nature of a *nunc stans* from whose all-too-knowing anoesis the intellectual expects a cure to his surfeit of intellection. The blissful forgetfulness intended but not realized by Hölderlin's poem is begotten of its name-giver Mnemosyne, the goddess of memory, not of Lethe.

The analysis of the polemic ventured in the foregoing chapter leads one to suspect, however, that there may be more to this now-time than just wishful thinking. Indeed, Adorno takes care to distinguish it from the anodyne visions of a better world being promulgated by the philosophers of hope at the time, barely a year after the Cuban missile crisis had threatened the species with extinction. The injunction not to look forward, he warns, amounts to a "taboo against abstract utopia";[119] the gently swaying boat represents not the telos of human striving but the momentary suspension of teleology. Hölderlin's ship is sailing nowhere, which is what makes its voyage utopian in a non-abstract, strictly literal sense. Likewise, the refusal to look backward rules out the yearning for the primitive, the naive, and the unspoiled that since Tacitus, or in modern times Rousseau, has gone hand in hand with the critique of civilization. The state of prelapsarian innocence never existed outside the heads of those who lament its passing, and even if it did, "the irretrievability of something once overthrown" thwarts in advance any attempt at its restitution, including the Heideggerian variety.[120] So if Adorno's dream of abandonment to pure presence equates to neither origin nor goal (whose identity in now-time had been posited by Benjamin), what role does it play in his philosophy of history?

The renunciation of synthesis envisaged by Hölderlin brings about a lull in the state of universal hostility, which Adorno traces back to a conflict between nature and the logos that seeks to dominate it. The image of this temporary ceasefire, for which he had earlier found the caption *Sur l'eau* — in 1945, to be exact, not by chance the year in which the catastrophe reached its nadir — affords a foretaste of peace to the philosopher-warrior caught up in the thick of battle.[121] As the calm in the eye of the storm, Adorno's now-time distils the redemptive impulse that fuels and legitimates the polemic. Lying outside or alongside history in a region inaccessible to cognition, which cannot do without synthesis, it owes more to the instantaneous release yearned for by mystics than to utopia, if we take the latter to mean a blueprint for the rational organization of society; in this it resembles the time of conversation. The political danger skirted by Adorno is similar in kind, for one can well imagine his chosen mantra causing those who chant it often enough to drift into the same quietist stupor he denounces in his adversary. This very charge would in fact be made against Adorno by several of his students. Yet unlike the preemptive daybreak talked into being by Heidegger's interlocutors, who seem to have wandered off into another temporal dimension, Adorno's "now" also stands for the polemical antithesis of synthesis, which is to say that it remains inextricably bound to the history from which it takes its leave. As he remarks in the next paragraph: "Hölderlin expects a state of freedom to be attained only in and through the synthetic principle, through its self-reflection."[122] Consequently, the time of polemic and the time of salvation are neither mutually exclusive, as they were for Benjamin, nor incompatible in essence, as they would be for Heidegger. The tendency in Hölderlin to disintegration into paratactic shards, shards then taken up by the negative dialectician and honed into weapons against identity thinking, flows from the idyll of "lying on the water and staring peacefully at the sky";[123] the ability of Hölderlin's work to rock the boat is inseparable from its metaphysical lassitude.

To the dialectical compulsion of the either/or driving history toward the precipice — either forward or backward, progress or regress, victory or defeat — Adorno thus opposes the non-synthetic coincidence of extremes in now-time. This is why Adorno, despite otherwise being at pains to emphasize the poet's critique of lyric immediacy, can argue that "the law of the present . . . in Hölderlin is the law of poetry"[124] — a claim that can be extended to the category of the late work in general, in which (according to Adorno's ex-student Carl Dahlhaus) "the aesthetic 'present' proves independent of the chronological distinctions between 'past' and 'future.'"[125] Now-time is the point of indifference of polemic, the volcanic eruption of meaning intrinsic to late style, and salvation, the aquatic nirvana of "being, nothing else"[126] in which the labor of the concept is brought to a standstill. The former effects the ruination of the work of art in *Widersinn*, the latter its dissipation in worklessness. Together, they withdraw the late work into a counter-time that attains to fleeting, impotent presence through its non-contemporaneousness with the successive time of historicism. Incapable of entering into a preexisting tradition or of founding a new one, Hölderlin's poetry calls to us from the never-never land of the entirely Other. It anticipates and instantiates the moment when the dynamic of history, whose hyperactive bustle both Adorno and Heidegger interpret as a symptom of terminal decline, passes over into post-historical stasis.

Brecht parts company with the two philosophers, moving closer to Benjamin's original position, in his evaluation of the emancipatory potential of now-time. Two distinct versions of now-time are presented in his *Antigone* adaptation, corresponding to the two temporal layers that go together to make up the citation. For the sake of convenience, I will call them the "now" of the cited material (that is, the time of *Antigone*) and the "now" of the recital (that is, the time of *Die Antigone des Sophokles*). The former, mythic and catastrophic, comes into its own in the dying seconds of the adaptation: "Thus Thebes *now* falls," "But we / all follow him *now*, / Plunging into the abyss"; "But she who saw everything / Could only help the enemy, who is coming / *Now* to annihilate us [my italics]."[127] The latter is thematized in an important passage that immediately precedes the citation. The first sister, shortly to be translated into Ismene, has just denied knowing the deserter executed by the SS man, who thereupon asks her: "Then what does she want the knife for?" She replies — they are the last words spoken in the *Vorspiel* — "Then I looked at my sister. / Should she in mortal danger / *Now* go to release our brother? / He might not have died [my italics]."[128]

Let me try to answer the question dodged by the future Ismene, whose talent for evasion will keep her out of trouble later, too (at least until the barbarians have reached the gates). Her sister, it will be recalled, had fetched the knife in order to cut their brother down from the butcher's hook: "The knife, give me the knife / To cut him down so he hangs no more."[129] With the SS man back on the scene, she realizes she will have to kill him first in order to carry out her intention. The tool initially chosen to *release* her brother from the hook has become, in her hands, a weapon of *liberation* from the forces that brought about his death; "befrein" supports both readings. While it was still possible to understand the former deed solely in terms of family obligation, the latter spills beyond the domestic sphere and onto the political stage on which, in the garb of Antigone, she will henceforth "walk / Before us a while."[130] In this it parallels and completes her earlier movement from the interior of the apartment, where she had first heard her brother's cries, to the landing outside, where she finds his body. The "now" marks the moment in which the opposition of private and public worlds to which *Antigone* is often (and wrongly) reduced is canceled in revolutionary action,[131] the caesura that cuts the beloved free while cutting into enemy flesh.

The sister's "now," however, remains a prospective present. We do not hear a response from her own lips to the guard's question, nor do we learn whether she subsequently risks her life to challenge him. Instead, "at the sound of a gong the two actresses, Helene Weigel and Martia Glenck, handed their coats to an assistant and returned as Antigone and Ismene to play their opening scene."[132] Brecht's decision to withhold this moment from his audience can be understood in one of two ways. First, it can be seen to demonstrate the limits of theater by pointing to what lies beyond it. The play brings us to the threshold of now-time without itself being able to cross that threshold. It dismisses us, after an hour or two spent in willing surrender to its ontological frivolity, back to the seriousness of life outside, there to work with fresh resolve toward building a new, more humane Germany from out of the rubble. I will set aside this interpretation, which accords with a deeply engrained, quasi-Schillerian belief in the lightheartedness of art informing Brecht's concept of "didactic theater," to pursue another, in my view more promising, avenue of inquiry. According to this second approach, the sister's parting words prompt us to suppose that whatever transpires next will take place in the "now" to which she refers. They therefore lead us to assume the equivalence of the decision left hanging at the end of the scene with the citation of *Antigone* that follows. The agonizing choice apparently put on hold through the insertion of the citation *is in fact actualized in that citation;* the now-time of intervention and the time of recital are one and the same.

To articulate the past historically, writes Benjamin, means "to seize hold of a memory as it flashes up at a moment of danger."[133] Such a moment is given in exemplary fashion in the tableau vivant that closes the *Vorspiel*. At this critical point, with the sisters' fate balanced on a knife-edge, the memory of Antigone is revived and transfixed in the form of a citation.[134] The cut from Berlin to Thebes — in Benjamin's terms, the flash of a memory wrenched from its context in a successive chain of events — structurally enacts the stab wound that the sister may or may not be about to inflict upon her brother's murderer. *Die Antigone des Sophokles* thus accommodates the unvarying, fatalistic "now" of the cited material, with its innumerable reprisals of the same calamitous refrain (chorus: "thus Thebes now falls"), within the performative, antimythological "now" of the recital, in which traditional texts and practices are put on the stand and interrogated for their current use-value. Both "nows" are co-present in the time of citation, in which, as Eva Geulen points out, "the old and the new attain the status of simultaneity."[135] Analogously, Brecht requested that when not on stage, his actors remain seated on pew-like benches positioned directly behind it, where the audience would have full view of them "reading, unobtrusively making minor gestures, applying their make-up," and generally acting out of character.[136] Here as there, the play of framing has as its effect the framing of the play as an instance of what Benjamin calls *citation à l'ordre du jour*. Moreover, because the *novum* that emerges in the now-time of citation is not something unheard-of and unique, resulting instead from the defamiliarizing transformation of the long-familiar into a precedent whose validity is at issue, now-time can be ushered in at any moment. It requires nothing more than a keen sense for the "actual" (Benjamin again) backed up by a certain tactical finesse: in a word, Brechtian cunning.

It follows that the relationship to tradition entailed in citation will be of a different order from that articulated in conversation and polemic. I asserted earlier that each paradigm presupposes a rupture in the transmissibility of tradition, a rupture that necessitates reflection upon the changed circumstances under which Hölderlin is now to be received. Heidegger grasps this rupture in terms of the *unhomeliness* of Dasein, which prevents it from entering into an authentic relation with its past and future possibilities. According to Heidegger, unhomely (that is, modern) Dasein typically experiences the present as a bare now-point in a series of such points stretching in both directions into infinity. Similarly, we tend to view the patch of turf on which we take up residence as a fungible resource standing at our disposal rather than as the irreplaceable site of disclosure of our being-in-the-world. This impoverishment in our connection to time and place, which Heidegger believes to have attained planetary dimensions since the victory of "Americanist" technocracy, cuts us off from the source of our history, degrading the diachronic vitality of our common heritage — *echte Überlieferung* or "handing over," the prerequisite for any future renaissance — into a vapid synchrony, wherein the great works of our people appear to us as cultural goods suited to entertain or edify us in our hours of leisure. Regardless of whether our lifestyle is peripatetic or sedentary, Heidegger contends that we are already lost at sea, in dire need of a spiritual compass from which to take our bearings.

Hölderlin shows us the way home: "If, however, the historicality of any humankind resides in being homely, and if being homely is a becoming homely in being unhomely; and if, furthermore, such being homely can be determined only poetically and must be said poetically, then Hölderlin is the first to experience poetically, that is, to say poetically, the German need of being unhomely."[137] The "law of becoming homely" parsed in Heidegger's writings on the poet from 1942 to 1948 finds its clearest expression in the Ister hymn, and it is this poem that guides the philosopher, more deeply unsettled by the events of those years than he cares to let on, into the heartland of the secret Germany. He will barricade himself there for the rest of his life. Whereas Heidegger had earlier explored the capacity for violent acts of historical founding that sets man apart as the most monstrous of all beings, his thinking in this period comes to center upon the hearth where, according to Heraclitus's saying, gods are also to be found.[138] In order to return to the hearth, and so recover the meaning of being (German), Heidegger demands of his fellow travelers that they first recognize the singularity of the poet's calling. They must understand that Hölderlin is a jealous demigod who bars entry to the promised land to all but those who worship at his shrine. Because the recuperation of tradition is thus seen to depend upon the renunciation of what ordinarily goes by that name, the category of tradition has for Heidegger become unusable. We have Hölderlin — or rather, he has us — and that is enough for now.

Heidegger's conversationalists have no need for haste, because they are already right where they want to be, dwelling close to the origin. Adorno refuses to join them there. Hölderlin offers the polemicist no such prospect of eventual homeliness, no destination from which to launch his attack, and no stable identity guaranteed by tradition, only an exposed and extraterritorial nowhere — now figured as scorched earth, now as circumambient water — maintained through its antagonism toward each and every position of enunciation. The *homelessness* of Hölderlin's late work militates against its domestication after 1945, even as it secures the homeless poet his rightful place at the forefront of the modernist avant-garde. For Hölderlin registered in his poetry the same lesson Adorno saw exemplified in the history of aesthetic innovation in the "heroic years" of the early twentieth century,[139] a lesson that finds its most pointed formulation in a letter he wrote to Thomas Mann shortly after his arrival in bombed-out Frankfurt: "that in a central sense there is no such thing as a return."[140] Heidegger's failure to grasp this fundamental experience of modernity, his inability or unwillingness to perceive that Hölderlin marks a point of no return, gives occasion to some of the most bitter invective in "Parataxis." "Hardly anywhere did Hölderlin prove his posthumous champion more wrong than in his relationship to what is foreign," argues his posthumous avenger. "Hölderlin is driven up hill and down dale in the service of a conception of love that circles around inside what one is anyway, fixated narcissistically on one's own people; Heidegger betrays utopia to imprisonment in selfhood"; "the exiled Hölderlin" is transformed for transparently nationalistic purposes into "a trustworthy German living abroad."[141] Such accusations, whose justice or injustice is of no concern to me here, indirectly salvage Hölderlin for postwar Germany by locating the continued actuality of his work in its power to disrupt the mechanisms of identificatory actualization. Precisely his intransigence to his reclamation by and for his people makes him their contemporary today, after the catastrophe has unveiled the nightmarish reality to Heidegger's "endogamous ideal."[142] Far from annihilating tradition, polemic rescues it for the present by seizing hold of it in extremis, making its loss of binding force the condition of whatever authority it can still muster.

Brecht shares neither the sublime patriotism of the conversationalists nor Adorno's partisanship for the expatriate poet. *Die Antigone des Sophokles* is a work of *homecoming*, in the broadest possible sense of the term: to a disappropriated language, to an estranged country, to a corrupted dramaturgy, and to a compromised literary tradition. It stands at a turning point in Brecht's career, representing the last in a string of productions of exile dealing with the etiology (*Arturo Ui*) and psychopathology (*Furcht und Elend des Dritten Reiches*) of fascism, and the first in a series of adaptations of "classics" undertaken after the war — others include Molière's *Don Juan* and Goethe's *Urfaust* — in which he sought to build up a repertoire, and a repertory theater, for his self-elected homeland. It also signals a shift in his public standing from the iconoclast outsider of the Weimar years, who once declared everything new to be better than everything old, to the reluctant insider of the 1950s, who went on to draft a list of canonic works (including poems by Hölderlin) to be made compulsory reading for East German schoolchildren.

The adaptation is in like measure a case of work *on* homecoming, insofar as it problematizes, estranges, and provides running commentary on its own bid at repatriation. When Heidegger hears Hölderlin singing: "Hier aber wollen wir bauen" (But here we wish to build), his thoughts turn immediately to settlement in the homeland.[143] Brecht takes his words at face value, setting to work on the Hölderlinian text itself and transforming it into a busy construction site that is both product and process in one. No occidental destiny, no quest to return to the source dictated Brecht's choice of abode, the "here" at which he pitched camp upon his arrival in Europe. A number of more or less contingent biographical factors — a chance encounter on the streets of Zurich, an improvised offer, an impulsive decision — determined that this "here" lay in Chur and in the *Antigone* of Sophocles; it could just as easily have been elsewhere. The passage of home-coming displaces the destination by opening it up to a general nomadism of which it is revealed to be the local effect: the quiet domesticity enjoyed by the conversationalists is the exception, not the rule. Citation undermines their sense of groundedness in their native soil through its *selective mobilization* of tradition, its repositioning of the tradition in preparation for active service in the next phase of the class struggle.

Commenting on Benjamin, Giorgio Agamben remarks that "the interruption of tradition, which is for us now a *fait accompli*, opens up an era in which no link is possible between old and new, if not the infinite accumulation of the old in a sort of monstrous archive or the alienation effected by the very means that is supposed to help with the transmission of the old."[144] Heidegger and Adorno, to whom modernity presents itself as the history of the decline and fall of history, are the nay- and doomsayers of this era of unlimited citability, Brecht its yea-sayer. Unencumbered by their romantic predilection for great beginnings and endings, he offers his citation of Hölderlin as a work in (and of) progress, to be continued, tinkered with, improved upon, taken apart, and thrown on the scrapheap once it has outlived its usefulness. Asked by a journalist after the premiere whether he promised himself anything for the future from such a dramaturgy, Brecht was quick-witted enough to reply: "For a couple of hundred years at any rate!"[145] In an obvious and trivial sense, his confidence has proved unwarranted. *Die Antigone des Sophokles* was something of a box-office flop, and the theoretical apparatus of "epic theater" he brought to the production, for all the influence it exerted upon later theater-makers, has come to look ever more rickety. But beneath its ironic bombast and bluster, there is perhaps a kernel of truth to the quip. Despite the lack of interest that has been shown in the adaptation, the philological method brought to bear upon it has a good claim to be judged more flexible, more sensitive to the historical moment, more durable, and more enduring than the two others examined in this study. We live in a present for which the dreams of salvation spun out into philosophical concepts by Heidegger and Adorno are but a distant memory. Those dreams live on, broken and desacralized, in the citation. Brecht's now-time may well be our time, too.

Notes

[1] Brecht, *BFA* 27:248.

[2] "Der Flug war angenehm, und es war angenehm, abzufliegen." Brecht, *BFA* 29:425.

[3] "die wenig oder nicht gespielt wird, da sie für zu dunkel gilt" Brecht, *BFA* 27:255.

⁴ Ruth Berlau, *Brechts Lai-Tu: Erinnerungen und Notate von Ruth Berlau*, ed. Hans Bunge (Darmstadt: Luchterhand, 1985), 210.

⁵ See the contemporary reviews cited in Werner Hecht, *Brechts Antigone des Sophokles* (Frankfurt am Main: Suhrkamp, 1988), 197 and 203.

⁶ Cited in Hecht, *Brechts Antigone des Sophokles*, 198, 208–9.

⁷ Werner Hecht, *Brecht Chronik, 1898–1956* (Frankfurt am Main: Suhrkamp, 1997), 803.

⁸ Berlau writes: "The role of Antigone was as if made for Miss Weigel." Berlau, *Brechts Lai-Tu*, 211. In a letter to Feuchtwanger, Brecht calls the play "a try out for Berlin." Brecht, *BFA* 29:445.

⁹ "Vermutlich ist es die Rückkehr in den deutschen Sprachbereich, was mich in das Unternehmen treibt." Brecht, *BFA* 27:255.

¹⁰ "in eine neue Arbeit hineingefallen." Hecht, *Brecht Chronik*, 803.

¹¹ Brecht, *BFA* 12:115. Eisler was just as unimpressed as Brecht by the Left's refunctioning of Hölderlin during the war, sharing neither "the German pathos cultivated by the exiled Communists . . . nor the emasculation of Hölderlin into an elegiac dreamer," as Claudia Albert puts it in her study on his *Hollywooder Liederbuch*. Albert, *Das schwierige Handwerk des Hoffens: Hanns Eisler's "Hollywooder Liederbuch" (1942/43)* (Stuttgart: Metzler, 1991), 105. The new approach to Hölderlin first presented in this wartime song cycle involved subjecting his poems to drastic cuts before setting them to music, with the aim of producing a new poem that addressed the needs of the present in a way the original did not. Eisler explained his procedure in conversation with Hans Bunge: "Particularly in the case of Hölderlin, who overwrites — incidentally, that was Schiller's objection, Hölderlin's superabundance — I seek out what I can read today." Brecht's response was enthusiastic. Hans Bunge, *Fragen Sie mehr über Brecht: Hanns Eisler im Gespräch* (Munich: Rogner & Bernhard, 1970), 116.

¹² Cf. *Die heilige Johanna*, in which Brecht placed a cynical pastiche of "Hyperions Schicksalslied" in the mouth of the stockyard tycoon Graham. Brecht, *BFA* 3:211–12. We can perhaps also hear a parody of the oft-cited line "Wo aber Gefahr ist / wächst das Rettende auch" (But where danger threatens / that which saves from it also grows) in Mackie McHeath's "Wo die Not am größten, ist die Hilfe am nächsten" (where the need is greatest, help is closest), uttered just after his miraculous escape from the gallows. Brecht, *BFA* 2:307.

¹³ Brecht, *BFA* 26:416.

¹⁴ Brecht, *BFA* 27:181.

¹⁵ Walter Benjamin, "The Task of the Translator," trans. Harry Zohn, in *Illuminations* (London: Fontana, 1970), 82.

¹⁶ "erstaunliche radikalität"; "ziemlich getreu." Brecht, *BFA* 27:258; *BFA* 29:440. On the "more than thousand errors" that mar the translations of Sophocles, see Jochen Schmidt's commentary in Hölderlin, *Sämtliche Werke und Briefe*, ed. Jochen Schmidt (Frankfurt am Main: Deutscher Klassiker Verlag, 1994), 2:1326–28.

[17] "Selbst wenn man sich verpflichtet fühlte, für ein Werk wie die 'Antigone' etwas zu tun, können wir das nur so tun, indem wir es etwas für uns tun lassen." Brecht, *BFA* 25:75.

[18] Walter Benjamin, *Understanding Brecht*, trans. Stanley Mitchell (London: New Left Books, 1973), 108.

[19] On Brecht and citation in general, see Claudette Sartiliot, *Citation and Modernity: Derrida, Joyce, and Brecht* (Norman: Oklahoma UP, 1993).

[20] "One can call it a premiere," argued Bruno Snell after the premiere, "for Bert Brecht has changed Sophocles' structure and Hölderlin's poetry so much that to all intents and purposes a new Antigone has been created." Cited in Hecht, *Brechts Antigone des Sophokles*, 205.

[21] See Brecht's 1929 fragment "Plagiat als Kunst" (Plagiarism as Art): "[In the adaptations] citation finds the high position that is its right. Thus it is the most important stylistic feature. Citability." Brecht, *BFA* 21:318.

[22] For example, *Die Antigone des Sophokles* is missing from the standard one-volume edition of Brecht's plays; see *Die Stücke von Bertolt Brecht in einem Band* (Frankfurt am Main: Suhrkamp, 1981). Fredric Jameson has remarked that in a sense, "everything in Brecht is plagiarism in one way or another." Jameson, *Brecht and Method* (London: Verso, 1998), 105.

[23] Anouilh's play, which profiles Antigone's wittingly absurd defiance of her uncle's edict against the background of a kitschy upper-middle-class soap opera, can be regarded as a counter-pole to Brecht's adaptation. Whereas Anouilh presents Antigone as a compulsive naysayer whose death drive Créon, despite his best efforts, proves unable to check, Brecht derives her rebellion from her rational insight into the strategies of exploitation and military aggression that allow a hated tyrant to cling to power. Anouilh privatizes and psychologizes, even pathologizes, her deed; Brecht construes it as a symbolic protest against a proto-fascist regime. Volker Riedel concludes: "Whether Brecht wrote his adaptation *consciously* in reaction to Anouilh is not clear from the sources; however, it is in fact an early and particularly striking indicator of the contradictory relationship between the socialist and the late-bourgeois reception of ancient Greek literature." Riedel, "Antigone-Rezeption in der DDR," in Hecht, *Brechts Antigone des Sophokles*, 269. See also Jean Anouilh, *Antigone* (Paris: Éditions de la Table Ronde, 1946).

[24] "so etwas wie eine deutsche Literatur." Brecht, *BFA* 27:227.

[25] See Herman Meyer, *Das Zitat in der Erzählkunst: Zur Geschichte und Poetik des europäischen Romans* (Frankfurt am Main: Fischer, 1988).

[26] "Was nützen die schönsten und dringendsten Sprüche, aufgemalt auf die verlockendsten Täfelchen, wenn sie sich so rasch verbrauchen?" Brecht, *BFA* 2:233–34; Brecht, *Plays, Volume I* (London: Methuen, 1960), 102.

[27] In 1938, at the height of the realism debate, Eisler's selective, supposedly disrespectful treatment of the *Erbe* had come under fire from Lukács, who accused him of handling the "illustrious literary past of the German people" with arrogance and contempt. Lukács, "Es geht um den Realismus," in *Essays über den Realismus* (Neuwied and Berlin: Luchterhand, 1971), 339. At the time, Brecht had defended Eisler with a wit all the more caustic because not intended for the public eye: "*Lukács* took my friend Eisler, whom few consider to be a pale aesthete, to the

cleaners, as they say, because he supposedly did not show the appropriate pious emotion in relation to the inheritance when the will was executed. He dug around in it, so to speak, and refused to take over *everything*. Well, perhaps as an exile he is not in a position to cart so much around with him." Brecht, *BFA* 22.1:420–21. See also Helen Fehervary, *Hölderlin and the Left: The Search for a Dialectic of Art and Life* (Heidelberg: Carl Winter, 1977), 50.

[28] Adorno, *GS* 11:326.

[29] "die Besitzfrage, die in der Bourgeoisie, sogar was geistige Dinge betrifft, eine (überaus komische) Rolle spielt." Brecht, *BFA* 21:285.

[30] Hermann Meyer, *Das Zitat in der Erzählkunst*, 12.

[31] "aber die Mauer / Setzt er ums Eigene, und die Mauer / Niedergerissen muss sie sein!" Brecht, *BFA* 8:209.

[32] See George Steiner, *Antigones* (Oxford: Oxford UP, 1984), 288: "The full meaning of Creon's deeds (errors) has come home to us as it cannot have to any spectator or reader before our present danger."

[33] See Alfred Döblin, *November 1918: Dritter Teil; Karl und Rosa* (Munich: dtv, 1978), esp. book 8 ("Auf den Spuren der Antigone," "König Kreon").

[34] Brecht, *BFA* 8:205; Hölderlin, *StA* 5:232.

[35] Hölderlin, *StA* 5:272; Hölderlin, *Essays and Letters on Theory*, trans. Thomas Pfau (Albany: State U of New York P, 1988), 115.

[36] "Für das vorliegende theatralische Unternehmen wurde das Antigonedrama ausgewählt, weil es stofflich eine gewisse Aktualität erlangen konnte und formal interessante Aufgaben stellte. Was das stofflich Politische betrifft, stellten sich die Analogien zur Gegenwart, die nach der Durchrationalisierung überraschend kräftig geworden waren, eher nachteilig heraus: die große Figur des Widerstands im antiken Drama repräsentiert nicht die Kämpfer des deutschen Widerstandes, die uns am bedeutendsten erscheinen müssen." Brecht, *BFA* 25:74.

[37] "*Antigones* Tat kann nur darin bestehen, dem Feind zu helfen, was ihre moralische Kontribution ausmacht; auch sie hatte allzulange vom Brot gegessen, was im Dunkeln gebacken ward." Brecht, *BFA* 27:264.

[38] Brecht, *BFA* 15:191.

[39] Brecht, *BFA* 25:75.

[40] Knopf argues that by 1949, when Brecht was working on the foreword, his conception of *Antigone* had shifted from one of popular resistance to one of intra-aristocratic struggle. Jan Knopf, *Brecht-Handbuch: Theater* (Stuttgart: Metzler, 1980), 274.

[41] Brecht, *BFA* 27:255.

[42] Bernard Knox, "Introduction" to Sophocles, *The Theban Plays*, trans. Robert Fagles (Harmondsworth, UK: Penguin, 1984), 37. See also the entries in Brecht's journal from the last months of the war: "Still nothing from Upper Silesia on the attitude of the workers"; "Ruins and no sign of life from the workers." Brecht, *BFA* 27:219, 221.

[43] Sibylle Benninghoff-Lühl, *Figuren des Zitats: Eine Untersuchung zur Funktionsweise übertragener Rede* (Stuttgart: J. B. Metzler, 1998), 26.

[44] Mr. Peachum is also familiar with this meaning. In 1948, the same year he cited *Antigone*, Brecht added a new stanza to Peachum's *Morität:* "Und die Fische, sie verschwinden / doch zum Kummer des Gerichts: / Man zitiert am End den Haifisch / doch der Haifisch weiß von nichts" (And the fish disappear / but to the consternation of the court: / In the end the shark is cited / but the shark knows nothing at all). Brecht, *BFA* 2:309.

[45] In the poem, however, the tables have been turned: Antigone is now called up as a witness for the prosecution, while her one-time accusers themselves stand accused.

[46] Lacan's interpretation is to be found in Jacques Lacan, *The Seminar of Jacques Lacan,* book 7: *The Ethics of Psychoanalysis, 1959–1960,* ed. Jacques-Alain Miller, trans. Dennis Porter (New York: Norton, 1992), 243–87.

[47] "Ce qui importait pour elle, c'est de refuser et de mourir." Jean Anouilh, *Antigone* (Paris: Éditions de la Table Ronde, 1946), 102.

[48] Sophocles, *The Theban Plays,* 104.

[49] "Ich aber ruf euch an, daß ihr mir helft im Bedrängnis / Und helft euch auch dabei noch." Brecht, *BFA* 8:213. Brecht's notes to the production, published in the *Antigonemodell,* stipulate that this, her most impassioned appeal, is to be spoken "like a citation." Brecht, *BFA* 25:104.

[50] In a revised version of the prologue written for a later production, the actor who plays the part of Tiresias, the personification of omniscience, urges the audience "Nachzusuchen in euren Gemütern nach ähnlichen Taten / Näherer Vergangenheit oder dem Ausbleiben / Ähnlicher Taten" (To search in your hearts for similar deeds / Of recent time or the omission / Of similar deeds). Brecht, *BFA* 8: 242.

[51] "Ihr also duldet's. Und haltet das Maul ihm. / Und sei's nicht vergessen!" Brecht, *BFA* 8:213.

[52] "Und wir umarmten uns und waren frohgemut / Denn unser Bruder war im Krieg und 's ging ihm gut." Brecht, *BFA* 8:195–96.

[53] "Wer sehn will, wird gesehn." Brecht, *BFA* 8:197.

[54] "Und wir lachten, waren frohgemut: / Aus dem Krieg war unser Bruder. 's ging ihm gut." Brecht, *BFA* 8:197.

[55] "Schwester, sie haben gehänget ihn / Drum hat er laut nach uns geschrien." Brecht, *BFA* 8:198.

[56] "Lieber Herr, mit uns geh nicht ins Gericht / Denn wir kennen den Menschen nicht." Brecht, *BFA* 8:198.

[57] "einen Aktualitätspunkt zu setzen und das subjektive Problem zu skizzieren." Brecht, *BFA* 25:74–75.

[58] It remains unclear, however, whether the sisters will attain the insight into their mistake prescribed by Aristotle in the wake of the peripeteia. Brecht's conception of didactic drama dictates that it is up to the audience to reflect upon the situation in which the protagonists find themselves hopelessly embroiled: the likes of Mother

Courage are condemned to repeat their errors because they will never learn for themselves. The *Kleines Organon*, also composed during Brecht's sojourn in Switzerland, was directed against a dominant strand of Aristotle reception, inherited from French neoclassicism, rather than against Aristotle himself. There is no evidence that Brecht ever read a line of the *Poetics*.

59 "ein Stalingrad von heute." Brecht, *BFA* 24:350. Ronald Gray aptly calls Brecht's Creon "a flatly rapacious caricature of Hitler." Gray, *Brecht* (Edinburgh: Oliver & Boyd, 1961), 95.

60 Quoted in Steiner, *Antigones*, 194.

61 Adorno observes that the liquidation of the individual under late capitalism compels Brecht to fall back on pre-modern fables. Adorno, *GS* 11:420–21.

62 "Das Antigonedrama rollt dann objektiv, auf der fremden Ebene der Herrschenden, das Gesamtgeschehen auf." Brecht, *BFA* 25:75.

63 "Das Herz bleibt einem stehen, wenn man von den Luftbombardements Berlins liest. Da sie nicht mit militärischen Operationen verknüpft sind, sieht man kein Ende des Krieges, nur ein Ende Deutschlands." Brecht, *BFA* 27,168.

64 Sophocles, *The Theban Plays*, 65.

65 "recht dünn." Brecht, *BFA* 8:231.

66 "Der totale materielle und geistige Zusammenbruch hat zweifellos in unserem unglücklichen und Unglück schaffenden Land einen vagen Durst nach Neuem erzeugt, und was die Kunst anbetrifft, wird sie . . . hie und da ermutigt, Neues zu versuchen. Da freilich große Verwirrung darüber zu bestehen scheint, was alt und was neu ist, auch Furcht vor der Rückkehr des Alten mit der Furcht vor der Einkehr des Neuen mischt, und überdies die Besiegten vielerorts angewiesen werden, den Nazismus lediglich geistig und seelisch zu überwinden, werden die Künstler gut tun, nicht blindlings auf die Beteuerung zu vertrauen, daß Neues willkommen sei. . . . So mag es gerade in der Zeit des Wiederaufbaus nicht eben leicht sein, fortschrittliche Kunst zu machen. Dies sollte uns anfeuern." Brecht, *BFA* 25:73. See also Brecht's journal entry from 5 Aug. 1940, *BFA* 26:409.

67 See Hans Mayer, *Brecht* (Frankfurt am Main: Suhrkamp, 1996), 110.

68 Brecht, *BFA* 25:73.

69 "Jedoch kann die Kunst sich nur orientieren, indem sie fortschreitet, und sie muß . . . aus dem Zustand des Wartens auf Behandlung kommen und in dem allgemeinen Verfall an irgendeinem Ort beginnen." Brecht, *BFA* 25:73.

70 "Schwester, Ismene, Zwillingsreis / Aus des Ödipus Stamm." Brecht, *BFA* 8:200.

71 Hans Bunge, *Antigone-Modell 1948 von Bertolt Brecht und Caspar Neher: Zur Praxis und Theorie des epischen (dialektischen) Theaters Bertolt Brechts* (PhD diss., Greifswald University, Germany, 1957). Pohl remarks that these figures seem somewhat too precise, given the philological complexity of the situation. Rainer Pohl, *Strukturelemente und Entwicklung von Pathosformen in der Dramensprache Bertold Brechts* (Bonn: Bouvier, 1969), 165.

72 Hölderlin, *StA* 2:172.

[73] "Die Änderungen, die mich zum Schreiben ganz neuer Partien zwangen, sind gemacht, um die griechische 'moira' (das Schicksalhafte) herauszuschneiden; das heißt ich versuche da, zu der zugrunde liegenden Volkslegende vorzustoßen." Brecht, *BFA* 29:440. The letter was written some time in December 1948. See also his entry in the Arbeitsjournal from 16 December: "Nach und nach, bei der fortschreitenden Bearbeitung der Szenen, taucht aus dem ideologischen Nebel die höchst realistische Volkslegende auf" (Bit by bit, as I continue to work on the scenes, the highly realistic folk legend is emerging from the ideological mist). *BFA* 27:255.

[74] Hellmuth Karasek, for example, considers Brecht's historical parables to be "examples of acute and current problems translated into different times and different cultural environments, whose different conditions they cannot and do not intend to take into account." Hellmuth Karasek, *Bertolt Brecht: Der jüngste Fall eines Theaterklassikers* (Munich: Kindler, 1978), 99.

[75] On Hölderlin's "return to the occult source," see Steiner, *Antigones*, 74–75. I borrow the terms "hypotext" and "hypertext" from Gérard Genette, *Palimpseste: Die Literatur auf zweiter Stufe*, trans. Wolfram Bayer and Dieter Hornig (Frankfurt am Main: Suhrkamp, 1993), 14.

[76] See Hans Blumenberg, *Arbeit am Mythos* (Frankfurt am Main: Suhrkamp, 1979), 28.

[77] Hellmut Flashar, *Inszenierung der Antike: Das griechische Drama auf der Bühne der Neuzeit, 1585–1990* (Munich: C. H. Beck, 1991), 190.

[78] Walter Benjamin, *Gesammelte Schriften*, ed. Rolf Tiedemann and Herrmann Schweppenhäuser (Frankfurt am Main: Suhrkamp, 1974–89), 1.2:701.

[79] See Andrew Benjamin, "Being Roman Now: The Time of Fashion; A Commentary on Walter Benjamin's 'Theses on the Philosophy of History' XIV," *Thesis Eleven* 75 (2003): 39–53; here, 45.

[80] "haben wir doch immer noch den vergotzten Staat der Klassenkämpfe!" Brecht, *BFA* 27:261.

[81] "Benutzt ist die Hölderlinsche (ziemlich getreue) Übertragung aus dem Griechischen; sie hat etwas Hegelisches, das Du erkennen wirst und einen Dir wohl nicht erkennbaren schwäbischen Volksgestus (die 'Volksgrammatik' geht bis in die höchst artistischen Chöre hinein!)." Brecht, *BFA* 29:400.

[82] Brecht, *BFA* 27:258–59. Berlau recalled in her memoirs: "He considered the "Antigonä" more than a literary translation. Merely on the basis of its 'Swabian popular gestus,' which Brecht pointed out to me again and again as he was reading it to me, Hölderlin's text was for him the 'most powerful and most amusing.'" Berlau, *Brechts Lai-Tu*, 210. Even the adaptation's departures from the text are couched in a pseudo-Hölderlinian style, establishing a continuity of tone that smooths over the deep cuts inflicted upon the fable. Several commentators have noted the extent to which Brecht remains faithful to the arcane diction of the translation. Reinhold Grimm, for instance, remarks that the rationalization of the fable "seems by no means violent," finding the cause in the "linguistic affinity of the Swabian Brecht with the Swabian Hölderlin." Reinhold Grimm, *Brecht und die Weltliteratur* (Nürnberg: Verlag Hans Carl, 1961), 39.

[83] See Werner Mittenzwei, *Das Leben des Bertolt Brecht* (Frankfurt am Main: Suhrkamp, 1987), 1:11; André Müller and Gerd Semmer, *Geschichten vom Herrn Brecht: 99 Brecht-Anekdoten*, (Frankfurt am Main: Insel, 1967), 31.

[84] Hans Curjel, who commissioned the adaptation, speculated in 1961: "The ancient little city of Chur may well have seemed familiar to Brecht, who came from Augsburg." Cited in Hecht, *Brechts Antigone des Sophokles*, 188.

[85] "schwäbische Tonfälle und gymnasiale Latein-Konstruktionen." Brecht, *BFA* 27:255.

[86] See Ulrich Weisstein, "Imitation, Stylization, and Adaptation: The Language of Brecht's *Antigone* and its relation to Hölderlin's version of Sophocles," *German Quarterly* 46 (1973), 590: "Hölderlin's equivalents often (and characteristically) carry an archaic flavor which restores metaphorical meaning in a drama that is otherwise relatively poor in imagery. This is one trait of the 1803 *Antigone* which must have attracted Brecht, who in all likelihood saw the possibility of equating linguistic archaism with socio-political barbarism."

[87] Knopf detects in Brecht "a differentiation, one that started here with *Antigone*, between Schiller/Goethe on the one hand . . . and Hölderlin on the other." Knopf, *Brecht-Handbuch*, 276.

[88] Walter Jens, *Statt einer Literaturgeschichte* (Tübingen: Neske, 1957), 227.

[89] Peter Sloterdijk, *Nicht gerettet: Versuche nach Heidegger* (Frankfurt am Main: Suhrkamp, 2002), 51.

[90] "die alten / Heimischen Ulmen und Dächer"; "Tränenschleier." Brecht, *BFA* 8:202.

[91] "Ich hass dich." Brecht, BFA 8:202; "Magst du so etwas sagen, haß ich dich." Hölderlin, *StA* 5:209.

[92] Heidegger, *GA* 13:11.

[93] "wie die Stadt voll ist von Trauer um die Jungfrau." Hölderlin, *StA* 5:233.

[94] "Wisse, die Stadt ist voll mit innerer Unlust." Brecht, *BFA* 8:220.

[95] See Genette, *Palimpseste*, 440.

[96] "Der großnamige Sieg ist aber gekommen, / Der wagenreichen günstig, der Thebe." Hölderlin, *StA*:211.

[97] "Der großbeutige Sieg ist aber gekommen, / Der Wagenreichen günstig, der Thebe." Brecht, *BFA* 8:203. See also the ensuing victory address by Creon: "Ihr Männer, teilt's mit allen: Argos / Ist nicht mehr. Abrechnung war / Völlige." (You men, tell everyone: Argos / is no more. Accounts have been / cleared.) Brecht, *BFA* 8:203. Brecht's retrospective projection of the language of fascist genocide (*Abrechnung* is taken from the vocabulary of a desktop murderer) upon the mythic ruler of an ancient Greek city-state is not dissimilar to the manner in which Horkheimer and Adorno telescope bourgeois categories of self-understanding onto the figure of Odysseus: it provokes the shock of recognition from across a vast historical distance.

[98] Werner Frick, *"Die mythische Methode": Komparatistische Studien zur Transfo: mation der griechischen Tragödie im Drama der klassischen Moderne* (Tübingen: Max Niemeyer, 1998), 542–51.

[99] "Nicht, ich bitt euch, sprecht vom Geschick. / Das weiß ich. Von dem sprecht / Der mich hinmacht, schuldlos; dem / Knüpft ein Geschick!" Brecht, *BFA* 8:227.

[100] Jean Cocteau, *The Infernal Machine*, trans. Carl Wildman (London: Oxford UP, 1936), 4.

[101] See Brecht, *BFA* 24:350.

[102] "Halt für ein Beispiel." Brecht, *BFA* 8:212.

[103] "Aus ist die Stadt uns, Zügel gewohnt und / Ohne Zügel." *BFA* 8:240.

[104] "Denn kurz ist die Zeit / Allumher ist Verhängnis, und nimmer genügt sie / Hinzuleben, undenkend und leicht / Von Duldung zu Frevel und / Weise zu werden im Alter." Brecht, *BFA* 8:241.

[105] "sie haben im Alter gelehrt, zu denken." Hölderlin, *StA* 5:262.

[106] See Dieter Baldo, *Bertolt Brechts "Antigonemodell 1948": Theaterarbeit nach dem Faschismus* (Cologne: Pahl-Rugenstein Verlag, 1987), 17–18.

[107] Edward Said, *Beginnings: Intention and Method* (New York: Basic Books, 1975), 22.

[108] Max Frisch, *Gesammelte Werke in zeitlicher Folge*, vol. 2 (Frankfurt am Main: Suhrkamp, 1976), 597.

[109] See Richard Wagner, *Opera and Drama*, trans. William Ashton Ellis (Lincoln: U of Nebraska P, 1995), 190: "*O holy Antigone! on thee I cry! Let wave thy banner, that beneath it we destroy and yet redeem!*"

[110] Visibly "carried away" by his friend Eisler's wartime Hölderlin compositions, Brecht, Eisler reports, congratulated him "that I had 'liberated' — I am quoting him — certain Hölderlin poems 'from plaster.' I had 'unplastered' Hölderlin." Hanns Eisler, *Fragen Sie mehr über Brecht: Gespräche mit Hans Bunge* (Munich: Rogner & Bernhard, 1976), 66:195. In an essay from 1926, "Weniger Gips!!!" (Less Plaster!!!), Brecht had attacked those who contributed to the irrelevance and harmlessness of the theater through the zealous application of plaster, dreaming instead of "something bolder," a "freer, more objective, more focused" art (Brecht, *BFA* 21:186). One can conclude from his comments to Eisler that Brecht numbered Hölderlin among those from whose work a bourgeois public had sculpted a monument to its own ideology. Eisler's *Entgipsung* of Hölderlin was of the first importance for the later *Antigone* project, for it showed Brecht that the poet was good for something other than the nationalist mystification he had been used to authorize up to that point. Werner Mittenzwei is right to point out that Brecht's subsequent occupation with the poet is unthinkable without Eisler's example. Mittenzwei, *Brechts Verhältnis zur Tradition* (Berlin: Akademie-Verlag, 1972), 228. Nonetheless, Brecht transcended the model provided him by Eisler's *Hollywooder Liederbuch* through his modifications and additions to Hölderlin's text, which went far beyond anything contemplated by his friend. Eisler, himself something of an expert on Hölderlin, was one of few to appreciate the significance of the adaptation, enthusing: "There's been nothing since Brecht, let me say since he 'doctored' Sophocles, the Sophocles of Hölderlin, since he fixed up the plaster verses, the genial verses of Hölderlin, the genial translation — there's been nothing like it ever since!" Eisler, *Fragen Sie mehr über Brecht*, 72.

[111] "D. J. Das Maß der Mitte bestimmt das Verweilenkönnen, das nicht in die Verzögerung ausweicht, aber auch nicht zur Übereilung entflieht. / D. Ä. Dieses Maß betrifft die Zeit im Sinne der rechten Zeit, jene Zeit, zu der es jedesmal die Zeit ist, daß . . . / D. J. Jene Zeit, die wir nennen, wenn wir eigens sagen und gar rufen 'Jetzt.' / D. Ä. Wie der Ister-Gesang zum Beginn anhebt: 'Jezt komme, Feuer!' / D. J. 'Jezt' — wir sagen dies erste Wort des Gesanges nur, wenn wir es klingen lassen und ausklingen in ein Verweilen, darin sich ein langes Warten gesammelt hat . . . D. Ä. und jetzt sich vollendet." Heidegger, *GA* 75:67–68.

[112] "Diese Auszeichnung des 'Jezt' fordert, daß wir in diesem Zeit-Wort auch etwas Ausgezeichnetes vernehmen und eine verborgene Fülle der dichterischen Zeit und ihrer Wahrheit erwarten. . . . Das 'Jezt' nennt ein Ereignis." Heidegger, *GA* 53:9; *Hölderlin's Hymn "The Ister,"* trans. William McNeill and Julia Davis (Bloomington: Indiana UP, 1996), 9.

[113] "dieses 'Jezt' . . . ein plötzlich aufgegangener Stern, der alles überleuchtet." Heidegger, *GA* 53:8; *Hölderlin's Hymn "The Ister,"* 8.

[114] On Heidegger's reading of the "now" that opens the Ister hymn, see also Stanley Cavell, "Night and Day: Heidegger and Thoreau," in *Appropriating Heidegger*, ed. James E. Faulconer and Mark A. Wrathall (Cambridge: Cambridge UP, 2000), 30–49, esp. 40–41. Cavell suggestively compares Heidegger's river to Thoreau's pond, and the former's rhetoric of daybreak to the closing image of *Walden:* "There is more day to dawn. The sun is but a morning star."

[115] See Nietzsche's opening remarks on the unhistorical animal in his untimely meditation on the use and abuse of history. *Werke*, section 3, vol. 1 (Berlin: Walter de Gruyter, 1977), 244.

[116] See Robert Savage, "Adorno's Family and Other Animals," *Thesis Eleven* 78 (2004): 102–12.

[117] Hölderlin, *StA* 2:206.

[118] "ist wie ein Vorsatz, der Synthesis sich zu entschlagen, der reinen Passivität sich anzuvertrauen, um Gegenwart ganz zu erfüllen. Denn alle Synthesis — keine wußte das besser als Kant — geschieht wider die reine Gegenwart, als Beziehung aufs Vergangene und Künftige, das von Hölderlins Tabu ereilt wird." Adorno, *GS* 11:483; *Notes to Literature*, trans. Shierry Weber Nicholsen, 2 vols. (New York: Columbia UP, 1992), 2:142.

[119] "Tabu gegen die abstrakte Utopie." Adorno, *GS* 11:483; *Notes to Literature* 2:142.

[120] "Unwiederbringlichkeit des einmal Gestürzten." Adorno, *GS* 11:483; *Notes to Literature* 2:142.

[121] Adorno, *GS* 4:175–77.

[122] "Einen Stand von Freiheit erwartet Hölderlin nur durchs synthetische Prinzip hindurch, durch dessen Selbstreflexion." Adorno, *GS* 11:484; *Notes to Literature* 2:143.

[123] Adorno, *GS* 4:177.

[124] "dem Gesetz des Gegenwärtigen, bei Hölderlin dem der Dichtung." Adorno, *GS* 11:483; *Notes to Literature* 2:142.

[125] Carl Dahlhaus, *Ludwig van Beethoven: Approaches to His Music*, trans. Mary Whittall (Oxford: Clarendon, 1991), 220.

[126] "Sein, sonst nichts." Adorno, *GS* 4:179.

[127] "So fällt jetzt Thebe"; "Wir aber / Folgen auch jetzt ihm all, und / Nach unten ist's"; "Aber die alles sah / Konnte nur noch helfen dem Feind, der jetzt / Kommt und uns austilgt gleich." Brecht, *BFA* 8:241.

[128] "Da sah ich meine Schwester an. / Sollt sie in eigner Todespein / Jetzt gehn, den Bruder zu befrein? / Er mochte nicht gestorben sein." Brecht, *BFA* 8:198–99.

[129] "Das Messer, das Messer gib her / Daß ich ihn abschneid und er hängt nicht mehr." Brecht, *BFA* 8:198.

[130] Brecht, *BFA* 15:191.

[131] "True, in Sophocles' *Antigone* an extreme, a tragic form of opposition was acted out between Antigone and Creon. Contrary to run-of-the-mill interpretations, however, the tragedy did not involve an opposition between the private sphere and piety, on the one hand, and the 'public' sphere and politics, on the other: to obey a divine law is *also* a law of the city; to obey the laws of the city is *also* a divine injunction." Cornelius Castoriadis, *World in Fragments: Writings on Politics, Society, Psychoanalysis and the Imagination*, trans. David Ames Curtis (Stanford, CA: Stanford UP, 1997), 117.

[132] Keith A. Dickson, *Towards Utopia: A Study of Brecht* (Oxford: Clarendon, 1978), 200.

[133] Benjamin, *Gesammelte Schriften*, 1.2:695. For Benjamin's comments on the Brechtian technique of citation, see Benjamin, *Understanding Brecht*, 19.

[134] Brecht's notes to the production specify that the stage, hitherto "placed in half-darkness," should now be bathed in "full light." Benjamin's flash is thus sustained for the duration of the citation: the entire theatrical presentation fills up the moment of now-time. Brecht, *BFA* 25:88.

[135] Eva Geulen, "Zeit zur Darstellung: Walter Benjamins 'Das Kunstwerk im Zeitalter seiner technischen Reproduzierbarkeit.'" *MLN* 107.3 (1992): 602.

[136] Cited in Hecht, *Brechts Antigone des Sophokles*, 80.

[137] "Wenn aber die Geschichtlichkeit eines Menschentums im Heimischsein beruht und wenn das Heimischsein nur dichtend bestimmt werden kann und dichterisch gesagt werden muß, dann ist Hölderlin der erste, der die deutsche Not des Unheimischseins dichterisch erfährt und d.h. dichtend sagt." Heidegger, *GA* 53:155; *Hölderlin's Hymn "The Ister,"* 125.

[138] Several commentators have explored this shift by comparing the interpretation of the first stasimon from *Antigone* offered in Heidegger's 1935 lecture course *Einführung in die Metaphysik* with that ventured in his 1942 course on "Der Ister." See in particular Michael Zimmerman, *Heidegger's Confrontation with Modernity: Technology, Politics, and Art* (Bloomington: Indiana UP, 1990), 120–21, and Clare Pearson Geiman, "Heidegger's *Antigones*," in *A Companion to Heidegger's Introduction to Metaphysics*, ed. Richard Polt and Gregory Fried (New Haven: Yale UP, 2001), 161–82.

[139] On Adorno's idealized view of the "revolutionary" artistic movements in turn-of-the-century Vienna, see Heinz Steinert, *Adorno in Wien: Über die (Un)möglichkeit von Kunst, Kultur und Befreiung* (Frankfurt am Main: Fischer, 1993).

[140] "daß es in einem zentralen Sinn eine Rückkunft nicht gibt." Theodor Adorno and Thomas Mann, *Der Briefwechsel, 1943–1955*, ed. Christoph Gödde and Thomas Sprecher (Frankfurt am Main: Suhrkamp, 2000), 103.

[141] "Kaum anderswo dürfte Hölderlin seinen nachgeborenen Protektor schroffer Lügen strafen als im Verhältnis zum Fremden"; "Hölderlin wird über Stock und Stein für eine Vorstellung von Liebe eingespannt, die in dem kreist, was man ohnehin ist, narzißtisch fixiert ans eigene Volk; Heidegger verrät die Utopie an Gefangenschaft in der Selbstheit"; "de[r] exiliert[e] Hölderlin . . . ein zuverlässiger Auslandsdeutscher." Adorno, *GS* 11:456–57; *Notes to Literature* 2:17.

[142] Adorno, *GS* 11:456; *Notes to Literature* 2:117.

[143] Hölderlin, *StA* 2:190; *Poems and Fragments*, trans. Michael Hamburger (London: Routledge & Kegan Paul, 1966), 493.

[144] Giorgio Agamben, *The Man without Content*, trans. Georgia Albert (Stanford. CA: Stanford UP, 1999), 108.

[145] "Für ein paar hundert Jahre auf alle Fälle!" Cited in Mayer, *Brecht*, 285.

Epilogue: Three Anniversaries

Möcht' ich ein Komet seyn? Ich glaube.

[Would I like to be a comet? I think so.]
— Hölderlin, "In lieblicher Bläue"
(In lovely blueness)

THE JUBILEE OF A RENOWNED CULTURAL FIGURE may be likened to the long-expected appearance of a comet in the night sky. Much as the comet's approach transforms astronomy, however briefly, from a boffinish pursuit into a popular pastime, so the commemoration of an author ordinarily discussed by none but academics has the potential to bring him to the attention of a much broader reading public. As each celestial body shoots into view, it excites a flush of interest conditioned by the knowledge that decades may elapse before it again blazes across the firmament. Luther, Bach, and Nietzsche years follow one another in regular succession, observed with a solemnity that stands in inverse proportion to the arbitrariness of the occasion. Conferences are held, biographies published, and works reissued in accordance with the divinely prescribed calendar; appreciations and reevaluations appear by the dozen. Every so often a new comet emerges from the cosmic flotsam, or an old comet, hitherto unnoticed, veers closer to the earth in the course of its journey through the solar system.

Today comets give rise to different associations in the spectator than in the age of Hölderlin, who was not alone in regarding their elliptical trajectory — at once predetermined, aberrant, and dazzling to behold — as a figure of revolution.[1] Periodically recurring messengers from the beyond, they seem to offer the reassurance of historical continuity at times when evidence of such continuity has become ever more difficult to find on earth. When Halley's Comet last returned to the heavens, journalists sought out nonagenarians still able to recall its previous visit, while accounts of still earlier sightings, notably at the Battle of Hastings, established the pretense of a shared experience linking viewers of today with their ancestors. In a similar fashion, the jubilees of iconic writers such as Shakespeare and Goethe, while being used to affirm the timelessness of their achievement, have also increasingly come to prompt reflection on how previous jubilees were registered. Perhaps the sense of mild disappointment that the spectacle leaves in its wake is the same in both cases, too. Inevitably, an event that promised to serve as a reminder of permanence comes to pass as a demonstration of ephemerality: a non-event. Those who stayed up late to catch the show now retire to their beds, bleary-eyed and yawning, wondering whether it had been worth all the fuss.

One should not underestimate the influence of such jubilees upon the cultural politics of Germany, where they seem to be celebrated with unusual fervor. It is tempting to speculate upon the fate that might have befallen Hölderlin had he died around 1810, as Dr Autenrieth predicted when he was discharged from the clinic, rather than in 1843.[2] To be sure, he would still have been conscripted by the Party ideologists, a process that was already well underway by the time the Nazis seized power, but the worst excesses of the wartime reception might have been avoided. There would, almost certainly, have been no society founded under the aegis of Goebbels, no field edition, no Hitler wreath laid at the poet's grave, and perhaps no need for more than a token rescue operation after the war. As it happened, Heidegger marked the 100th anniversary by delivering a speech in Freiburg, at the same time publishing a long essay on "Andenken" — what else? — in the memorial volume brought out by the city of Tübingen. Both texts, fitted out with the same date, found their way into his *Erläuterungen zu Hölderlins Dichtung*, and as we have seen, Adorno chose the 120th anniversary to attack them, alluding at one stage to their context in the centenary festivities in none too flattering terms: "Clearly, in 1943, when the philosophical commentator was working with 'Andenken,' he must have feared even the appearance of French women as something subversive; but he did not change anything in this strange excursus later."[3] Simply by addressing a group of people gathered together to commemorate Hölderlin on the day of his death, both thinkers adopt the discursive stance of the eulogist, that is, the person considered best qualified to speak well of the deceased, a task that for Adorno extends to speaking ill of those who profane his memory. Ineluctably drawn to the seventh of June, they both presume to say the truth about Hölderlin that he cannot say for himself, a truth first released through the speaking engagement of the philosopher. Not by chance was Brecht the only member of the trio to withstand the allure of the funerary oration, for he alone never aspired to speak *for* Hölderlin (as his *Vormund* or mouthpiece), electing instead to speak *through* him (as his souffleur). The battle for Hölderlin's legacy in the postwar period, insofar as it concerns the authorization to speak in his name and on his behalf, may be regarded in part as a struggle for the right to eulogize him.

Pierre Bertaux's address to the Hölderlin Society in 1968, delivered on the occasion of the 125th anniversary of Hölderlin's death, marks another caesura in the history of the poet's reception. The remarkably intense, if relatively short-lived, wave of left-wing interest in Hölderlin stimulated by that address swept away the models of reception I have set up in this study, leaving them to be salvaged from the deep by later intellectual historians. These models, each incapable of refutation on its own terms, were made apparently defunct by a line of questioning that thematized in a new way the relationship between Hölderlin's poetic calling and the still incomplete project of political emancipation. The "red," revisionist poet presented by Bertaux and those who came after him did not necessarily cut a more lifelike, more imposing, or even more interesting figure than the Hölderlin(s) of Heidegger, Adorno, and Brecht, but he was without doubt more *timely*, in both the positive and negative senses of the word. And while the image of the firebrand poet they disseminated was to grow obsolete within a decade of its appearance, they set a full stop to the period with which this study is concerned, thereby allowing it to be perceived in its unity (just as, in hindsight, the lasting achievement of the 68 movement as a whole was not that it established some new socio-political order to replace the vaguely defined "establishment" but that it broke the hold of previously hegemonic cultural codes and assignations). I will conclude, then, with three further well-documented sightings of the comet Hölderlin as it continues on its "eccentric course," those of 1968, 1970, and 1983, in each case focusing on those eyewitness reports that most clearly indicate the distance separating the pre- from the post-68 reception.

1968, or, The (Re-)Birth of Hölderlin from the Spirit of the French Revolution

Pierre Bertaux, the son of Heinrich Mann's great friend Felix and professor at the newly established Institut d'Allemand at the Nouvelle Sorbonne, had been researching and publishing on Hölderlin for decades by the time he came to address the society's convention in Düsseldorf, and the main thesis he advanced there — "that Hölderlin was and, in his heart of hearts, always remained an enthusiastic supporter of the French Revolution, a Jacobin"[4] — was hardly novel. As Bertaux himself acknowledged, most of his findings had been anticipated years before in the writings of Georg Lukács, Werner Kirchner, Maurice Delorme, and Robert Minder,[5] while any unbiased reader of Hölderlin's correspondence is left in no doubt as to his republican sympathies. So why did Bertaux's speech prove so provocative that, in the words of one audience member, "immediately after his presentation there began an impassioned discussion in small circles and groups, which continued until the end of the conference and was still being followed in the press for a long time thereafter"?[6] What was the source of the controversy, considering that the Hölderlin community must already have been familiar with Bertaux's central claim?

During his years as a theology student in Tübingen, Hölderlin had followed with keen interest the events of the French Revolution as they unfolded, hoping with his friends that the states of Germany, too, might soon be liberated from the yoke of despotism. Now history seemed to be repeating itself. The civil unrest that had exploded in the *événements* of May 1968 was still simmering on the streets of Paris when Bertaux took to the podium, flanked by a retinue of socialist students he had brought with him from France.[7] Their counterparts in West Germany, whose own battle with the state had cranked up a gear following the formation of the Great Coalition and the death of Benno Ohnesorg the previous year, looked across the border for inspiration, little realizing that the movement would never again experience such a groundswell of popular support. They were searching for a native hero who embodied the simultaneously anti-capitalist and anti-Stalinist (or "anti-anticommunist")[8] spirit of the age, a standard-bearer of unblemished character and unquestioned revolutionary credentials who had already been legitimated by tradition, and who could in turn lend some much-needed legitimacy to their cause. They found him in Hölderlin. Identifying with his youthful idealism, they saw in his descent into madness the historical precedent and incentive for their own struggle against the forces of reaction. He taught them that the temporal disjunction between spirit and deed upon which he had foundered might finally be overcome through a praxis that took its cue directly from poetry, circumventing the ponderous mediations recommended by their mentors in Frankfurt. Had not Hölderlin himself proclaimed: "and if the kingdom of darkness should break upon us with violence, then we will throw our quills under the table and go in God's name to where the need is greatest, and we are most needed"?[9]

While Bertaux was blessed by circumstance, like all gifted publicists he also demonstrated a canny knack for seizing the moment. Deliberately pitching his message over the heads of his audience in Düsseldorf, many of whom must have found his rhetoric inappropriate to the occasion, Bertaux was casting around for a wider interested public. Ten years later, he would dedicate his biography of the poet, with a characteristically histrionic locution, to "MY GERMAN FRIENDS / *in Hölderlin's name!*"[10] His awareness that Hölderlin *mattered*, as he had not mattered since the darkest days of the war, came through in the infectious sense of urgency with which he pressed his argument. Countering the hypothetical objection that as a Frenchman he lacked the essential prerequisite to understanding the most German of all poets, he asserted at the beginning of the speech: "Today I would like to turn the tables and ask: 'What can a German understand about Hölderlin?' With this paradox I simply want to say that the Germans lack *one* prerequisite for understanding Hölderlin entirely, in all his aspects. They lack the Frenchman's innate familiarity with the history of the French Revolution and its revolutionary pathos."[11] This must have been galling news for Bertaux's listeners, many of whom had spent a lifetime trying to understand Hölderlin, only to be told they were congenitally unfit for the task. More evidence of the Frenchman's predisposition to pathos was to come: "If a color is missing from a four-color print, no matter how sharp the picture may be — it is badly distorted. The German picture of Hölderlin, which 'blossoms in lovely blueness,' is missing a color: the color red. As if German scholarship were red-blind, or perhaps red-shy."[12] In the remainder of his speech, Bertaux set about correcting the received image with bold and vivid brushstrokes, and while the portrait's official curator, Adolf Beck, subsequently took issue with several of his individual retouchings, the reddish tint was allowed to stand.[13]

Not only Heidegger but also such ostensibly leftist critics as Adorno and Brecht would not have recognized the restoration as a fair likeness. It is true that in his biography, Bertaux praised "Parataxis" as belonging "to the very best . . . that has been written about Hölderlin's poetry."[14] But Bertaux could only marshal Adorno's remarks on the late work's quasi-musical technique of syntactic seriation in support of his psychological and political contestation of Hölderlin's madness by ignoring the insight from which they sprang: that the truth-content of a poem is inseparably bound up with its semblance character. By short-circuiting the constitutive distance between poetic model and utopian vision, Bertaux canceled what was, for Adorno, the precondition for the valid cognition of artworks, transforming Hölderlin's poetry into a coded manifesto, a more or less legible testament to the author's state of mind at the time of composition. The scholars who followed him, freshly attuned to the political resonances that reach right down into the mythic stratum of the hymnic work, were inclined to show even less tolerance for Adorno's abstruse reservations.

For Brecht, meanwhile, Hölderlin's political leanings were a matter of relative indifference. His scattered comments on the poet up to 1948 all suggest that he accepted the rumors being spread about him by Nazis and Communists alike without bothering to check them against the source: in part because the air of studied ignorance he liked to adopt when dealing with the classics precluded a more thoroughgoing engagement; more importantly because he tended, good pragmatist that he was, to equate the intrinsic value of a literary commodity with the uses to which it had been, or could be, put. While I suspect Brecht would have been happy to concede Adorno's point that when Hölderlin and Hitler use the word *Vaterland*, they are not referring to the same thing,[15] he still complained at the height of the centenary celebrations in 1943: "The nationalistic element in Schiller, Goethe, Hölderlin is for us quite unbearable."[16] The "truth" of Hölderlin was for Brecht coterminous with his near-universal exploitation by the nationalists. Far from signaling a fundamental shift in his views, the *Antigone* adaptation of five years later represented a practical demonstration (no doubt spurred by the example of Eisler's *Hollywooder Liederbuch*) that Hölderlin was good for something other than the patriotic saber-rattling he had been used to sanction hitherto. In this respect, the salient difference between Brecht and Bertaux is that between a revolutionary refunctioning of the poet and his rehabilitation *as* a revolutionary poet, between dramaturgy and hermeneutics.

Bertaux thus permits us to grasp after the event the epochal co-belonging of our three authors, who can now be seen to stand united in their principled aversion to reading Hölderlin's poetry as the self-expression (the *Aussage*) of a historical subject, "committed" or otherwise. At the same time, the break with the past effected by Bertaux was not a clean one, remaining secretly indebted to the paradigm established by the George Circle even as it set about debunking its central mythologeme of the "pure poet." As in the 1910s, when the cult of Hölderlin had been fueled by the disaffection of the younger generation, the turn to "the poet as leader" — Kommerell's phrase is apposite here, even if its connotations of Boy Scout romanticism are not — implied a turning away from bourgeois literary culture and its attendant values, now perceived in Marxist terms as an instrument of mystification and class domination. The same students who interrupted their lecturers with the cry, "Schlagt die Germanistik tot, färbt die blaue Blume rot!" (Strike German Studies dead, paint the blue flower red!)[17] congregated afterwards to read aloud from *Hyperion*. Although unaware of it at the time, they were staging the last hurrah of the aesthetic ideology in Germany, according to which works of art were expected to provide the impetus for the kind of sweeping change that a moribund parliamentary system, irredeemably bound to conventions and beholden to vested interests, was thought incapable of implementing. What was concretely envisaged under such change was always of secondary importance, almost a matter of technical concern when compared to the clarion call to action that issued irresistibly from the poet's work. Those interpellated by Hölderlin in this manner felt impelled to generalize their own aesthetic state into a future Aesthetic State, a *Gemeinschaft* in which the deficiency of meaning felt to be constitutive of modernity would be replenished from the fount of poetry;[18] hence the astonishing consistency with which Germans of all political persuasions were drawn to Hölderlin, over the course of the century, as the common focal point of their ambitions for national renewal. Bertaux and his successors imagined themselves dispersing, with a blast of fresh air from the streets, the clouds of incense that had enveloped the poet since before the First World War. It would be more accurate to say that they were bringing to term — both culminating and driving to exhaustion — the process of actualization set in motion by Hellingrath, and so failing to recognize the caesura of 1945 writ large by Heidegger, Adorno, and Brecht.

In order to fathom what that process entailed, it is necessary to look beyond Bertaux at some of the ways in which the Jacobin thesis was taken up elsewhere. For the most striking hallmark of the post-68 reception was that it no longer took place exclusively, or even predominantly, within the academic sphere, but in newspapers, student assemblies, happenings, novels, and plays. Hölderlin had slipped from the protective custody of the Hölderlin Society to emerge as a public figure in his own right. This became evident, at the very latest, during celebrations of his 200th birthday in 1970.

1970, or, Storming the Tower

1970 was the most important Hölderlin jubilee since 1943, and expectations were running high. The society had made plans for a three-day party in and around Stuttgart, opting to convene on 21 March rather than on the usual date in June, to give members the chance to offer their birthday greetings in unison. The timing was auspicious. Whereas earlier conferences had taken place under the sign of death, whether that of the poet or of the people he was leading into battle at the time, the recent upsurge of interest in "Hölderlin and the French Revolution" (the title of Bertaux's speech and follow-up book) had given him a new lease on life appropriate to the festive occasion. Martin Walser, still very much an angry young(ish) man of the Left at the time, set the tone in his keynote speech, "Hölderlin zu entsprechen" (Corresponding to Hölderlin). To correspond to Hölderlin, it became clear as the speech progressed, meant to respond to him in such a way that the impulse sent out from his poetry escaped the cloistering confines of "the history of fine literature" to inform the everyday conduct of his readers.[19] For Walser, as for Heidegger, the collective failure of the Germans to take up that impulse was the sad proof that they had not yet begun to understand him. In contrast to Heidegger, for whom withdrawal into the cell of contemplative reading established the conditions for an adequate response to the poet's word, immersion in that word is now seen to lead beyond it, into the hurly-burly of political engagement.

Walser was too good a student of Beißner, his former academic mentor and the speech's dedicatee, not to voice his misgivings about any attempted one-to-one conversion of the poet's dream of community into political reality: "He is singing on the side of the revolution, no doubt about it, but nonetheless: singing."[20] Such precautionary statements led the correspondent of the conservative *Frankfurter Allgemeine Zeitung* to heave a sigh of relief: "Not a Jacobin after All," ran the headline of her report.[21] Nonetheless, Walser went considerably further than Bertaux in applying the lessons he drew from his reading of Hölderlin to an analysis of the contemporary political situation in West Germany, which he characterized as one of stagnation and complacency. Giving a surprising twist to Hölderlin's historical-poetological principle that the danger of petrifying into abstract identity can only be countered through the opposite risk of self-abandonment, of exposure to the foreign, Walser proclaimed: "We have learned so little from him that we believe to have arrived without further ado at the end point of history. We think ourselves capable of outwitting the historical process. Two parties rotate, immobile. Locked in their embrace, the process will at last be stilled. And yet the opposing power, socialism, has its foot in the German door."[22] Following the logic of this passage, the harmony parodied in the *mésalliance* of the CDU and the SPD is to be concretely won by plunging headlong into the danger of socialism. Walser leaves unspecified whether this means pursuing a more conciliatory policy toward its "real existing" variety in the East, along the lines of the policy being tried out by the new Brandt government, or whether, as seems more likely, he is demanding the reform of the free market economy to ensure a fairer distribution of the means of production; the two possibilities do not rule each other out. What is more important is that Hölderlin is aligned here with a radical politics that operates outside of, and in opposition to, the entrenched two-party system in West Germany. He is to be found consorting, not with the distinguished guests whom Walser was addressing at the time (among them representatives of the Ministry of Culture), but with the students, dancing around the liberty tree in the Tübingen town square.

As it happened, the students of Tübingen did not let him down. Greeting delegates on 22 March as they assembled there to resume their activities, Mayor Gmelin remarked in passing that "Tübingen's secret Jacobins, too, have adopted and usurped him as one of their own."[23] He was referring to an incident that had taken place at the local cemetery at noon the previous day, the poet's birthday. A group calling itself the "secret tübingen jacobin club" had marched from the town center to Hölderlin's grave, where its members proceeded to hold speeches, lay a wreath plaited from barbed wire, and plant a red flag in front of his gravestone. As the official proceedings were getting underway downriver in Stuttgart, a speaker of the club proclaimed:

> we are no longer willing to leave the revolutionary tradition to the stranglehold of the ruling class and their hired lackeys. therefore we proclaim here at his gravesite that hölderlin belongs in the ranks of german revolutionaries, whose struggle for the downfall of the ruling class we are continuing at the historically higher level of the socialist class struggle.[24]

His twenty or so comrades, sporting red caps adorned with tricolor cockades, rounded off the occasion with a spirited rendition of the Marseillaise.

Small in number as it may have been, and farcical as its parallel action may appear in retrospect, the club had launched the first serious assault upon the discursive monopoly enjoyed by the Hölderlin Society since its reconstitution in 1947. As such, it brought into the open an antagonism that had become ever more perceptible at the three previous conventions,[25] an antagonism that threatened to reintroduce into the "garden" Beck and his colleagues had been cultivating since war's end "the tumultuous time" from which it was designed to provide shelter.[26] In the past, rival interpretations such as those of Heidegger and Adorno had been accommodated, if not always resolved, within the same institutional space. The scholars who addressed the society at its biennial meetings might not always have agreed with each other, but they were still prepared to talk through their differences during the plenary session at the end; Adorno's failure to do so had arguably caused as much offense as his polemic against Heidegger. Even Bertaux had sought to reform the society from within, taking up a seat on its directorial panel not long after stirring up its membership from the podium. Now (the) society as a whole stood accused of orchestrating a "reactionary falsification" of the poet comparable to that practiced in the Second World War.[27] It is not difficult to see the birth of this counter-institutional movement as mirroring, albeit on a much smaller and more innocuous scale, the increasing militancy of the extra-parliamentary opposition during the same period.[28] The Tübingen Jacobins were challenging precisely Hölderlin's institutionalization at the hands of those who purported to be acting in his best interests, the latter-day wardens who took care of society business from its headquarters in the tower in which he had spent his twilight years. The poet of the revolution, long since tended and contained by the academic establishment, demanded no less revolutionary methods of his followers if he were to be broken out of his confinement and given back to his people. The Jacobins' goal was thus, figuratively speaking, to storm the tower and release its inmate, thereby righting the injustice that had befallen him during his lifetime and ever since.

The most concerted effort in this direction was begun four years later by Dietrich Sattler, whose Frankfurt Edition, appearing under the imprint of the aptly named Red Star publishing house, contested the previously undisputed authority of Beißner's project. According to Sattler, Beißner and his collaborators had systematically smoothed over the traces of Hölderlin's freely associative, open-ended, and inchoate creative process through the preparation of spurious, sanitized "final" versions, which they had culled from a profusion of textual variants. In each case, Beißner had elected to prioritize a particular wording as definitive rather than leaving the choice to the reader, who was forced to consult the supplementary volumes of the edition in search of any material judged to be extraneous. But what if the assumption underlying this procedure — that Hölderlin's fragmentary texts were "works in progress," waiting to be purified of their surface flaws — remained trapped in an idealist aesthetics that those texts had already left behind them? On this occasion, then, the tower to be stormed resembled a clinic staffed by doctors in white coats, trained to wield the tools of philology with surgical precision, while the poet upon whom they were operating displayed marked anarchist tendencies.[29] After a heated internal debate, the society eventually reasserted its hegemony by assimilating the threat, voting to relinquish the affiliation with the Stuttgart Edition stipulated in its constitution.[30] Here, too, parallels can be drawn with the broader societal developments of the 1970s.

The tower cast a long shadow over the poet's reception from 1970 right up to the publication of Bertaux's biography in 1978, which argued that Hölderlin had feigned insanity in order to escape arrest for his part in a republican plot. Whether construed as a symbol of political impotence, the marginalization of dissent, the incarceration of non-conformists, the retreat into madness, compartmentalization in the annals of literary history, obscurantism, enforced silence, or the irrelevance of text-immanent criticism, the tower presented itself as an ideal target to writers interested in exploring how Hölderlin's poetry intersected with the concerns of a present-day audience. I want to illustrate this claim by briefly looking at two of the tower's most prominent appearances in the literature of the period, one from the GDR, the other from the FRG. For it should be pointed out that the bicentennial commemorations, while centered in Stuttgart, extended well beyond the boundaries of the poet's Swabian homeland. Those that took place behind the Iron Curtain, although generally more subdued in tone and more modest in extent, showed themselves no less affected by the paradigm shift inaugurated by Bertaux. Günther Deicke, for example, drew upon Bertaux's research in pronouncing it a "curious coincidence that we are observing in this year the 200th birthdays of Hölderlin, Hegel and Beethoven and, concurrently with the same patriotic engagement — to borrow one of Hölderlin's concepts —, the 100th birthday of Lenin. In this apparently purely external sequence," adduced Deicke in his birthday address to the Berlin Academy of Arts, "is revealed . . . the continuity of revolutionary development."[31]

Stephan Hermlin's radio play *Scardanelli*, broadcast in the same year, was concerned less with celebrating Hölderlin as a patron saint of the workers' state than with piecing together the stages of his descent into madness. "His standpoint was the most advanced," we hear at one point; "but he proved unable to stand there."[32] Hermlin was interested in examining how the headstrong idealist saluted by Deicke became the schizophrenic old man vegetating by the river. The latter figure is introduced at the beginning of the play by two passers-by, one of them his first biographer Wilhelm Waiblinger, in lines strongly reminiscent of the opening of *Empedokles*. The audio cues indicate that the conversationalists are taking a stroll down the alley of plane trees on the Neckar island, located directly opposite Hölderlin's living quarters, as they speak:

Rushing water. From afar, the creaking of a carriage. Approaching steps.
VOICE 1   So, up there? *A window closes*
WAIBLINGER   Up there. . . .
VOICE 1   Here then. And for how long?
WAIBLINGER   Almost twenty years now.[33]

There follow thirteen loosely interconnected scenes that chart, through a montage of quotations interspersed with fictive dialogue, the frustration of Hölderlin's revolutionary aspirations and the failure of his efforts to carve a niche for himself in his native land. The same voices return toward the end of the play, after the main characters in his life have faded one by one into silence, in a kind of wistful coda:

A VOICE	Hölderlin!
A SECOND VOICE	Holderle!
CHILD'S VOICE	Dear Hölder!
A FOURTH VOICE	Holderlen!
FEMALE VOICE	My Holder . . .
A SIXTH VOICE	Hölterlein!
Pause	
HÖLDERLIN	But he's far off; is no longer there.[34]
VOICE 1	Who is up there?
HÖLDERLIN	Your humble servant Scardanelli.

The window closes. Rushing water crescendo.[35]

The exaggerated obsequiousness with which Hölderlin received his visitors in the tower under the assumed name of Scardanelli is thus shown to be the consequence of his withdrawal from the claims of the world around him, which he had once hoped to rid of such forms of servility. By closing his window upon that world, Hölderlin paradoxically causes the gentle murmuring of the river flowing beneath to build up into a roar, drowning out the voices that crowd his head and leaving him alone with the question: "What did I want? What went wrong? What will they answer when you are gone and people ask: what did he lack?"[36] Hermlin does not provide any easy answers to this question. Instead, the strategy of biographical *Annäherung* or approximation made audible in the approaching steps of the opening reaches its limit at the window slammed shut by Hölderlin at both ends of the play. We are invited to peer through this window into the room beyond, hoping to catch a glimpse of its occupant, but we are forbidden from entering. To make matters worse, the impartiality and reliability of the voices we hear during our tour around the tower, including that of our guide Waiblinger, are by no means to be taken for granted. Such perspectival distortions and limitations seem to be overcome in the last words of the play, when we hear Hölderlin, now completely isolated in the turret, speaking to and for himself. But as the quote from "Ganymed" following the general pause suggests, the impression of intimacy created by eavesdropping on him is illusory: at the very moment when we appear to have arrived "up there," in the interior of his chamber and the privacy of his innermost thoughts, it is to find him "no longer there," represented in his absence by the empty sign "Scardanelli." In prohibiting us unrestricted access to the poet within, the play itself comes ever more to resemble the tower around which it circles.[37]

If Hermlin suggests that the tower stands in the way of the poet's ever attaining to the living presence invoked by the students, Peter Weiss views it as an obstacle still to be overcome through revolutionary struggle. In his play *Hölderlin*, conceived in the bicentenary year and premiered, to great popular success, the following season in Stuttgart, Hölderlin is portrayed as a tragic figure who remained true to the ideals of his youth while they were being betrayed by those around him. Whereas Hermlin had treated the poet's madness as a riddle which, although conditioned by oppressive social factors, is ultimately not explicable in terms of such factors, Weiss is in no doubt as to its etiology: Hölderlin was the victim of the general backwardness of his age. Historical accuracy is thrown to the winds in order that the duress against which he struggled may appear all the more obdurate, his martyrdom all the more exemplary. None too subtle correspondences to later political developments abound. Thus Fichte, who made a deep and positive impression on Hölderlin during his stay in Jena, is caricatured as a rabble-rouser urging his students to purge the Fatherland of foreign elements, "especially Jews."[38] Hölderlin and his friends stage a sit-in at one of his lectures, whereupon they are led off in handcuffs at the behest of a certain "Privy Ducal Counsellor von Göthe." The latter joins the throng at the end of the scene, standing hand in hand with Schiller in the immortal pose, while on the dais above them Fichte raises his arm — one understands what kind of gesture is intended — to salute the chorus of nationalist students. Even Adorno comes in for a posthumous whipping: "So after / all that fuss / philosophy makes common cause with / the police."[39] The hero of the morality play, meanwhile, goes underground once he realizes that the time is not yet ripe for revolution. In the sixth and longest scene, Weiss transfigures him into a forerunner to Che Guevara, a guerilla of the Swabian foothills who laid down his life for the disenfranchised and underfed, blithely ignoring the recalcitrance of Hölderlin's late work to such claims. Indeed, for Weiss his development seems to reach a halt with the republican drama *Empedokles*.[40]

Each character in the play stands under the spell of what he will subsequently become: the young Hegel is already the apologist for state power, Schelling already the preacher of revelation and irrationalism, Fichte already the author of the *Reden an die deutsche Nation* (Addresses to the German Nation), and so on. This technique of retrojecting much later consequences onto their nascent causes, which serves to profile more sharply the differences separating Hölderlin from his contemporaries, is applied with equally drastic effect to the title character. His destiny is summed up in the tower, much as Christ's path of sorrows leads inexorably to the cross, and it is the tower that looms before him from the outset:

SINGER When he arrived in town
for the first time the tower was already there
right by the Neckar to which he looked down
through the low window of his chamber
his cell lay there and he perceived it.[41]

Having taken up residence there in the final scene, a potted history of his reception in the nineteenth and twentieth centuries is paraded before his (and our) eyes, a premonition of things to come (for him) or remembrance of things past (for us) that runs parallel to the poet's own process of ageing during the decades he spent languishing in the tower. Three distinct periods in his biographical and literary afterlife may be discerned here. The first, which coincides with the relative lack of interest shown in Hölderlin up to the eve of the First World War, is signaled by the initial silence that descends upon his room, granting him some respite from the torments he has just suffered in the clinic. "The stream flows quietly by," Hölderlin's carer tells him as she opens the window looking out to the river, the same window that Hermlin had barricaded against the outside world; "and there's not a boat to be seen."[42] At this stage, the tower still affords Hölderlin the sanctuary of seclusion.

The next phase, which covers the age of catastrophe from 1914 to the end of the Second World War, begins with the entrance into his room of members of a local student fraternity, come to pay homage to the genius of his people. Conservative and fascist appropriations alike are telescoped onto the 1817 demonstration for national unity on the Wartburg in a single, phantasmagoric episode that illustrates, in the garish colors of nightmare, Michelet's precept that each epoch dreams its successor. Upon proclaiming: "Hölderlin we carry your odes / in our backpacks when we break through / the trenches beyond the Rhine / and invade the land of the archenemy,"[43] the students proceed to denounce and consign to the flames books by free-thinking authors, all of them favorites of Hölderlin's, which they have brought with them in a basket: "In praise of Hölderlin / Against the mad dogs / who want to destroy the world / with communist revolution / we consign to the flames / Buonarotti."[44] At this stage, the tower functions as a sign of the poet's helplessness in the face of those who would twist into its opposite everything he stood for. Its idyllic solitude, which had earlier granted him temporary asylum from the barbarians outside, condemns him to speechlessness once they have succeeded in breaching his defenses: "*Sobbing, Hölderlin buries his face in his hands.*"[45]

Finally, when all hope seems lost, another visitor is announced: the young (or perhaps one should say: the early) Karl Marx. In an essay from 1923, Thomas Mann had famously pronounced that all would stand well in Germany if Marx were to read Hölderlin.[46] As the context makes clear, he was expressing the wish that the grubbily materialist doctrine with which he identified socialism at the time might be purified through its subsumption under the conservative cultural ideal he found epitomized in the works of the poet (and Ernst Bloch was to interpret the comment in just this manner).[47] What Mann had envisaged as a hypothetical meeting of contraries Weiss dramatizes as the real-life reunion of long-lost soulmates. His Marx *has* read Hölderlin, and with such zealous attentiveness that the experience set him on the road to his mature thinking. "It was the encounter / with your poetry, / above all Hyperion / which smashed my own efforts / with a single blow."[48] The stage direction that follows this confession, "*Hölderlin has moved closer to Marx*," could stand as motto for both the play as a whole and the general tendency of the post-68 reception, of which this third tableau is emblematic.[49] The direction betrays, moreover, that it is Hölderlin who has been drawn into the more powerful orbit of socialism, and not the other way around, as Mann would have preferred (even if we are left in no doubt that Marx first had to seek him out: Hölderlin's recovery for the Left presupposes his discovery by the Left). This is the condition under which the comet's erratic voyage through the centuries, one section of which I have plotted in this study, may terminate in a fixed constellation.

From the vantage point of its achieved telos, the history of the poet's reception stands revealed as a detour of alienation culminating in the coming-to-itself of revolutionary spirit. The fictive meeting in the tower represents Weiss's attempt to bring the myth to an end, not by propagating a "Hölderlin without myth,"[50] but by precluding the possibility of future recensions.[51] Marx is not simply the latest in a long line of visitors to have filed through the poet's room; he is the One sent to open that line onto eternity. Weiss cites several tropes of messianic discourse to bring this point across, including the initial failure of the prophet, grown frail with age, to see through his savior's incognito. Like the Messiah, Marx arrives late on the scene, although not too late, infiltrating the tower at the moment when he is least expected — who indeed would have expected Marx to make a guest appearance in a play about Hölderlin? — to liberate its captive from the bonds of mortality. As Lotte Zimmer opens the window to let in a gust of fresh air, Hölderlin breathes his last, secure in the knowledge that his life's work will not have been in vain. Hölderlin, whom Eich had depicted just three years before as a spectral figure loitering in pedestrian tunnels, has nothing more to wait for. For he realizes now that his entire afterlife will have been spent in preparation for this encounter, which will have imbued with meaningfulness the travesty that still awaits him. The combined efforts of Weiss, Bertaux, Walser, and their comrades have ensured that Hölderlin will now be able to rest in peace: with his message received and acted upon, the messenger is free to retire. Just as his living death in the tower was accompanied and prolonged by the paeans of the Tübingen *Burschenschaftler*, so his real death corresponds to the symbolic rites of burial officiated by their antipodes, the Tübingen *Jakobiner*. The history of his reception, which is that of a series of misconceptions, cancels itself out at the moment when authorial intention and reader response meet on common ground.

Yet Hölderlin's interment, the fulfillment of his long-frustrated death wish, also heralds a new beginning. More specifically, it frames his exodus from the tower as the figuration and confirmation of a transition to praxis, the "preparation / of fundamental changes" in which, as Marx tells him, their two paths converge.[52] The hard work of revolution remains to be done. But while those who carry it out will continue to draw inspiration from his example, the mission with which they are entrusted is no longer the poet's prerogative (or the prerogative of poetry, for that matter). Hölderlin's spell in purgatory, represented by the flames that licked the walls of his cell during the book-burning ceremony, now makes way for a *vita nuova*, the natural light that floods his room upon Marx's departure. Deathday and birthday, 1843 and 1970, valediction and resurrection come full circle in the image of a "circle of living voices" — at once refulgent constellation, revolutionary council, and metamorphosed tower — in which Hölderlin will henceforth stand "as one who is alive."[53] The tower, so long a death sentence pending execution, has become a rallying cry for the cause he fought for, the cause his readership has at last made its own:

SINGER   When he had sunk away from the town
and lay in the earth the tower was still there
and when he had turned to dust
and you could only see his gravestone
his cell remained standing by the Neckar
you can still see it today[54]

1983, or, Hölderlin as Pop Star

The euphoria of the bicentennial celebrations fizzed out into the long hangover of the 1970s. "Every last godforsaken town of 10,000 people set up a pedestrian zone in the Seventies, . . . no one knows why? what for? against what? Pedestrian zones broke out in the German provinces like a divine punishment."[55] In 1983 Rainald Goetz stood nonplussed in the middle of the pedestrian zone in Marbach am Neckar, having traveled there to visit the exhibition "Klassiker in finsteren Zeiten" (Classics in Dark Times) at the German Literature Museum. The exhibition catalogue, two hefty volumes that document the reception under fascism of canonic literary figures, does not name a particular occasion for the six-month show. While it was most likely put on to coincide with the fiftieth anniversary of Hitler's accession to the chancellorship, the front cover of the catalogue suggests another, no less plausible, explanation for the timing.[56] The cover depicts a book lying open to show side-by-side versions of the last page of "Germanien," a format familiar from bilingual editions of poetry. The two versions differ only in the typeface used: the version on the left-hand side is printed in Gothic script, that on the right in Roman. The latter, however, has been additionally tampered with by a human hand. The predicate "defenseless" (*wehrlos*), attributed to Germania as she dispenses counsel to the peoples gathered round about her, has been crossed out with a red pen; in addition, the page is defaced around the edges with sticky black finger-prints — so many, in fact, that whoever touched it must have had ink seeping out of his pores. This is presumably meant to be a facsimile reproduction, albeit an obviously contrived one, of the copy of the poem recited by Gerhard Schumann in 1943 at the end of his inaugural address as President of the Hölderlin Society, when in deference to his audience he deliberately left out that crucial qualifier. It might be remembered that the Stuttgart Edition whose launch he oversaw, unlike previous editions, was likewise printed in Roman type, and that the colors featured on the right-hand page — red and black against a white background — are also those of the swastika flag. Furthermore, one of the most substantial sections of the catalogue was devoted to the Hölderlin jubilee of 1943, in particular the events surrounding the founding of the Society. It does not seem far-fetched to conclude that the exhibition may have been held, in part at least, to mark the fortieth anniversary of the centenary commemorations (as well as, by extension, the 140th anniversary of the poet's death).

Goetz purports to have made the pilgrimage to Marbach to find out what a classic is, and as he leafs through this catalogue of fascist crimes against literature he hits upon an answer. Here are the inky traces of his perusal:

> What's best about the classics, I understood the next day as I flicked through the amply-documented catalogue, is that they are far too well-known to far too many people and that any twit can do with them whatever he wants. That's why the classic is a pop phenomenon. It can be used for the most contradictory purposes, a source of citations that is there to be plundered, and what is truly subversive is the open affirmation it encounters, from a Nazi idiot just as much as from the decent responsible democratic "working through the past" idiots, who there in Marbach are responsibly and democratically working through things, above all darkness.[57]

Goetz gauges what might previously have been regarded as the most troubling aspect of Hölderlin's poetry, the seemingly indiscriminate compliance with which it caters to the demands of its clientele, to be its principal strength. His reevaluation bids farewell to the truth content of poetry and celebrates in its stead the eternal return of the evergreen hit. For the pathos of revolution it substitutes the bathos of recycling. By 1983 the comet Hölderlin has dwindled, disastrously, to a pop star, twinkling in the firmament alongside such luminaries as "Andreas Dorau," "Neger Negersen," "Grace Jones," "Charlotte von Kalb," and "Frieda Grafe."[58] Unthinkable that such a proposition could have been seriously entertained before the 1968 reception; inevitable that it should be voiced after it. For with the benefit of hindsight, the efforts of Bertaux and company to remix the poet's song to the beat of the present can be seen to have had as their unintended consequence the exhaustion of its relation to the past and future. Hölderlin's now-time had been sapped of the tension between the demands of the hour and the unfulfilled promise of salvation, a tension that still persisted in the writings of Heidegger, Adorno, and Brecht and lent them their sense of purpose. With every conceivable use having been made of him, the question as to the respective merits of each interpretation has become, quite literally, academic — for the time being, at least.

What remains, then, after Hölderlin after the catastrophe? I will give Goetz the final word: "In the best case scenario, the classic is logically what pop is in the best case scenario as well: a hit. . . . For a chief characteristic, practically a cardinal symptom of both the hit and the classic is ultimately that it instills courage, gives you new force, new strength, new New and new fury for the next and newest attack."[59]

Notes

[1] See Alexander Honold, "Krumme Linie, exzentrische Bahn: Hölderlin und die Astronomie," in *Erschriebene Natur: Internationale Perspektive auf Texte des 18. Jahrhunderts*, ed. Michael Scheffel (Bern: Peter Lang, 2001), 309–33.

[2] See Adolf Beck, ed. *Hölderlin: Chronik seines Lebens mit ausgewählten Bildnissen* (Frankfurt am Main: Insel, 1975), 102.

[3] "Offenbar mußte der philosophische Kommentator, als er 1943 mit dem 'Andenken' sich beschäftigte, bereits die Erscheinung französischer Frauen als subversiv fürchten; er hat aber auch später an dem putzigen Diskurs nichts geändert." Adorno, *GS* 11:458; *Notes to Literature* 2:118.

[4] Pierre Bertaux, "Hölderlin und die Französische Revolution," *HJb* 15 (1967/68): 2.

[5] See Georg Lukács, "Hölderlins Hyperion," in *Der andere Hölderlin: Materialien zum "Hölderlin"-Stück von Peter Weiss*, ed. Thomas Beckermann and Volker Canaris (Frankfurt am Main: Suhrkamp, 1972), 19–47; Robert Minder, "Hölderlin und die Deutschen," *HJb* 14 (1965/66): 1–19; Werner Kirschner, *Der Hochverratsprozess gegen Sinclair: Ein Beitrag zum Leben Hölderlins* (Marburg: Simons Verlag, 1949); Maurice Delorme, *Hölderlin et la Révolution française* (Monaco: Éditions du Rocher, 1959). Delorme's book, all but ignored in Germany at the time, had already said the essentials on the matter: "l'oeuvre brève de Hölderlin était profondément imprégnée de l'idéal de civisme régénéré que la Révolution avait suscité en lui" (Hölderlin's small body of work was deeply imbued with the revitalized civic ideal that the French Revolution had aroused in him; 222).

[6] Klaus Betzen, "Bericht über die Jahresversammlung in Düsseldorf," *HJb* 15 (1967/68), 312.

[7] See Betzen, "Bericht," 312: "Above all, the French students brought a moment of present-day reality in with them, when they reported on the student unrest in Paris that had just come to an end."

[8] Claus Offe, "Repercussions of 68," *Thesis Eleven* 68 (2002): 83.

[9] "und wenn das Reich der Finsterniß mit Gewalt einbrechen will, so werfen wir die Feder unter den Tisch, und gehen in Gottes Nahmen dahin, wo die Noth am grösten ist, und wir am nöthigsten sind." Hölderlin, *StA* 6:307.

[10] Pierre Bertaux, *Friedrich Hölderlin: Eine Biographie* (Frankfurt am Main: Suhrkamp, 1978), 7.

[11] Bertaux, "Hölderlin und die Französische Revolution," 1.

[12] Bertaux, "Hölderlin und die Französische Revolution," 3.

[13] See Adolf Beck, "Hölderlin als Republikaner," *HJb* 15 (1967/68): 28–52.

[14] Pierre Bertaux, *Friedrich Hölderlin: Eine Biographie* (Frankfurt am Main: Suhrkamp, 1978), 361.

[15] Adorno, *GS* 11:458; *Notes to Literature* 2:119.

[16] "Das Nationalistische ist bei Schiller, Goethe, Hölderlin für uns schon unerträglich." Brecht, *BFA* 27:181.

[17] Quoted in Günter Mieth, "Ein Rückblick auf öffentliche Hölderlin-Ehrungen 1970," in *Im Zwielicht des Jahrhunderts: Beiträge zur Hölderlin-Rezeption*, ed. Alfred Klein, Günter Mieth, and Klaus Pezold (Leipzig: Rosa-Luxemburg-Verein, 1994), 51.

[18] Scharfschwerdt sees in Hölderlin the founder of the idea of a German special path or *Sonderweg* that remains virulent in the reception history all the way up to 1968 and beyond. Jürgen Scharfschwerdt, *Friedrich Hölderlin: Der Dichter des "deutschen Sonderweges"* (Stuttgart: Kohlhammer, 1994), 157. For an alternative genealogy, see Josef Chytry, *The Aesthetic State: A Quest in Modern German Thought* (Berkeley: U of California P, 1989).

[19] Martin Walser, *Umgang mit Hölderlin: Zwei Reden* (Frankfurt am Main: Insel, 1997), 50, 54.

[20] Walser, *Umgang mit Hölderlin*, 35–36.

[21] Clara Menck, "Doch kein Jakobiner," *Frankfurter Allegemeine Zeitung*, 24 Mar 1970, 24.

[22] Walser, *Umgang mit Hölderlin*, 53. Compare the rhetoric of Peter Härtling's address "Mein Hölderlin": "We have fallen behind his insights," in Härtling, *Zwischen Untergang und Aufbruch: Aufsätze, Reden, Gespräche* (Berlin: Aufbau, 1990), 305.

[23] Hans Gmelin, "Anrede des Tübinger Bürgermeisters Gmelin," *HJb* 16 (1969/70): 367.

[24] I draw here upon Günter Mieth's helpful "Rückblick auf öffentliche Hölderlin-Ehrungen 1970," in Klein, Mieth, and Pezold, *Im Zwielicht des Jahrhunderts*, 49–65.

[25] In addition to Adorno's "Parataxis" speech of 1963 and Bertaux's address five years later, Robert Minder's speech "Hölderlin unter den Deutschen," delivered at the 1965 convention, deserves mention here.

[26] Adolf Beck, "Die Hölderlin-Forschung in der Krise, 1945–1947," *HJb* 3 (1948/49): 212; see "Whitewash," section 3 of my introduction.

[27] Mieth, "Rückblick," 54.

[28] One terrorist jailed in Cologne went so far as to call upon the poet as his patron saint. My source is an undated flier I inspected while in Tübingen in early 2003.

[29] See Stephan Wackwitz, "Text als Mythos: Zur Frankfurter Hölderlin-Ausgabe und ihrer Rezeption." *Merkur* 44.2 (1990): 134–43.

[30] See the protocol of the discussion in the 1975–77 yearbook. Theodor Pfizer, "Bericht über die 14. Jahresversammlung der Hölderlin-Gesellschaft in Bad Homburg," *HJb* 19 (1975–77): 577–78.

[31] Günther Deicke, "Zum 200. Geburtstag von Friedrich Hölderlin," *Sinn und Form* 22.4 (1970): 865.

[32] Stephan Hermlin, *Scardanelli*, in *Hörspiele aus der DDR*, ed. Stefan Bodo Würffel (Frankfurt am Main: Fischer, 1982), 159.

[33] Hermlin, *Scardanelli*, 146. Compare Panthea's opening words in "Der Tod des Empedokles": "Dies ist sein Garten! Dort im geheimen / Dunkel, wo die Quelle springt, dort stand er / jüngst, als ich vorüberging. — Du / hast ihn nie gesehen?" Hölderlin, *StA* 4:3.

[34] This line is a quotation from Hölderlin's poem "Ganymede": "Der ist aber ferne; nicht mehr dabei"; see Hölderlin, *Poems and Fragments*, 209.

[35] Hermlin, *Scardanelli*, 167.

[36] Hermlin, *Scardanelli*, 167.

[37] Peter Härtling would generate a similar effect, albeit without Hermlin's economy of means, in his novel *Hölderlin* (1976) by constantly interrupting his narrative to comment on the fictitiousness of his reconstructive enterprise: "I am inventing figures that have been" Peter Härtling, *Hölderlin: Ein Roman* (Darmstadt: Luchterhand, 1976), 79.

[38] Peter Weiss, *Hölderlin* (Frankfurt am Main: Suhrkamp, 1971), 76.

[39] "So mache / nach all dem Geschrey / die Filosofie mit der Polizey / gemeinsame Sache." Weiss, *Hölderlin*, 77.

[40] See Reinhard Baumgart, "Ein linkes Helden Lied — ein rother Schimmel," in Beckermann and Canaris, *Der andere Hölderlin*, 162.

[41] "SÄNGER Als hingekommen in die Stadt er war / zum ersten Mahl da lag der Thurm schon da / ganz nah am Nekar drauf er runtersah / durchs nidre Fenster seiner Cammer sonderbar / lag dort sein Kercker und er nahm ihn wahr." Weiss, *Hölderlin*, 13.

[42] "Ganz still fließt das Wässerle, und ist kein Boot zu sehn." Weiss, *Hölderlin*, 156–57.

[43] "Hölderlin deine Oden im Ranzen / tragen wir wenn wir die Schantzen / durchbrechen jenseits des Rhein / und falln ins Land des ErbFeindes ein." Weiss, *Hölderlin*, 157.

[44] "Für die LobPreisung Hölderlins / Gegen die tollen Hunde / die mit communistischer Revoluzion / die Welt zerstören wolln / Wir übergeben dem Feuer / Buonarotti." Weiss, *Hölderlin*, 161.

[45] "*Hölderlin schlägt schluchzend die Hände vors Gesicht.*" Weiss, *Hölderlin*, 161.

[46] Thomas Mann, "Goethe und Tolstoi: Fragmente zum Problem der Humanität," in Mann, *Bemühungen: Neue Folge der Gesammelten Abhandlungen und kleinen Aufsätze* (Berlin: S. Fischer, 1925), 137.

[47] See Ernst Bloch, *Spuren* (Frankfurt am Main: Suhrkamp, 1969), 141.

[48] "Es war die Begegnung / mit Ihrer Dichtung, vor allem dem Hyperion / die mir die eigenen Versuche / mit einem Schlag zerschmetterte." Weiss, *Hölderlin*, 172.

[49] "*Hölderlin ist Marx näher getreten.*" Weiss, *Hölderlin*, 173.

[50] See Ingrid Riedel, ed., *Hölderlin ohne Mythos* (Göttingen: Vandenoeck & Ruprecht, 1973).

[51] On bringing myth to an end, see Hans Blumenberg, *Arbeit am Mythos* (Frankfurt am Main: Suhrkamp, 1979), 291–326.

[52] "Vorbereitung / grundlegender Veränderungen." Weiss, *Hölderlin*, 175.

[53] "Krais lebendger Stimmen"; "als Lebender." Weiss, *Hölderlin*, 181.

[54] "SÄNGER Als weggesunken aus der Stadt er war / und in der Erde lag da war der Thurm noch da / und als zu Erde er geworden ganz und gar / und man von ihm nur noch den GrabStein sah / stand nah am Nekar immerdar /sein Kercker nimmst ihn heut noch wahr." Weiss, *Hölderlin*, 181.

[55] Rainald Goetz, "Was ist ein Klassiker," in *Hirn* (Frankfurt am Main: Suhrkamp, 1986), 23.

[56] Bernhard Zeller, ed. *Klassiker in finsterer Zeit, 1933–1945* (Marbach: Schiller-Nationalmuseum, 1983).

[57] Goetz, "Was ist ein Klassiker," 24.

[58] Goetz, "Was ist ein Klassiker," 22 and 24.

[59] Goetz, "Was ist ein Klassiker," 24–25.

Works Cited

Adorno, Theodor W. "The Actuality of Philosophy." Translated by Benjamin Snow. In *The Adorno Reader*, edited by Brian O'Connor, 23–39. Oxford: Blackwell, 2000.

———. *Aesthetic Theory*. Translated by Robert Hullot-Kentor. London: Athlone, 1997.

———. *Beethoven: Philosophie der Musik*. Edited by Rolf Tiedemann. Frankfurt am Main: Suhrkamp, 1993.

———. *Critical Models: Interventions and Catchwords*. Translated by Henry W. Pickford. New York: Columbia UP, 1998.

———. *Einleitung in die Musiksoziologie*. Frankfurt am Main: Suhrkamp, 1975.

———. *Einleitung in die Soziologie*. Edited by Christoph Gödde. Frankfurt am Main: Suhrkamp, 1993.

———. *Essays on Music*. Edited by Richard Leppert. Translated by Susan Gillespie. Berkeley: U of California P, 2002.

———. *Gesammelte Schriften*. 20 vols. Edited by Rolf Tiedemann, with the collaboration of Gretel Adorno, Susan Buck-Morss, and Klaus Schultz. Frankfurt am Main: Suhrkamp, 1970–86.

———. *Minima Moralia*. Translated by E. F. N. Jephcott. London: New Left Books, 1974.

———. *Negative Dialectics*. Translated by E. B. Ashton. New York: Seabury, 1973.

———. *Notes to Literature*. Translated by Shierry Weber Nicholsen. 2 vols. New York: Columbia UP, 1992.

———. *Ontologie und Dialektik*. Edited by Rolf Tiedemann. Frankfurt am Main: Suhrkamp, 2002.

———. *Philosophische Terminologie*. Vol. 1. Frankfurt am Main: Suhrkamp, 1973.

Adorno, Theodor W., and Walter Benjamin. *Briefwechsel, 1928–1940*. Edited by Henri Lonitz. Frankfurt am Main: Suhrkamp, 1994. In English, *The Complete Correspondence, 1928–1940*. Translated by Nicholas Walker. Cambridge MA: Harvard UP, 1999.

Adorno, Theodor W., and Max Horkheimer. *Briefwechsel, 1927–1969. Band 1: 1927–1937*. Edited by Christoph Gödde and Henri Lonitz. Frankfurt am Main: Suhrkamp, 2003.

Adorno, Theodor W., and Thomas Mann. *Briefwechsel, 1943–1955*. Edited by Christoph Gödde and Thomas Sprecher. Frankfurt am Main: Suhrkamp, 2002.

Agamben, Giorgio. *The Man without Content*. Translated by Georgia Albert. Stanford: Stanford UP, 1999.

Albert, Claudia, ed. *Deutsche Klassiker im Nationalsozialismus: Schiller; Kleist; Hölderlin*. Stuttgart: Metzler, 1994.

———. "'Dient Kulturarbeit dem Sieg?' Hölderlin-Rezeption von 1933–1945." In *Hölderlin und die Moderne: Eine Bestandsaufnahme*, edited by Gerhard Kurz, Valérie Lawitschka, and Jürgen Wertheimer, 153–73. Tübingen: Attempto, 1995.

———. *Das schwierige Handwerk des Hoffens: Hanns Eislers "Hollywooder Liederbuch" (1942/43)*. Stuttgart: Metzler, 1991.

Allemann, Beda. *Hölderlin und Heidegger*. Zurich: Atlantis, 1954.

Alt, Peter-André. "Das Problem der inneren Form: Zur Hölderlin-Rezeption Benjamins und Adornos." *Deutsche Vierteljahresschrift* 61.3 (1987): 531–63.

Anderle, Martin. "Hölderlin in der Lyrik Günter Eichs." *Seminar: Journal of Germanic Studies* 7.2 (1971): 99–113.

Andersch, Alfred. "Das junge Europa formt sein Gesicht." *Der Ruf: Unabhängige Blätter der jungen Generation* 1.1 (1946): 2.

Anouilh, Jean. *Antigone*. Paris: Éditions de la table ronde, 1946.

Baldo, Dieter. *Bertolt Brechts "Antigonemodell 1948": Theaterarbeit nach dem Faschismus*. Cologne: Pahl-Rugenstein Verlag, 1987.

Bate, Johnathan. *The Song of the Earth*. London: Picador, 2001.

Baumgart, Reinhard. "Ein linkes Helden Lied — ein rother Schimmel." In Beckermann and Canaris, *Der andere Hölderlin*, 161–70.

Becher, Johannes R. *Publizistik IV: 1952–1958*. Berlin: Aufbau-Verlag, 1981.

Beck, Adolf. "Hölderlin als Republikaner." *HJb* 15 (1967/68): 28–52.

———, ed. *Hölderlin: Chronik seines Lebens mit ausgewählten Bildnissen*. Frankfurt am Main: Insel, 1975.

———. "Die Hölderlin-Forschung in der Krise, 1945–1947." *HJb* 1948/49: 211–40.

Beckermann, Thomas, and Volker Canaris, ed. *Der andere Hölderlin: Materialen zum 'Hölderlin'-Stück von Peter Weiss*. Frankfurt am Main: Suhrkamp, 1972.

Beißner, Friedrich, and Paul Kluckhohn, eds. *Iduna: Jahrbuch der Hölderlin-Gesellschaft*. Tübingen: J. C. B. Mohr, 1944.

Benjamin, Andrew. "Being Roman Now: The Time of Fashion; A Commentary on Walter Benjamin's 'Theses on the Philosophy of History' XIV." *Thesis Eleven* 75 (2003): 39–53.

Benjamin, Walter. *Gesammelte Briefe III*. Edited by Christoph Gödde and Henri Lonitz. Frankfurt am Main: Suhrkamp, 1996.

———. *Gesammelte Schriften*. Edited by Rolf Tiedemann and Hermann Schweppenhäuser. 7 vols. Frankfurt am Main: Suhrkamp, 1974–89.

———. *Illuminations.* Translated by Harry Zohn. London: Fontana, 1970.

———. *The Origin of German Tragic Drama.* Translated by John Osborne. London: New Left Books, 1977.

———. *Selected Writings.* Translated by Howard Eiland and Gary Smith. Edited by Michael W. Jennings et al. 4 vols. Cambridge, MA: Harvard UP, 1996–2003.

———. *Understanding Brecht.* Translated by Stanley Mitchell. London: New Left Books, 1972.

Benn, Gottfried. *Doppelleben.* Munich: dtv, 1967.

Benninghof-Lühl, Sibylle. *'Figuren des Zitats': Eine Untersuchung zur Funktionsweise übertragener Rede.* Stuttgart: J. B. Metzler, 1998.

Berlau, Ruth. *Brechts Lai-Tu: Erinnerungen und Notate von Ruth Berlau.* Edited by Hans Bunge. Darmstadt: Luchterhand, 1985.

Bernstein, J. M. *The Fate of Art: Aesthetic Alienation from Kant to Derrida and Adorno.* Cambridge: Polity, 1992.

———. "Why Rescue Semblance? Metaphysical Experience and the Possibility of Ethics." In *The Semblance of Subjectivity: Essays in Adorno's Aesthetic Theory,* edited by Tom Huhn and Lambert Zuidevaart, 177–212. Cambridge, MA: MIT P, 1997.

Bertaux, Pierre. *Friedrich Hölderlin: Eine Biographie.* Frankfurt am Main: Suhrkamp, 1978.

———. "Hölderlin und die französische Revolution." *HJb* 15 (1967/68): 1–27.

Betzen, Klaus. "Bericht über die Jahresversammlung in Berlin." *HJb* 13 (1963/64): 172–84.

———. "Bericht über die Jahresversammlung in Düsseldorf." *HJb* 15 (1967/68): 311–17.

Binder, Wolfgang. "Bericht über die Diskussion." *HJb* 13 (1963/64): 185–86.

———. "Bericht über die Gründung der 'Friedrich-Hölderlin-Gesellschaft.'" *HJb* 2 (1947): 240–42.

———. *Hölderlin-Aufsätze.* Frankfurt am Main: Insel, 1970.

———. "Hölderlins Namenssymbolik." *HJb* 11 (1958–60): 95–204.

Blanchot, Maurice. *The Work of Fire.* Translated by Charlotte Mandell. Stanford, CA: Stanford UP, 1995.

Bloch, Ernst. *Atheismus im Christentum.* Frankfurt am Main: Suhrkamp, 1968.

———. *Spuren.* Frankfurt am Main: Suhrkamp, 1969.

Blumenberg, Hans. *Arbeit am Mythos.* Frankfurt am Main: Suhrkamp, 1979.

Bogumil, Sieghild. "Celans Hölderlinlektüre im Gegenlicht des schlichten Wortes." *Celan-Jahrbuch* 1 (1987): 81–126.

Bonacker, Thorsten. "Dabei sein ist alles: Kulturindustrie und die Polemik Adornos." Unpublished MS, 2003.

Borchert, Wolfgang. *Das Gesamtwerk*. Hamburg: Rowohlt, 1949.

———. *The Man Outside: The Prose Works of Wolfgang Borchert*. Translated by David Porter. London: Calder & Boyars, 1966.

Böschenstein, Bernhard. "Arbeit an Hölderlins Griechenland. Zwei Tage im März 1959 am Rötebuckweg." In Trawny, *"Voll Verdienst doch dichterisch wohnet / Der Mensch auf dieser Erde": Heidegger und Hölderlin*, 221–26.

———. "Celan als Leser Hölderlins und Jean Pauls." In *Argumentio e Silencio: International Paul Celan Symposium*, edited by Amy D. Colin, 183–98. Berlin: Walter de Gruyter, 1987.

———. "Hölderlin und Celan." In *Paul Celan*, edited by Werner Hamacher and Winfried Menninghaus, 191–200. Frankfurt am Main: Suhrkamp, 1988.

Bothe, Henning. *"Ein Zeichen sind wir, deutungslos": Die Rezeption Hölderlins von ihren Anfängen bis zu Stefan George*. Stuttgart: Metzler, 1992.

Brecht, Bertolt. *Große kommentierte Berliner und Frankfurter Ausgabe*. 30 vols. Edited by Werner Hecht, Jan Knopf, Werner Mittenzwei, and Klaus-Detlef Müller. Frankfurt am Main: Suhrkamp, 1988–98.

———. *Plays, Volume I*. London: Methuen, 1960.

———. *Die Stücke von Bertolt Brecht in einem Band*. Frankfurt am Main: Suhrkamp, 1981.

Breuer, Dieter. "Wörter so voll Licht so finster: Hölderlingedichte von Günter Eich bis Rolf Haufs." In *Deutsche Lyrik nach 1945*, edited by Dieter Breuer, 354–93. Frankfurt am Main: Suhrkamp, 1988.

Brunkhorst, Hauke. *Theodor W. Adorno: Dialektik der Moderne*. Munich: Piper, 1990.

Bubner, Rüdiger. "Kann Theorie ästhetisch werden? Zum Hauptmotiv der Philosophie Adornos." In *Materialien zur ästhetischen Theorie: Th. W. Adornos Konstruktion der Moderne*, edited by Burkhardt Lindner and W. Martin Lüdke, 108–37. Frankfurt am Main: Suhrkamp, 1980.

Bunge, Hans. *Antigone-Modell 1948 von Bertolt Brecht und Caspar Neher: Zur Praxis und Theorie des epischen (dialektischen) Theaters Bertolt Brechts*. PhD diss., Greifswald University, Germany, 1957.

Burte, Hermann. "Rede auf Hölderlin." In Beißner and Kluckhohn, *Iduna: Jahrbuch der Hölderlin-Gesellschaft*, 160–76.

Butler, E. M. *The Tyranny of Greece over Germany: A Study of the Influence Exercised by Greek Art and Poetry over the Great German Writers*. Cambridge: Cambridge UP, 1935.

Caputo, John. *Demythologizing Heidegger*. Bloomington: Indiana UP, 1993.

Cassirer, Ernst. "Hölderlin und der deutsche Idealismus." In *Hölderlin: Beiträge zu seinem Verständnis in unserm Jahrhundert*, edited by Alfred Kelletat, 79–118. Tübingen: J. C. B. Mohr, 1961.

Castoriadis, Cornelius. *World in Fragments: Writings on Politics, Society, Psychoanalysis, and the Imagination*. Translated by David Ames Curtis. Stanford, CA: Stanford UP, 1997.

Cavell, Stanley. "Night and Day: Heidegger and Thoreau." In *Appropriating Heidegger*, edited by James E. Faulconer and Mark A. Wrathall, 30–49. Cambridge: Cambridge UP, 2000.

Celan, Paul. *Gesammelte Werke*. 5 vols. Edited by Beda Allemann and Stefan Reichert. Frankfurt am Main: Suhrkamp, 1983.

———. *Selected Poems and Prose*. Translated by John Felstiner. New York: Norton, 2001.

Chytry, Josef. *The Aesthetic State: A Quest in Modern German Thought*. Berkeley: U of California P, 1989.

Cocteau, Jean. *The Infernal Machine*. Translated by Carl Wildman. London: Oxford UP, 1936.

Corngold, Stanley, and Geoffrey Waite. "A Question of Responsibility: Nietzsche with Hölderlin at War, 1916–1946." In *Nietzsche, Godfather of Fascism? On the Uses and Abuses of a Philosophy*, edited by Jacob Golomb and Robert S. Wistrich, 196–210. Princeton: Princeton UP, 2002.

Dahlhaus, Carl. *Ludwig van Beethoven: Approaches to His Music*. Translated by Mary Whittall. Oxford: Clarendon, 1991.

———. *Richard Wagners Musikdramen*. Reclam: Stuttgart, 1996.

Dallmayr, Fred. *The Other Heidegger*. Ithaca, NY: Cornell UP, 1993.

Dastur, Françoise. "Europa und der 'andere Anfang.'" In *Europa und die Philosophie*, edited by Hans-Helmuth Gander, 185–96. Schriftenreihe der Martin-Heidegger Gesellschaft 2. Frankfurt am Main: Klostermann, 1993.

Deicke, Günther. "Zum 200. Geburtstag von Friedrich Hölderlin." *Sinn und Form* 22.4 (1970): 865–72.

Delorme, Maurice. *Hölderlin et la Révolution française*. Monaco: Éditions du Rocher, 1959.

De Man, Paul. *Blindness and Insight: Essays in the Rhetoric of Contemporary Criticism*. Minneapolis: U of Minnesota P, 1983.

Demetz, Peter. *After the Fires: Recent Writing in the Germanies, Austria, and Switzerland*. San Diego: Harcourt Brace Jovanovich, 1986.

Derrida, Jacques. "Heidegger's Ear: Philopolemology (*Geschlecht* IV)." In *Reading Heidegger: Commemorations*, edited by John Sallis, 160–217. Bloomington: Indiana UP, 1993.

———. *Of Spirit: Heidegger and the Question*. Translated by Geoff Bennington and Rachel Bowlby. Chicago: Chicago UP, 1989.

Dickson, Keith A. *Towards Utopia: A Study of Brecht*. Oxford: Clarendon, 1978.

Dilthey, Wilhelm. *Das Erlebnis und die Dichtung*. Göttingen: Vandenhoeck & Ruprecht, 1965.

Döblin, Alfred. *November 1918: Dritter Teil; Karl und Rosa*. Munich: dtv, 1978.

Düttmann, Alexander García. *Between Cultures: Tensions in the Struggle for Recognition*. Translated by Kenneth Woodgate. London: Verso, 2000.

Düttmann, Alexander García. *Das Gedächtnis des Denkens: Versuch über Heidegger und Adorno.* Frankfurt am Main: Suhrkamp, 1991.

Eich, Günter. *Gesammelte Werke.* 4 vols. Edited by Axel Vieregg. Frankfurt am Main: Suhrkamp, 1991.

———. *Pigeons and Moles: Selected Writings of Günter Eich.* Translated by Michael Hamburger. Columbia, SC: Camden House, 1990.

Eisler, Hanns. *Fragen Sie mehr über Brecht: Gespräche mit Hans Bunge.* Munich: Rogner & Bernhard, 1976.

Enzensberger, Hans Magnus. *Landessprache.* Frankfurt am Main: Suhrkamp, 1960.

Fehervary, Helen. *Hölderlin and the Left: The Search for a Dialectic of Art and Life.* Heidelberg: Carl Winter, 1977.

Felstiner, John. *Paul Celan: Poet, Survivor, Jew.* New Haven, CT: Yale UP, 1995.

Fenves, Peter. "Measure for Measure: Hölderlin and the Place of Philosophy." In Aris Fioreto, *The Solid Letter: Readings of Friedrich Hölderlin,* 25–43.

Fichte, J. G. "Reden an die deutsche Nation." In *Werke VII,* 259–499. Berlin: Veit, 1846.

Fioretos, Aris, ed. *The Solid Letter: Readings of Friedrich Hölderlin.* Stanford, CA: Stanford UP, 1999.

Flashar, Hellmut. *Inszenierung der Antike: Das griechische Drama auf der Bühne der Neuzeit, 1585–1990.* Munich: C. H. Beck, 1991.

Foucault, Michel. "Polemics, Politics, and Problematizations." In *Ethics: Subjectivity and Truth,* edited by Paul Rabinow, 111–20. London: Penguin, 2000.

Freud, Sigmund. *Introductory Lectures on Psychoanalysis.* Translated by James Strachey. Harmondsworth, UK: Penguin, 1973.

Frick, Werner. *"Die mythische Methode": Komparatistische Studien zur Transformation der griechischen Tragödie im Drama der klassischen Moderne.* Tübingen: Niemeyer, 1998.

Fried, Gregory. *Heidegger's Polemos: From Being to Politics.* New Haven, CT: Yale UP, 2000.

Frisch, Max. *Gesammelte Werke in zeitlicher Folge.* Vol. 2. Frankfurt am Main: Suhrkamp, 1976.

Froment-Meurice, Marc. *That Is to Say: Heidegger's Poetics.* Translated by Jan Plug. Stanford, CA: Stanford UP, 1998.

Fynsk, Christopher. *Heidegger: Thought and Historicity.* Ithaca, NY: Cornell UP, 1986.

Gadamer, Hans-Georg. *Heidegger's Ways.* Translated by John W. Stanley. Albany: SUNY P, 1994.

Gay, Peter. *Weimar Culture.* Harmondsworth, UK: Penguin, 1971.

Geiman, Clare Pearson. "Heidegger's *Antigones*." In Polt and Fried, *A Companion to Heidegger's Introduction to Metaphysics*, 161–82.

Genette, Gérard. *Palimpseste: Die Literatur auf zweiter Stufe.* Translated by Wolfram Bayer and Dieter Hornig. Frankfurt am Main: Suhrkamp, 1993.

George, Stefan. *Werke.* Vol. 1. Munich: Helmut Küpper, 1958.

———. *The Works of Stefan George.* Translated by Olga Marx and Ernst Morwitz. Chapel Hill: U of North Carolina P, 1974.

Gethmann-Siefert, Annemarie. "Heidegger und Hölderlin: Die Überforderung des 'Dichters in dürftiger Zeit.' " In *Heidegger und die praktische Philosophie*, edited by Annemarie Gethmann-Siefert and Otto Pöggeler, 191–227. Frankfurt am Main: Suhrkamp, 1988.

Gethmann-Siefert, Annemarie, and Otto Pöggeler, eds. *Heidegger und die praktische Philosophie.* Frankfurt am Main: Suhrkamp, 1988.

Geulen, Eva. *Das Ende der Kunst: Lesarten eines Gerüchts nach Hegel.* Frankfurt am Main: Suhrkamp, 2002.

———. "Zeit zur Darstellung. Walter Benjamins 'Das Kunstwerk im Zeitalter seiner technischen Reproduzierbarkeit.' " *MLN* 107.3 (1992): 580–605.

Gmelin, Hans. "Anrede des Tübinger Bürgermeisters Gmelin." *HJb* 16 (1969/70): 367–70.

Goetz, Rainald. *Hirn.* Frankfurt am Main: Suhrkamp, 1986.

Gray, Ronald. *Brecht.* Edinburgh: Oliver & Boyd, 1961.

Grimm, Reinhold. *Bertolt Brecht und die Weltliteratur.* Nuremberg: Hans Carl, 1961.

Haering, Hermann. "Hölderlin im Weltkrieg, 1914–1918." In Beißner and Kluckhohn, *Iduna*, 177–92.

Härtling, Peter. *Hölderlin: Ein Roman.* Darmstadt: Luchterhand, 1976.

———. "Mein Hölderlin." In *Zwischen Untergang und Aufbruch: Aufsätze, Reden, Gespräche.* Berlin: Aufbau, 1990.

Haverkamp, Anselm. *"Laub voll Trauer": Hölderlins späte Allegorie.* Munich: Wilhelm Fink, 1991. In English, *Leaves of Mourning: Hölderlin's Late Work — With an Essay on Keats and Melancholy.* Translated by Vernon Chadwick. Albany, NY: SUNY P, 1996.

Hecht, Werner. *Brecht-Chronik, 1898–1956.* Frankfurt am Main: Suhrkamp, 1997.

———, ed. *Brechts Antigone des Sophokles.* Frankfurt am Main: Suhrkamp, 1988.

Hegel, G. W. F. "Das älteste Systemprogramm des deutschen Idealismus." In *Mythologie der Vernunft: Hegels "ältestes Systemprogramm" des deutschen Idealismus*, edited by Christoph Jamme and Helmut Schneider, 7–17. Frankfurt am Main: Suhrkamp, 1984.

Heidegger, Martin. *Basic Writings.* Translated by David Farrell Krell. San Francisco: Harper, 1993.

Heidegger, Martin. *Contributions to Philosophy (from Enowning)*. Translated by Parvis Emad and Kenneth Maly. Bloomington: Indiana UP, 1999.

———. *Elucidations to Hölderlin's Poetry*. Translated by Keith Hoeller. New York: Humanity Books, 2000.

———. *Gesamtausgabe*. 103 vols. Edited by Friedrich-Wilhelm von Herrmann et al. Frankfurt am Main: Klostermann, 1976–.

———. *Hölderlin's Hymn "The Ister."* Translated by William McNeill and Julia Davis. Bloomington: Indiana UP, 1996.

———. "Vom Ursprung des Kunstwerks: Erste Ausarbeitung." *Heidegger Studies* 5 (1989): 5–22.

Heidegger, Martin, and Hannah Arendt. *Briefe, 1925 bis 1975*. Edited by Ursula Ludz. Frankfurt am Main: Klostermann, 1998.

Hellingrath, Norbert von. *Hölderlin-Vermächtnis*. Edited by Ludwig von Pigenot. Munich: Bruckmann, 1936.

Henrich, Dieter. *The Course of Remembrance and Other Essays on Hölderlin*. Edited by Eckhardt Förster. Stanford, CA: Stanford UP, 1997.

———. "Hegel und Hölderlin." In *Stuttgarter Hegel-Tage 1970*, edited by Hans-Georg Gadamer, 29–52. Bonn: Bouvier, 1974.

Hermlin, Stephan. *Scardanelli*. In *Hörspiele aus der DDR*, edited by Stefan Bodo Würffel, 146–67. Frankfurt am Main: Fischer, 1982.

Hofmannsthal, Hugo von. *Gesammelte Werke in zehn Einzelbänden*. Edited by Bernd Schoeller. Frankfurt am Main: Fischer, 1979.

Hölderlin, Friedrich. *Essays and Letters on Theory*. Translated by Thomas Pfau. Albany: SUNY P, 1988.

———. *Hyperion and Selected Poems*. Edited by Eric L. Santner. Translated by Willard Trask. New York: Continuum, 1990.

———. *Poems and Fragments*. Translated by Michael Hamburger. London: Routledge & Kegan Paul, 1966.

———. *Sämtliche Werke*. 8 vols. Edited by Friedrich Beißner and Adolf Beck. Stuttgart: W. Kohlhammer, 1943–85.

Honold, Alexander. "Krumme Linie, exzentrische Bahn: Hölderlin und die Astronomie." In *Erschriebene Natur: Internationale Perspektive auf Texts des 18. Jahrhundert*, edited by Michael Scheffel, 309–33. Bern: Peter Lang, 2001.

———. *Der Leser Walter Benjamin: Bruchstücke einer deutschen Literaturgeschichte*. Berlin: Verlag Vorwerk 8, 2000.

Husserl, Edmund. *Logische Untersuchungen*. Edited by Ursula Panzer. The Hague: Martinus Nijihoff, 1984.

Jameson, Fredric. *Brecht and Method*. London: Verso, 1998.

Janz, Curt Paul. *Friedrich Nietzsche: Biographie*. Munich: Carl Hanser, 1978.

Jens, Walter. *Statt einer Literaturgeschichte*. Tübingen: Neske, 1957.

Karasek, Hellmuth. *Bertolt Brecht: Der jüngste Fall eines Theaterklassikers*. Munich: Kindler, 1978.

Kirschner, Werner. *Der Hochverratsprozess gegen Sinclair: Ein Beitrag zum Leben Hölderlins.* Marburg, Germany: Simons Verlag, 1949.

Kisiel, Theodor. "Heidegger's Philosophical Geopolitics in the Third Reich." In *A Companion to Heidegger's Introduction to Metaphysics,* edited by Richard Polt and Gregory Fried, 226–49. New Haven, CT: Yale UP, 2001.

Klein, Alfred. "Im Zwielicht des Jahrhunderts: Johannes R. Bechers Hölderlinbilder." In Klein, Mieth, and Pezold, *Im Zwielicht des Jahrhunderts: Beiträge zur Hölderlin-Rezeption,* 7–32.

Klein, Alfred, Günter Mieth, and Klaus Pezold, eds. *Im Zwielicht des Jahrhunderts: Beiträge zur Hölderlin-Rezeption.* Leipzig: Rosa-Luxemburg-Verein, 1994.

Kluckhohn, Paul. "Bericht über die Veranstaltungen." In Beißner and Kluckhohn, *Iduna: Jahrbuch der Hölderlin-Gesellschaft,* 12–15.

———. "Hölderlin bei den Soldaten des zweiten Weltkriegs." In Beißner and Kluckhohn, *Iduna: Jahrbuch der Hölderlin-Gesellschaft,* 192–95.

———, ed. *Hölderlin: Gedenkschrift zu seinem 100. Todestag.* Tübingen: J. C. B. Mohr, 1943.

———. "Hölderlin im Bilde der Nachwelt." In Beißner and Kluckhohn, *Iduna: Jahrbuch der Hölderlin-Gesellschaft,* 1–11.

Knopf, Jan. *Brecht-Handbuch: Theater.* Stuttgart: Metzler, 1980.

Knox, Bernard. "Introduction to *Antigone.*" In Sophocles, *The Theban Plays,* 35–53.

Kohlenbach, Michael. *Günter Eichs späte Prosa: Einige Merkmale der Maulwürfe.* Bonn: Bouvier, 1982.

Kurz, Gerhard. "Hölderlin 1943." In *Hölderlin und Nürtingen,* edited by Peter Härtling and Gerhard Kurz, 103–28. Stuttgart: J. B. Metzler, 1994.

Kurz, Gerhard, Valérie Lawitschka, and Jürgen Wertheimer, eds. *Hölderlin und die Moderne: Eine Bestandsaufnahme.* Tübingen: Attempto, 1995.

Lacan, Jacques. *The Ethics of Psychoanalysis, 1959–1960.* Book 7 of *The Seminar of Jacques Lacan,* edited by Jacques-Alain Miller, translated by Dennis Potter. New York: Norton, 1992.

Lacoue-Labarthe, Philippe. *Heidegger: Art and Politics.* Translated by Chris Turner. Oxford: Blackwell, 1990.

———. *Musica Ficta (Figures of Wagner).* Translated by Felicia McCarren. Stanford, CA: Stanford UP, 1994.

———. *Poetry as Experience.* Translated by Andrea Tarnowski. Stanford, CA: Stanford UP, 1999.

———. "Poetry's Courage." In Fioretos, *The Solid Letter: Readings of Friedrich Hölderlin,* 74–93.

———. *Typography: Mimesis, Philosophy, Politics.* Translated by Christopher Fynsk. Stanford, CA: Stanford UP, 1998.

Lang, Berel. *Heidegger's Silence.* Ithaca, NY: Cornell UP, 1996.

Leppert, Richard. "Commentary." In Adorno, *Essays on Music*, 528–31.

Löwith, Karl. *Mein Leben in Deutschland vor und nach 1933.* Stuttgart: Metzler, 1986.

Lukács, Georg. *Essays über den Realismus.* Neuwied / Berlin: Luchterhand, 1971.

———. "Hölderlins Hyperion." In Beckermann and Canaris, *Der andere Hölderlin: Materialien zum 'Hölderlin'-Stück von Peter Weiss*, 19–47.

———. *The Theory of the Novel.* Translated by Anna Bostock. London: Merlin, 1971.

Lütkehaus, Ludger. "Mangel an Güte, objective Solidaritat." *Die Zeit*, 10 Apr. 2003, 17.

Mann, Thomas. "Goethe und Tolstoi: Fragmente zum Problem der Humanität." In *Bemühungen: Neue Folge der Gesammelten Abhandlungen und Aufsätze*, 7–140. Berlin: S. Fischer, 1925.

Martens, Gunter. "Hölderlin-Rezeption in der Nachfolge Nietzsches: Stationen der Aneignung eines Dichters." *HJb* 23 (1982/83): 54–78.

Martin, Bernd, ed. *Martin Heidegger und das dritte Reich.* Darmstadt: Wissenschaftliche Buchgesellschaft, 1989.

Mayer, Hans. *Brecht.* Frankfurt am Main: Suhrkamp, 1996.

———. *Das unglückliche Bewußtsein: Zur deutschen Literaturgeschichte von Lessing bis Heine.* Frankfurt am Main: Suhrkamp, 1990.

McNeill, Will. " 'A Scarcely Pondered Word': The Place of Tragedy; Heidegger, Aristotle, Sophocles." In *Philosophy and Tragedy*, edited by Miguel de Beistegui and Simon Sparks, 169–92. London: Routledge, 2000.

Mehring, Reinhard. *Heideggers Überlieferungsgeschick: Eine dionysische Selbstinszenierung.* Würzburg: Königshausen & Neumann, 1992.

Meinecke, Friedrich. *The German Catastrophe.* Translated by Sidney B. Fay. Boston: Beacon, 1963.

Menck, Clara. "Doch kein Jakobiner." *FAZ*, 24 Mar. 1970, 24.

Menke, Christoph. *Die Souveranität der Kunst: Ästhetische Erfahrung nach Adorno und Derrida.* Frankfurt am Main: Suhrkamp, 1991.

Menninghaus, Winfried. *Ekel: Theorie und Geschichte einer starken Empfindung.* Frankfurt am Main: Suhrkamp, 2002.

Meyer, Herman. *Das Zitat in der Erzählkunst: Zur Geschichte und Poetik des europäischen Romans.* Frankfurt am Main: Fischer, 1988.

Meyer, Jochen, ed. *Alfred Döblin: 1878–1978: Eine Ausstellung des Deutschen Literaturarchivs im Schiller-Nationalmuseum Marbach am Neckar.* Munich: Kösel Verlag, 1978.

Mieth, Günter. "Ein Rückblick auf öffentliche Hölderlin-Ehrungen 1970." In *Im Zwielicht des Jahrhunderts: Beiträge zur Hölderlin-Rezeption*, edited by Alfred Klein, Günter Mieth, and Klaus Pezold, 49–65. Leipzig: Rosa-Luxemburg-Verein, 1994.

Minder, Robert. "Heidegger und Hebbel oder die Sprache von Meßkirch." In *"Hölderlin unter den Deutschen" und andere Aufsätze zur deutschen Literatur*, 86–153. Frankfurt am Main: Suhrkamp, 1968.

———. "Hölderlin unter den Deutschen." *HJb* 14 (1965/66): 1–19.

Mittenzwei, Werner. *Brechts Verhältnis zur Tradition*. Berlin: Akademie-Verlag, 1972.

———. *Das Leben des Bertolt Brecht*. Frankfurt am Main: Suhrkamp, 1987.

Mörchen, Herrmann. *Adorno und Heidegger: Untersuchung einer philosophischen Kommunikationsverweigerung*. Stuttgart: Klett-Cotta, 1981.

———. *Macht und Herrschaft im Denken von Heidegger und Adorno*. Stuttgart: Klett-Cotta, 1980.

Müller, André, and Gerd Semmer. *Geschichten vom Herrn Brecht: 99 Brecht-Anekdoten*. Frankfurt am Main: Insel, 1967.

Müller-Doohm, Stefan. *Adorno: Eine Biographie*. Frankfurt am Main: Suhrkamp, 2003.

Muñoz, Breno Onetto. *Überschritt ins Unumgängliche: Heideggers dichterische Wende jenseits der Metaphysik*. Frankfurt am Main: Peter Lang, 1997.

Nicholsen, Shierry Weber. *Exact Imagination, Late Work: Adorno's Aesthetics*. Cambridge, MA: MIT P, 1997.

Niethammer, Lutz. *Posthistoire: Has History Come to an End?* Translated by Patrick Camiller. London: Verso, 1992.

Nietzsche, Friedrich. *Werke. Kristische Gesamtausgabe*. Edited by Giorgio Colli and Mazzino Montinari. Berlin: Walter de Gruyter, 1968–.

Norton, Robert E. *Secret Germany: Stefan George and His Circle*. Ithaca, NY: Cornell UP, 2002.

Offe, Claus. "Repercussions of 68." *Thesis Eleven* 68 (2002): 82–88.

Otto, Walter F. *Mythos und Welt*. Edited by Kurt von Fritz. Darmstadt: Wissenschaftliche Buchgesellschaft, 1963.

Pfizer, Theodor. "Bericht über die 14. Jahresversammlung der Hölderlin-Gesellschaft in Bad Homburg." *HJb* 19 (1975–77): 567–80.

Phillips, James. *Heidegger's Volk: Between National Socialism and Poetry*. Stanford, CA: Stanford UP, 2005.

Picht, Georg. "Die Macht des Denkens." In *Erinnerung an Martin Heidegger*, edited by Günther Neske, 197–205. Pfullingen: Neske, 1977.

Plato. *Phaedrus and Letters VII and VIII*. Translated by Walter Hamilton. Harmondsworth, UK: Penguin, 1973.

Pöggeler, Otto. *Der Denkweg Martin Heideggers*. Pfullingen, Germany: Neske, 1963.

———. "Heideggers Begegnung mit Hölderlin." *Man and World* 10 (1977): 13–61.

———. "Heideggers politisches Selbstverständnis." In Gethmann-Siefert and Pöggeler, *Heidegger und die praktische Philosophie*, 17–63.

Pöggeler, Otto. *Neue Wege mit Heidegger.* Freiburg: Alber, 1992.

———. *Philosophie und Politik bei Heidegger.* Freiburg: Alber, 1974.

———. *Spur des Worts: Zur Lyrik Paul Celans.* Freiburg: Alber, 1986.

Pohl, Rainer. *Strukturelemente und Entwicklung von Pathosformen in der Dramensprache Bertolt Brechts.* Bonn: Bouvier, 1969.

Polt, Richard, and Gregory Fried, eds. *A Companion to Heidegger's Introduction to Metaphysics.* New Haven, CT: Yale UP, 2001.

Pongs, Hermann. *Dichtung im gespaltenen Deutschland.* Stuttgart: Union, 1966.

———. "Einwirkungen Hölderlins auf die deutsche Dichtung seit der Jahrhundertwende." In Beißner and Kluckhohn, *Iduna: Jahrbuch der Hölderlin-Gesellschaft,* 114–59.

Prins, A. W. "Heideggers 'Andenken': Zwiesprache und Gewalt." In *Poesie und Philosophie in einer Tragischen Kultur,* edited by Heinz Kammerle, 73–86. Würzburg: Königshausen & Neumann, 1995.

Rabinbach, Anson. *In the Shadow of Catastrophe: German Intellectuals between Apocalypse and Enlightenment.* Berkeley: UCLA P, 1997.

Rath, Norbert. "Kriegskamerad Hölderlin: Zitate zur Sinngebungsgeschichte." In *Neue Wege zu Hölderlin,* edited by Uwe Beyer, 219–42. Würzburg: Königshausen & Neumann, 1994.

Rehm, Walter. *Orpheus: Der Dichter und die Toten.* Düsseldorf: L. Schwann, 1950.

Riedel, Ingrid, ed. *Hölderlin ohne Mythos.* Göttingen: Vandenoeck & Ruprecht, 1973.

Riedel, Manfred. "Seinserfahrung in der Dichtung: Heideggers Weg zu Hölderlin." In Trawny, *"Voll Verdienst, doch dichterisch wohnet / Der Mensch auf dieser Erde": Heidegger und Hölderlin,* 19–49.

Riedel, Volker. "Antigone-Rezeption in der DDR." In *Brechts Antigone des Sophokles,* edited by Werner Hecht, 261–75. Frankfurt am Main: Suhrkamp, 1988.

Rigby, Kate. *Topographies of the Sacred.* Richmond: U of Virginia P, 2005.

Roberts, David. *Art and Enlightenment: Aesthetic Theory after Adorno.* Lincoln: U of Nebraska P, 1991.

———. "Art and Myth: Adorno and Heidegger." *Thesis Eleven* 58 (1999): 19–34.

Roquette, Otto. *Geschichte der deutschen Literatur.* Stuttgart: Ebnert & Seubert, 1872.

Rosiek, Jan. *Maintaining the Sublime: Heidegger and Adorno.* Bern: Peter Lang, 2000.

Safranski, Rüdiger. *Ein Meister aus Deutschland: Heidegger und seine Zeit.* Munich: Carl Hanser, 1994.

Said, Edward. "Adorno as Lateness Itself." In *Adorno: A Critical Reader,* edited by Nigel Gibson and Andrew Rubin, 193–208. Oxford: Blackwell, 2002.

———. *Beginnings: Intention and Method.* New York: Basic Books, 1975.

Sartiliot, Claudette. *Citation and Modernity: Derrida, Joyce, and Brecht.* Norman: Oklahoma UP, 1993.

Savage, Robert. "Adorno's Family and Other Animals." *Thesis Eleven* 78 (2004): 102–12.

———. "Between Heidegger and Hölderlin: The 'Sacred' Speech of Maurice Blanchot." In *After Blanchot: Literature, Criticism, Philosophy,* edited by Leslie Hill, Brian Nelson, and Dimitris Vardoulakis, 149–67. Newark: U of Delaware P, 2005.

———. "My Own Private Swabia: On the Idiocy of Heidegger's Nationalism." *Thesis Eleven* 87 (2006): 112–21.

Scharfschwerdt, Jürgen. *Friedrich Hölderlin: Der Dichter des "deutschen Sonderweges."* Stuttgart: Kohlhammer, 1994.

Schmid, Holger. "Geschick und Verhältnis des Lebendigen: Die griechische Sphäre zwischen Heidegger und Hölderlin." In Trawny, *"Voll Verdienst, doch dichterisch wohnet / Der Mensch auf dieser Erde: Heidegger und Hölderlin,* 163–80.

Schmidt, Jochen. "Stellungnahme." *Deutsche Vierteljahresschrift* 63 (1989): 679–711.

Schmitt, Carl. *Glossarium: Aufzeichnungen der Jahre 1947–1951.* Edited by Eberhard Freiherr von Medem. Berlin: Duncker & Humblot, 1991.

Schmücker, Reinold. "Monologisches Gespräch: Heideggers Vorlesung über Hölderlins Hymne 'Andenken.'" *Zeitschrift für Germanistik* 2.3 (1992): 550–68.

Schnädelbach, Herbert. *Philosophie in Deutschland, 1831–1933.* Frankfurt am Main: Suhrkamp, 1983.

Scholem, Gershom. *Briefe II: 1948–1970.* Edited by Thomas Sparr. Munich: C. H. Beck, 1995.

Scholze, Britta. *Kunst als Kritik: Adornos Weg aus der Dialektik.* Würzburg: Königshausen & Neumann, 2000.

Schumann, Gerhard. "Ansprache des Präsidenten," In Beißner and Kluckhohn, *Iduna: Jahrbuch der Hölderlin-Gesellschaft,* 16–19.

Seel, Martin. *Aesthetics of Appearing.* Translated by John Farrell. Stanford, CA: Stanford UP, 2005.

Sloterdijk, Peter. *Kritik der zynischen Vernunft.* 2 vols. Frankfurt am Main: Suhrkamp, 1983.

———. *Nicht gerettet: Versuche nach Heidegger.* Frankfurt am Main: Suhrkamp, 2002.

Sophocles. *The Theban Plays.* Translated by Robert Fagles. Harmondsworth, UK: Penguin, 1984.

Steiner, George. *Antigones.* Oxford: Oxford UP, 1984.

Steinert, Heinz. *Adorno in Wien: Über die (Un)möglichkeit von Kunst, Kultur und Befreiung.* Frankfurt am Main: Fischer, 1993.

Suglia, Joseph. "On the Nationalist Reconstruction of Hölderlin in the George Circle." *German Life and Letters* 55.4 (2002): 387–97.

Szondi, Peter. *Briefe.* Edited by Christoph König and Thomas Sparr. Frankfurt am Main: Suhrkamp, 1993.

———. "Hölderlin 1943." *Die Zeit*, 20 Mar. 1970, 28.

———. *Hölderlin-Studien: Mit einem Traktat über philologische Erkenntnis.* Frankfurt am Main: Insel, 1967.

Taylor, Charles. *Sources of the Self: The Making of the Modern Identity.* Cambridge MA: Harvard UP, 1989.

Thomä, Dieter. "The Name on the Edge of Language: A Complication in Heidegger's Theory of Language and Its Consequences." In Polt and Fried, *A Companion to Heidegger's Introduction to Metaphysics*, 103–22.

Tiedemann, Rolf. "Concept, Image, Name: On Adorno's Utopia of Knowledge." In *The Semblance of Subjectivity: Essays in Adorno's Aesthetic Theory*, edited by Tom Huhn and Lambert Zuidevaart, 123–45. Cambridge, MA: MIT P, 1997.

Trawny, Peter, ed. *"Voll Verdienst, doch dichterisch wohnet der Mensch auf dieser Erde": Heidegger und Hölderlin.* Frankfurt am Main: Klostermann, 2000.

Van den Bergh, Gerhard. *Adornos philosophisches Deuten von Dichtung. Ästhetische Theorie und Praxis der Interpretation: Der Hölderlin-Essay als Modell.* Bonn: Bouvier, 1989.

Wackwitz, Stephan. "Text als Mythos: Zur Frankfurter Hölderlin-Ausgabe und ihrer Rezeption." *Merkur* 44.2 (1990): 134–43.

Wagner, Richard. *Opera and Drama.* Translated by William Ashton Ellis. Lincoln: U of Nebraska P, 1995.

Walser, Martin. *Ehen in Philippsburg.* Frankfurt am Main: Suhrkamp, 1997.

———. *Umgang mit Hölderlin: Zwei Reden.* Frankfurt am Main: Insel, 1997.

Warminski, Andrzej. "Monstrous History: Heidegger reading Hölderlin." In Fioretos, *The Solid Letter: Readings of Friedrich Hölderlin*, 201–15.

———. *Readings in Interpretation: Hölderlin, Hegel, Heidegger.* Minneapolis: U of Minnesota P, 1986.

Weiss, Peter. *Hölderlin.* Frankfurt am Main: Suhrkamp, 1971.

Weisstein, Ulrich. "Imitation, Stylization, and Adaptation: The Language of Brecht's *Antigone* and Its Relation to Hölderlin's Version of Sophocles." *German Quarterly* 46 (1973): 581–604.

Wellmer, Albrecht. "Wahrheit, Schein, Versöhnung: Adornos ästhetische Rettung der Modernität." In *Adorno-Konferenz 1983*, edited by Ludwig von Friedeburg and Jürgen Habermas, 138–76. Frankfurt am Main: Suhrkamp, 1983.

Wiggershaus, Rolf. *Die Frankfurter Schule: Geschichte — Theoretische Entwicklung — Politische Bedeutung.* Munich: Carl Hanser, 1986.

Wilke, Sabine. *Zur Dialektik von Exposition und Darstellung: Ansätze zu einer Kritik der Arbeiten Martin Heideggers, Theodor W. Adornos und Jacques Derridas.* New York: Peter Lang, 1988.

Wocke, Helmut. "Norbert von Hellingrath zum Gedächtnis." *Dichtung und Volkstum* 41 (1941): 352–60.

Zeller, Bernhard, ed. *Klassiker in finsterer Zeit, 1933–1945.* 2 vols. Marbach: Schiller-Nationalmuseum, 1983.

Zimmerman, Michael. *Heidegger's Confrontation with Modernity: Technology, Politics, and Art.* Bloomington: Indiana UP, 1990.

———. "The Ontological Decline of the West." In Polt and Fried, *A Companion to Heidegger's Introduction to Metaphysics,* 185–204.

Index